NORðNORðVESTUR,
INN Í SKÝJABAKKANN

Go with the Clouds, North-by-Northwest Vol. 2
Aki Irie

Norðnorðvestur,
inn í skýjabakkann

Aki Irie

He knows alone who has wandered wide,
and far has fared on the way,
what manner of mind a man doth own
who is wise of head and heart.

Table of Contents

Norðnorðvestur,
inn í skýjabakkann

GO WITH THE CLOUDS
NORTH-BY-NORTHWEST

AKI IRIE

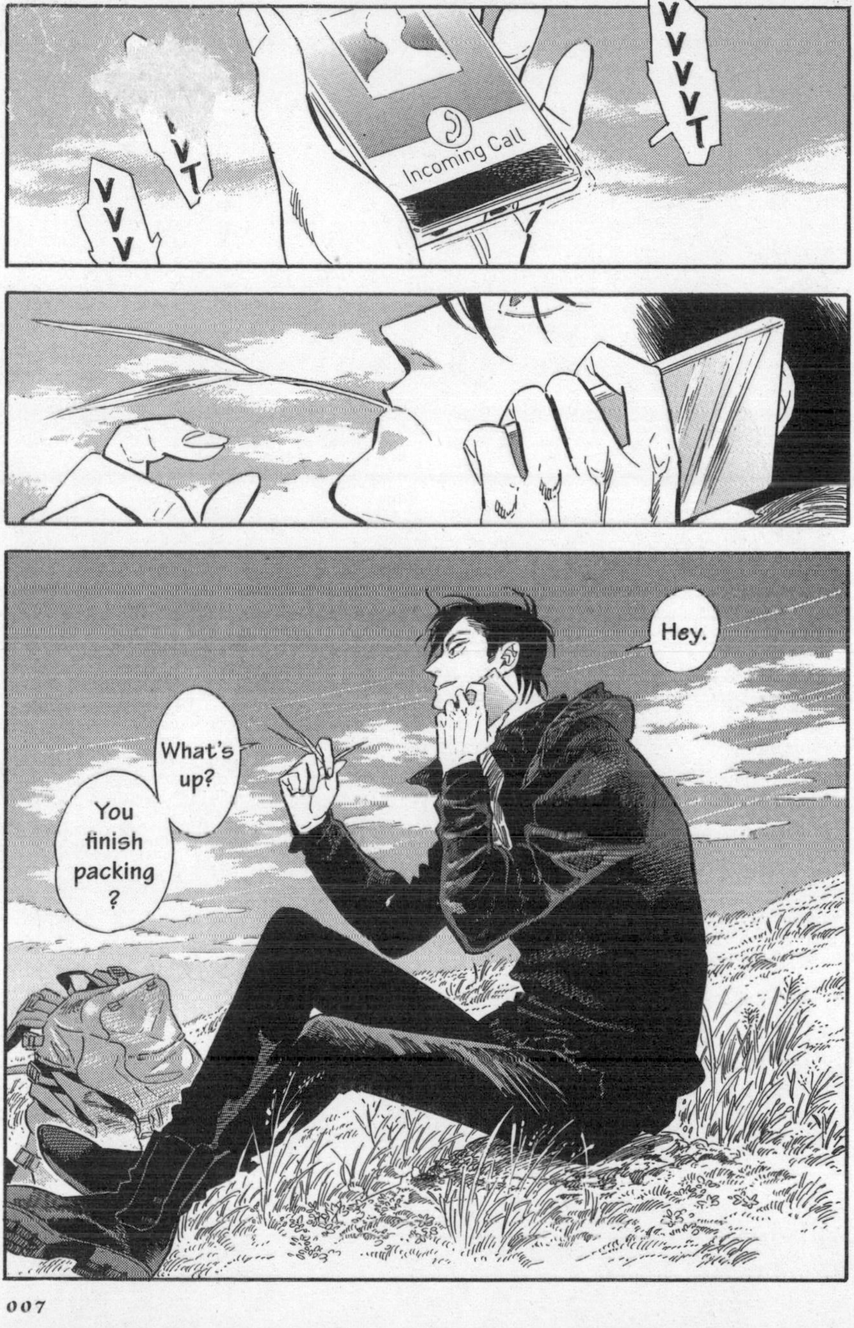
VVVVT
Incoming Call
VT
VVV
Hey.
What's up?
You finish packing?

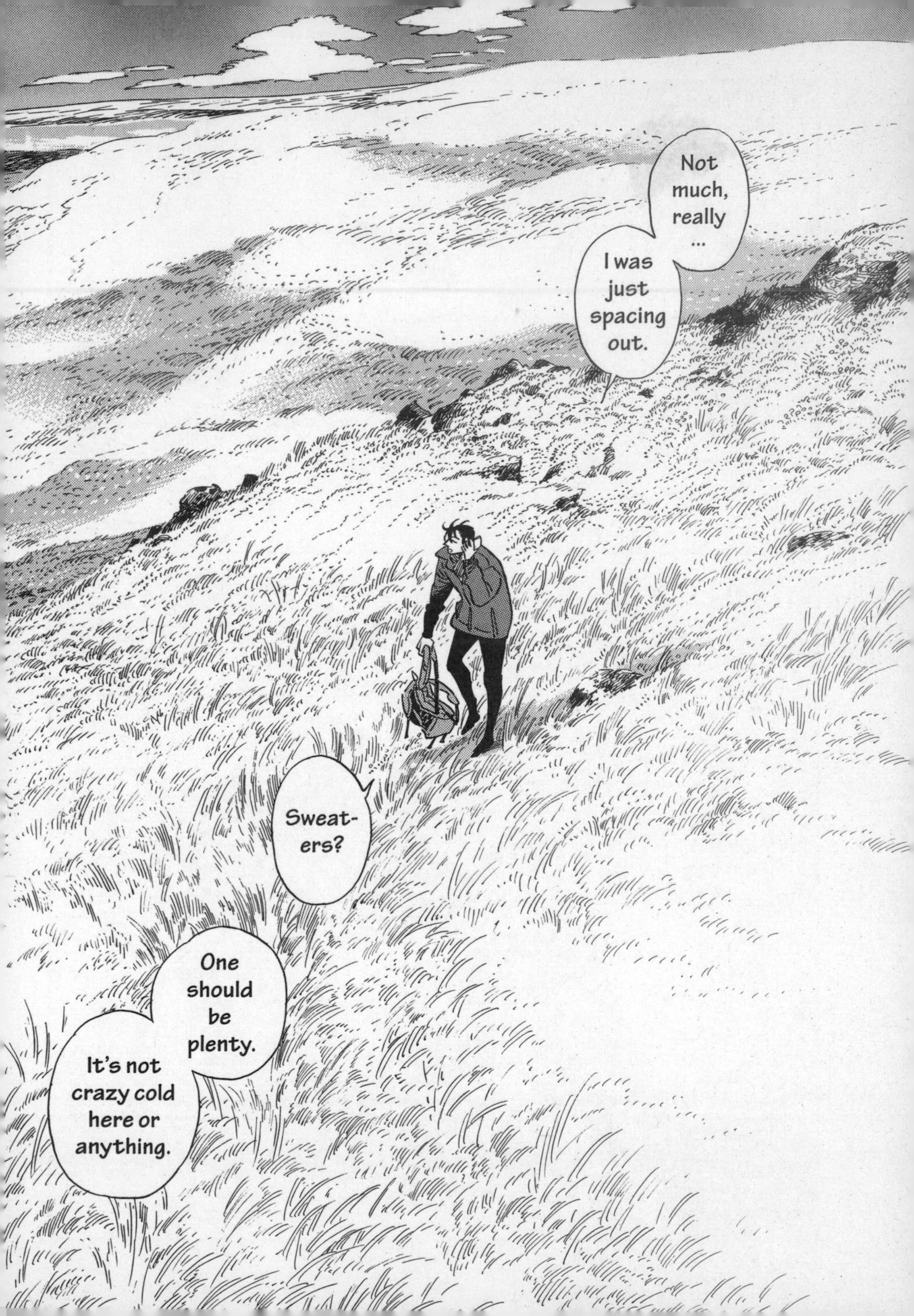
Not much, really ...
I was just spacing out.
Sweat-ers?
One should be plenty.
It's not crazy cold here or anything.

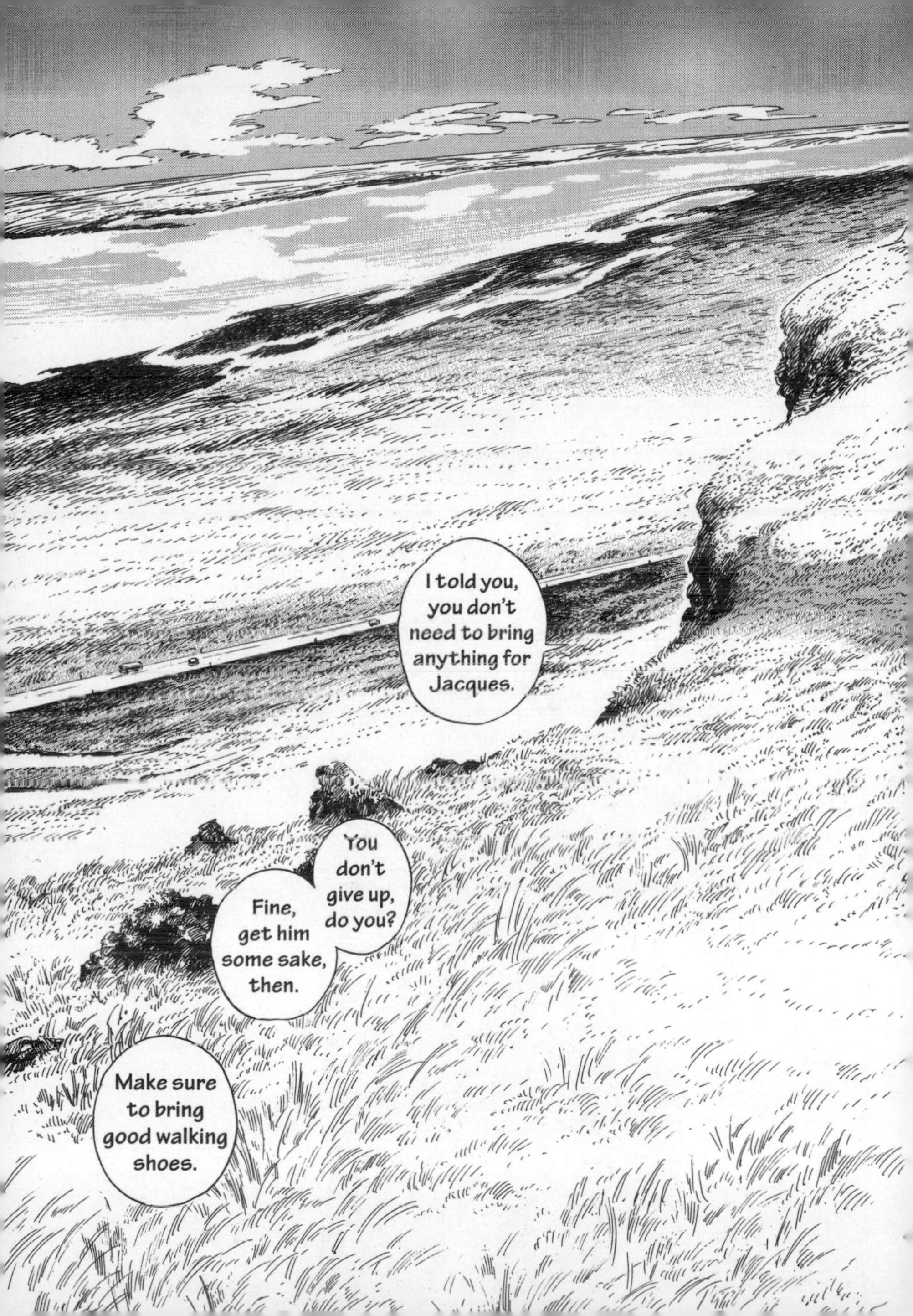
I told you, you don't need to bring anything for Jacques.
You don't give up, do you?
Fine, get him some sake, then.
Make sure to bring good walking shoes.

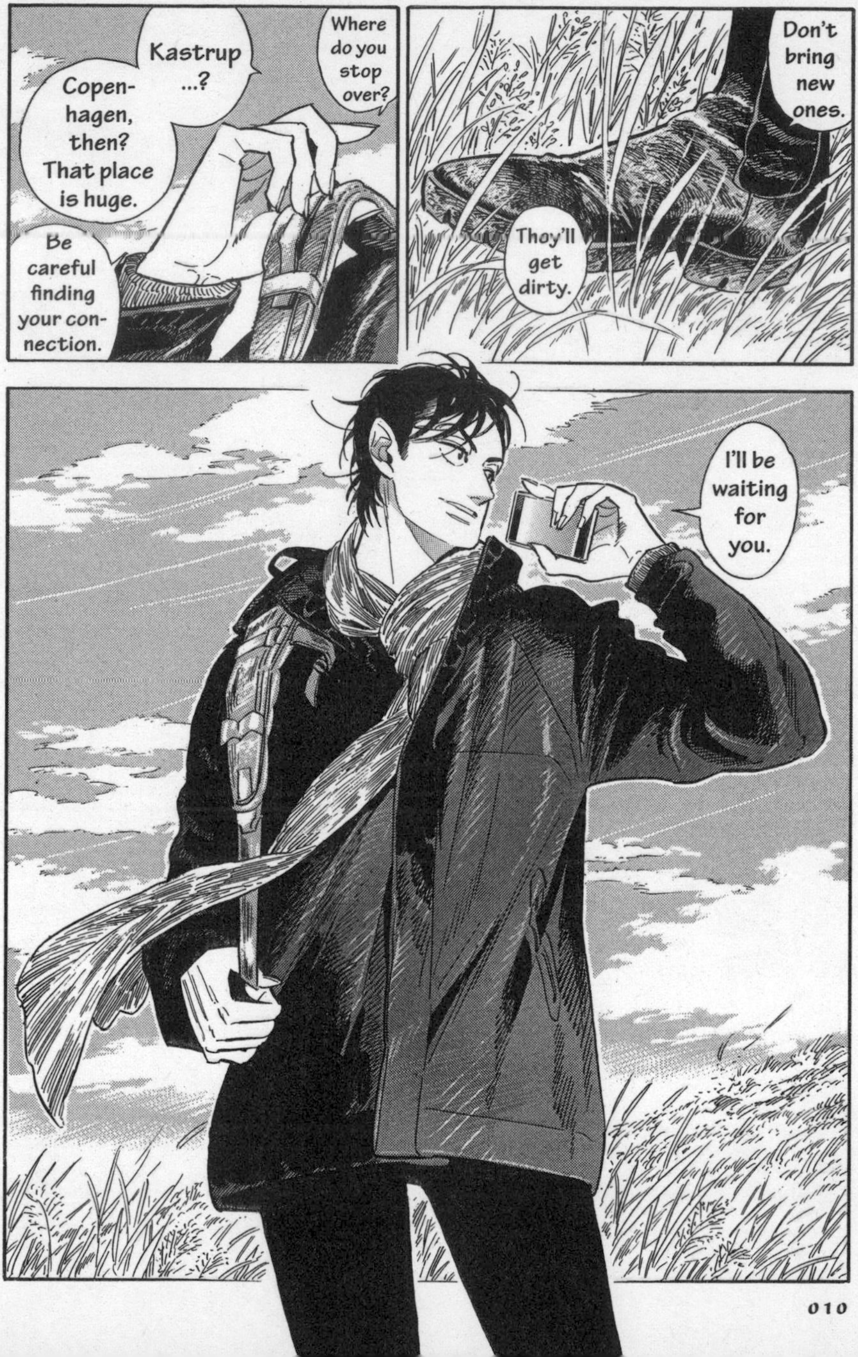
Don't bring new ones.
They'll get dirty.
Where do you stop over?
Kastrup ...?
Copenhagen, then? That place is huge.
Be careful finding your connection.
I'll be waiting for you.

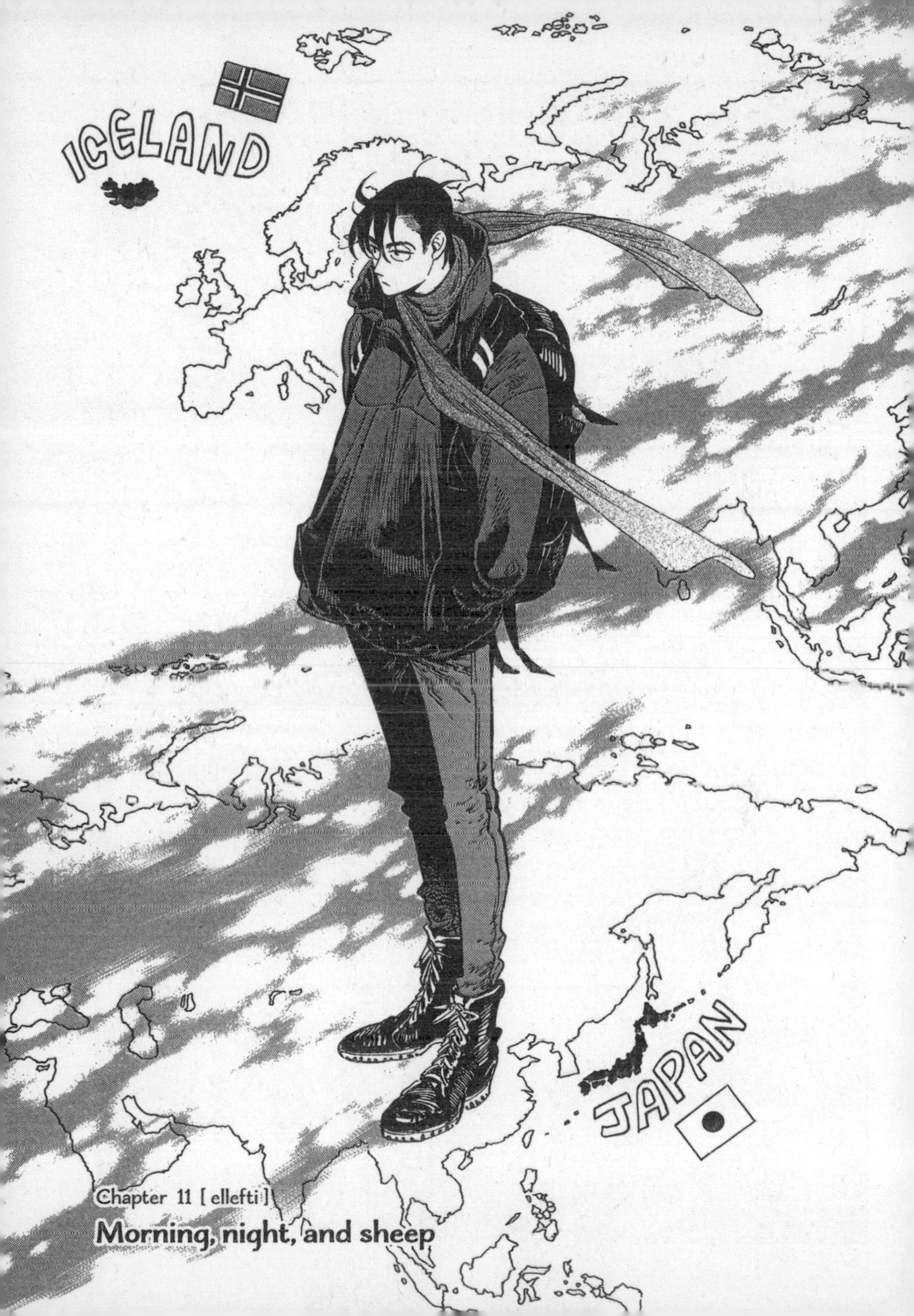
ICELAND
JAPAN

Chapter 11 [ellefti]
Morning, night, and sheep

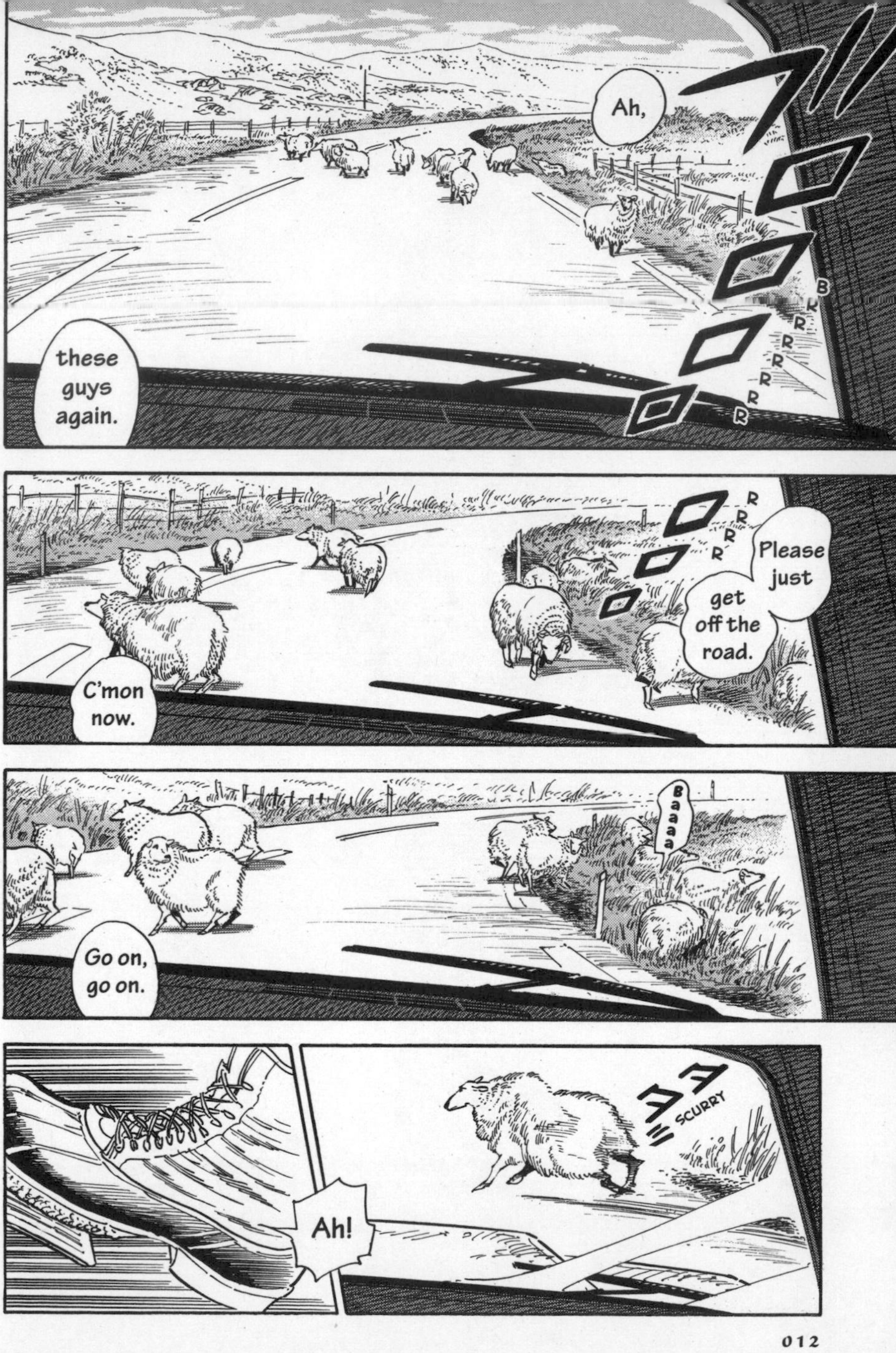
BRRRRRRR
Ah,
these guys again.
RRRRR
Please just get off the road.
C'mon now.
Baaaa
Go on, go on.
SCURRY
Ah!

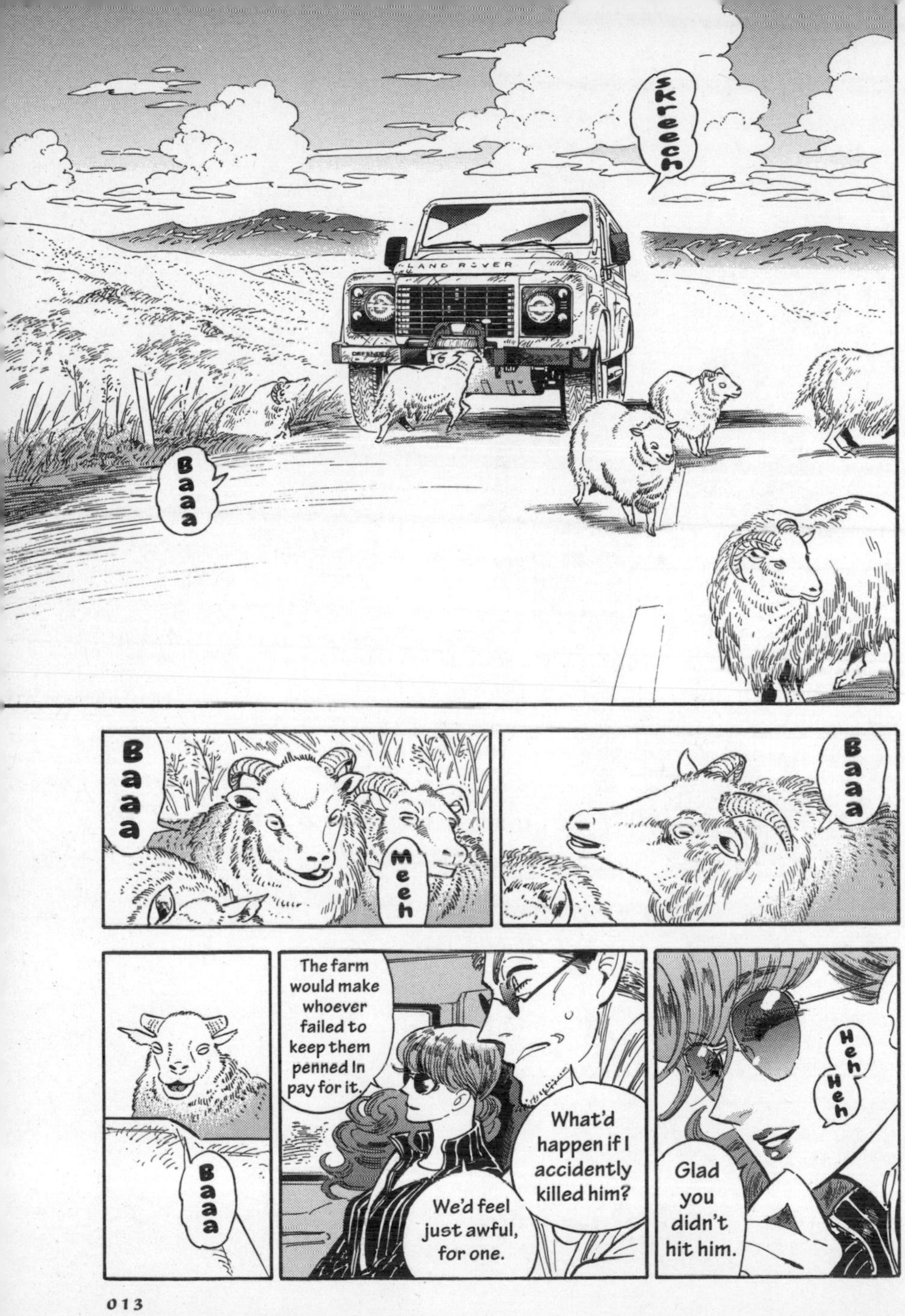
Skreech
Baaa
Baaa
Baaa
Meeh
Heh Heh
Glad you didn't hit him.
What'd happen if I accidently killed him?
We'd feel just awful, for one.
The farm would make whoever failed to keep them penned In pay for it.
Baaa

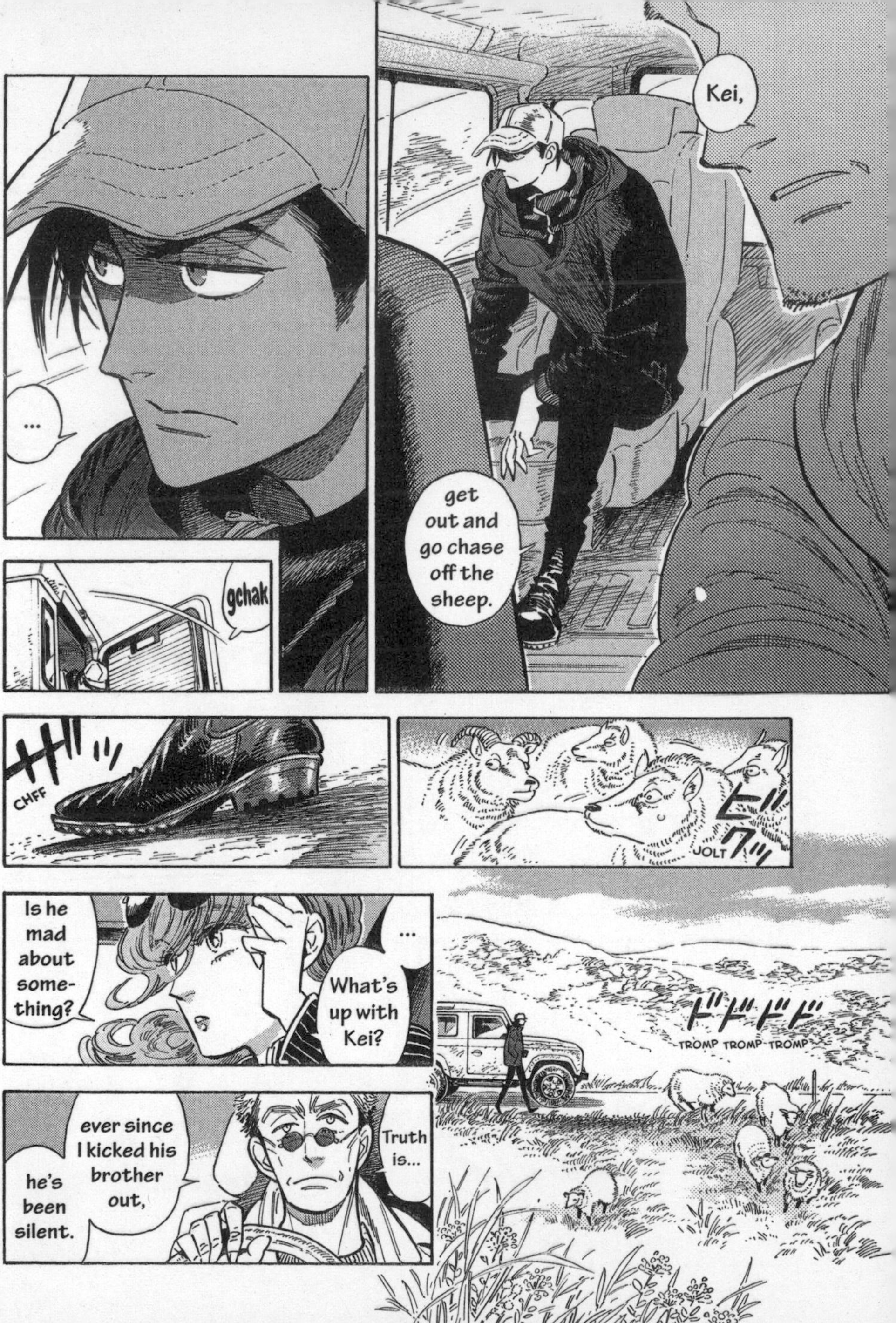
Kei,
get out and go chase off the sheep.
...
gchak
JOLT
CHFF
ドドドド
TROMP TROMP TROMP
...
What's up with Kei?
Is he mad about something?
Truth is...
ever since I kicked his brother out,
he's been silent.

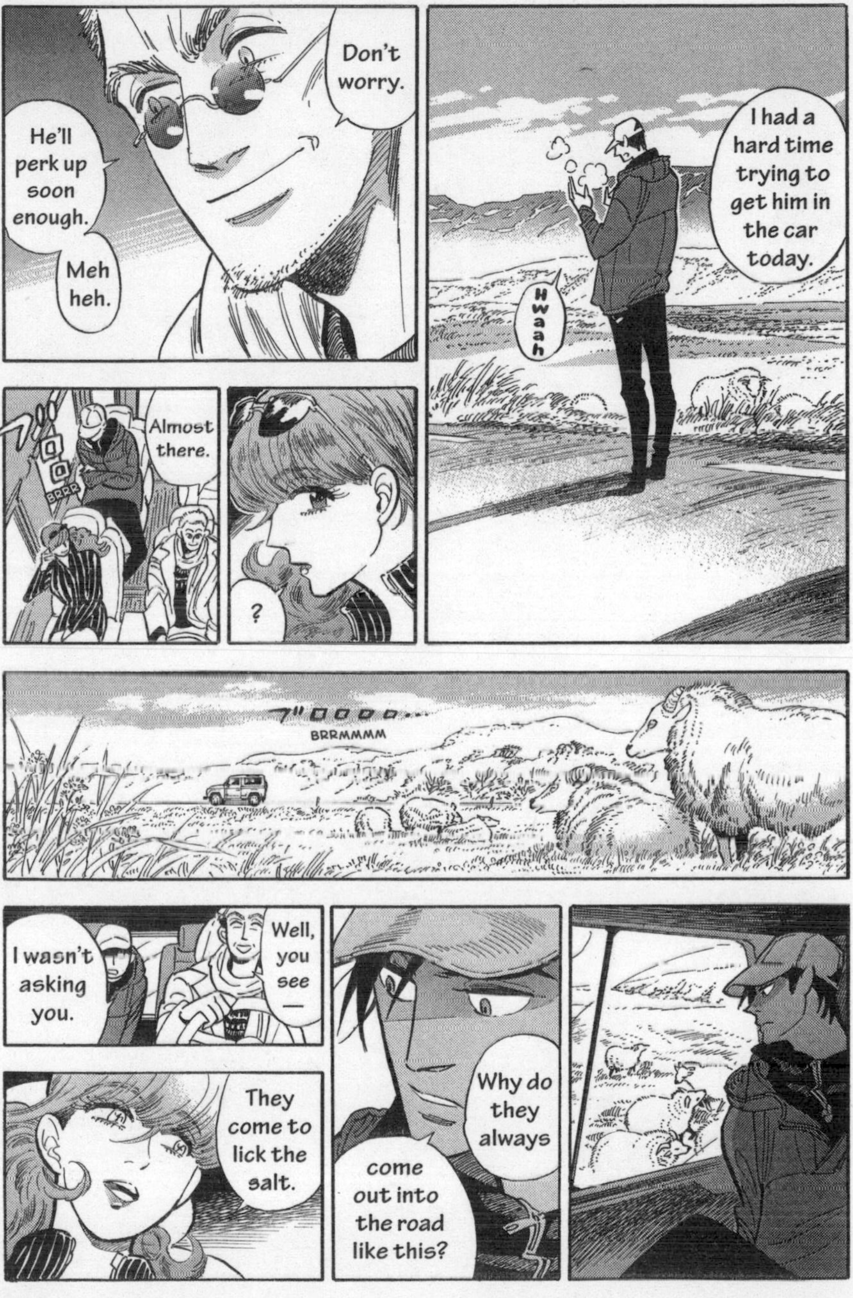
I had a hard time trying to get him in the car today.
Hwaah
Don't worry.
He'll perk up soon enough.
Meh heh.
?
Almost there.
BRRR
BRRMMM
Why do they always
come out into the road like this?
Well, you see—
I wasn't asking you.
They come to lick the salt.

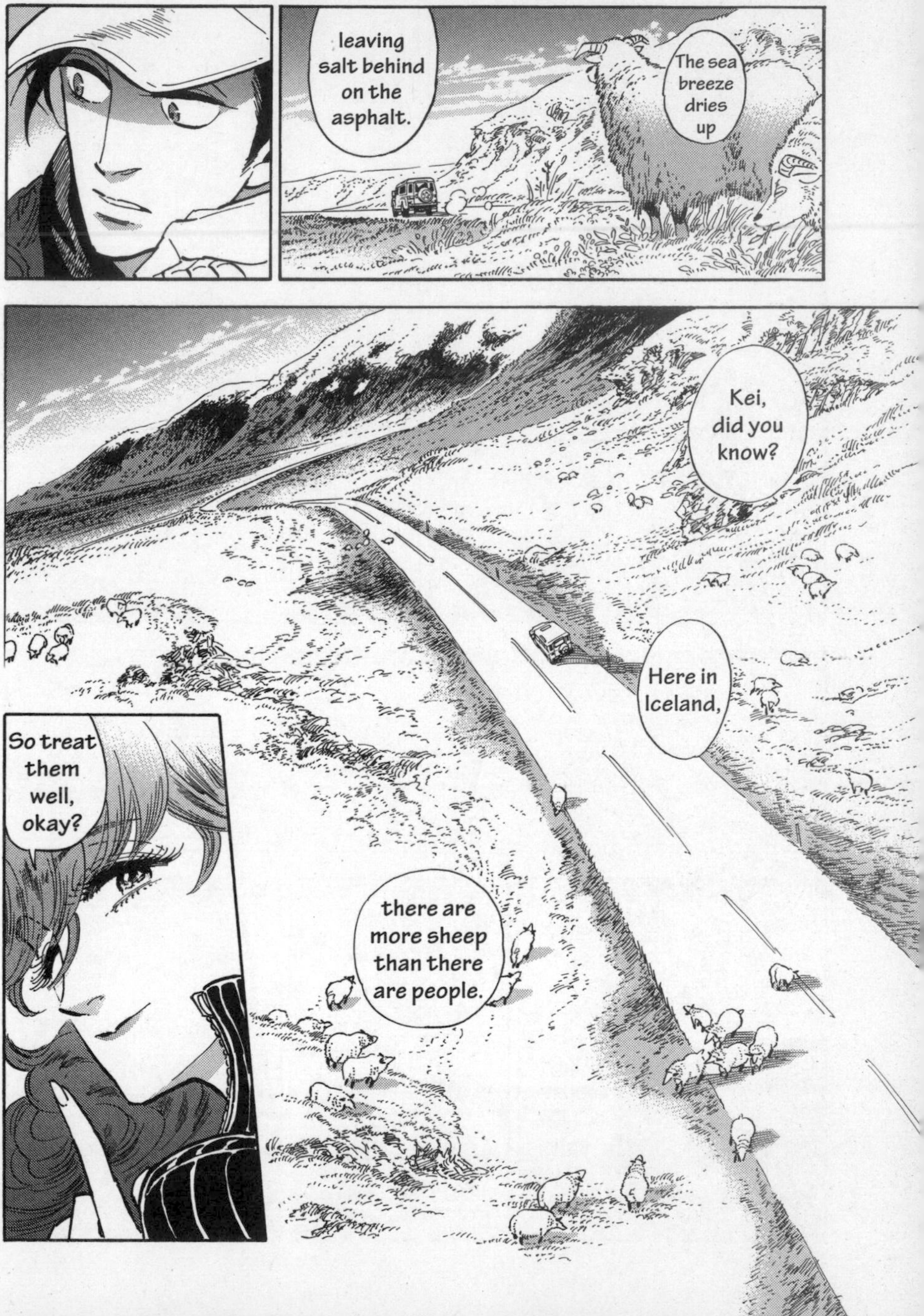
The sea breeze dries up
leaving salt behind on the asphalt.
Kei, did you know?
Here in Iceland,
there are more sheep than there are people.
So treat them well, okay?

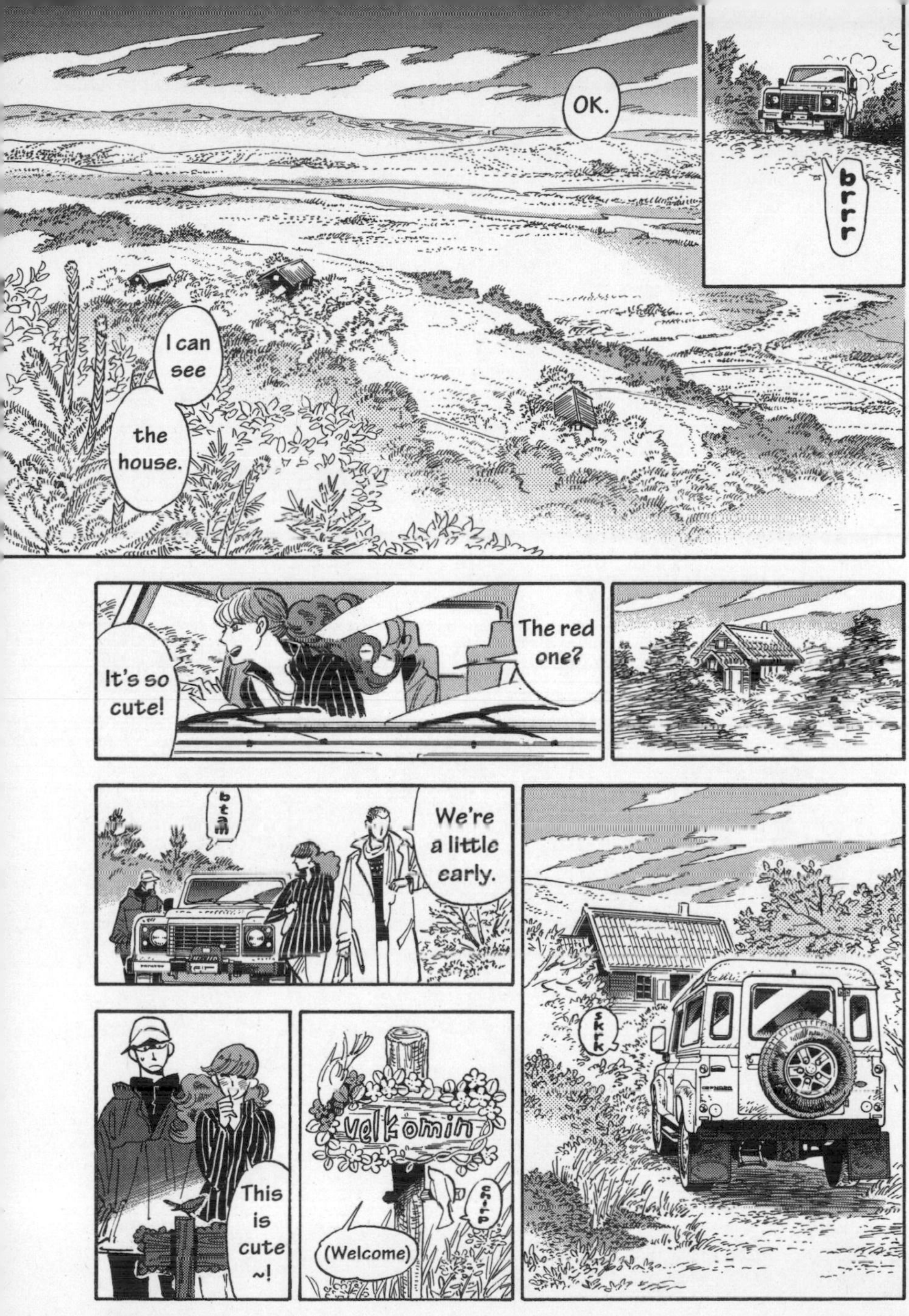
brrr
OK.
I can see
the house.
The red one?
It's so cute!
skrk
We're a little early.
velkomin
(Welcome)
chirp
This is cute ~!

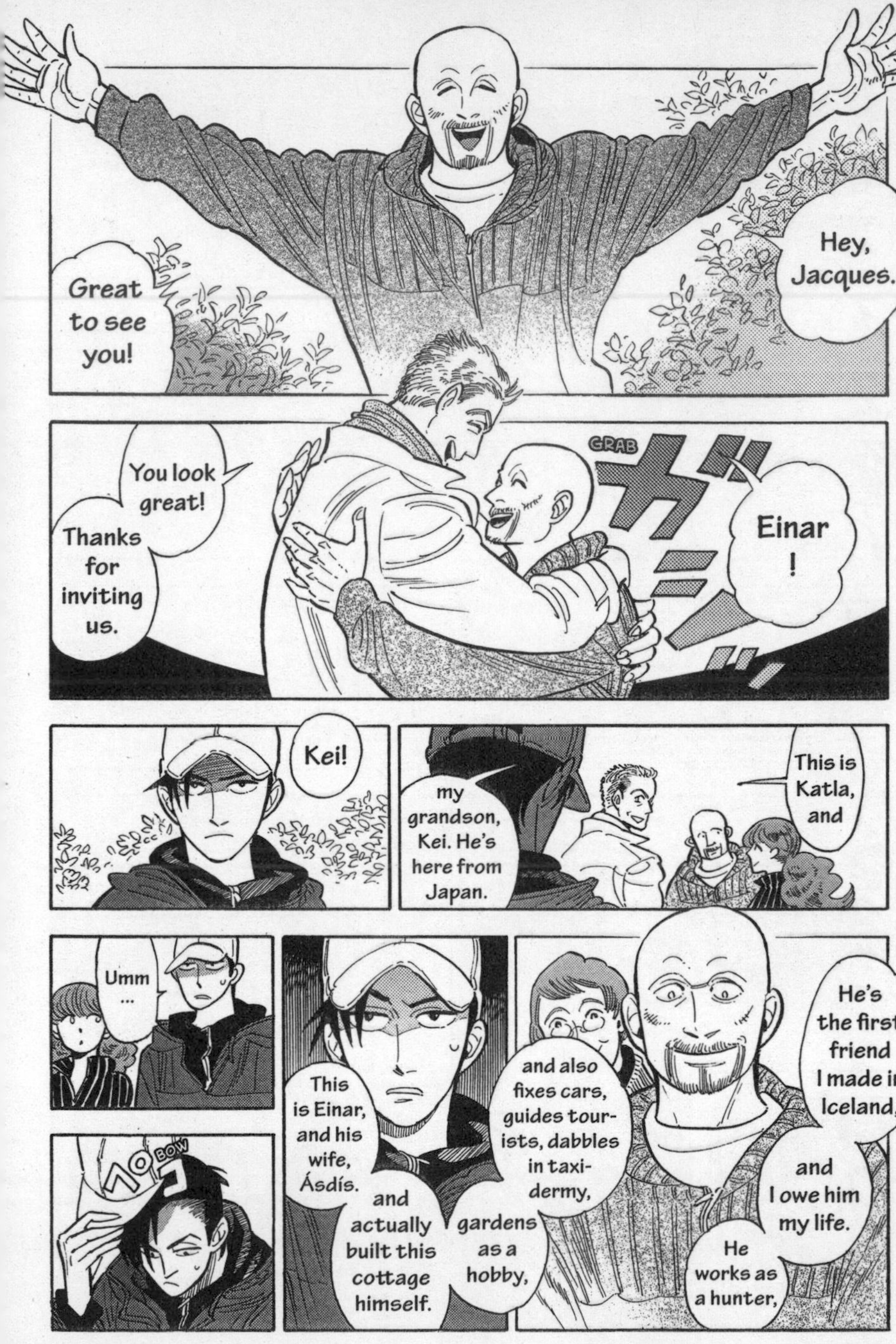
Hey, Jacques.
Great to see you!
GRAB
Einar!
You look great!
Thanks for inviting us.
This is Katla, and
my grandson, Kei. He's here from Japan.
Kei!
He's the first friend I made in Iceland,
and I owe him my life.
He works as a hunter,
and also fixes cars, guides tour-ists, dabbles in taxi-dermy,
gardens as a hobby,
and actually built this cottage himself.
This is Einar, and his wife, Ásdís.
Umm ...
BOW

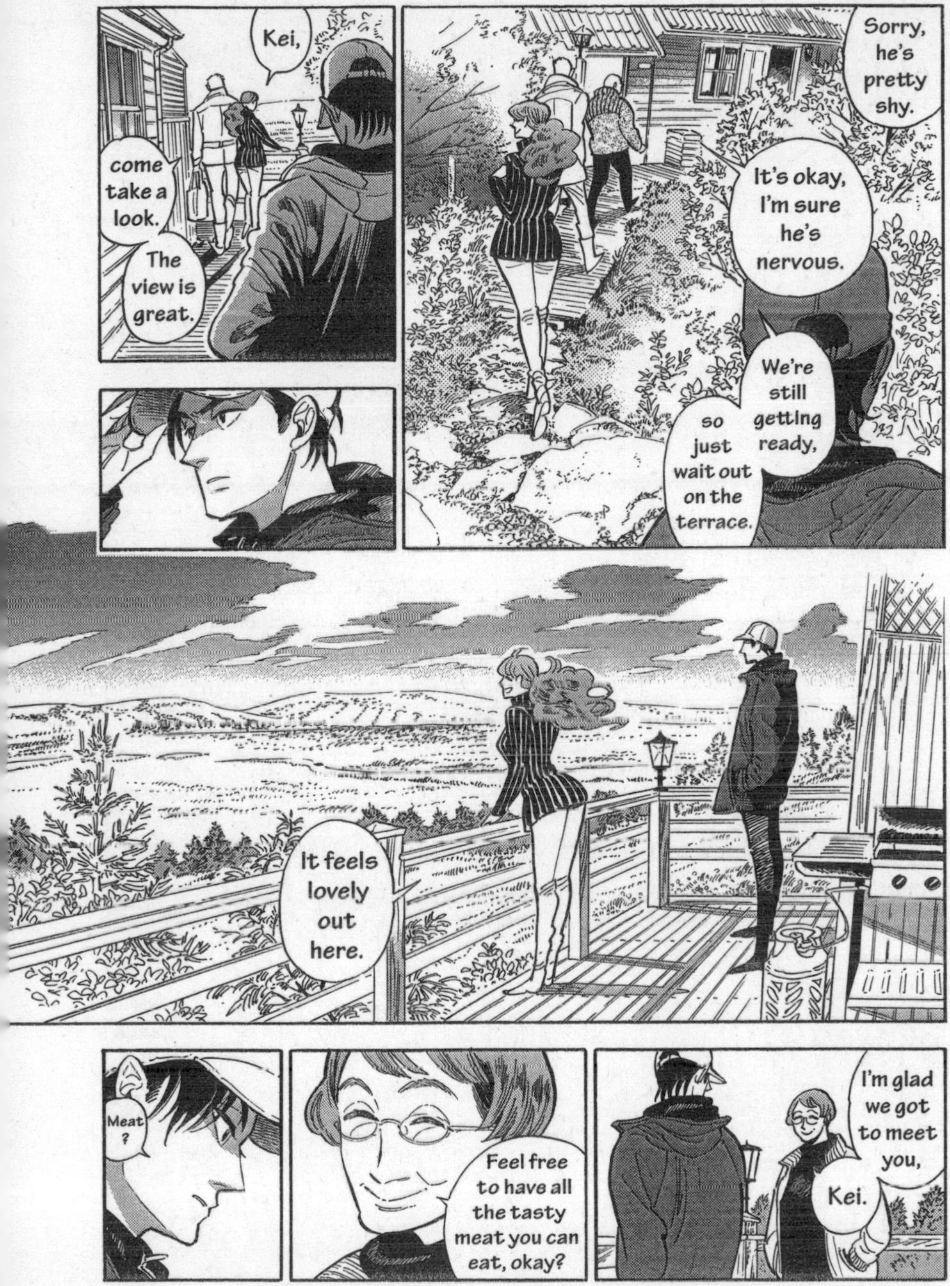

Sorry, he's pretty shy.
It's okay, I'm sure he's nervous.
We're still getting ready,
so just wait out on the terrace.
Kei,
come take a look.
The view is great.
It feels lovely out here.
I'm glad we got to meet you,
Kei.
Feel free to have all the tasty meat you can eat, okay?
Meat?

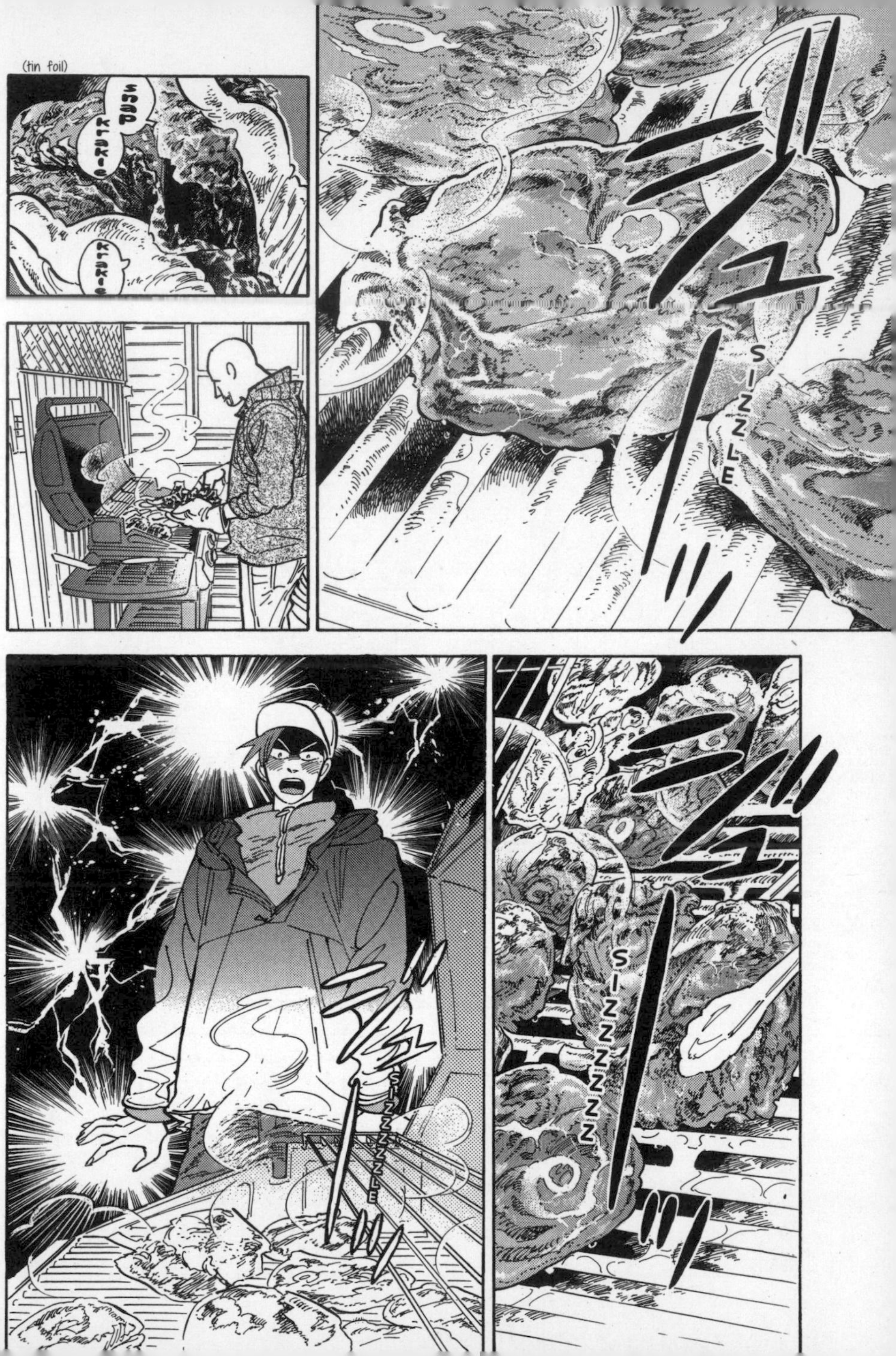

SIZZLE
(tin foil)
snap krakie
krakie
SIZZZZZZZ
SIZZZZZLE

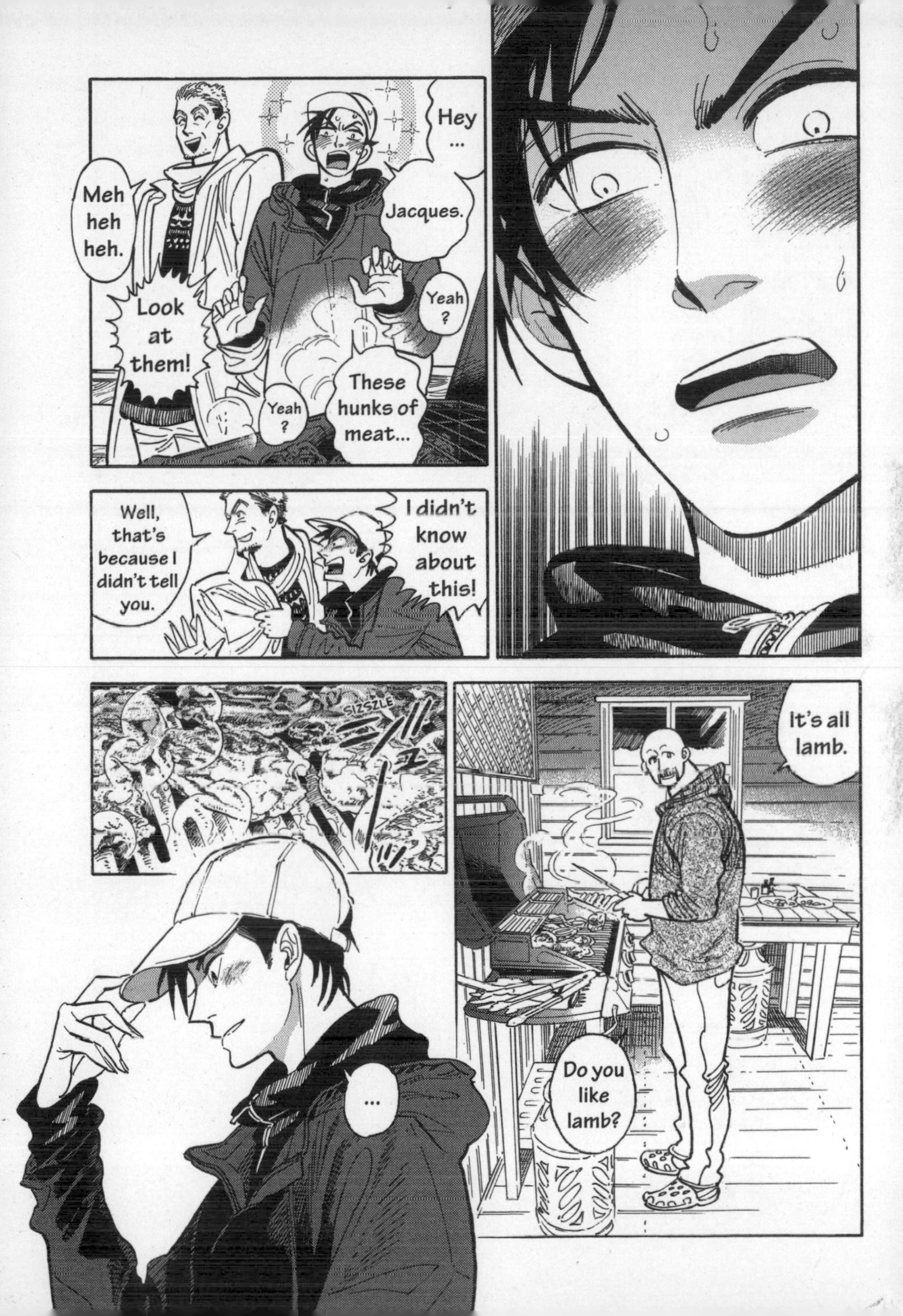

Hey ...
Jacques.
Yeah ?
Meh heh heh.
Look at them!
These hunks of meat...
Yeah ?
I didn't know about this!
Well, that's because I didn't tell you.
It's all lamb.
Do you like lamb?
SIZSZLE
...

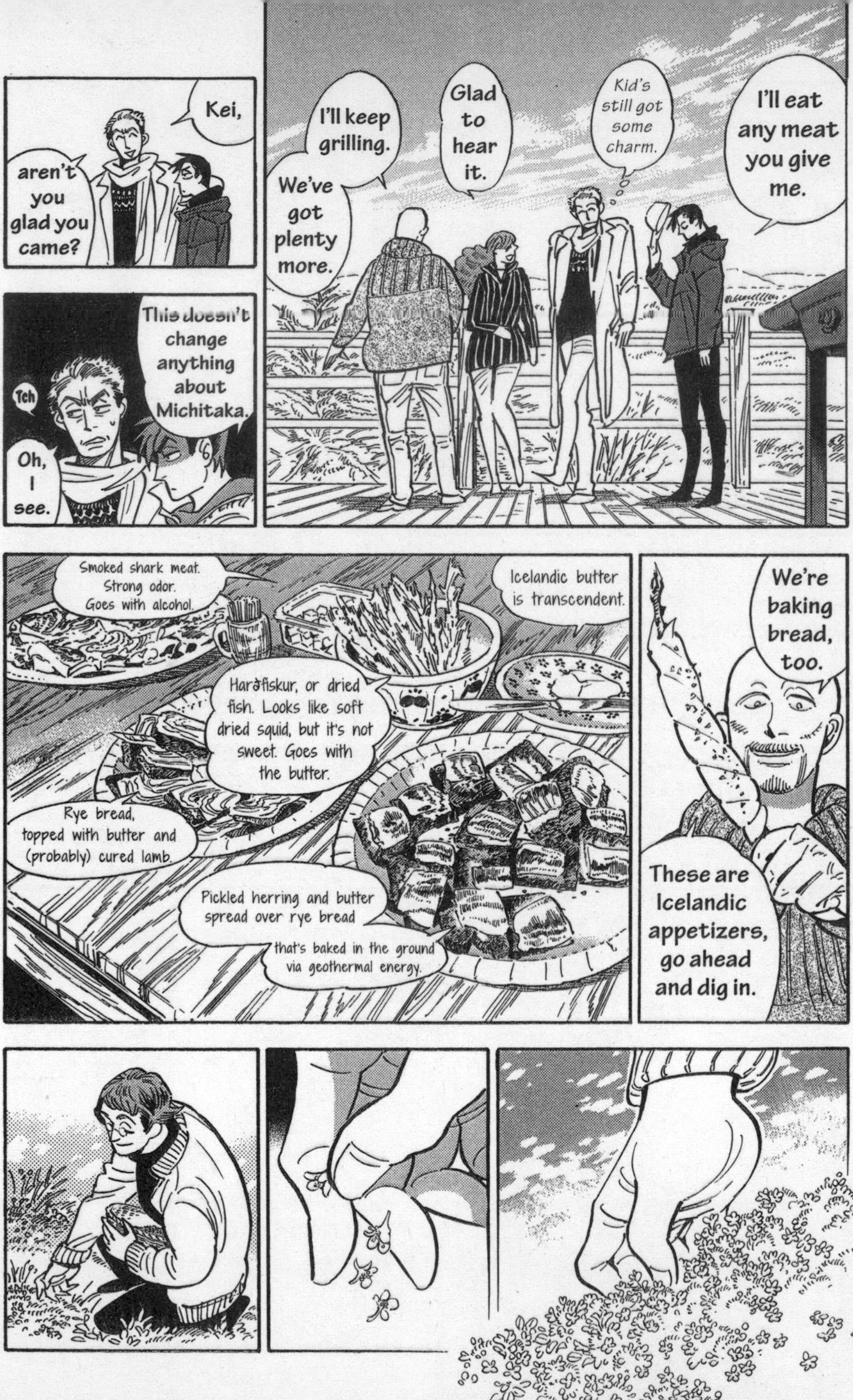
I'll eat any meat you give me.
Kid's still got some charm.
Glad to hear it.
I'll keep grilling.
We've got plenty more.
Kei,
aren't you glad you came?
This doesn't change anything about Michitaka.
Tch
Oh, I see.
We're baking bread, too.
These are Icelandic appetizers, go ahead and dig in.
Icelandic butter is transcendent.
Smoked shark meat. Strong odor. Goes with alcohol.
Harðfiskur, or dried fish. Looks like soft dried squid, but it's not sweet. Goes with the butter.
Rye bread, topped with butter and (probably) cured lamb.
Pickled herring and butter spread over rye bread
that's baked in the ground via geothermal energy.

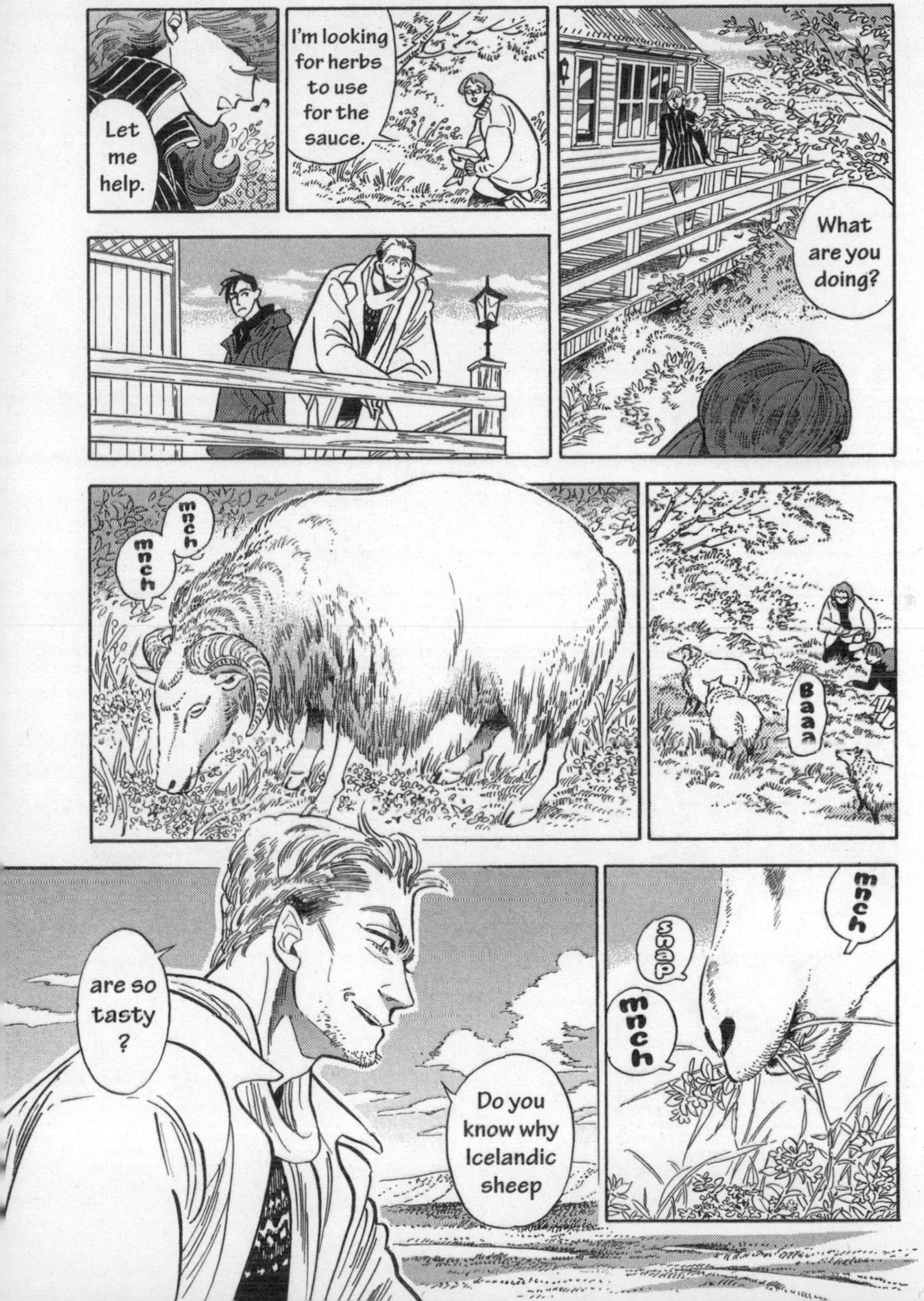
What are you doing?
I'm looking for herbs to use for the sauce.
Let me help.
Baaa
mnch
mnch
mnch
snap
mnch
Do you know why Icelandic sheep
are so tasty?

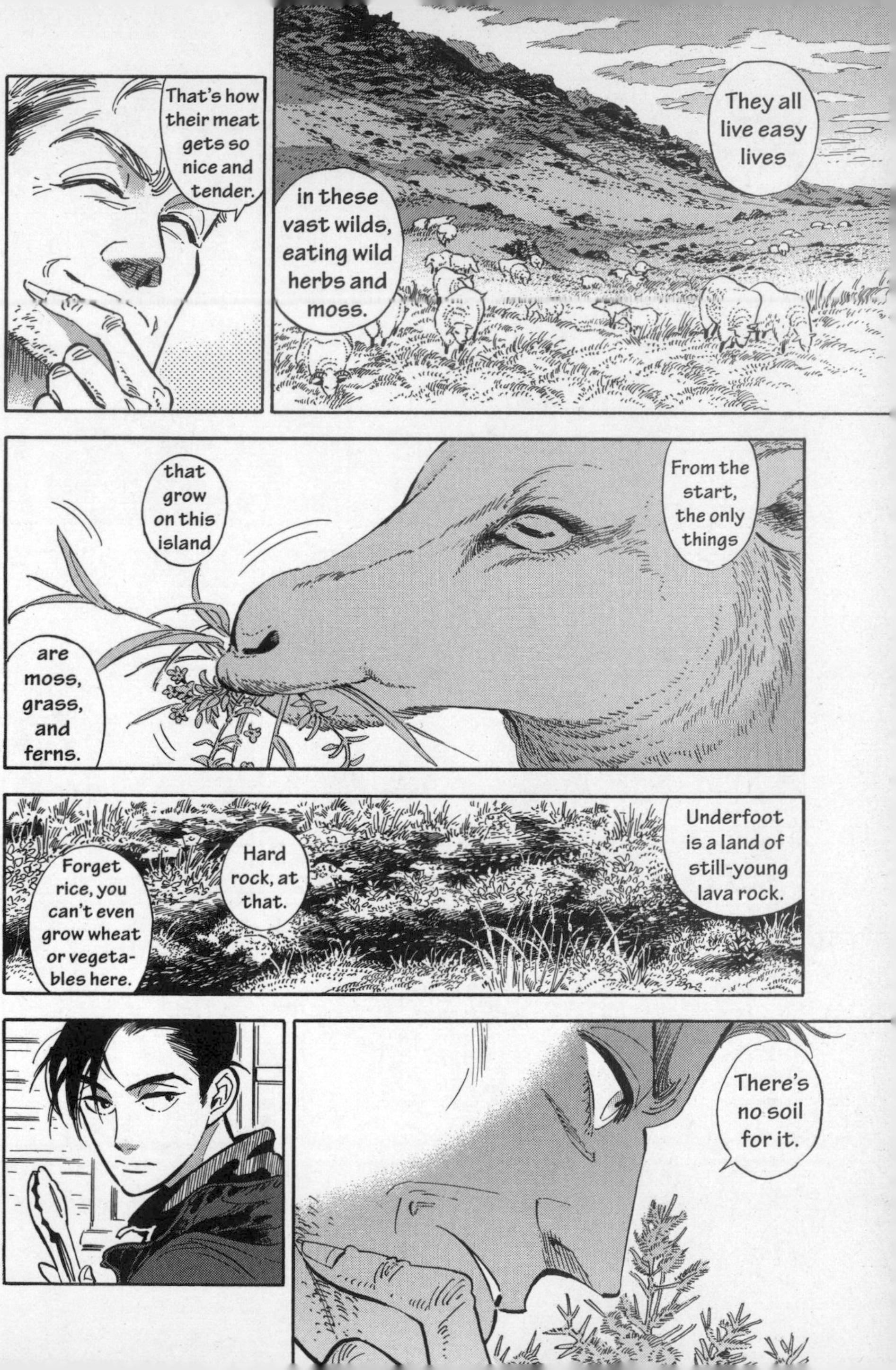
They all live easy lives
in these vast wilds, eating wild herbs and moss.
That's how their meat gets so nice and tender.
From the start, the only things
that grow on this island
are moss, grass, and ferns.
Underfoot is a land of still-young lava rock.
Hard rock, at that.
Forget rice, you can't even grow wheat or vegeta-bles here.
There's no soil for it.

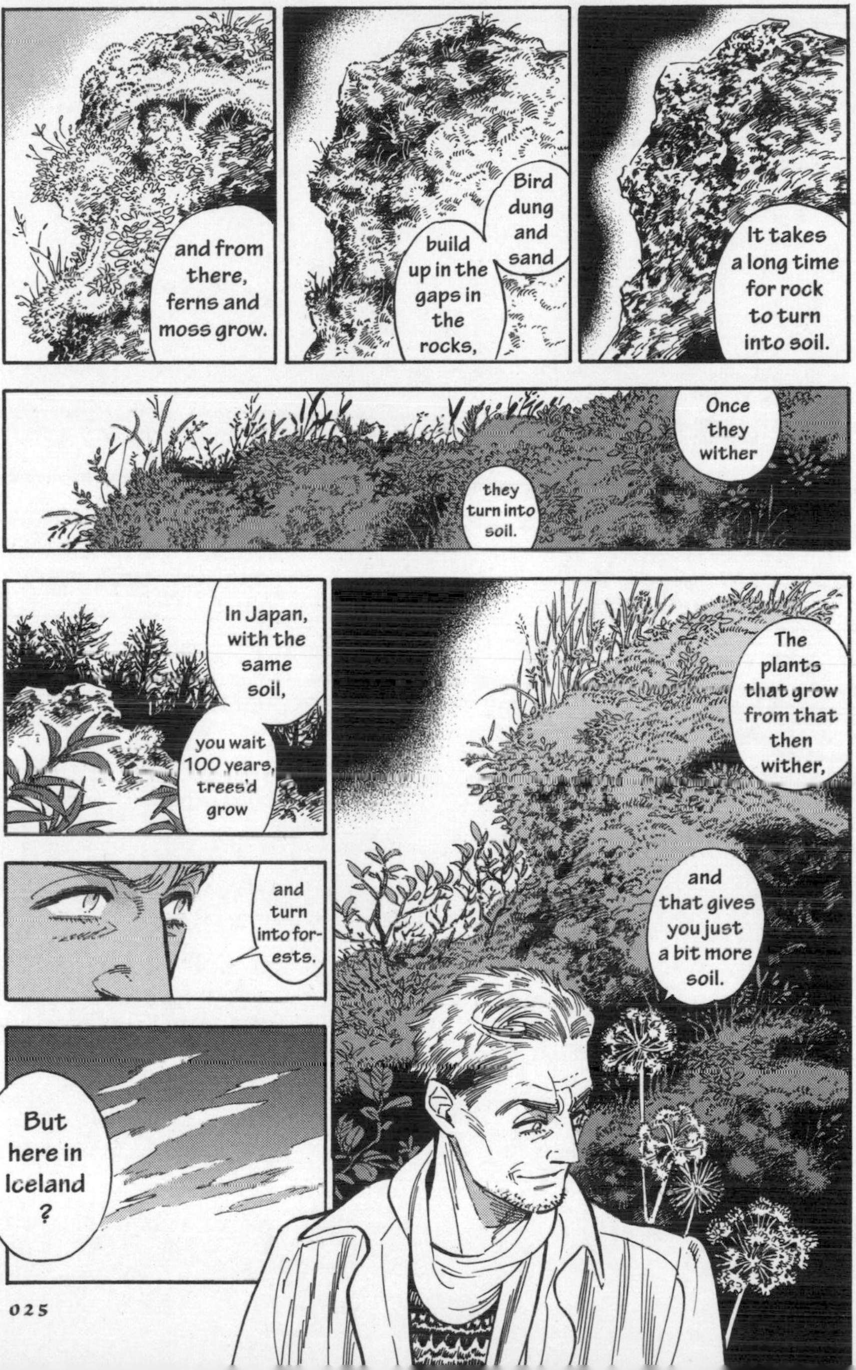
It takes a long time for rock to turn into soil.
Bird dung and sand
build up in the gaps in the rocks,
and from there, ferns and moss grow.
Once they wither
they turn into soil.
The plants that grow from that then wither,
and that gives you just a bit more soil.
In Japan, with the same soil,
you wait 100 years, trees'd grow
and turn into forests.
But here in Iceland ?

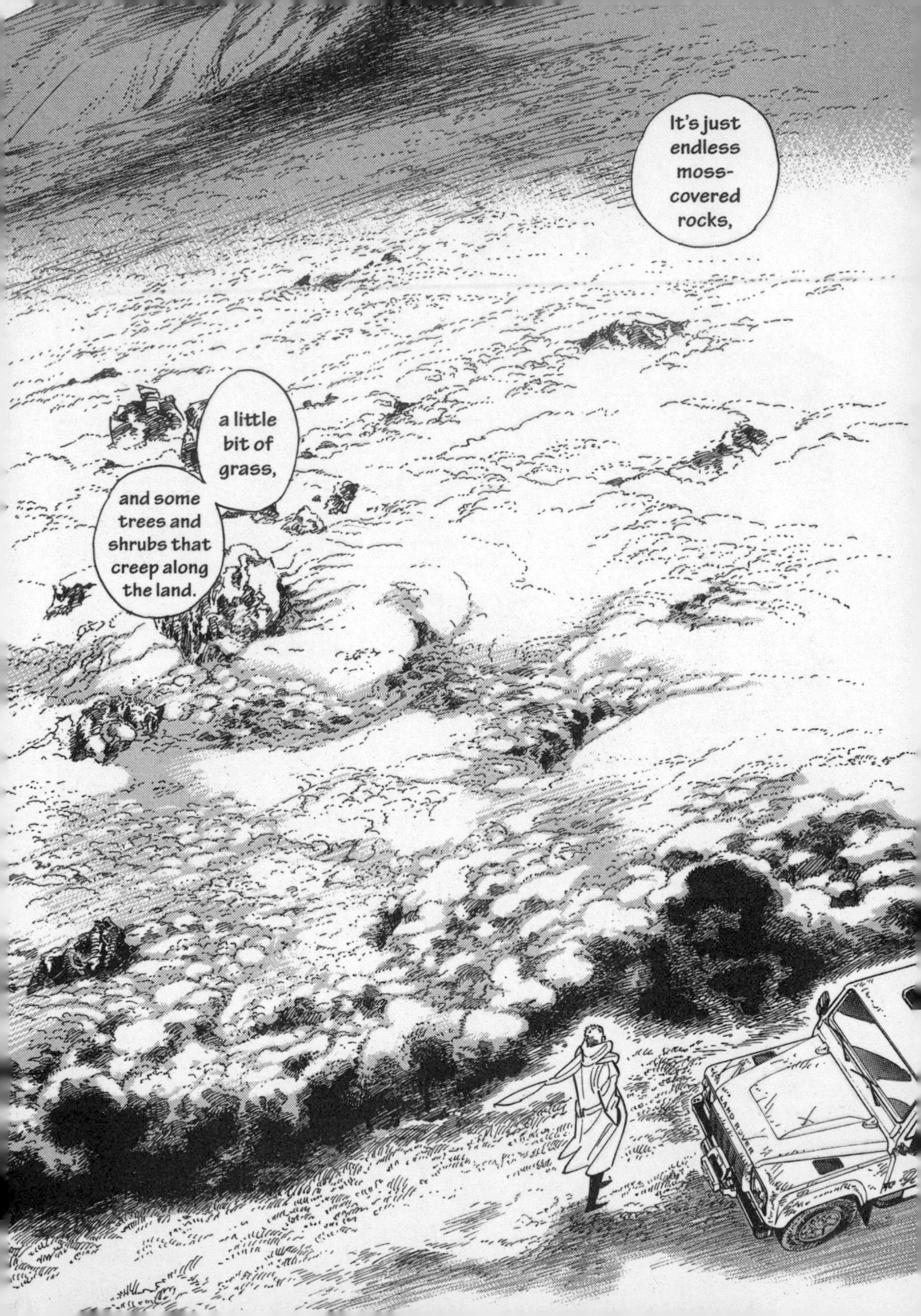
It's just endless moss-covered rocks,
a little bit of grass,
and some trees and shrubs that creep along the land.

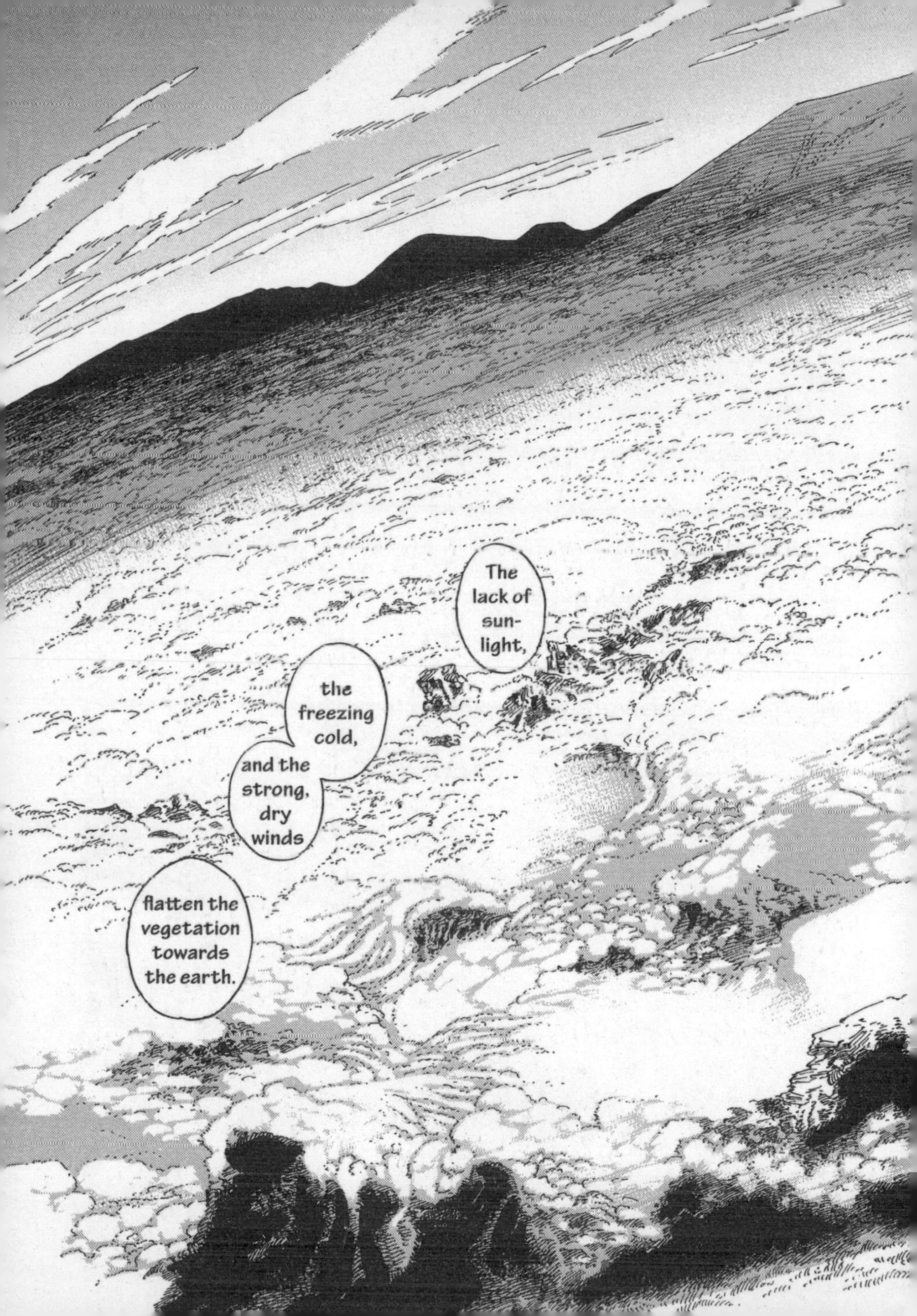
The lack of sun-light,
the freezing cold,
and the strong, dry winds
flatten the vegetation towards the earth.

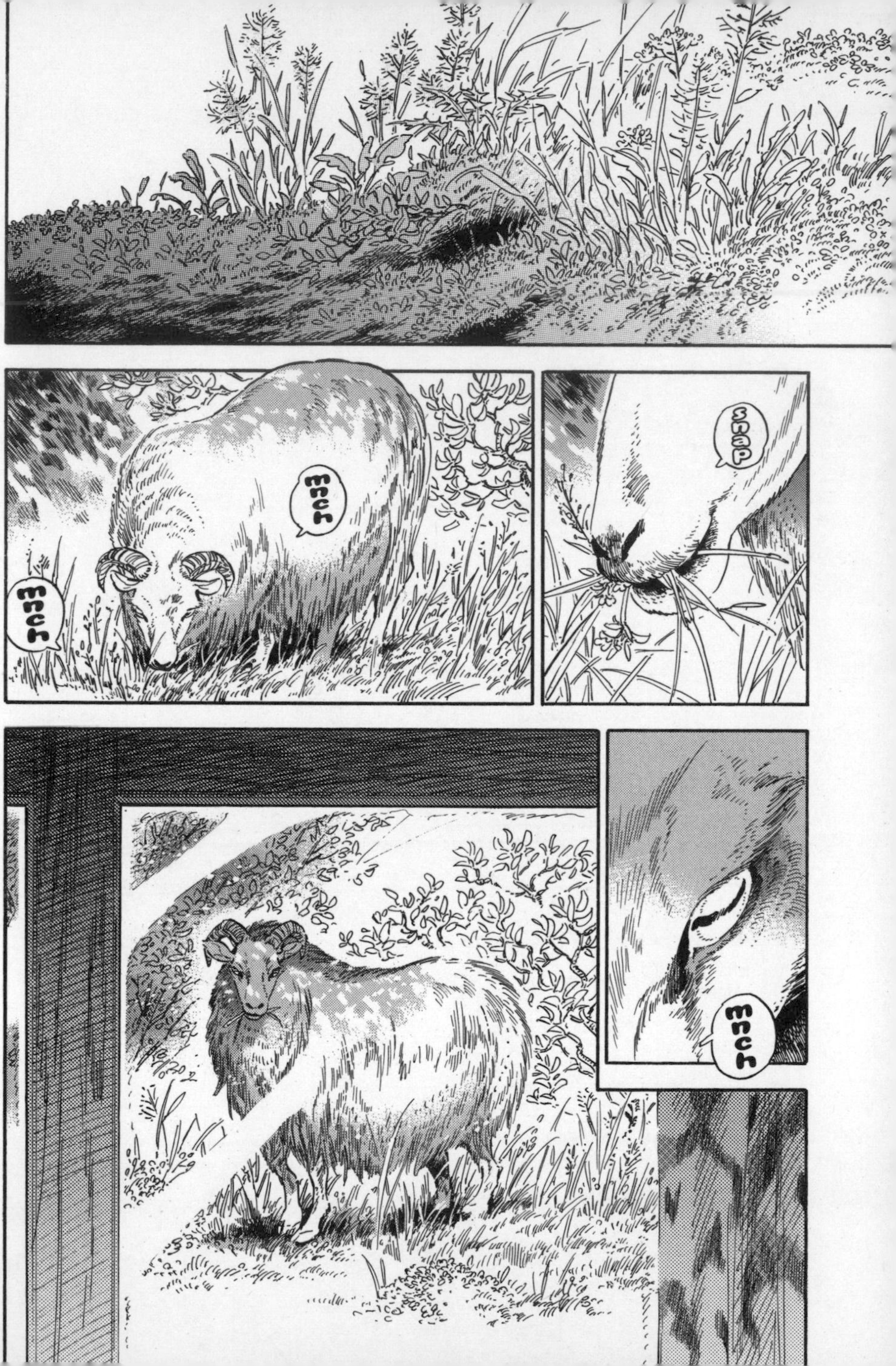
snap
mnch
mnch
mnch

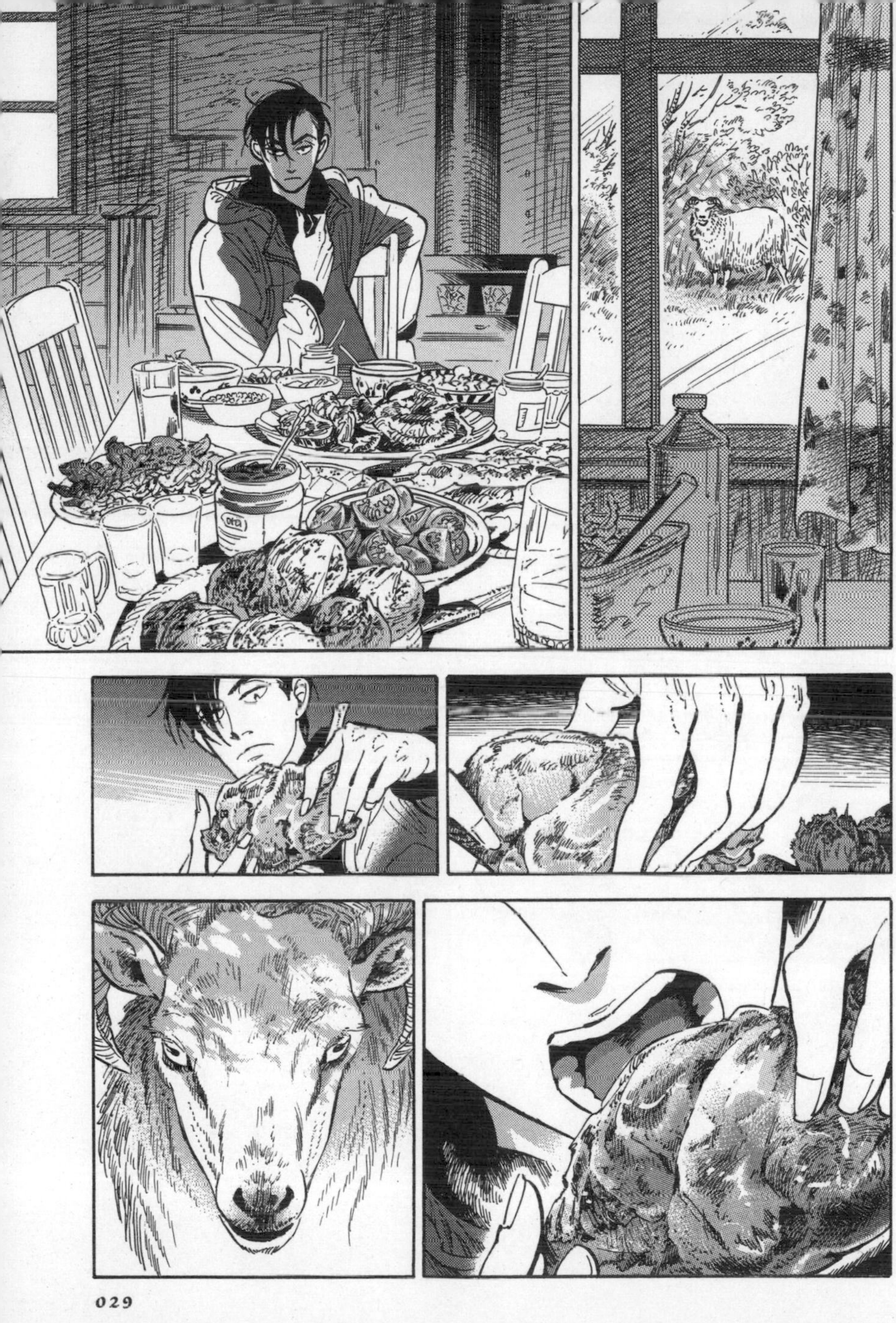

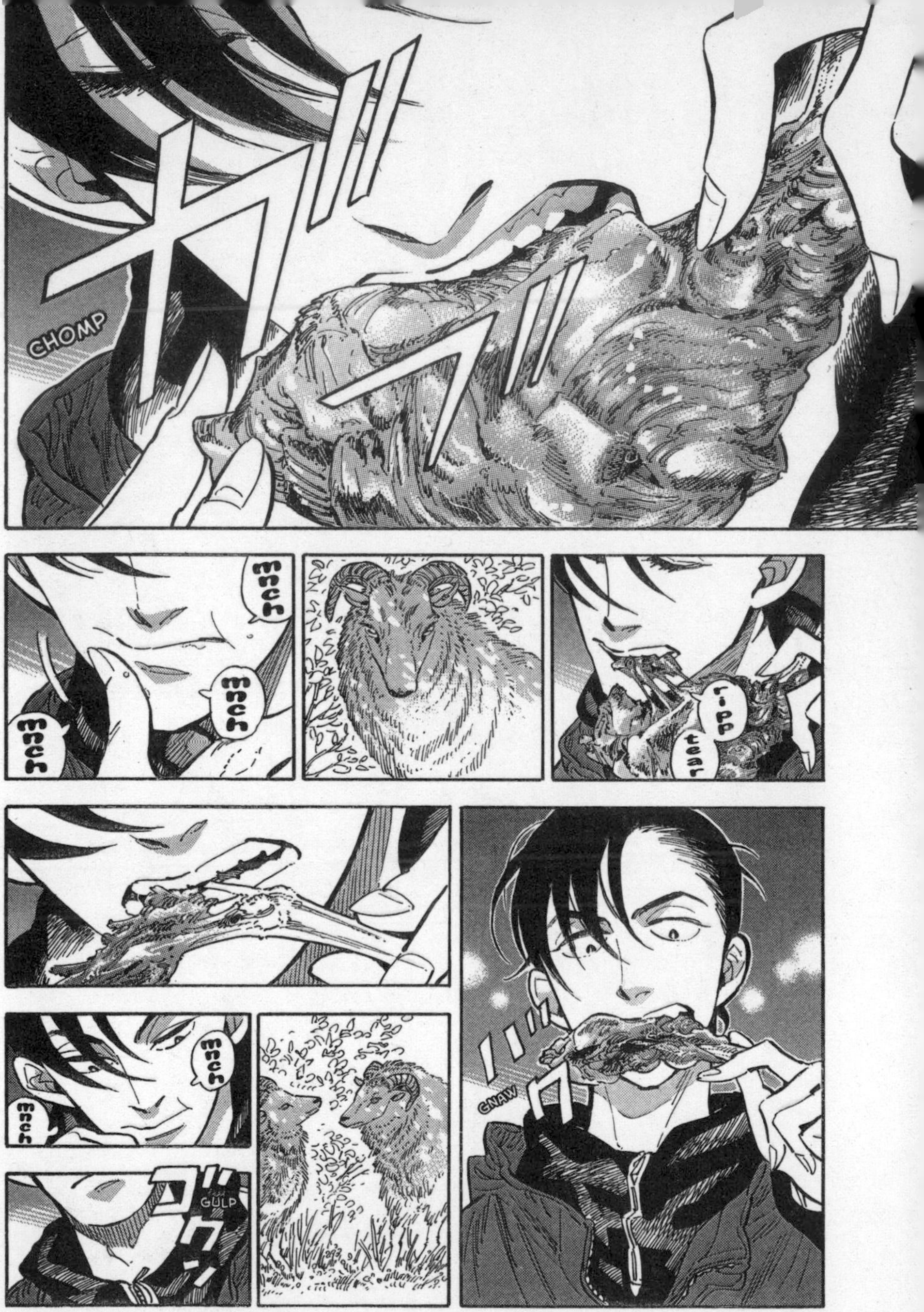
CHOMP
ripp
tear
mnch
mnch
mnch
GNAW
mnch
mnch
GULP

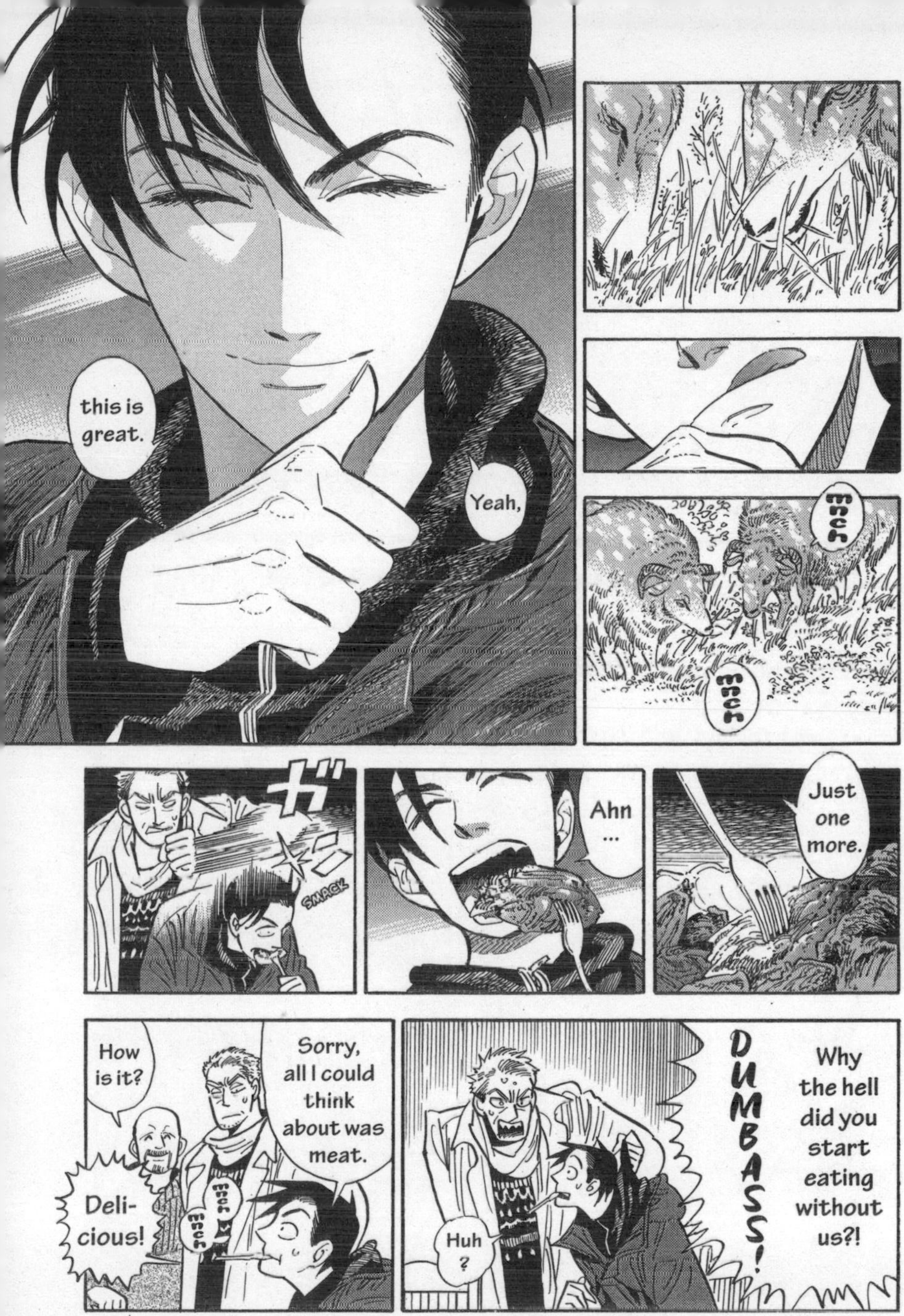
mnch
mnch
Yeah,
this is great.
Just one more.
Ahn ...
ガ
SMACK
Why the hell did you start eating without us?!
DUMBASS!
Huh?
Sorry, all I could think about was meat.
How is it?
mnch
mnch
Deli-cious!

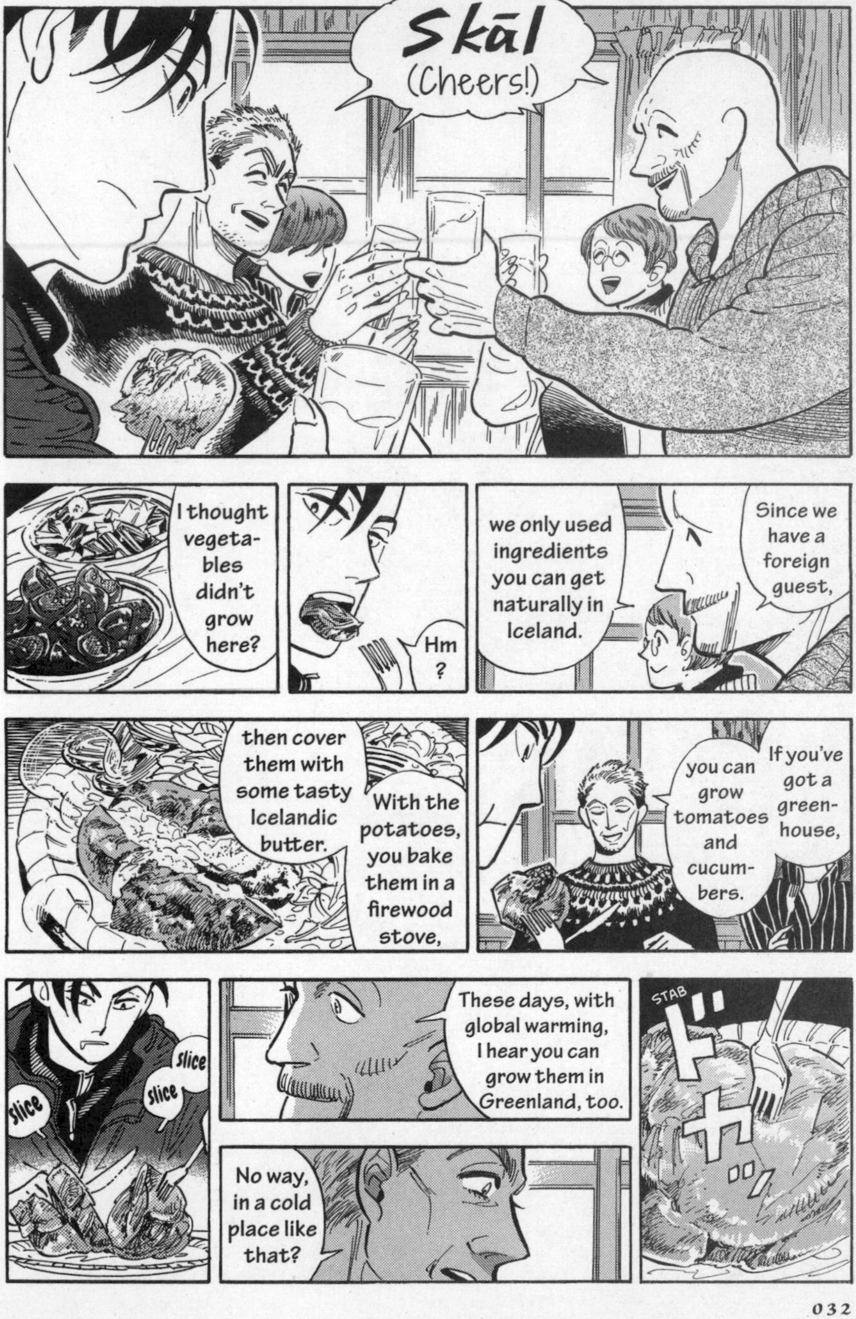
Skāl
(Cheers!)
Since we have a foreign guest,
we only used ingredients you can get naturally in Iceland.
Hm?
I thought vegeta-bles didn't grow here?
If you've got a green-house,
you can grow tomatoes and cucum-bers.
With the potatoes, you bake them in a firewood stove,
then cover them with some tasty Icelandic butter.
STAB
These days, with global warming, I hear you can grow them in Greenland, too.
No way, in a cold place like that?
slice
slice
slice

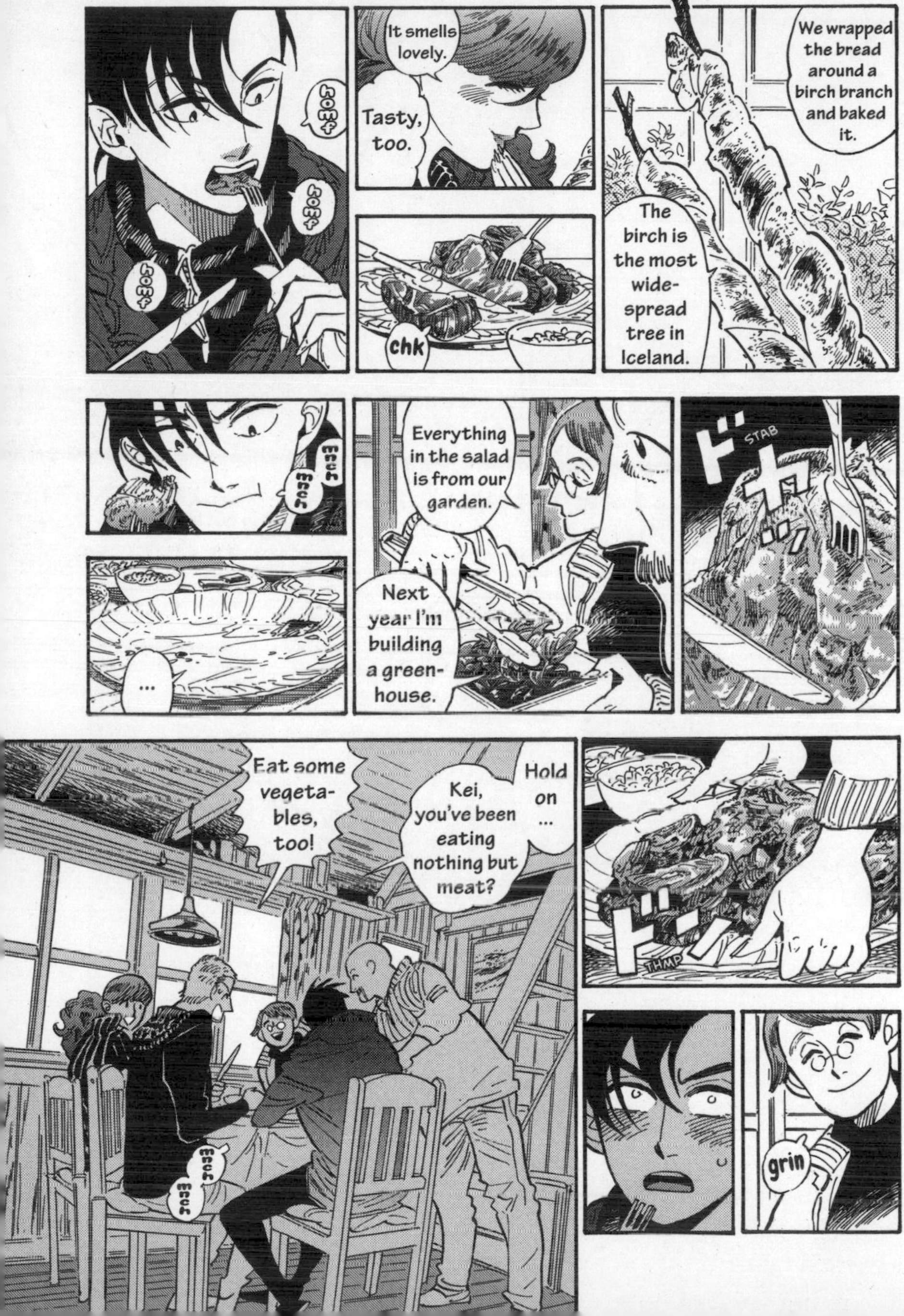
We wrapped the bread around a birch branch and baked it.
The birch is the most wide-spread tree in Iceland.
It smells lovely.
Tasty, too.
chk
nomf
nomf
nomf
ドカッ
STAB
Everything in the salad is from our garden.
Next year I'm building a green-house.
mnch
mnch
...
ドン
THMP
grin
Hold on ...
Kei, you've been eating nothing but meat?
Eat some vegeta-bles, too!
mnch
mnch

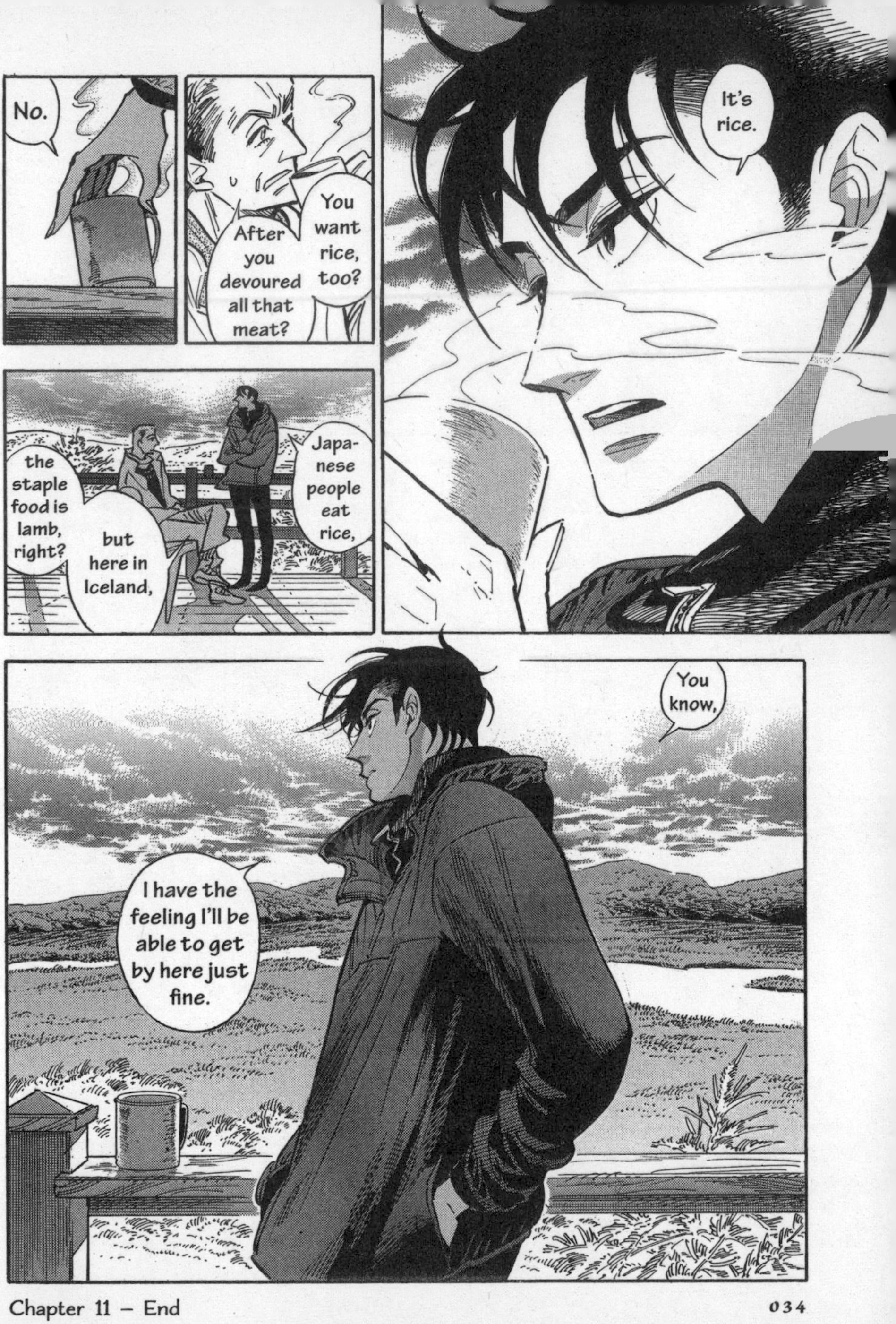
It's rice.
You want rice, too?
After you devoured all that meat?
No.
Japanese people eat rice,
but here in Iceland,
the staple food is lamb, right?
You know,
I have the feeling I'll be able to get by here just fine.

Chapter 12 [tólfti]

Rainbow shower welcome

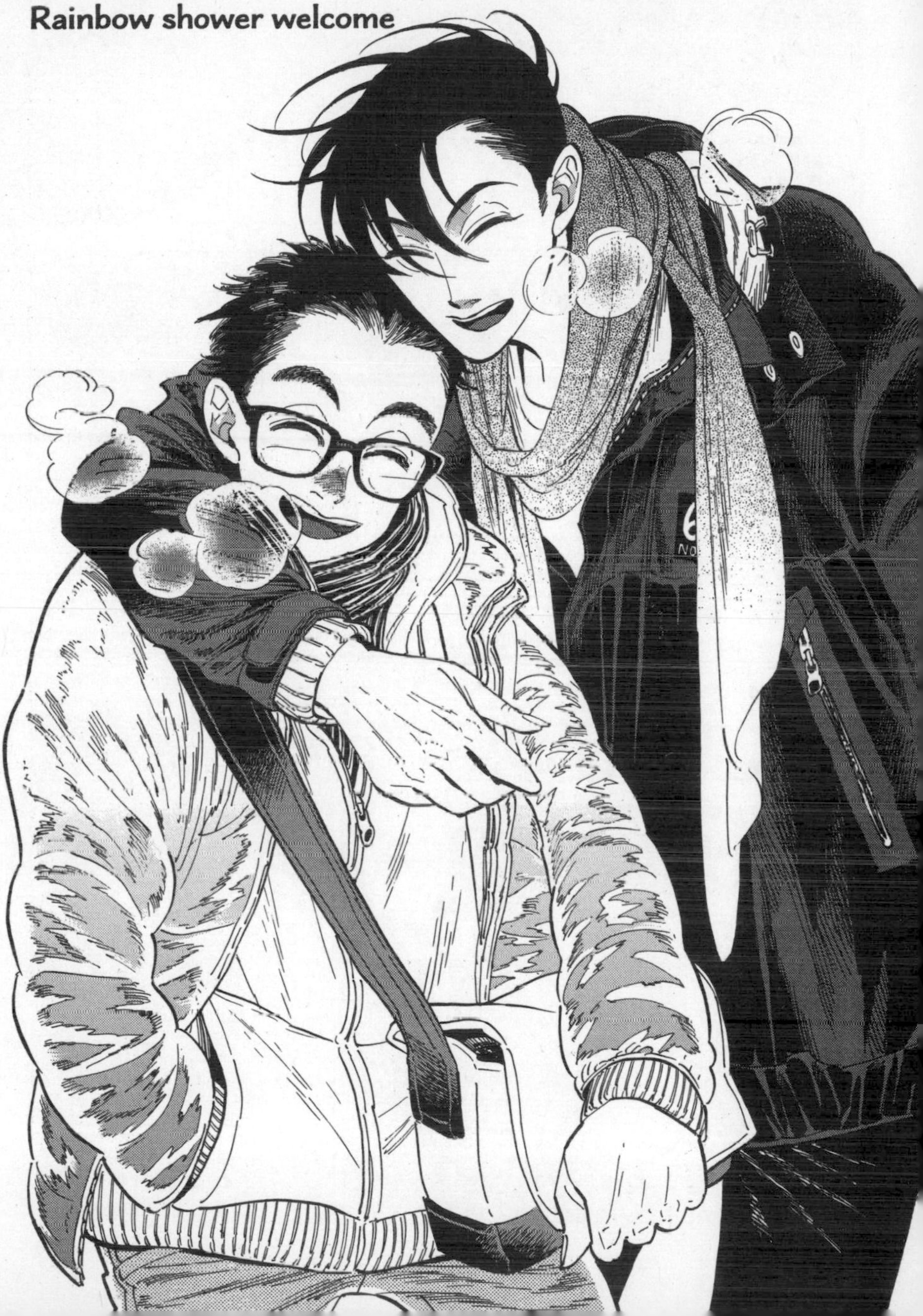

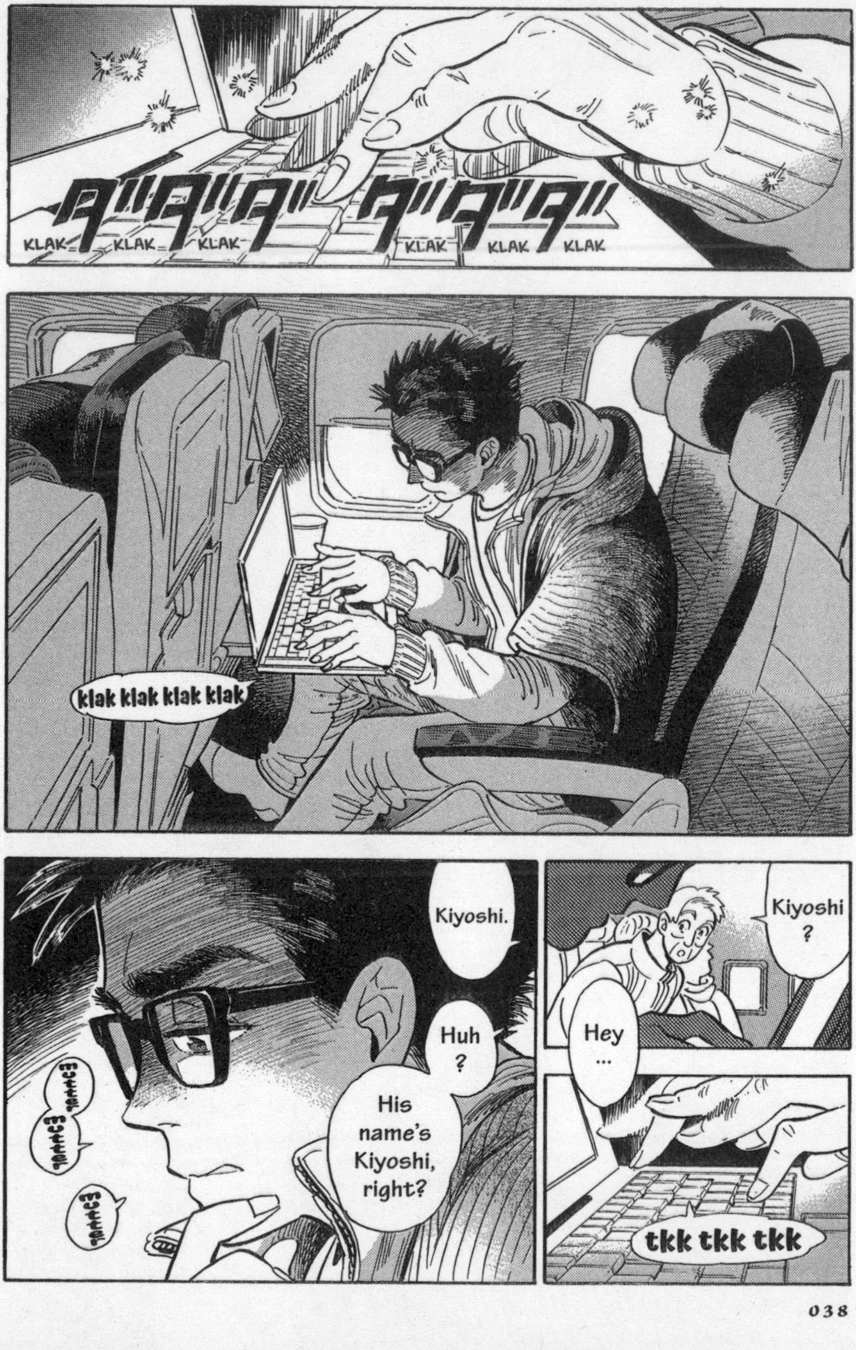
KLAK KLAK KLAK KLAK KLAK KLAK
klak klak klak klak
Kiyoshi ?
Hey ...
tkk tkk tkk
Kiyoshi.
Huh ?
His name's Kiyoshi, right?
mutter mutter
mutter

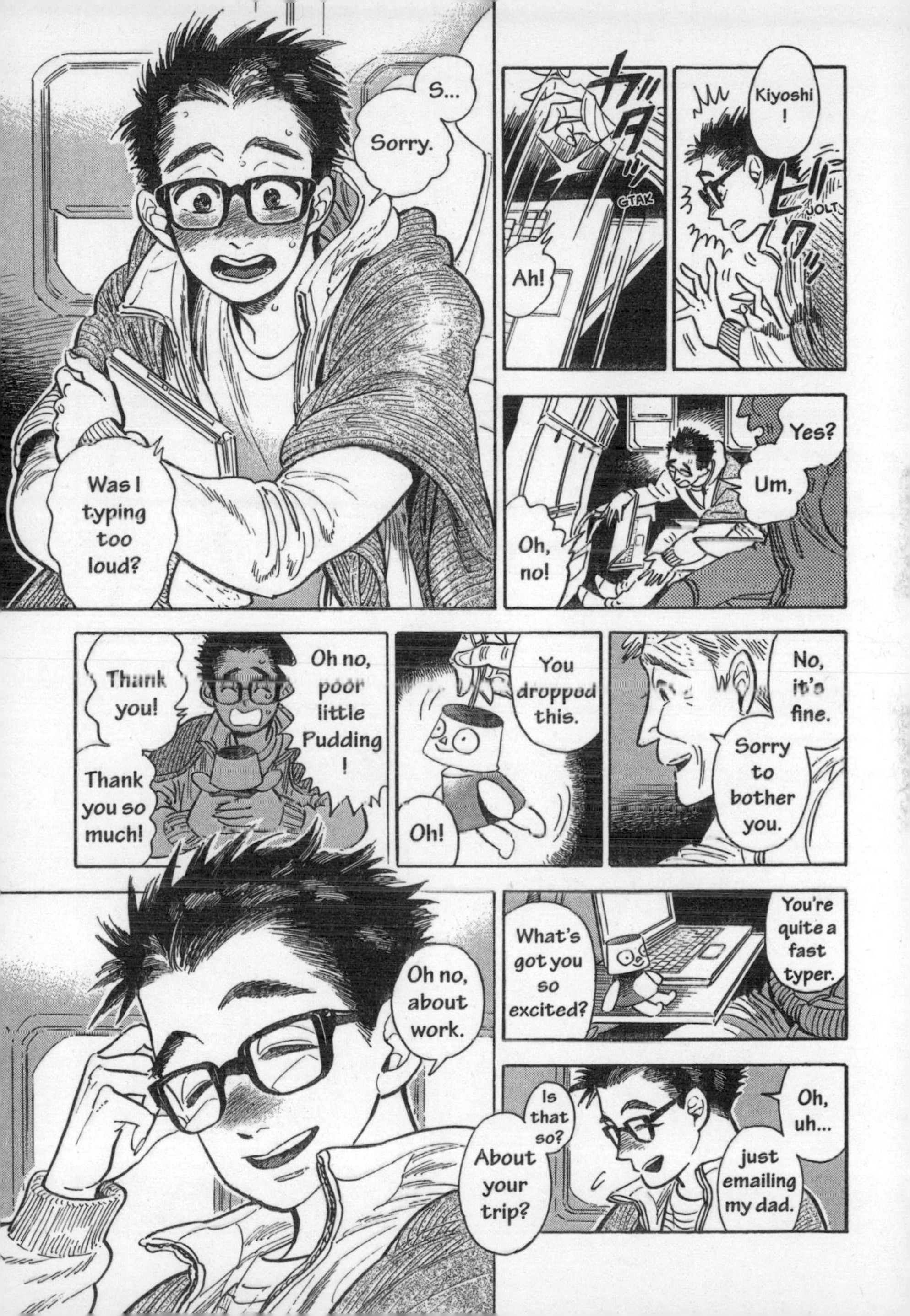
Kiyoshi!
JOLT
GTAK
Ah!
Yes?
Um,
Oh, no!
S...
Sorry.
Was I typing too loud?
No, it's fine.
Sorry to bother you.
You dropped this.
Oh!
Oh no, poor little Pudding!
Thank you!
Thank you so much!
You're quite a fast typer.
What's got you so excited?
Oh, uh...
just emailing my dad.
Is that so?
About your trip?
Oh no, about work.

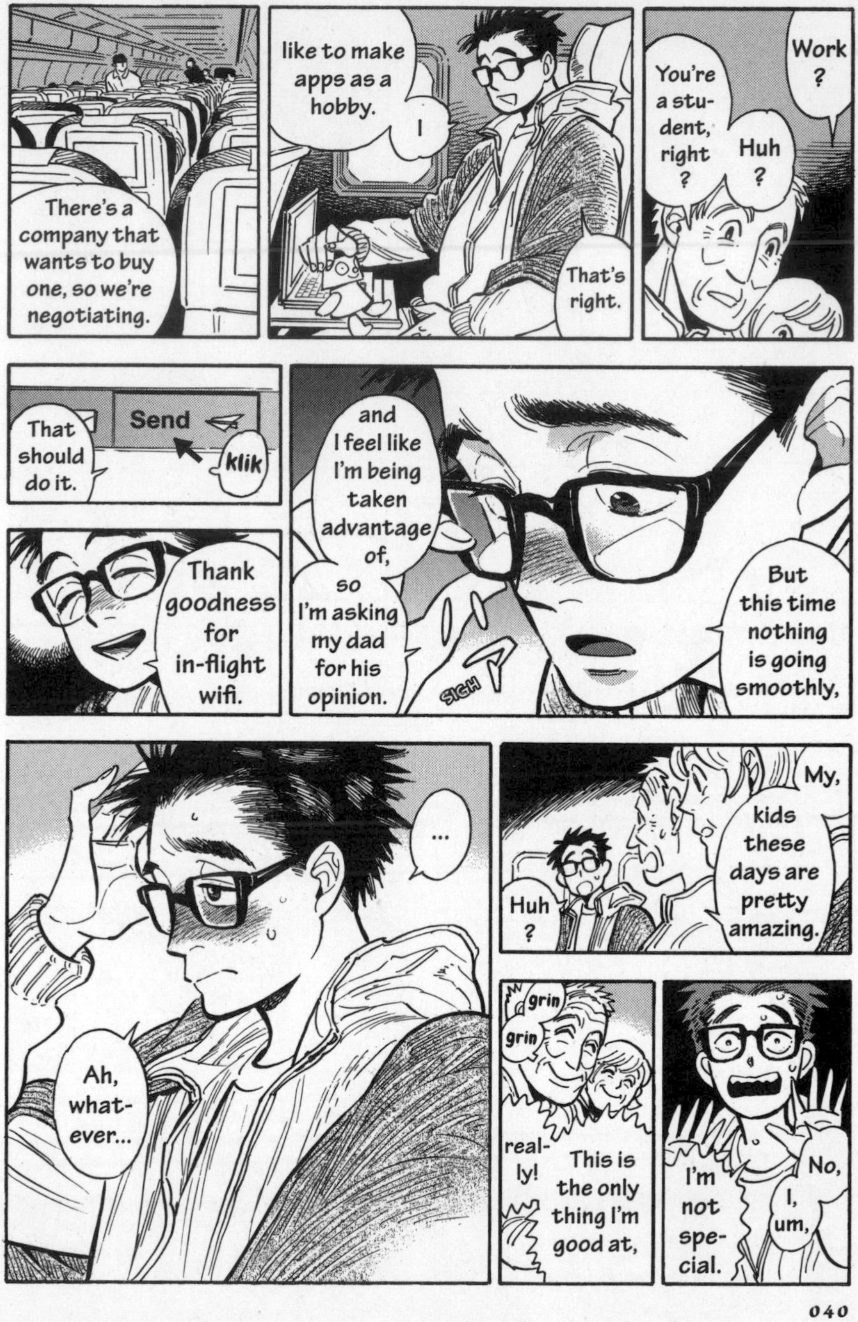
Work?
Huh?
You're a stu-dent, right?
That's right.
I
like to make apps as a hobby.
There's a company that wants to buy one, so we're negotiating.
But this time nothing is going smoothly,
and I feel like I'm being taken advantage of,
so I'm asking my dad for his opinion.
SIGH
Send
klik
That should do it.
Thank goodness for in-flight wifi.
My, kids these days are pretty amazing.
Huh?
No, I, um,
I'm not spe-cial.
This is the only thing I'm good at,
real-ly!
grin
grin
...
Ah, what-ever...

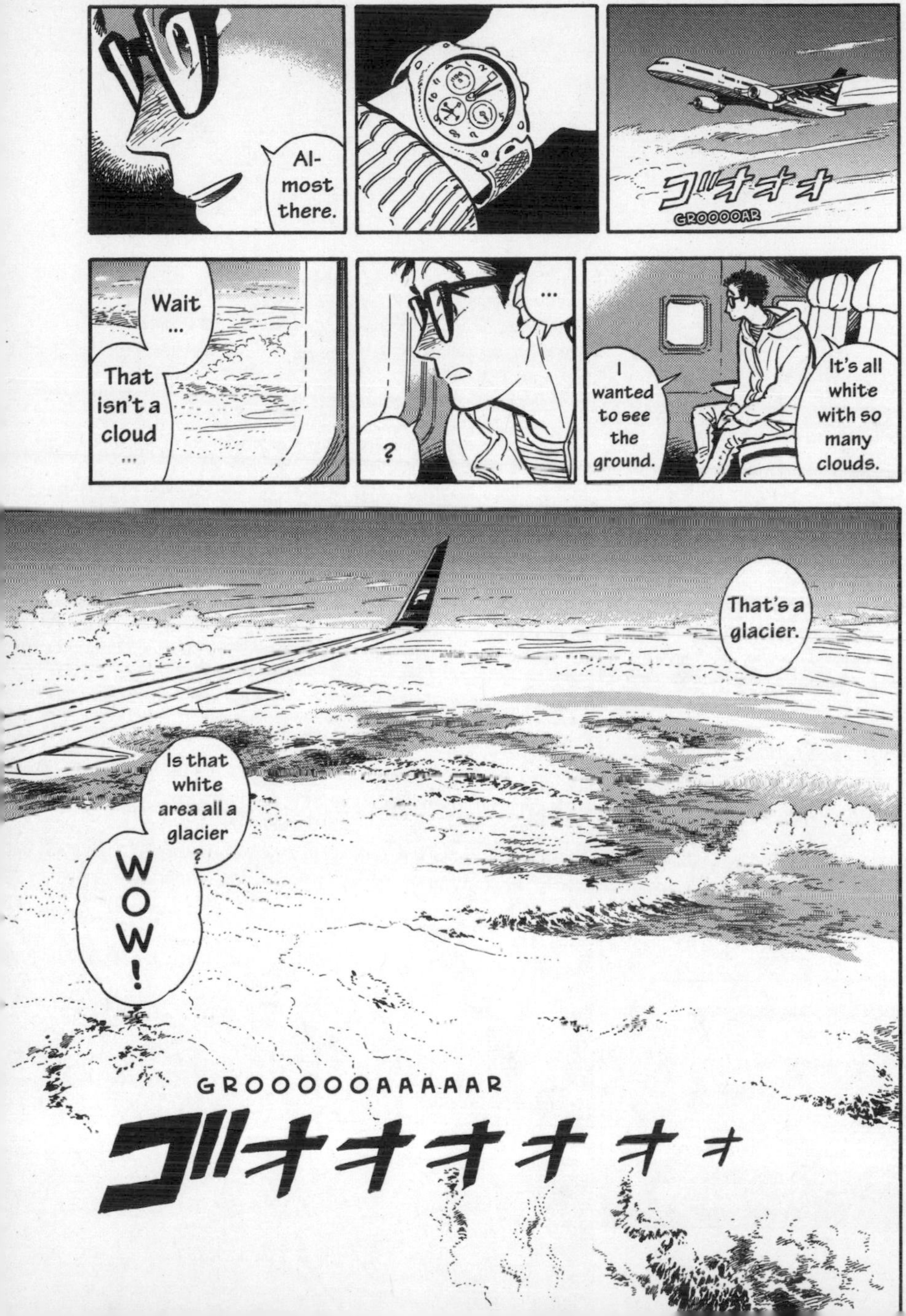
ゴオオオ
GROOOOAR
Al-most there.
It's all white with so many clouds.
I wanted to see the ground.
...
?
Wait ...
That isn't a cloud ...
That's a glacier.
Is that white area all a glacier?
WOW!
GROOOOOAAAAAR
ゴオオオオオオ

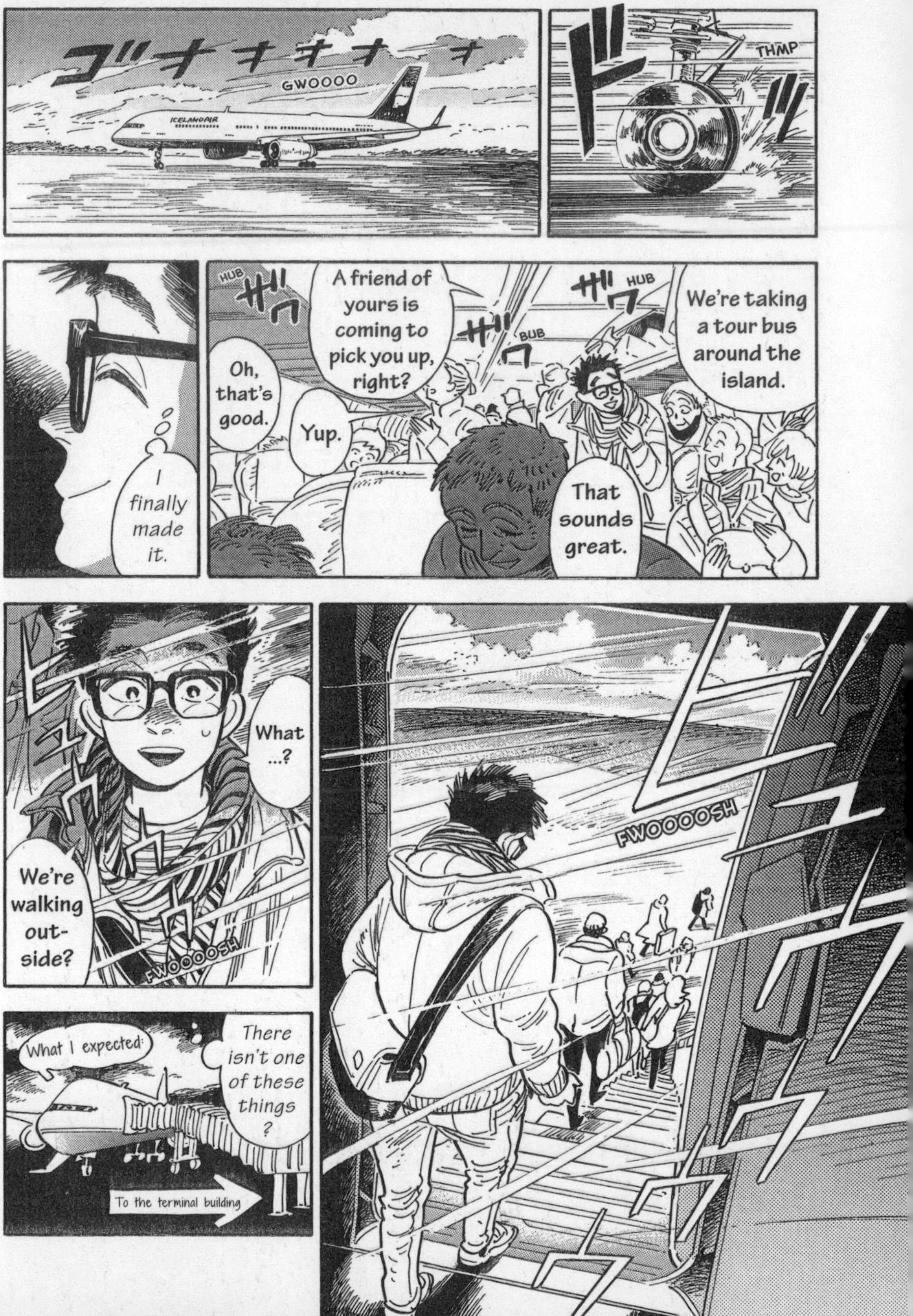
ドッ
THMP
ゴオオオオオ
GWOOOO
ICELANDAIR
HUB
BUB
We're taking a tour bus around the island.
That sounds great.
A friend of yours is coming to pick you up, right?
Yup.
Oh, that's good.
I finally made it.
FWOOOOSH
What ...?
We're walking out-side?
FWOOOOSH
What I expected:
There isn't one of these things?
To the terminal building

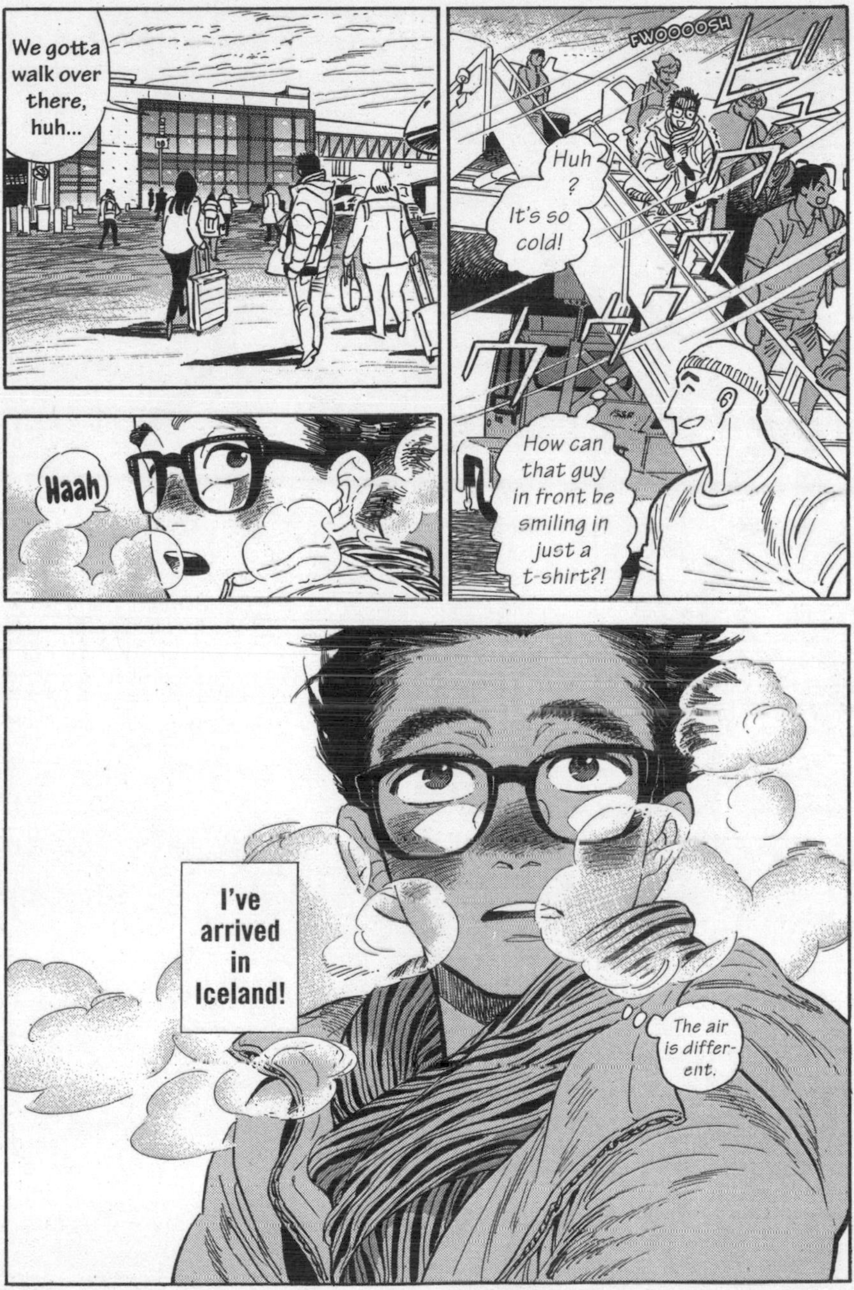
FWOOOOSH
Huh? It's so cold!
We gotta walk over there, huh...
How can that guy in front be smiling in just a t-shirt?!
Haah
I've arrived in Iceland!
The air is differ-ent.

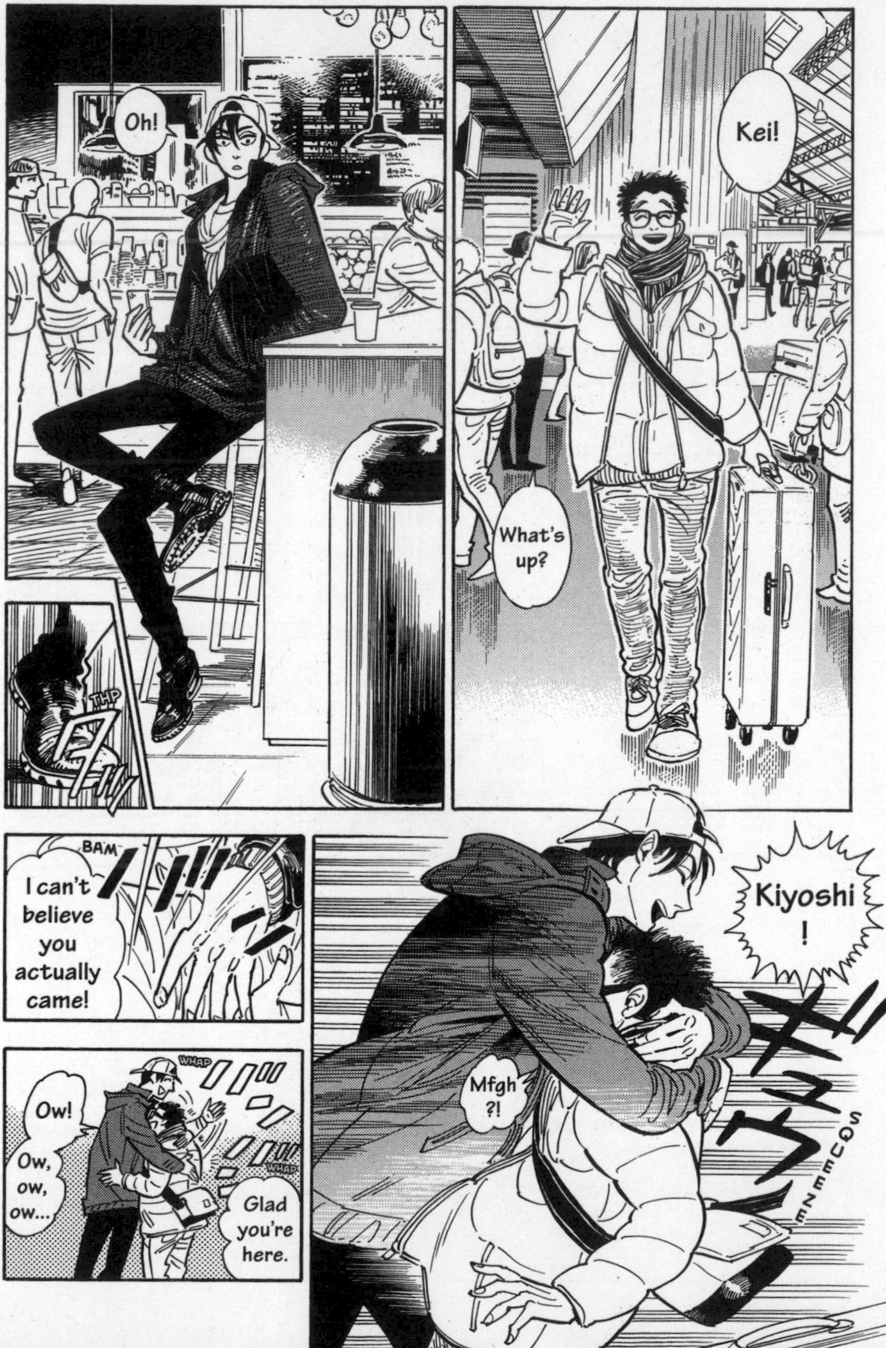
Kei!
What's up?
Oh!
THP
Kiyoshi!
SQUEEZE
Mfgh?!
BAM
I can't believe you actually came!
WHAP
WHAP
Glad you're here.
Ow!
Ow, ow, ow...

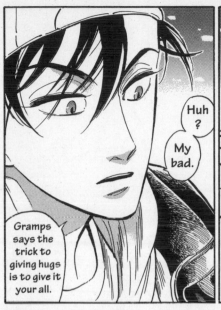

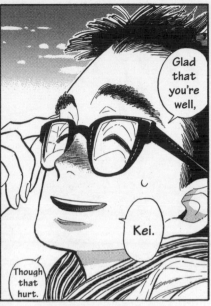

Glad that you're well,
Kei.
Though that hurt.
Huh?
My bad.
Gramps says the trick to giving hugs is to give it your all.
I see.
I guess overseas, you gotta hug people, huh.
You bet.
And I suck at it, too.
...
...
What're you getting all bashful about?
You're one to talk.

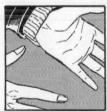

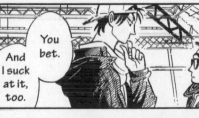

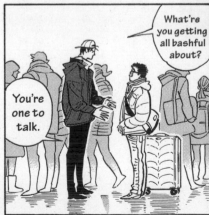

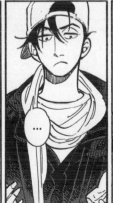

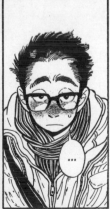

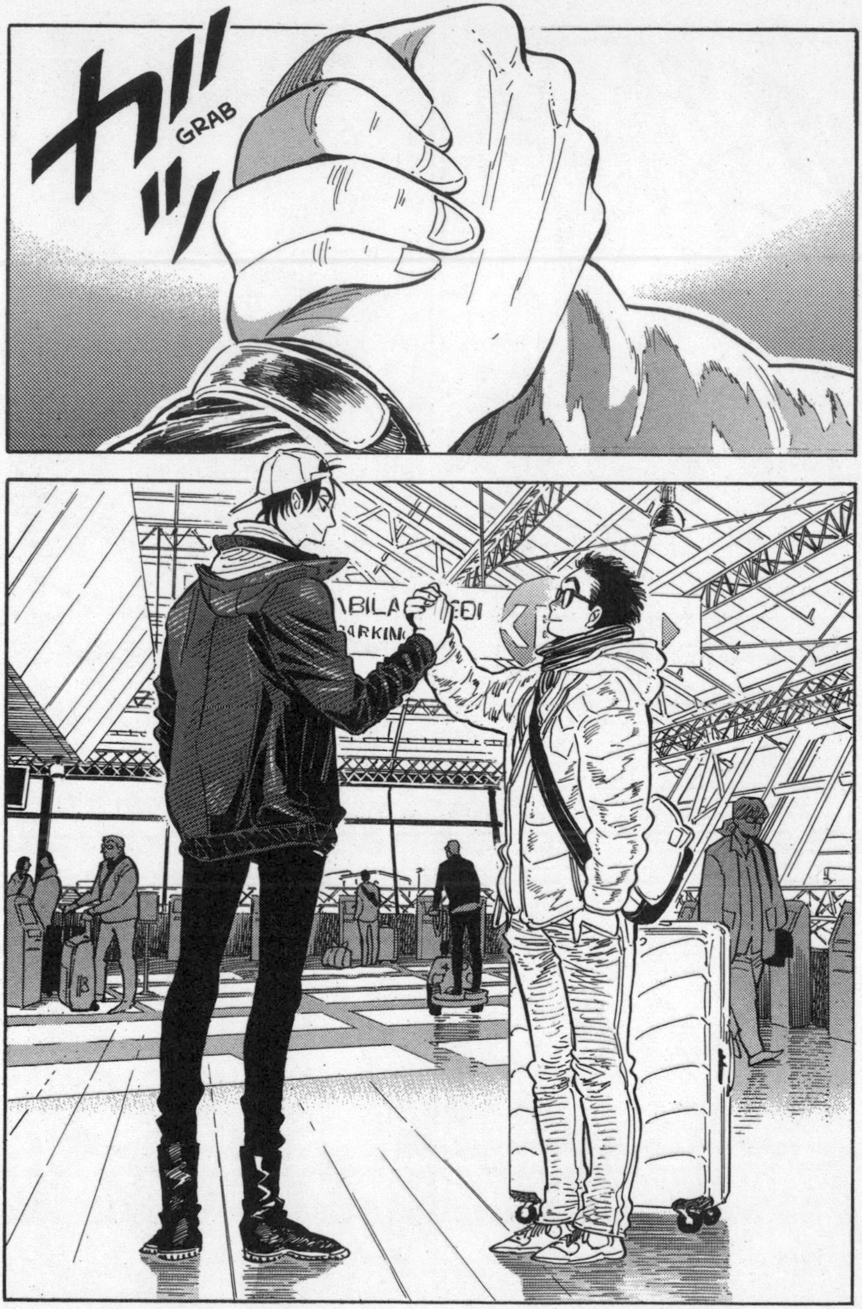
カッ
GRAB

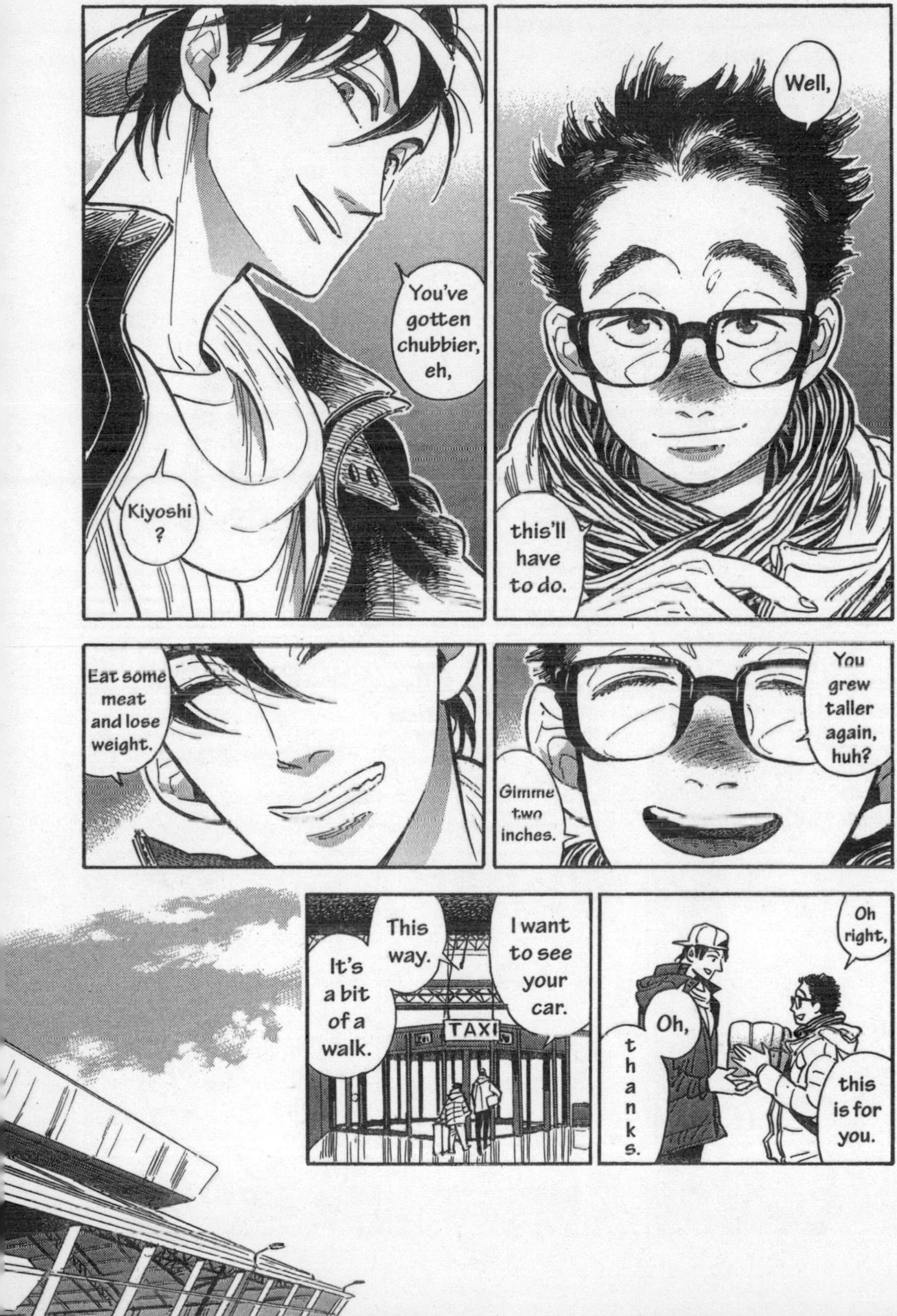
Well,
this'll have to do.
You've gotten chubbier, eh,
Kiyoshi?
You grew taller again, huh?
Gimme two inches.
Eat some meat and lose weight.
Oh right,
this is for you.
Oh,
thanks.
I want to see your car.
This way.
It's a bit of a walk.
TAXI

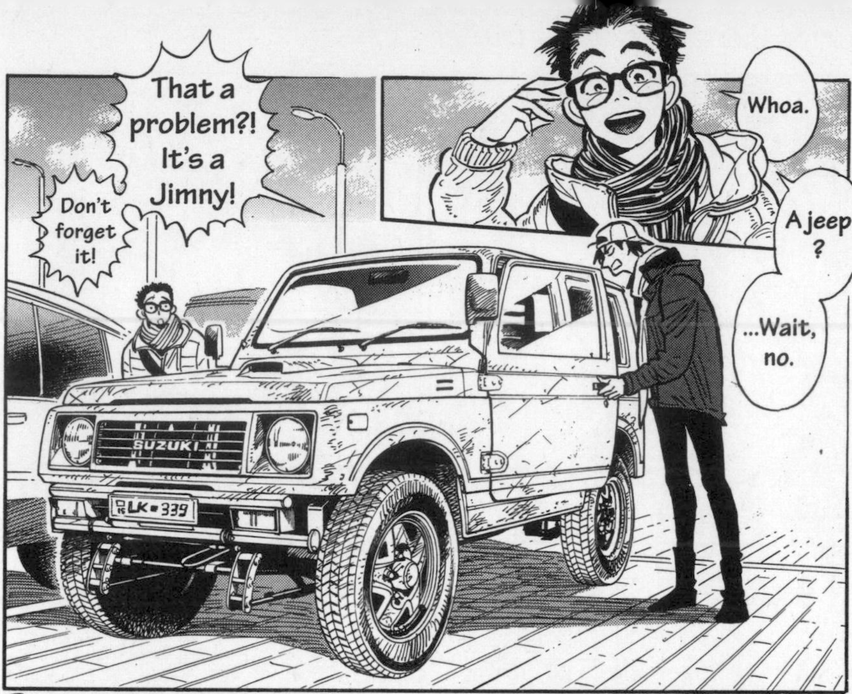
Whoa.
A jeep?
...Wait, no.
That a problem?! It's a Jimny!
Don't forget it!
SUZUKI

Overseas, it goes by the name Suzuki Samurai and is well-loved.

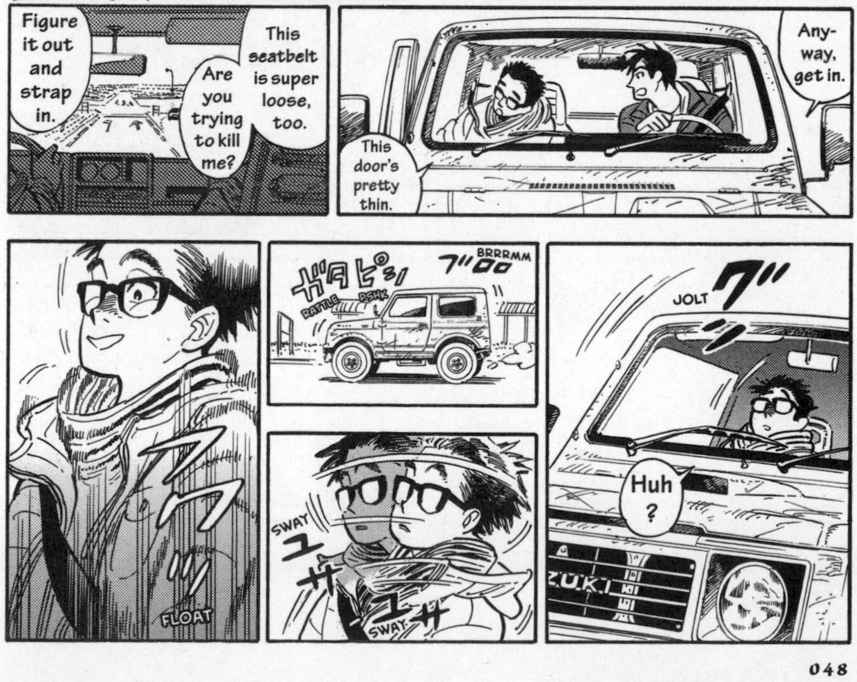
Any-way, get in.
This door's pretty thin.
This seatbelt is super loose, too.
Are you trying to kill me?
Figure it out and strap in.
JOLT
Huh?
BRRRMM
RATTLE
PSHK
SWAY
SWAY
FLOAT

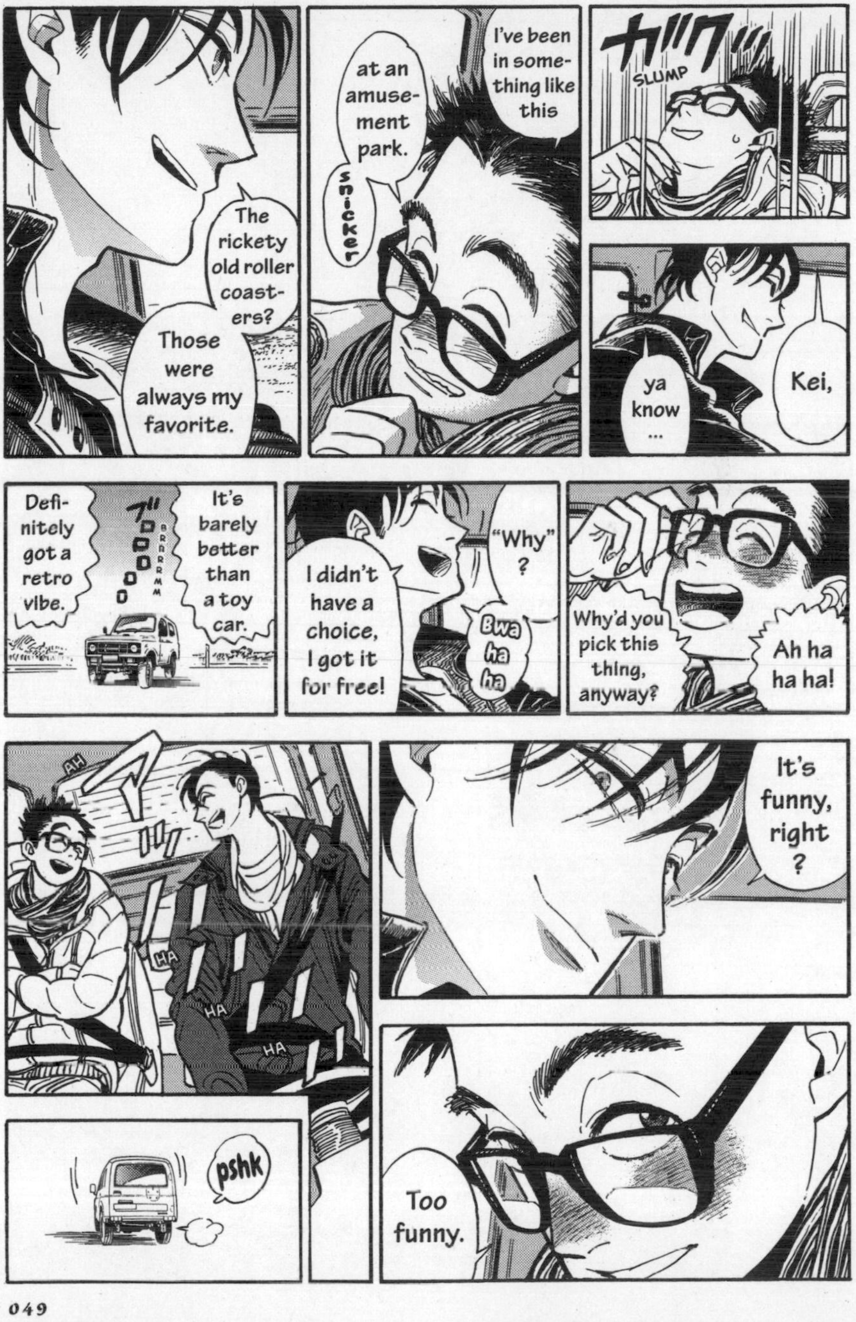
SLUMP
Kei,
ya know ...
I've been in something like this
at an amusement park.
snicker
The rickety old roller coasters?
Those were always my favorite.
Ah ha ha ha!
Why'd you pick this thing, anyway?
"Why"?
Bwa ha ha
I didn't have a choice, I got it for free!
It's barely better than a toy car.
BRRRRMM
Definitely got a retro vibe.
It's funny, right?
AH
HA
HA
HA
Too funny.
pshk

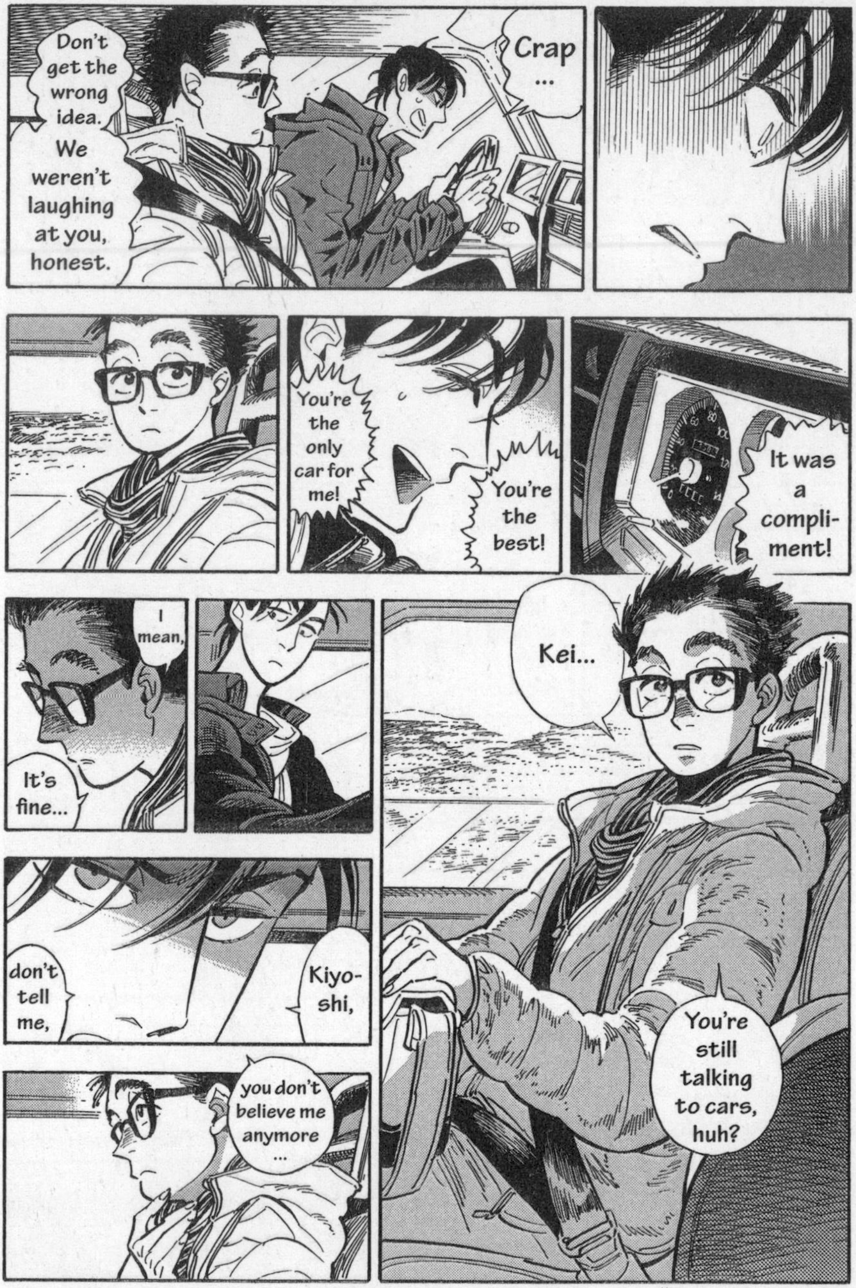
Crap ...
Don't get the wrong idea.
We weren't laughing at you, honest.
It was a compli-ment!
You're the best!
You're the only car for me!
Kei...
You're still talking to cars, huh?
I mean,
It's fine...
Kiyo-shi,
don't tell me,
you don't believe me anymore ...

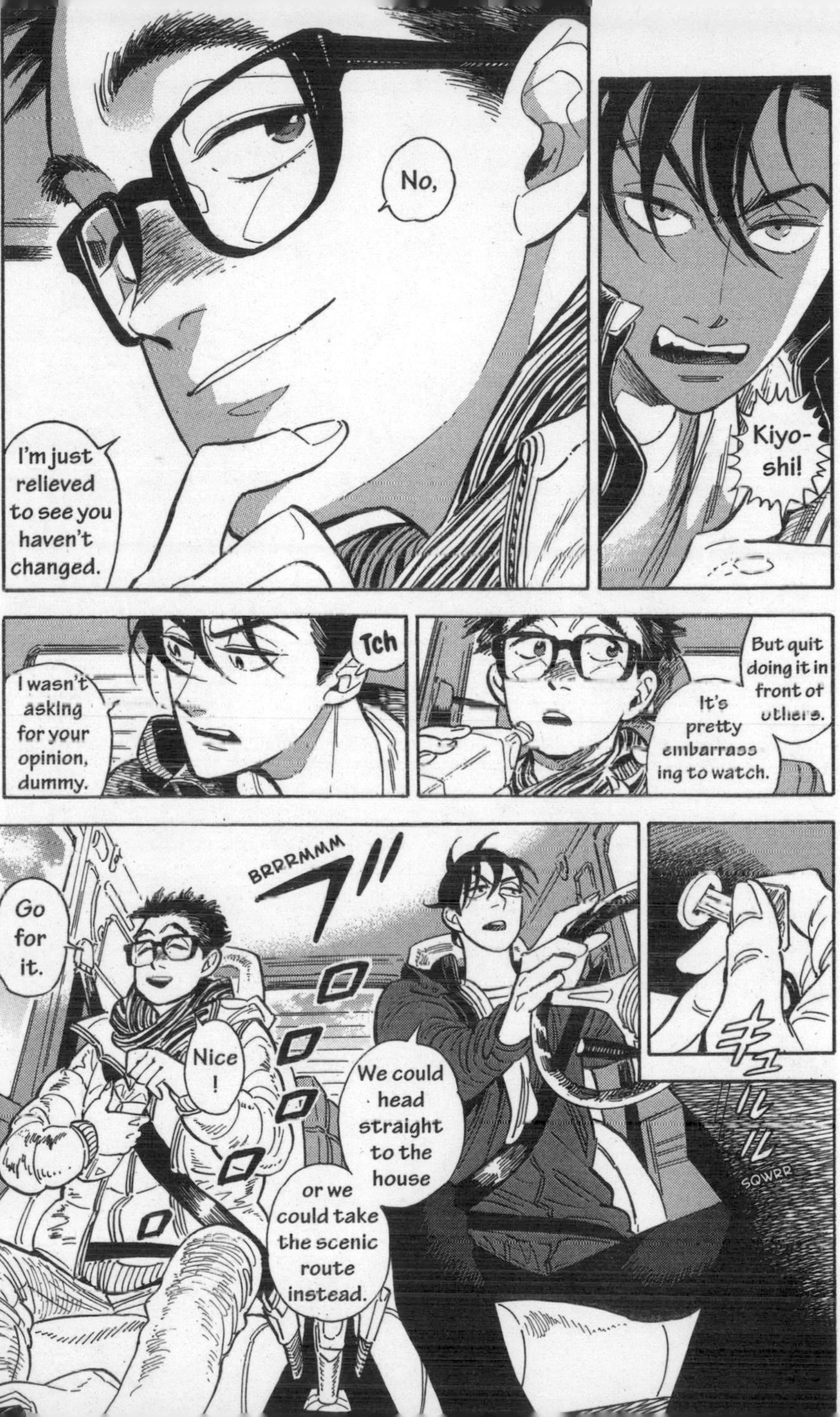
Kiyo-shi!
No,
I'm just relieved to see you haven't changed.
But quit doing it in front of others.
It's pretty embarrass ing to watch.
Tch
I wasn't asking for your opinion, dummy.
キュルル
SQWRR
BRRRMMM
ブ
We could head straight to the house
or we could take the scenic route instead.
Nice!
Go for it.

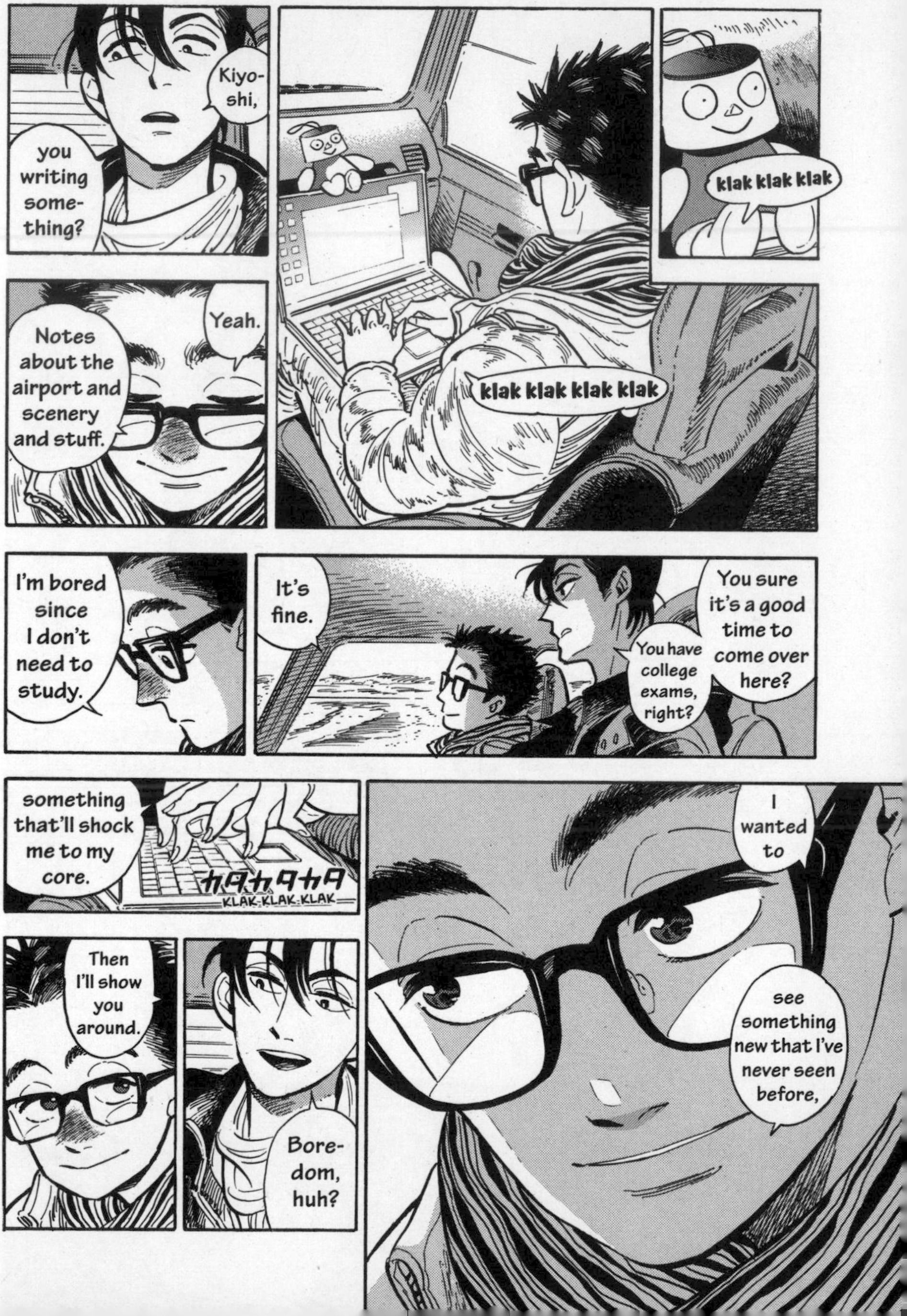
klak klak klak
klak klak klak klak
Kiyo-shi,
you writing some-thing?
Yeah.
Notes about the airport and scenery and stuff.
You sure it's a good time to come over here?
You have college exams, right?
It's fine.
I'm bored since I don't need to study.
I wanted to
see something new that I've never seen before,
something that'll shock me to my core.
カタカタカタ
KLAK-KLAK-KLAK
Bore-dom, huh?
Then I'll show you around.

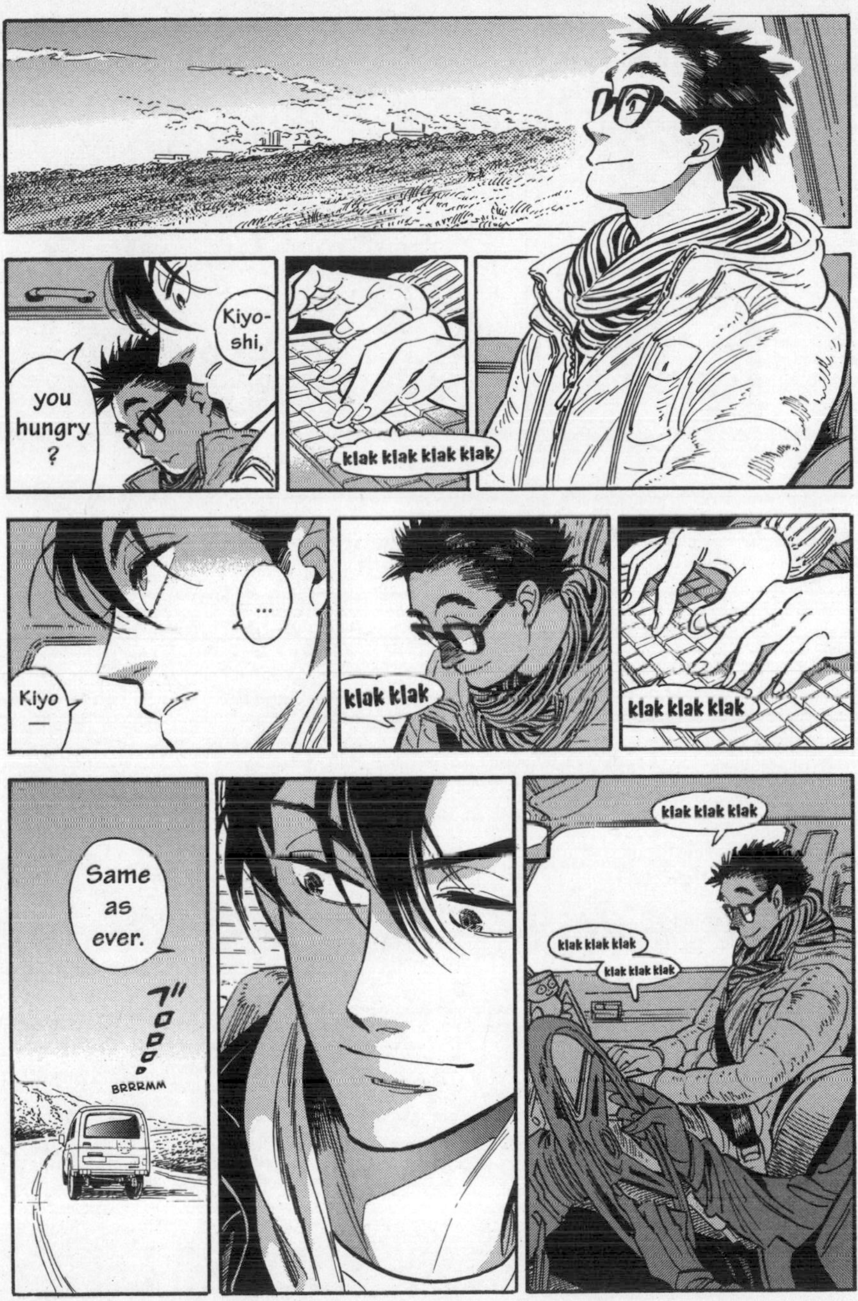
klak klak klak klak
Kiyo-shi,
you hungry ?
klak klak klak
klak klak
...
Kiyo —
klak klak klak
klak klak klak
klak klak klak
Same as ever.
ブロロロロ
BRRRMM

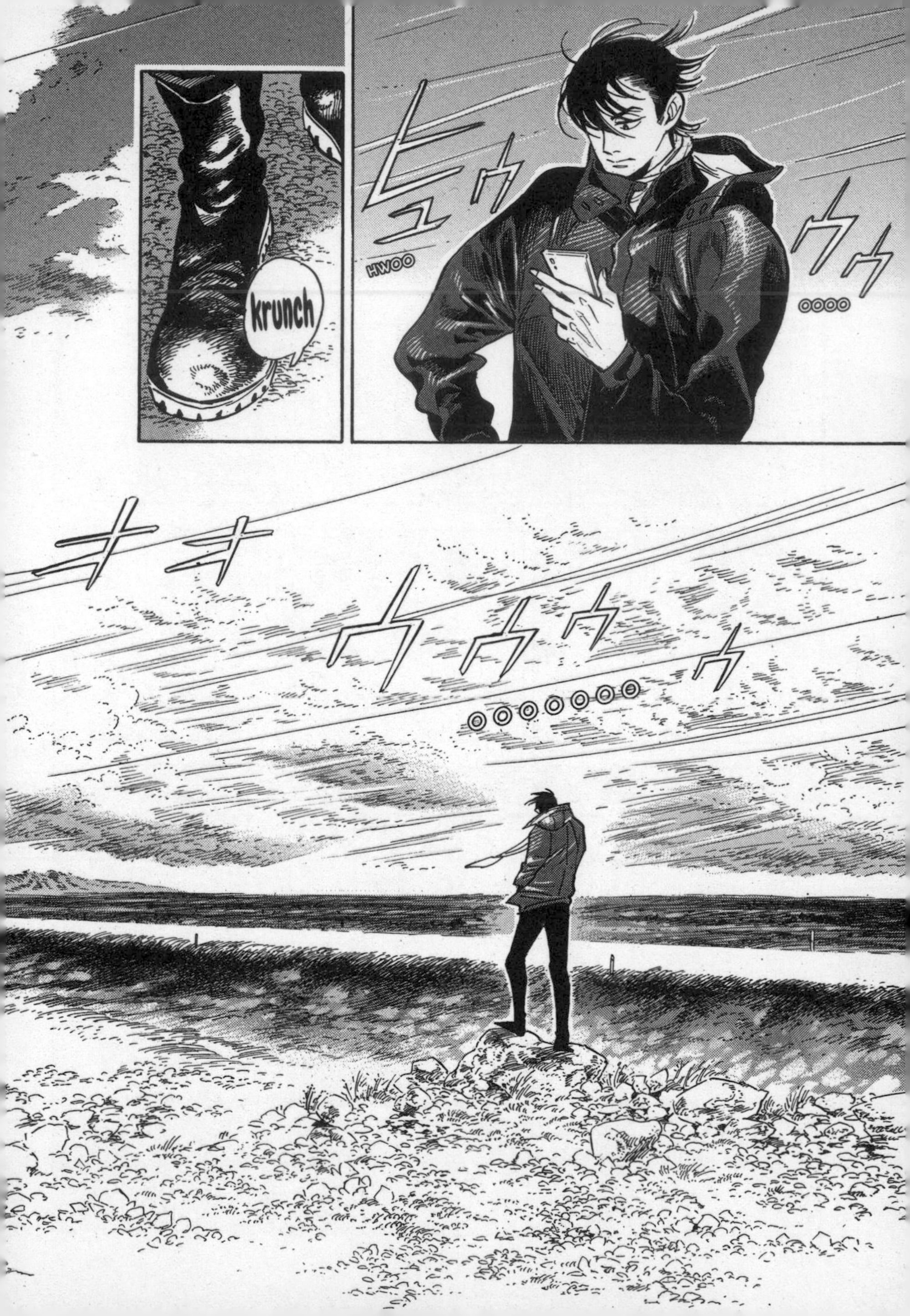
ヒュウ
HWOO
ウゥ
OOOO
krunch
オオウウウゥ
OOOOOOOO

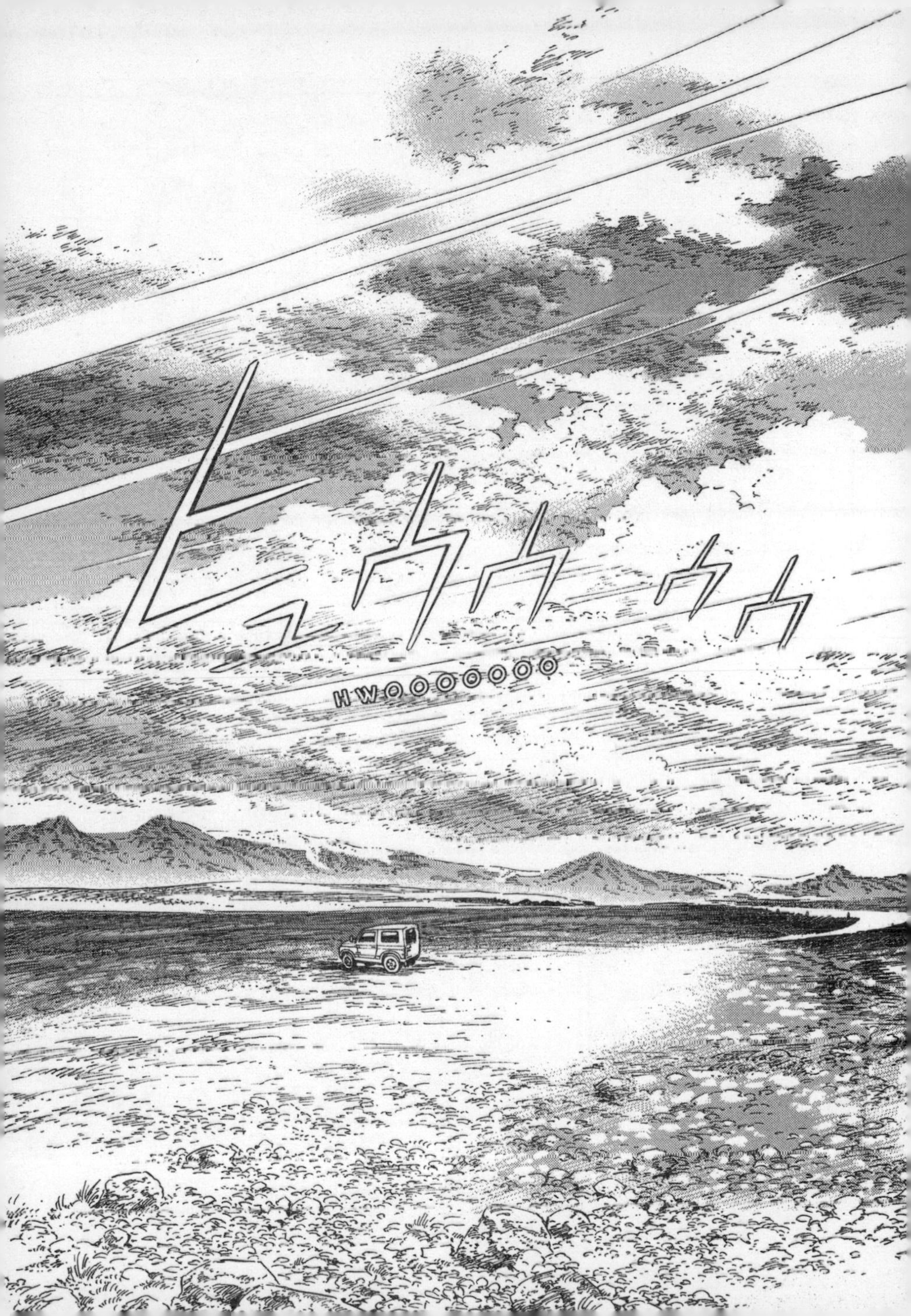
ヒュウウゥゥゥ
HWOOOOOOOO

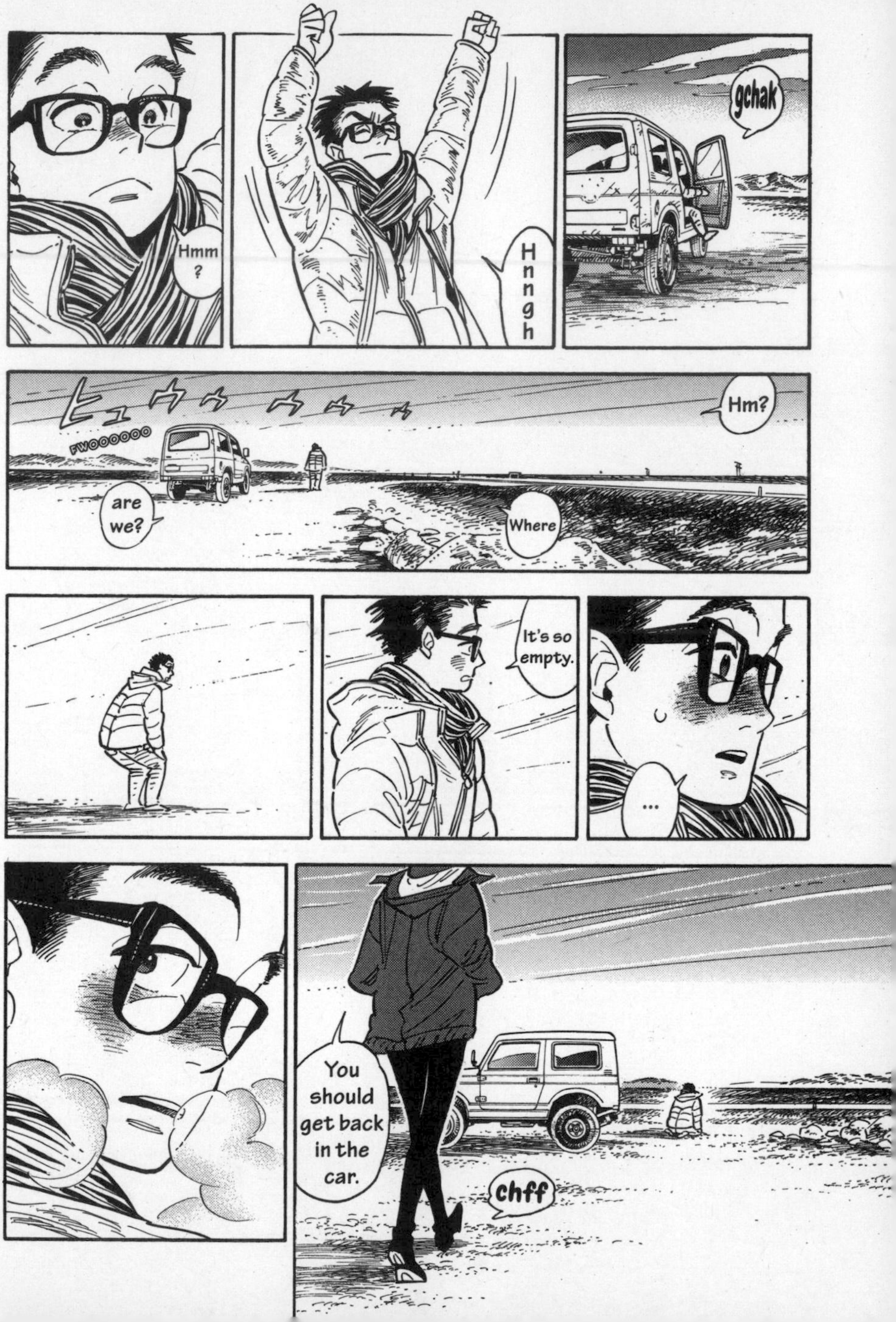
gchak
Hnngh
Hmm ?
Hm?
ヒュウゥゥ ゥゥゥ
FWOOOOOO
Where
are we?
...
It's so empty.
You should get back in the car.
chff

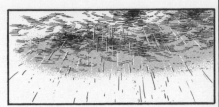

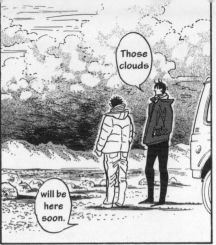

Those clouds
will be here soon.
pitter
patter
pitter
ZHAAAAAA
…
I'm starving.
Here.
Huh?
rstle
It's cold now, but...
There's two for each of us.
When did you get these?

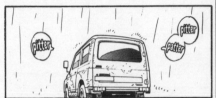

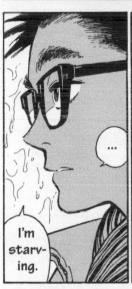

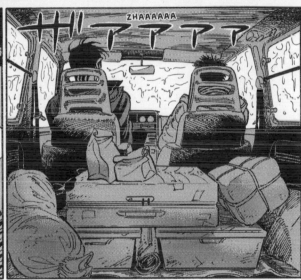

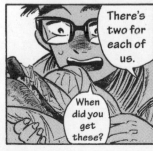

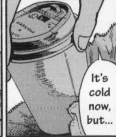

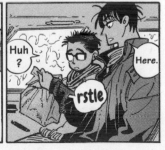

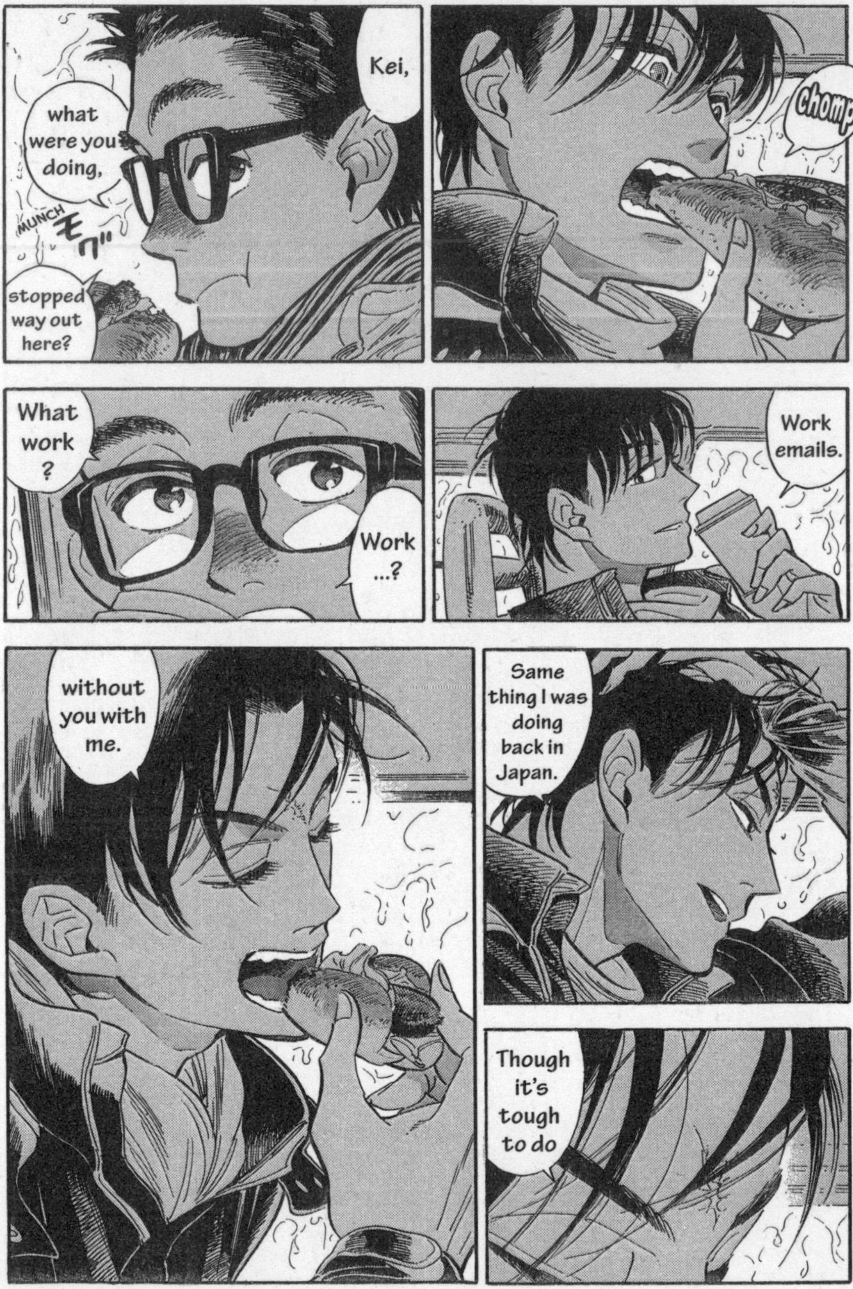
chomp
Kei,
what were you doing,
MUNCH モグ
stopped way out here?
Work emails.
Work ...?
What work ?
Same thing I was doing back in Japan.
Though it's tough to do
without you with me.

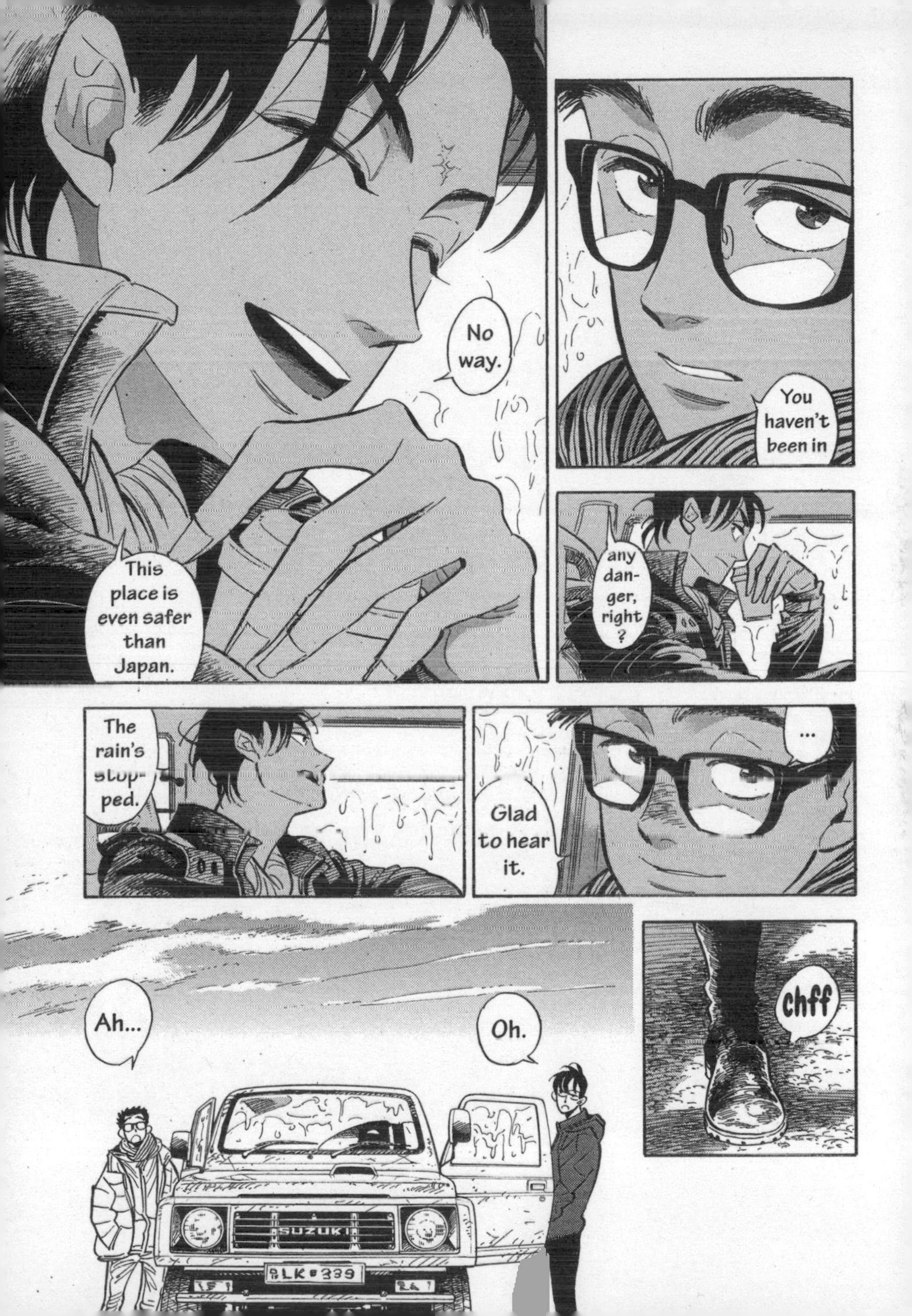
You haven't been in
any danger, right?
No way.
This place is even safer than Japan.
...
Glad to hear it.
The rain's stopped.
chff
Oh.
Ah...

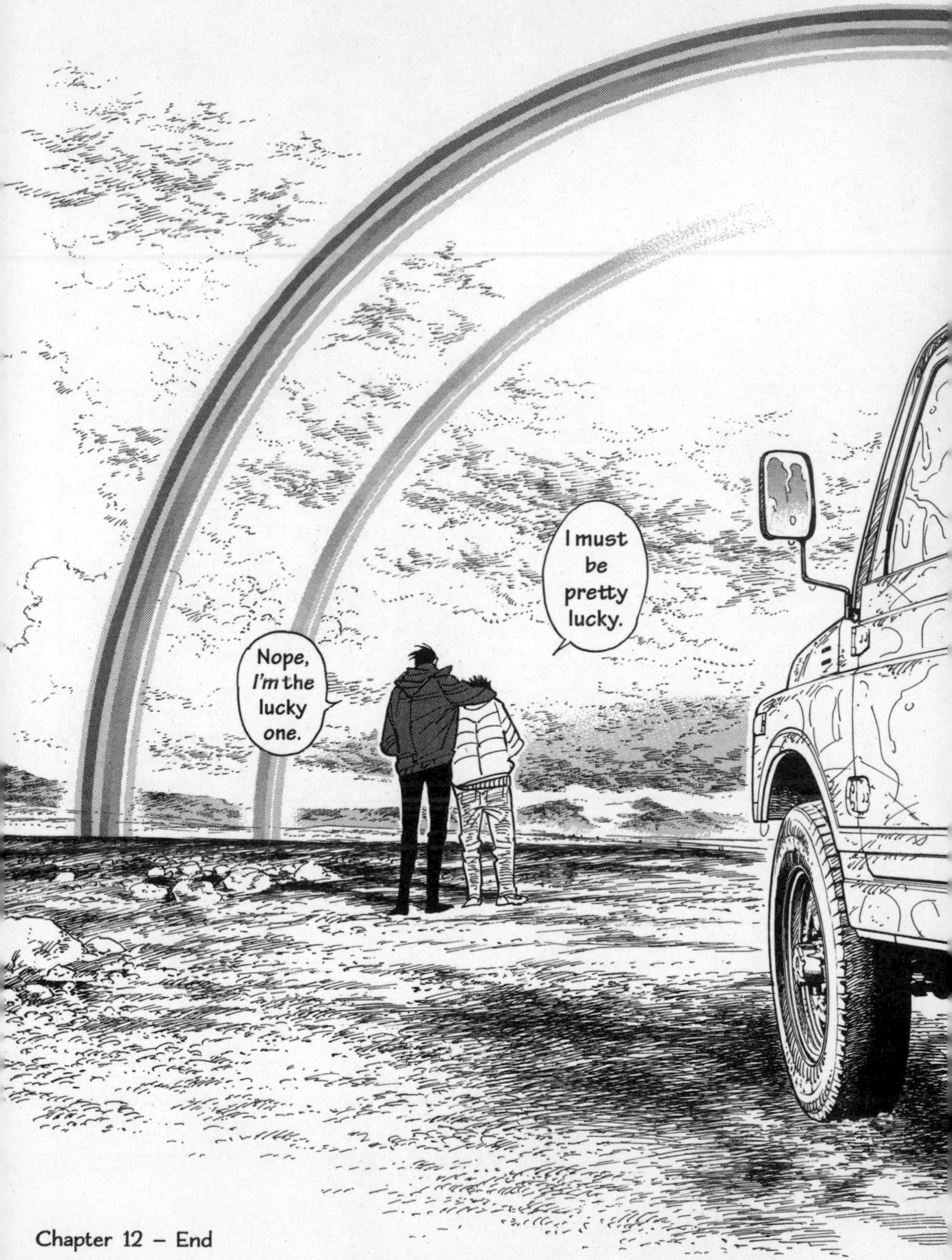
I must be pretty lucky.
Nope, *I'm* the lucky one.

Chapter 12 – End

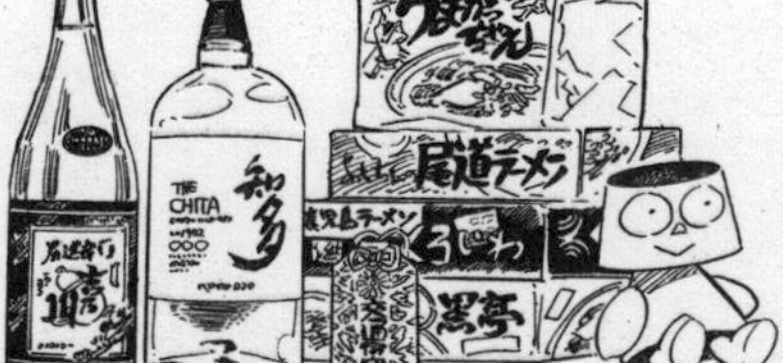
THE CHITA
知多
うまかっちゃん
尾道ラーメン
鹿児島ラーメン
黒亭

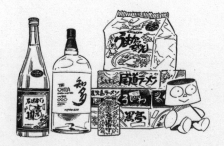

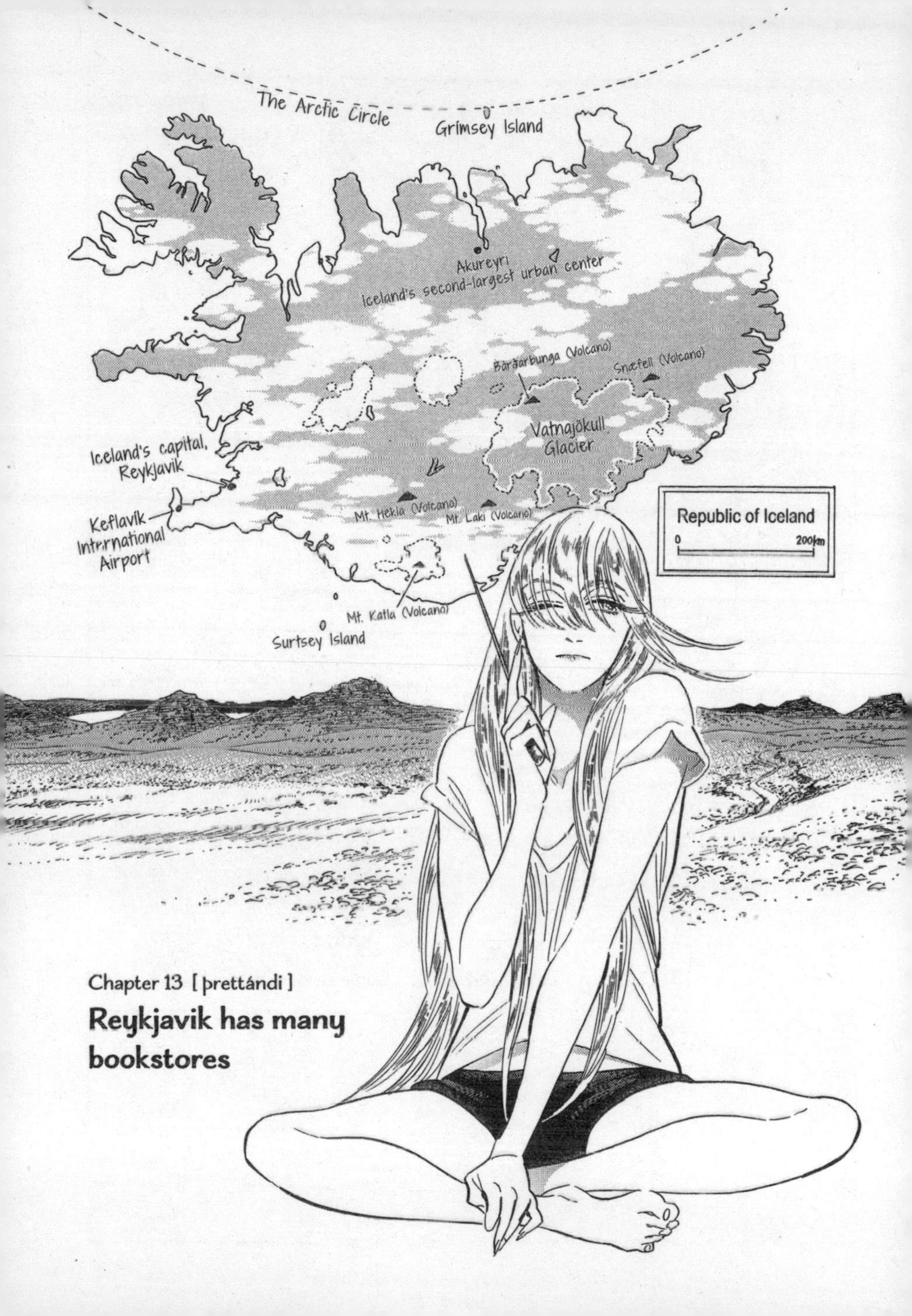
The Arctic Circle
Grímsey Island
Akureyri
Iceland's second-largest urban center
Bárðarbunga (Volcano)
Snæfell (Volcano)
Vatnajökull Glacier
Iceland's capital, Reykjavik
Keflavík International Airport
Mt. Hekla (Volcano)
Mt. Laki (Volcano)
Mt. Katla (Volcano)
Surtsey Island
Republic of Iceland
0
200km

Chapter 13 [þrettándi]

Reykjavik has many bookstores

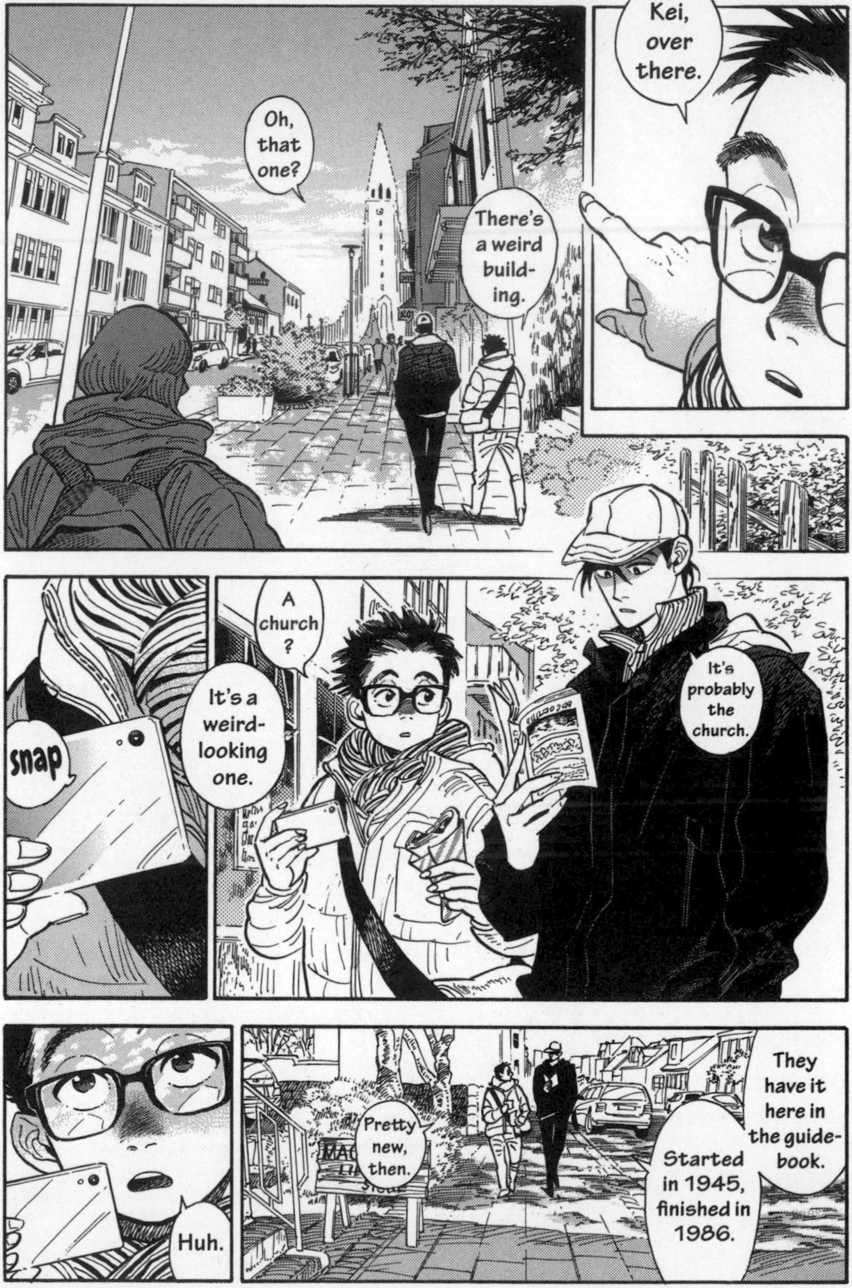
Kei, over there.
Oh, that one?
There's a weird building.
A church?
It's probably the church.
It's a weird-looking one.
snap
They have it here in the guide-book.
Started in 1945, finished in 1986.
Pretty new, then.
Huh.

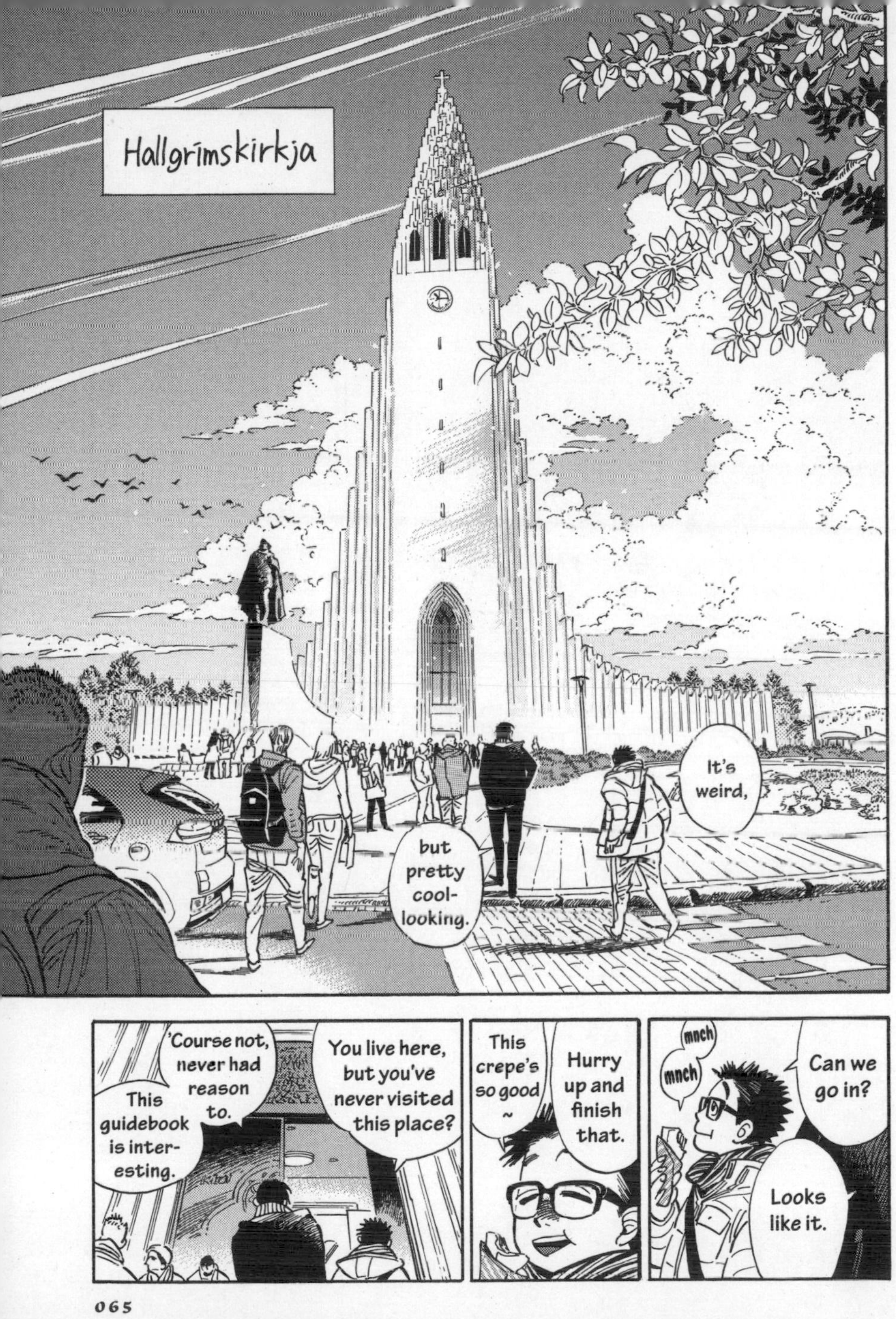
Hallgrímskirkja
It's weird,
but pretty cool-looking.
This guidebook is interesting.
You live here, but you've never visited this place?
'Course not, never had reason to.
This crepe's so good ~
Hurry up and finish that.
mnch
mnch
Can we go in?
Looks like it.

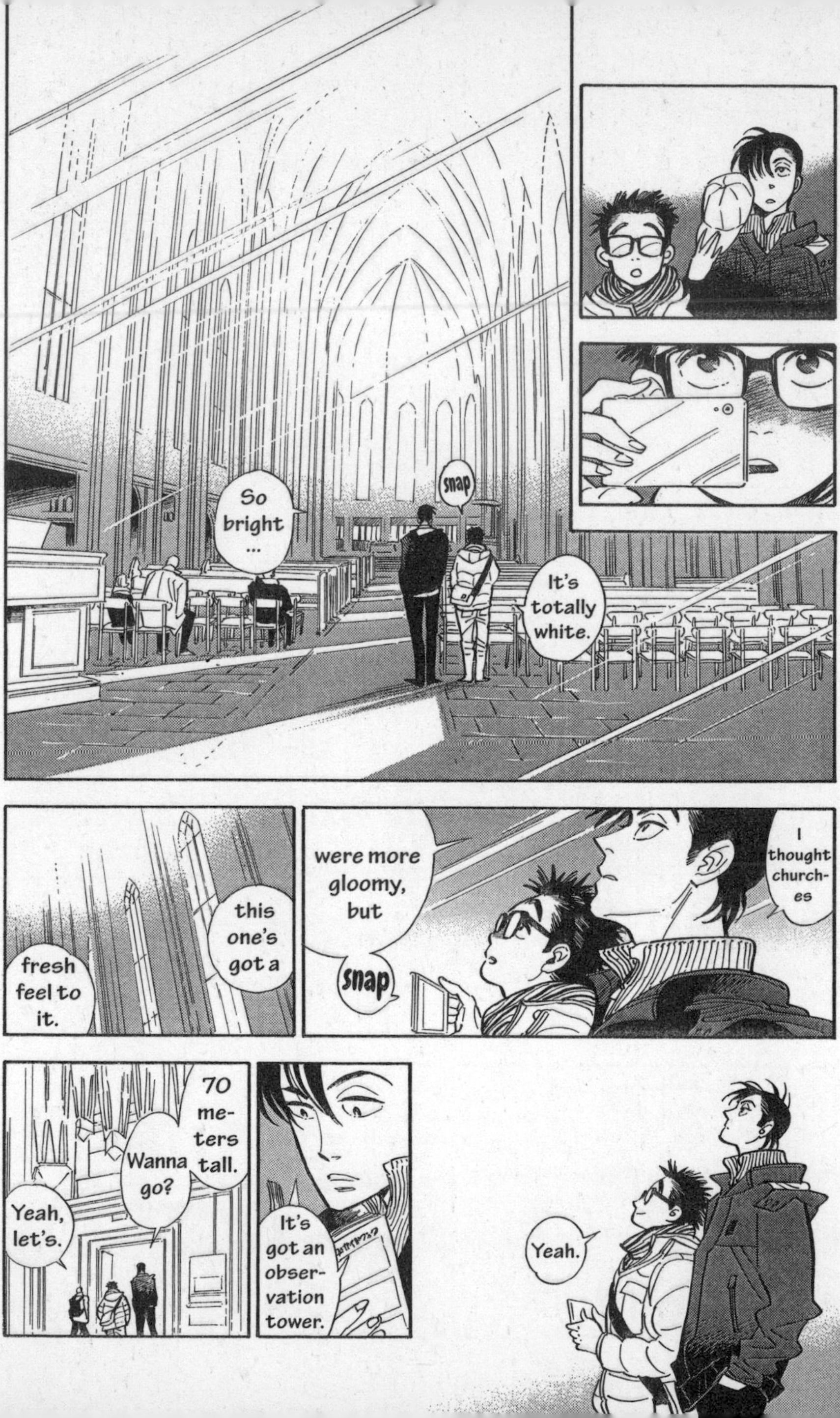
snap
So bright ...
It's totally white.
I thought church-es
were more gloomy, but
snap
this one's got a
fresh feel to it.
Yeah.
It's got an obser-vation tower.
70 me-ters tall.
Wanna go?
Yeah, let's.

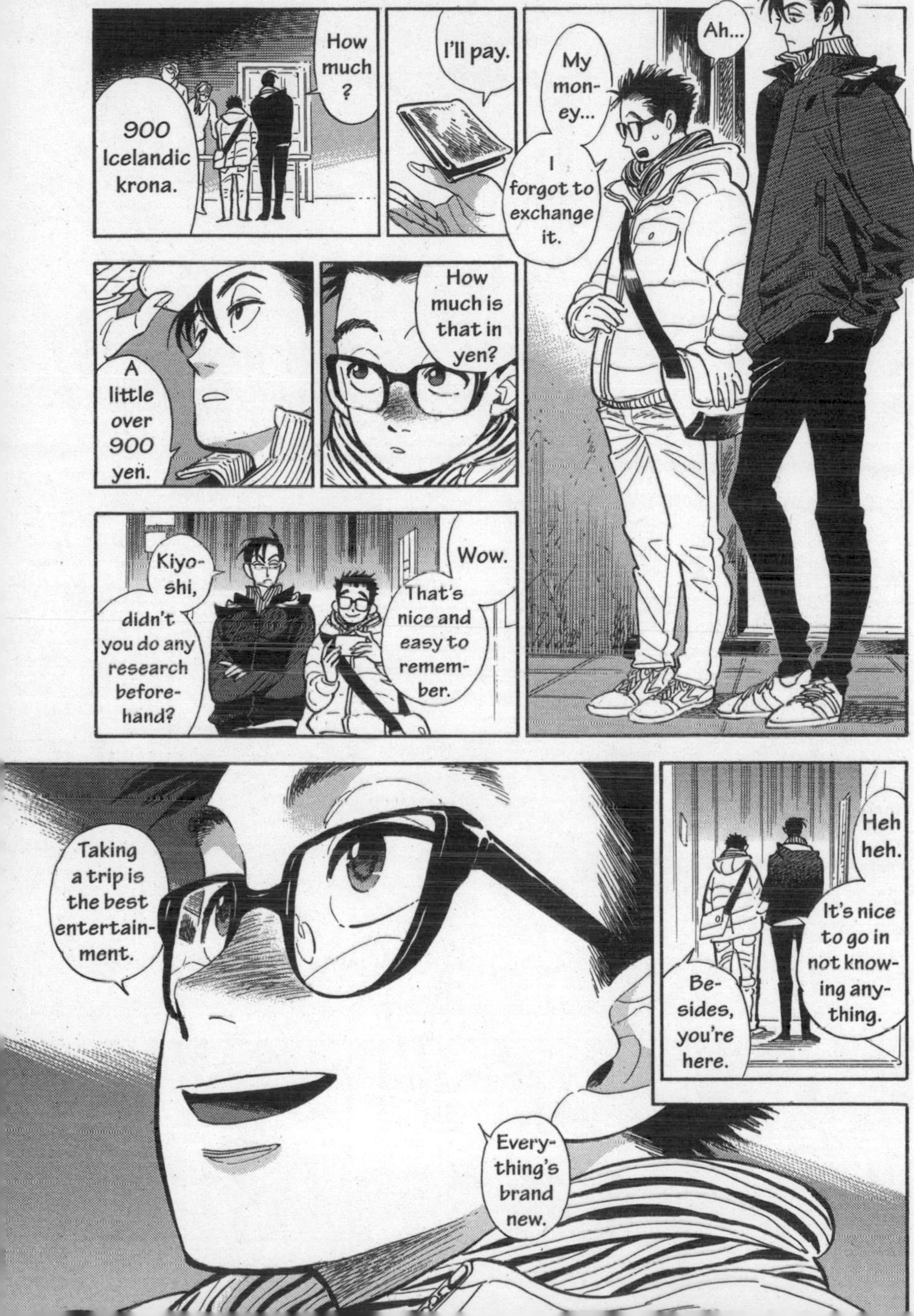
Ah...
My money...
I forgot to exchange it.
I'll pay.
How much?
900 Icelandic krona.
How much is that in yen?
A little over 900 yen.
Wow.
That's nice and easy to remember.
Kiyoshi, didn't you do any research beforehand?
Heh heh.
It's nice to go in not knowing anything.
Besides, you're here.
Taking a trip is the best entertainment.
Everything's brand new.

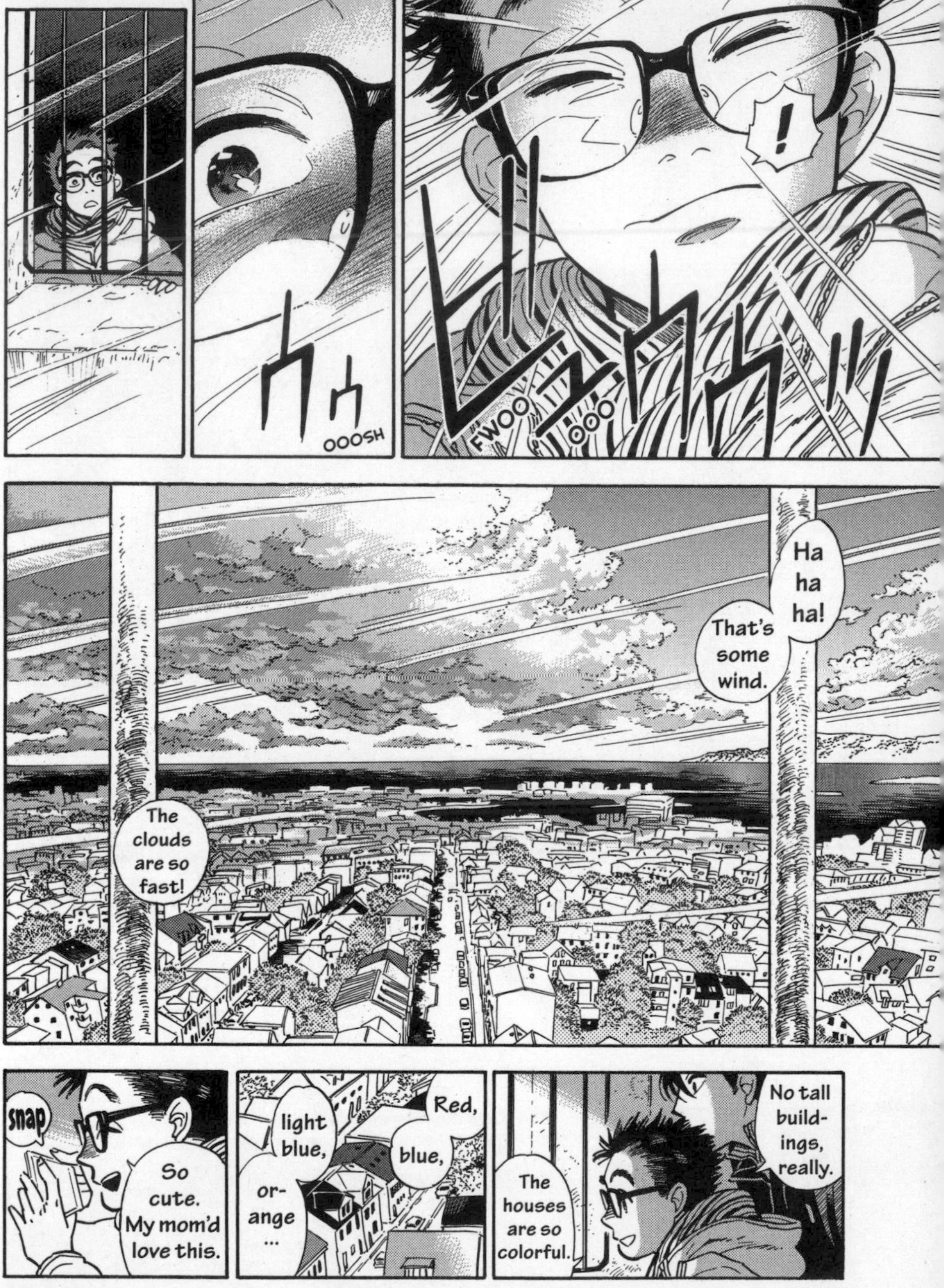
!
FWOOOOO
OOOSH
Ha ha ha!
That's some wind.
The clouds are so fast!
No tall build-ings, really.
The houses are so colorful.
Red,
blue,
light blue,
or-ange ...
snap
So cute. My mom'd love this.

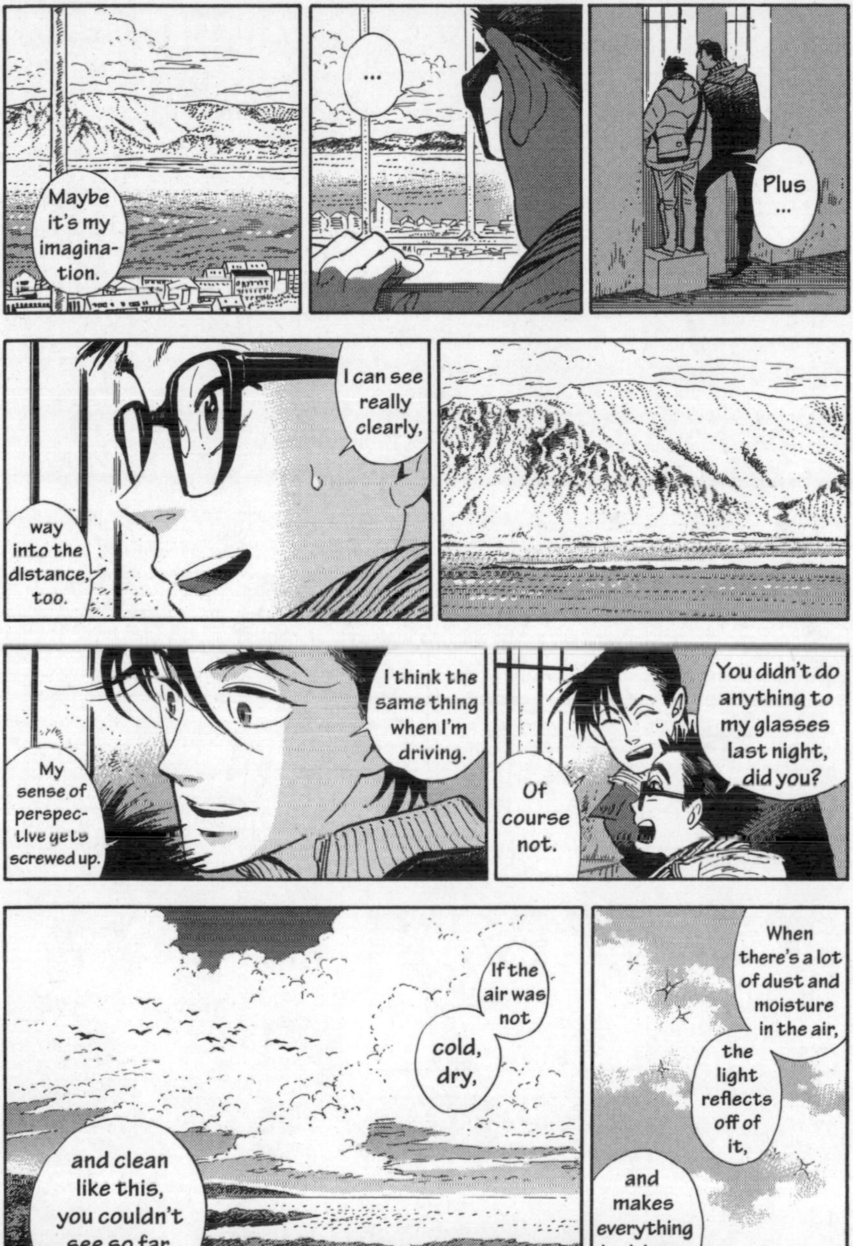
Plus ...
...
Maybe it's my imagination.
I can see really clearly,
way into the distance, too.
You didn't do anything to my glasses last night, did you?
Of course not.
I think the same thing when I'm driving.
My sense of perspective gets screwed up.
When there's a lot of dust and moisture in the air,
the light reflects off of it,
and makes everything look hazy.
If the air was not
cold, dry,
and clean like this, you couldn't see so far.

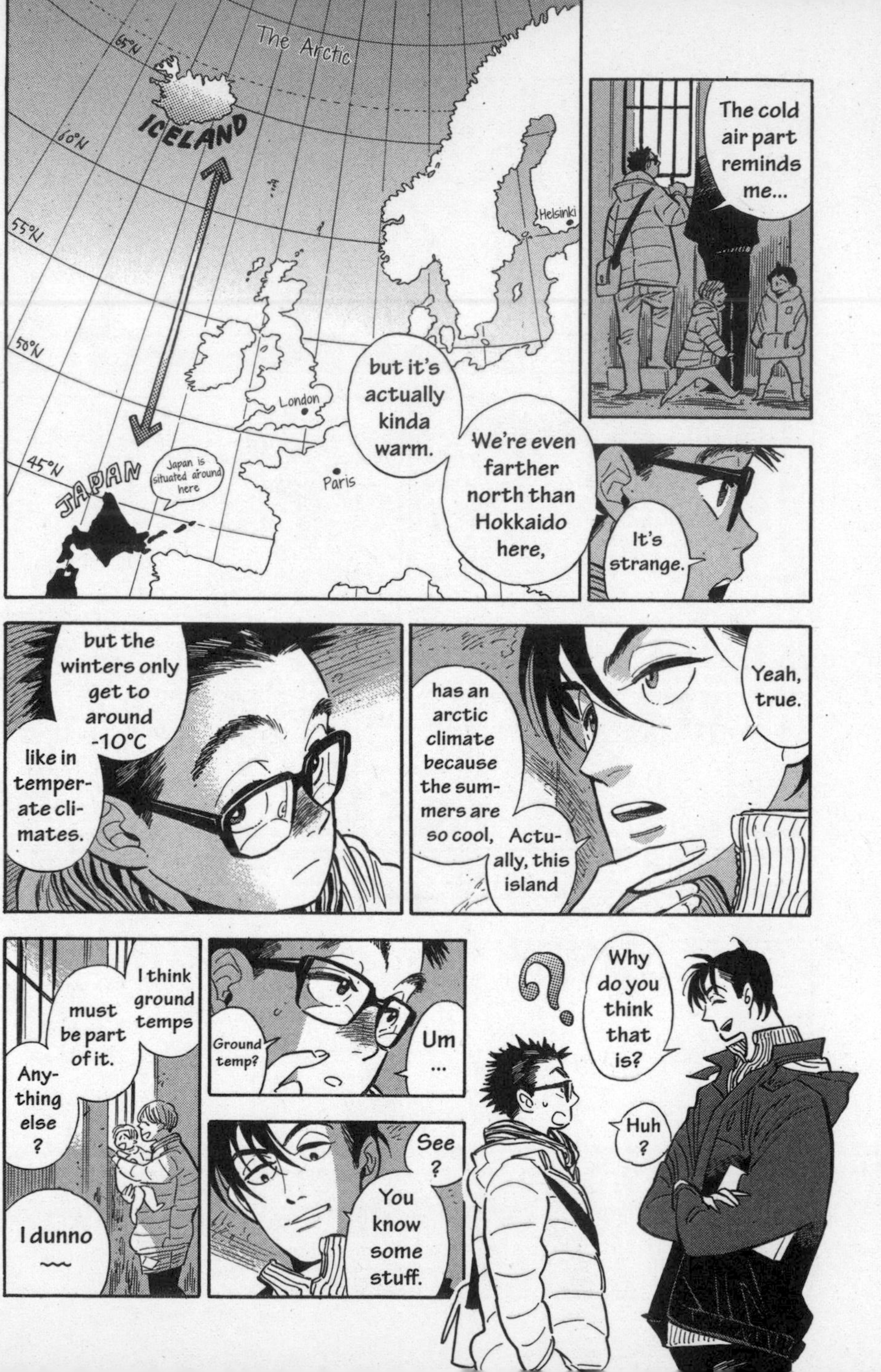
The cold air part reminds me...
It's strange.
We're even farther north than Hokkaido here,
but it's actually kinda warm.
The Arctic
65°N
ICELAND
60°N
55°N
50°N
45°N
Helsinki
London
Paris
JAPAN
Japan is situated around here
Yeah, true.
Actually, this island
has an arctic climate because the summers are so cool,
but the winters only get to around -10°C
like in temperate climates.
Why do you think that is?
Huh?
Um ...
Ground temp?
See?
You know some stuff.
I think ground temps
must be part of it.
Anything else?
I dunno ~~~

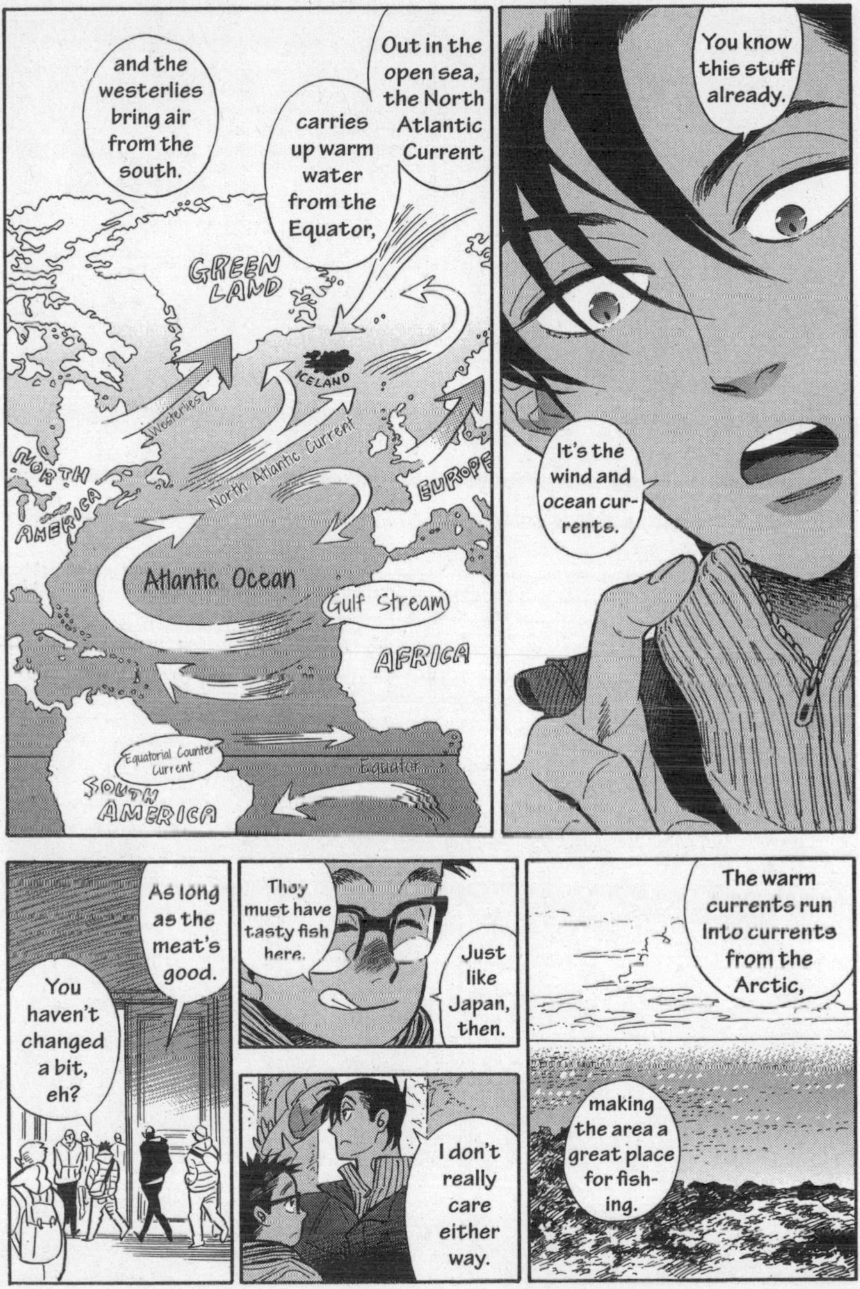
You know this stuff already.
It's the wind and ocean currents.
Out in the open sea, the North Atlantic Current
carries up warm water from the Equator,
and the westerlies bring air from the south.
GREEN LAND
ICELAND
Westerlies
North Atlantic Current
NORTH AMERICA
EUROPE
Atlantic Ocean
Gulf Stream
AFRICA
Equatorial Counter Current
Equator
SOUTH AMERICA
The warm currents run into currents from the Arctic,
making the area a great place for fishing.
They must have tasty fish here.
Just like Japan, then.
I don't really care either way.
As long as the meat's good.
You haven't changed a bit, eh?

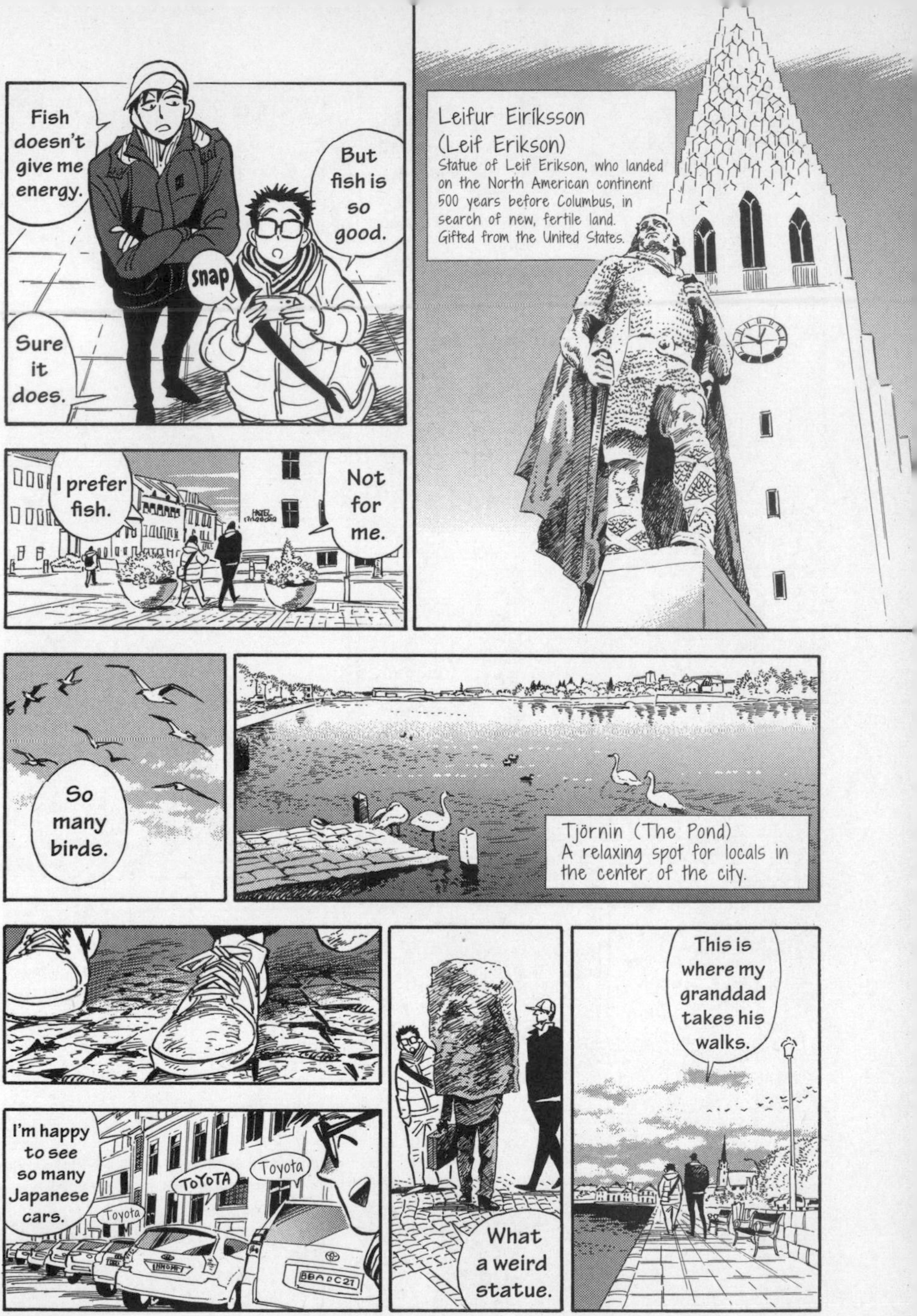
Leifur Eiríksson
(Leif Erikson)
Statue of Leif Erikson, who landed on the North American continent 500 years before Columbus, in search of new, fertile land. Gifted from the United States.
But fish is so good.
Fish doesn't give me energy.
snap
Sure it does.
Not for me.
I prefer fish.
Tjörnin (The Pond)
A relaxing spot for locals in the center of the city.
So many birds.
This is where my granddad takes his walks.
What a weird statue.
I'm happy to see so many Japanese cars.
Toyota
TOYOTA
Toyota

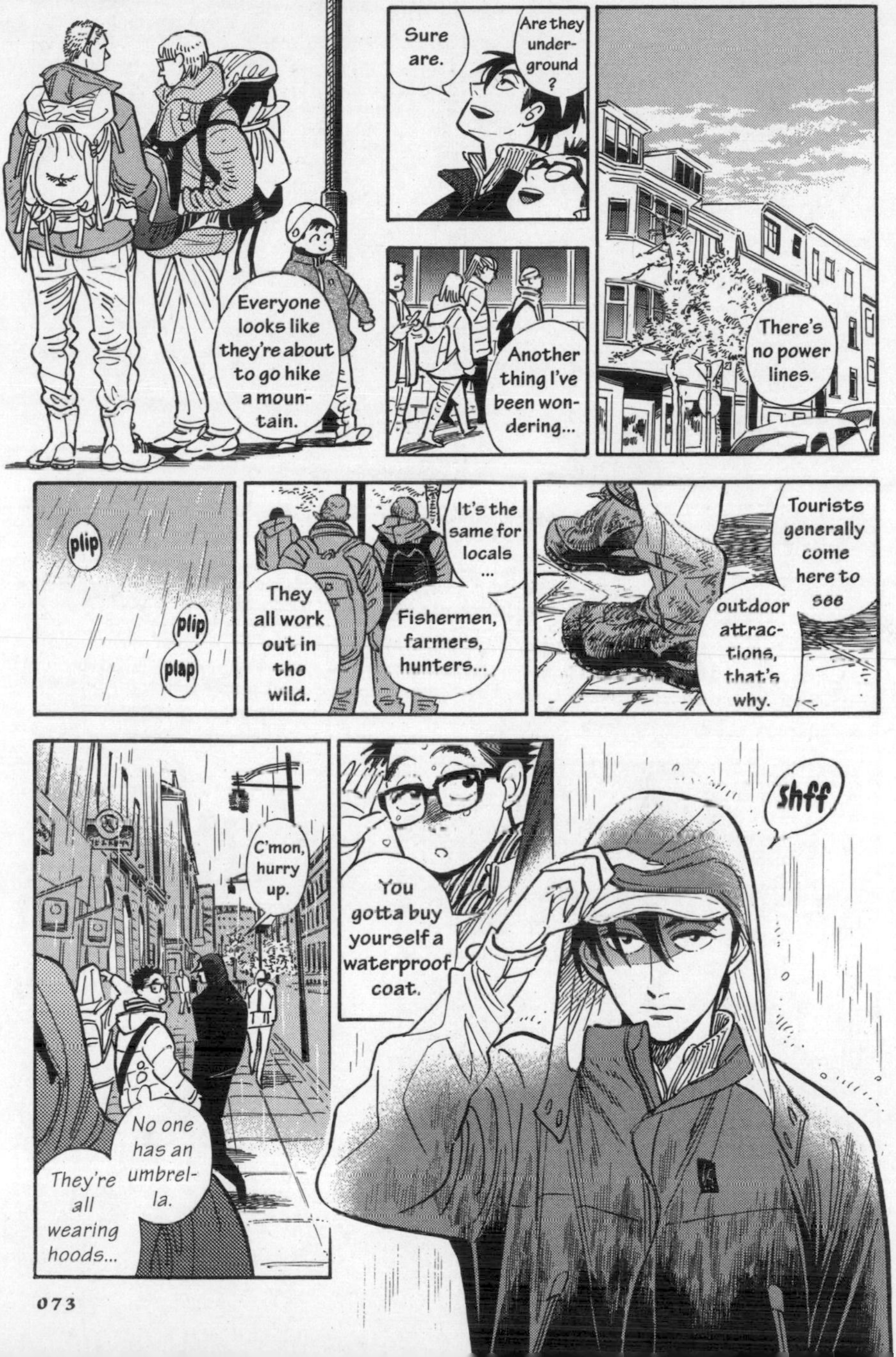
There's no power lines.
Are they underground?
Sure are.
Another thing I've been wondering...
Everyone looks like they're about to go hike a mountain.
Tourists generally come here to see
outdoor attractions, that's why.
It's the same for locals ...
Fishermen, farmers, hunters...
They all work out in the wild.
plip
plip
plap
shff
You gotta buy yourself a waterproof coat.
C'mon, hurry up.
No one has an umbrella.
They're all wearing hoods...

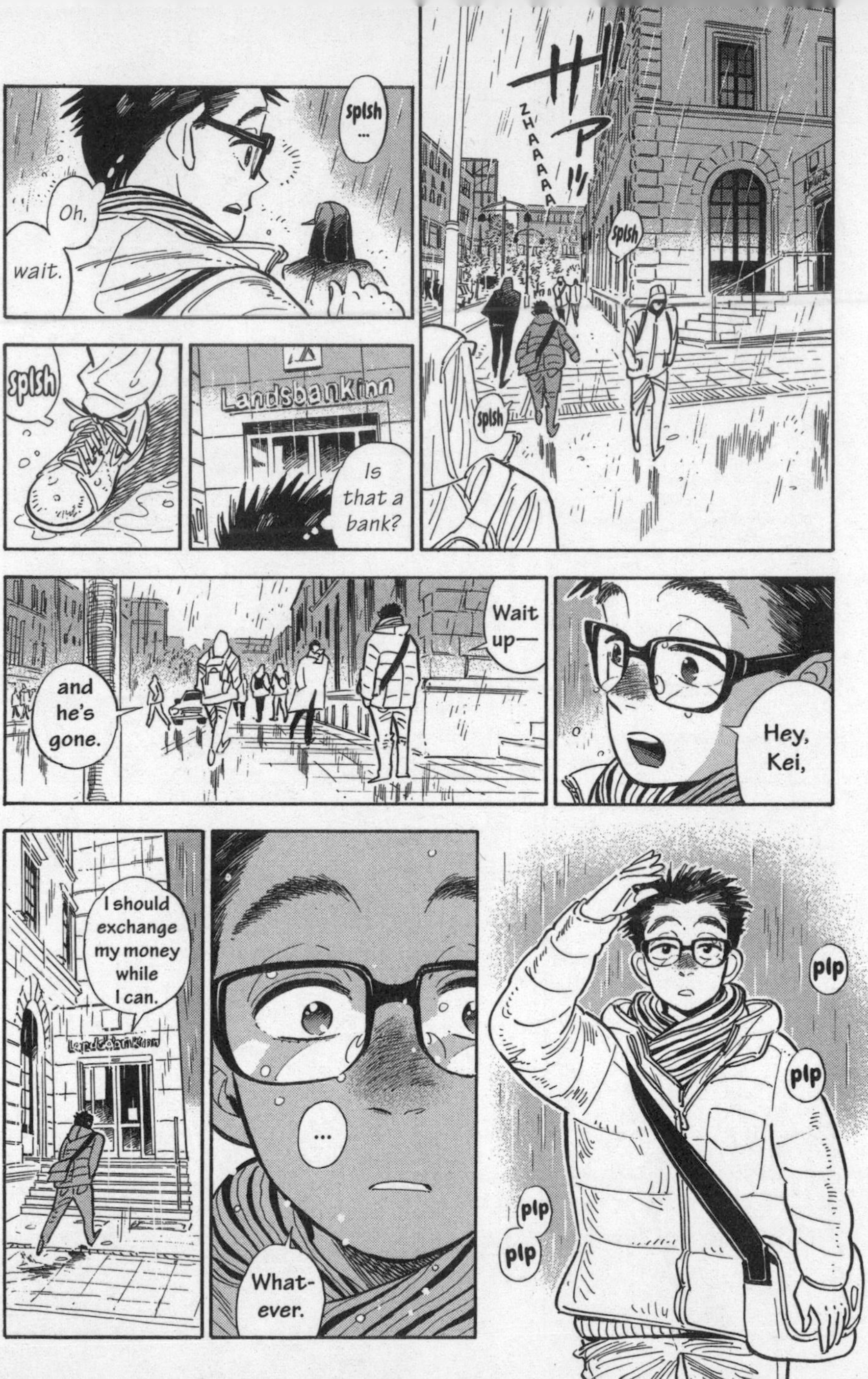
ZHAAAAAA
splsh
splsh
splsh...
Oh, wait.
Landsbankinn
Is that a bank?
splsh
Hey, Kei,
Wait up—
and he's gone.
plp
plp
plp
plp
...
What-ever.
I should exchange my money while I can.
Landsbankinn

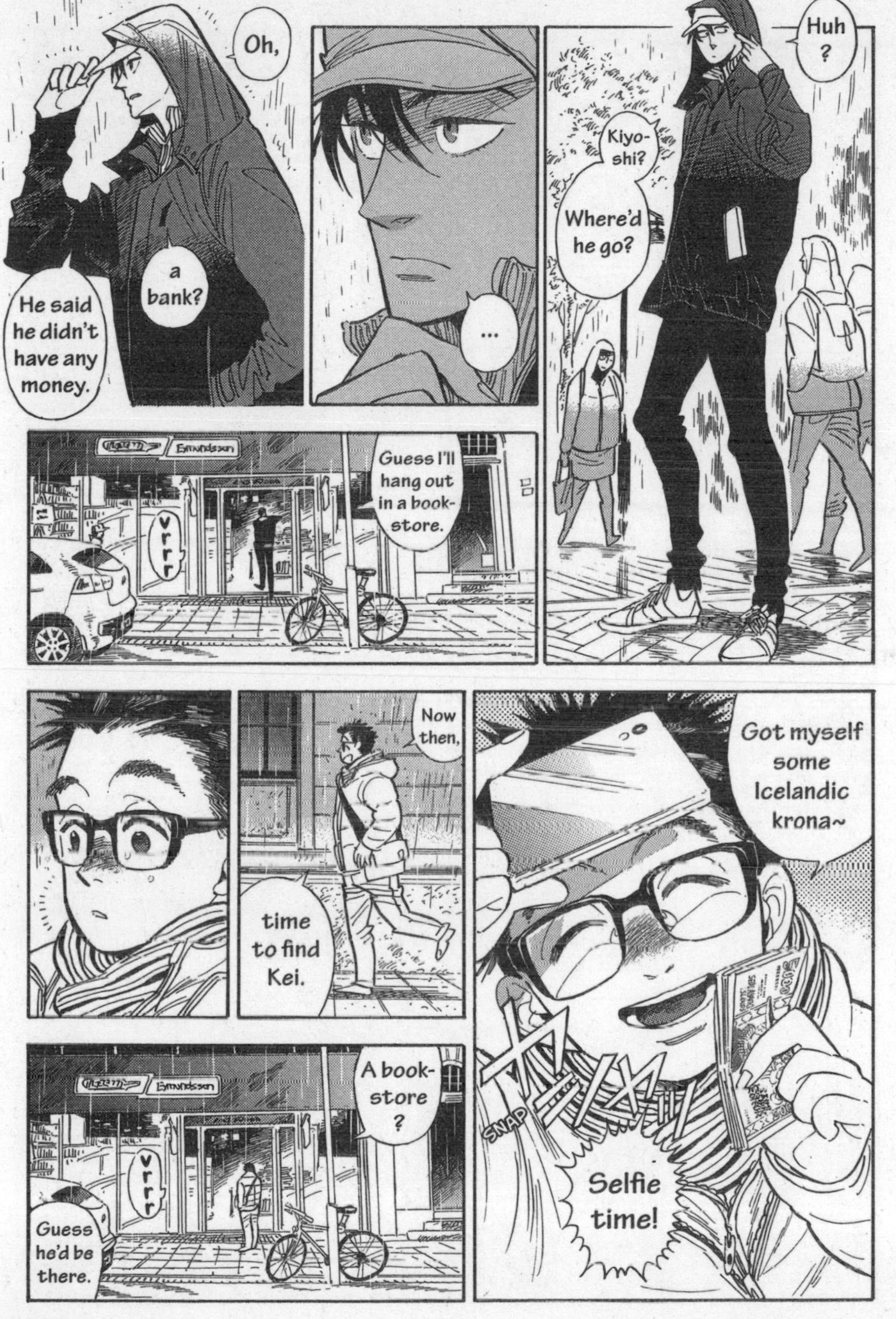
Huh?
Kiyo-shi?
Where'd he go?
...
Oh,
a bank?
He said he didn't have any money.
Guess I'll hang out in a book-store.
vrrr
Got myself some Icelandic krona~
SNAP
Selfie time!
Now then,
time to find Kei.
A book-store?
vrrr
Guess he'd be there.

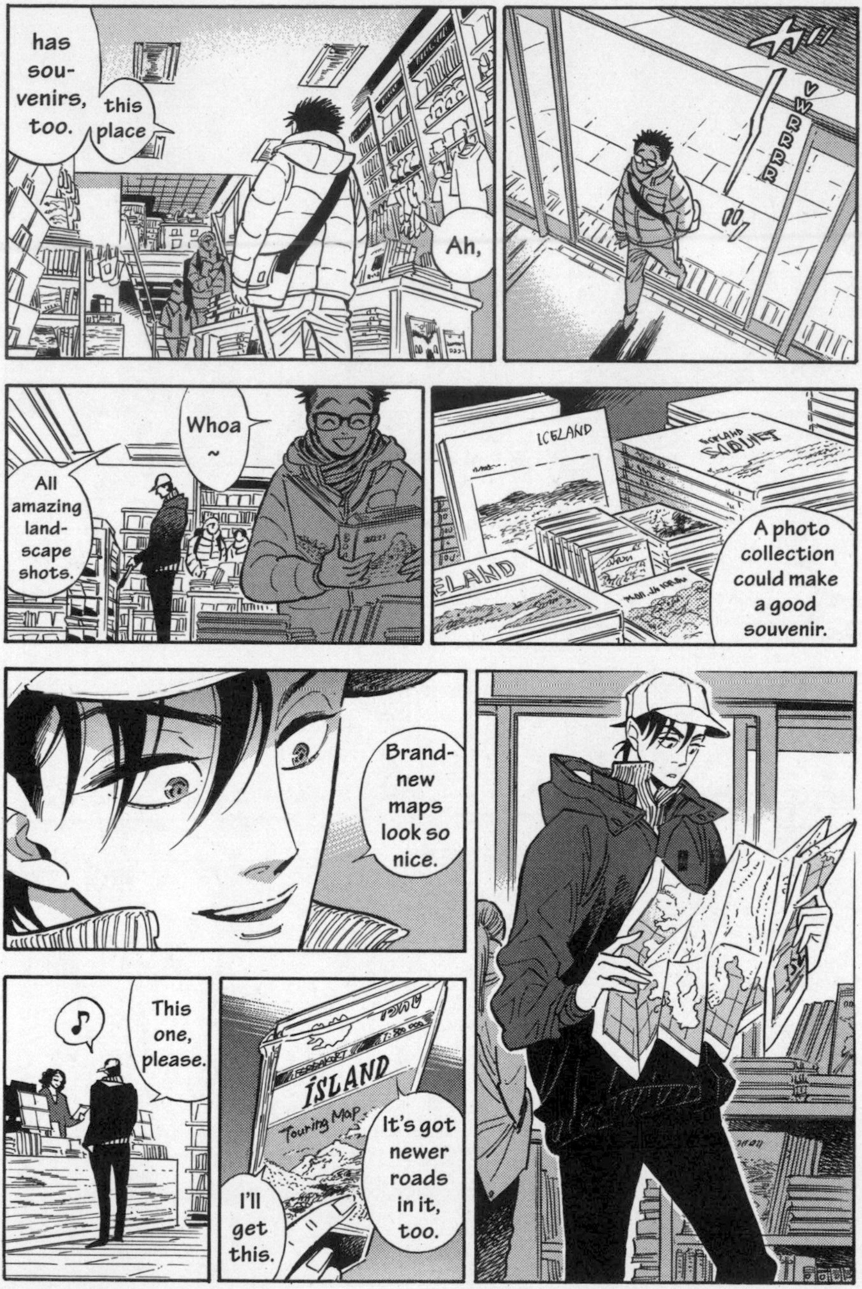
VWRRRR
Ah,
this place
has sou-venirs, too.
ICELAND
A photo collection could make a good souvenir.
Whoa ~
All amazing land-scape shots.
Brand-new maps look so nice.
ÍSLAND
Touring Map
It's got newer roads in it, too.
I'll get this.
♪
This one, please.

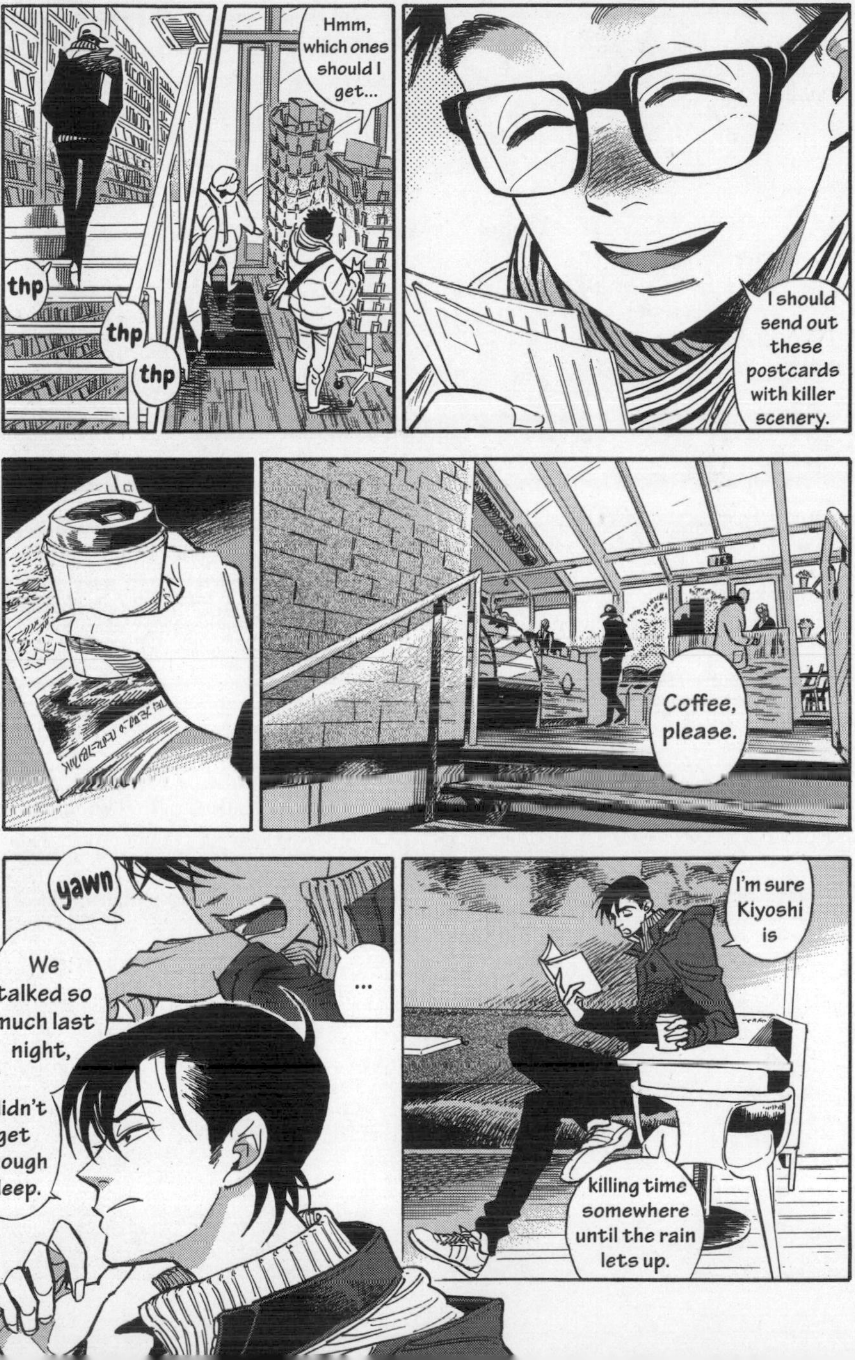
I should send out these postcards with killer scenery.
Hmm, which ones should I get...
thp
thp
thp
Coffee, please.
I'm sure Kiyoshi is
killing time somewhere until the rain lets up.
yawn
...
We talked so much last night,
I didn't get enough sleep.

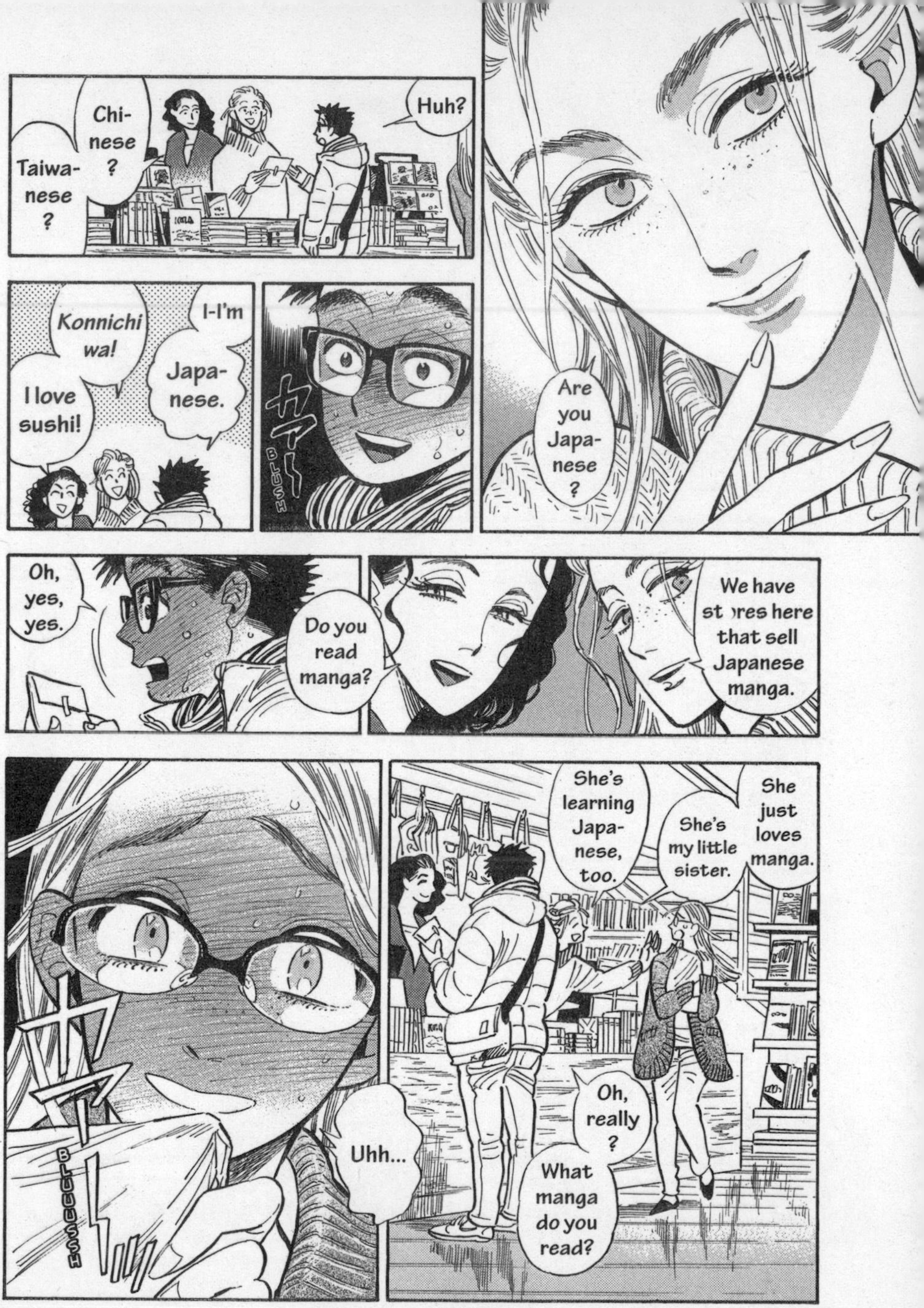
Are you Japanese?
Huh?
Chinese?
Taiwanese?
BLUSH
I-I'm Japanese.
Konnichiwa!
I love sushi!
We have stores here that sell Japanese manga.
Do you read manga?
Oh, yes, yes.
She just loves manga.
She's my little sister.
She's learning Japanese, too.
Oh, really?
What manga do you read?
Uhh...
BLUUUSH

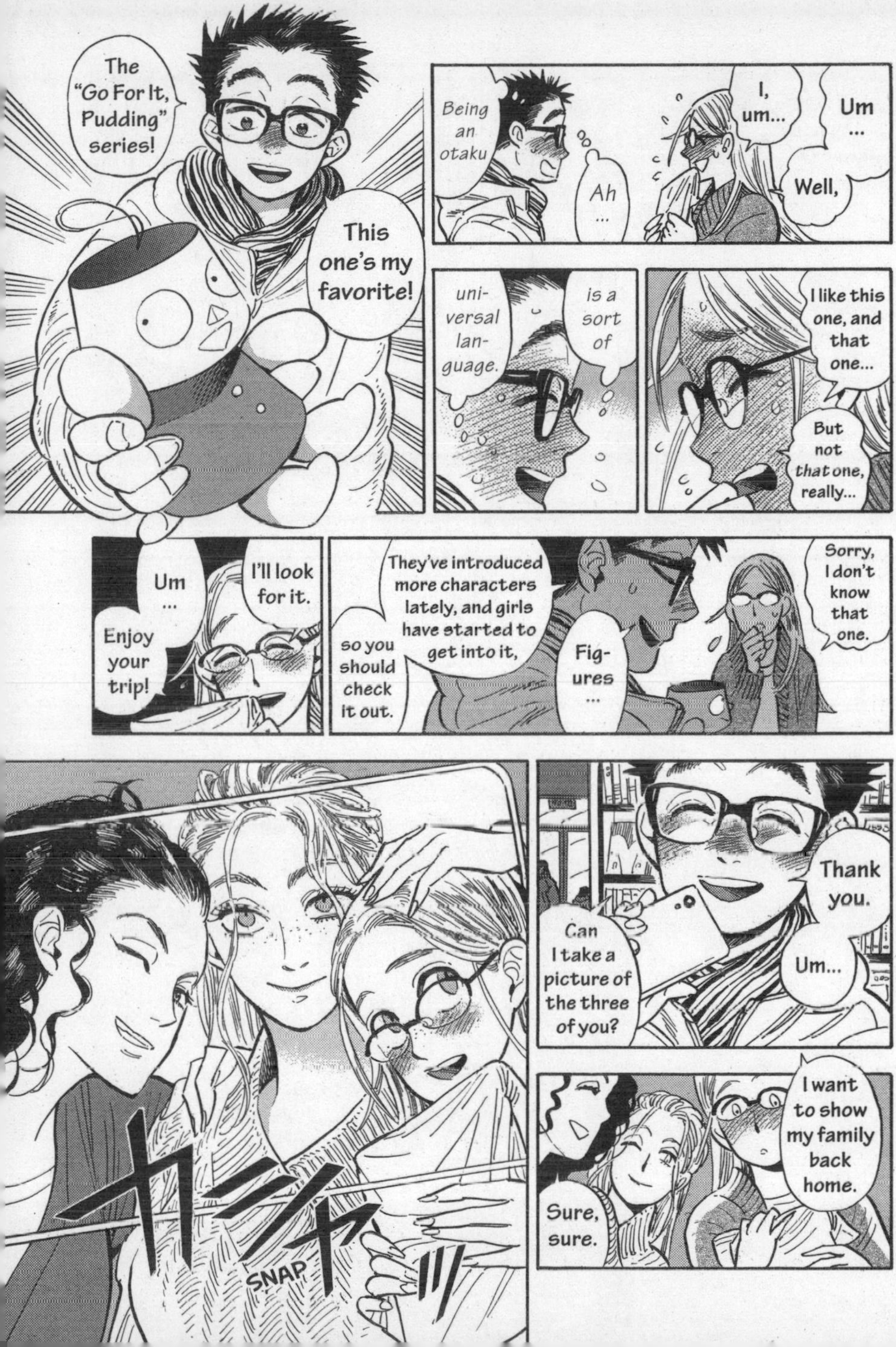
Um ...
I, um...
Well,
Ah ...
Being an otaku
I like this one, and that one...
But not that one, really...
is a sort of
universal language.
The "Go For It, Pudding" series!
This one's my favorite!
Sorry, I don't know that one.
They've introduced more characters lately, and girls have started to get into it,
so you should check it out.
Figures ...
I'll look for it.
Um ...
Enjoy your trip!
Thank you.
Um...
Can I take a picture of the three of you?
I want to show my family back home.
Sure, sure.
SNAP

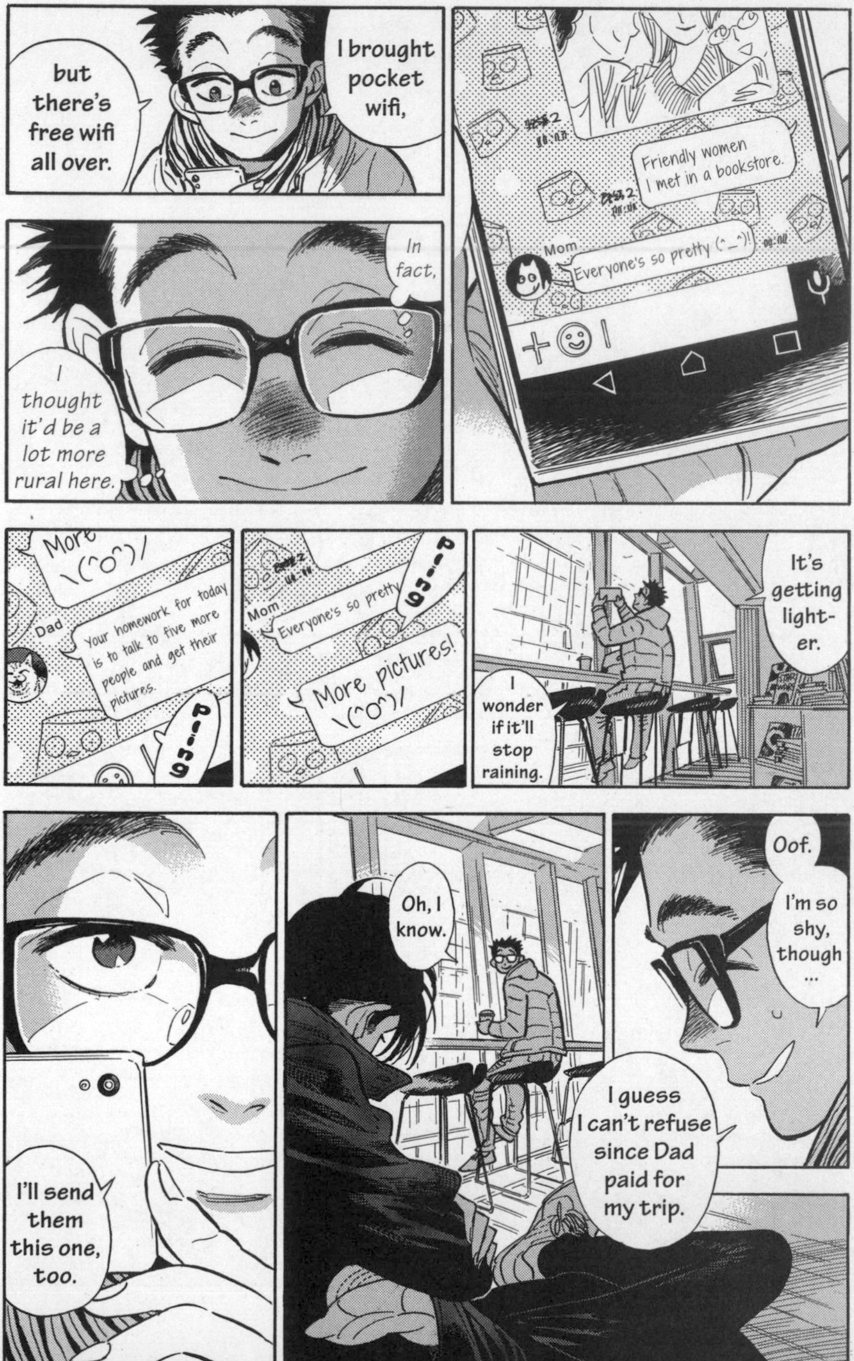
Friendly women I met in a bookstore.
Mom
Everyone's so pretty (^_^)!
I brought pocket wifi,
but there's free wifi all over.
In fact,
I thought it'd be a lot more rural here.
It's getting lighter.
I wonder if it'll stop raining.
Piing
Mom
Everyone's so pretty
More pictures! \(^O^)/
More \(^O^)/
Dad
Your homework for today is to talk to five more people and get their pictures.
Piing
Oof.
I'm so shy, though ...
I guess I can't refuse since Dad paid for my trip.
Oh, I know.
I'll send them this one, too.

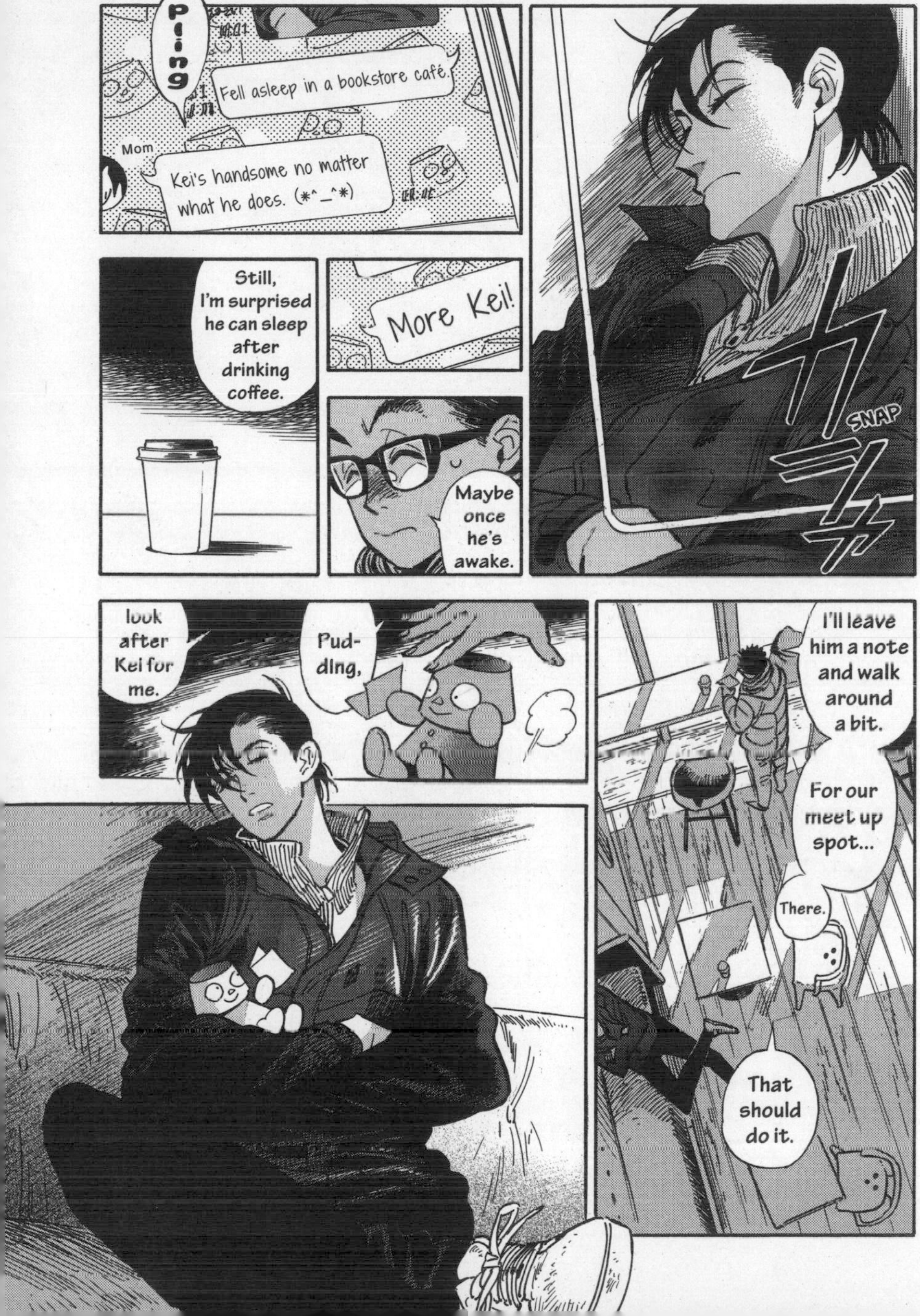
SNAP
Pling
Fell asleep in a bookstore café.
Mom
Kei's handsome no matter what he does. (*^_^*)
More Kei!
Maybe once he's awake.
Still, I'm surprised he can sleep after drinking coffee.
I'll leave him a note and walk around a bit.
For our meet up spot...
There.
That should do it.
Pud-ding,
look after Kei for me.

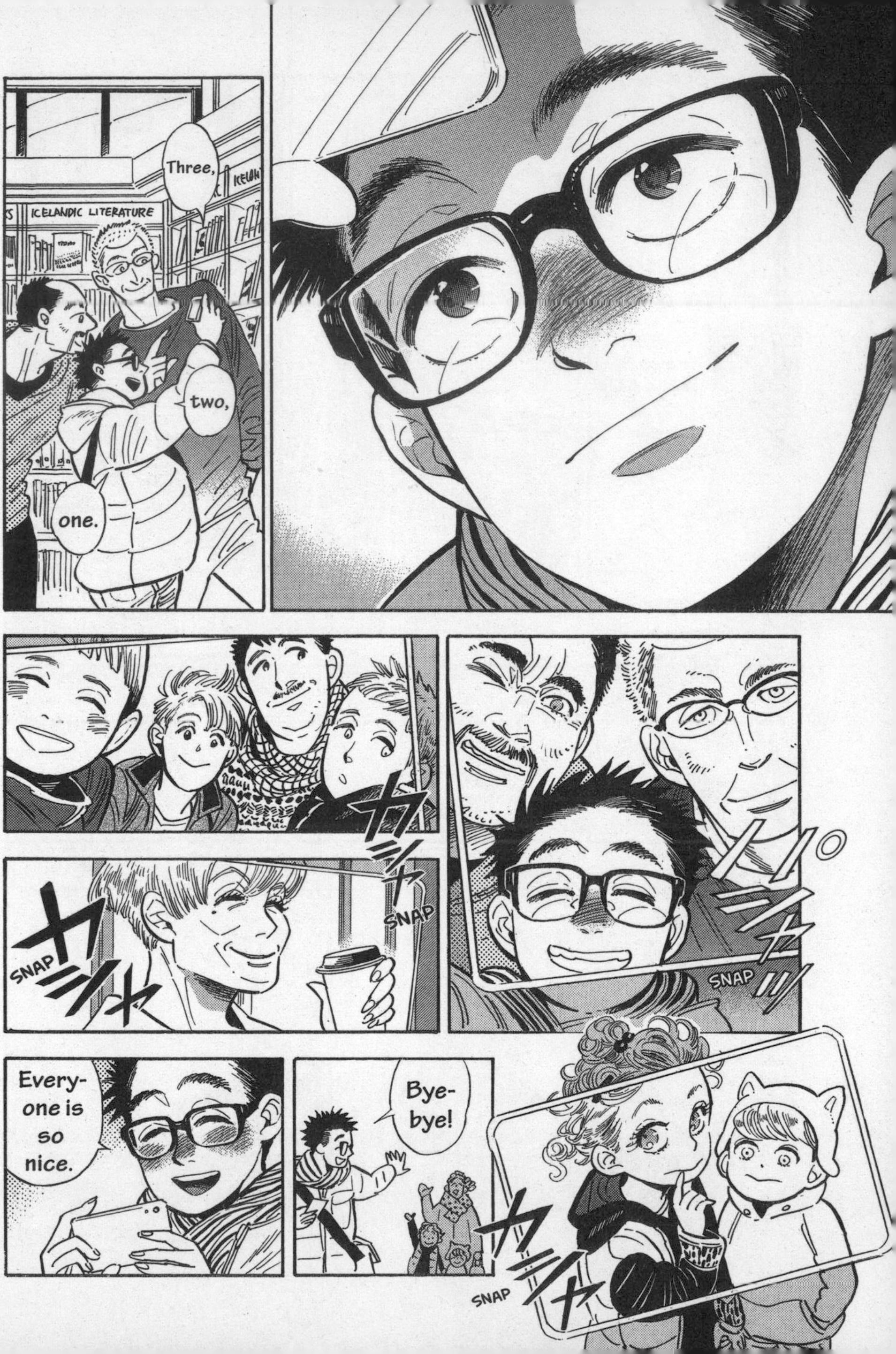
ICELANDIC LITERATURE
Three,
two,
one.
SNAP
SNAP
SNAP
SNAP
Bye-bye!
Everyone is so nice.

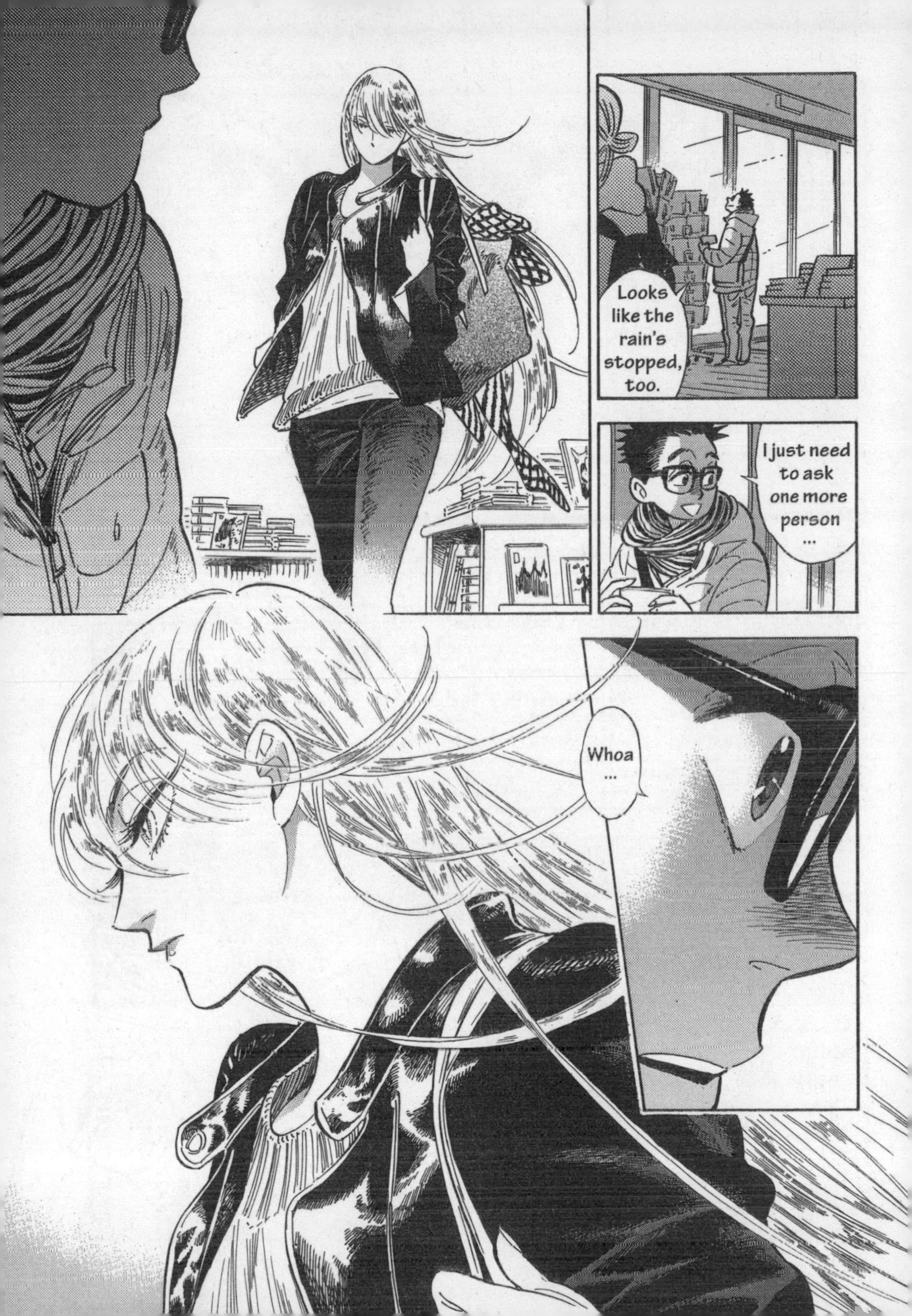
Looks like the rain's stopped, too.
I just need to ask one more person ...
Whoa ...

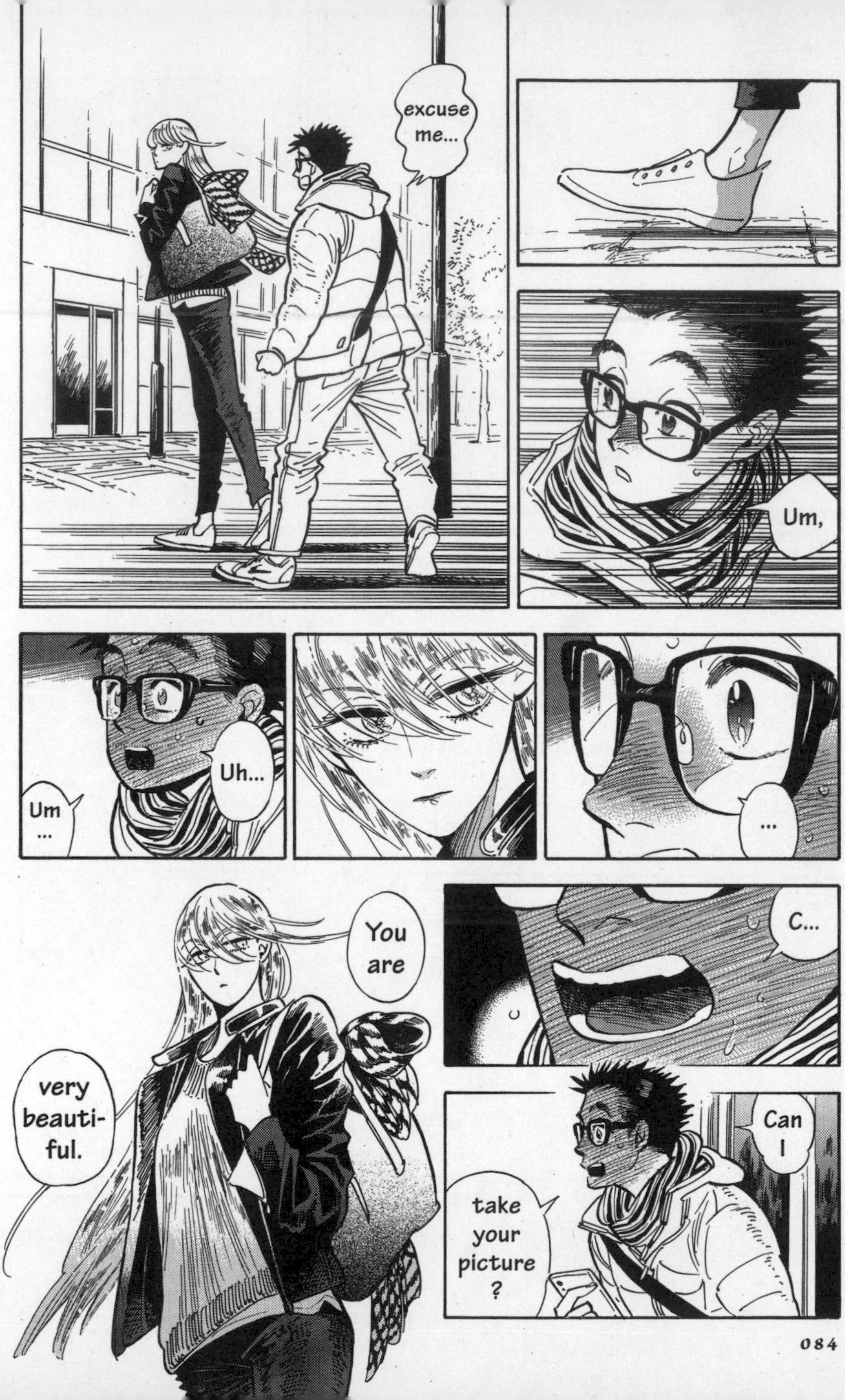
Um,
excuse me...
...
Uh...
Um ...
C...
Can I
take your picture ?
You are
very beauti-ful.

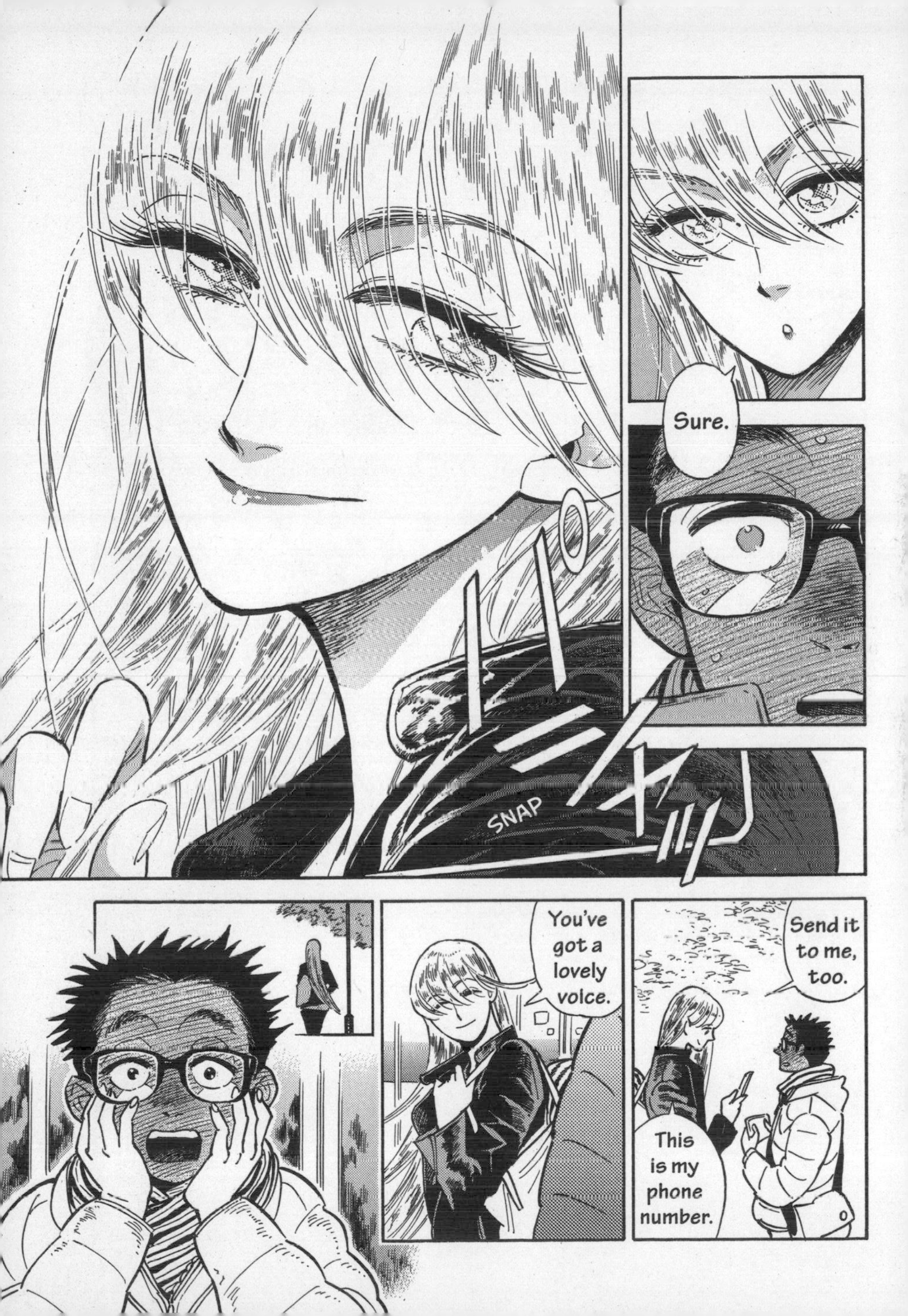
Sure.
SNAP
Send it to me, too.
This is my phone number.
You've got a lovely voice.

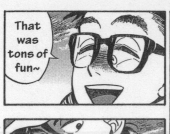

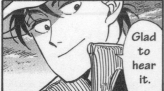

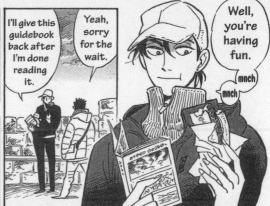

Well, you're having fun.
mnch
mnch
Yeah, sorry for the wait.
I'll give this guidebook back after I'm done reading it.
That was tons of fun~
Glad to hear it.
Really,
really fun ~~~!
Tell me about it later. Let's go home.
I'm starv-ing.

Chapter 13 – End

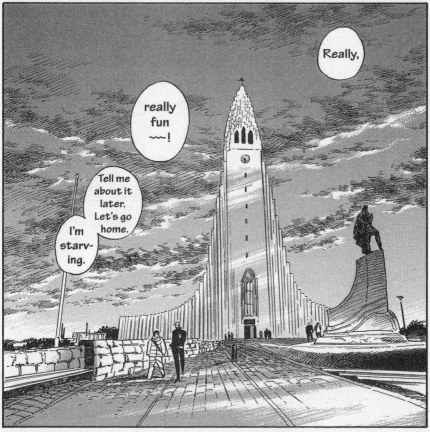

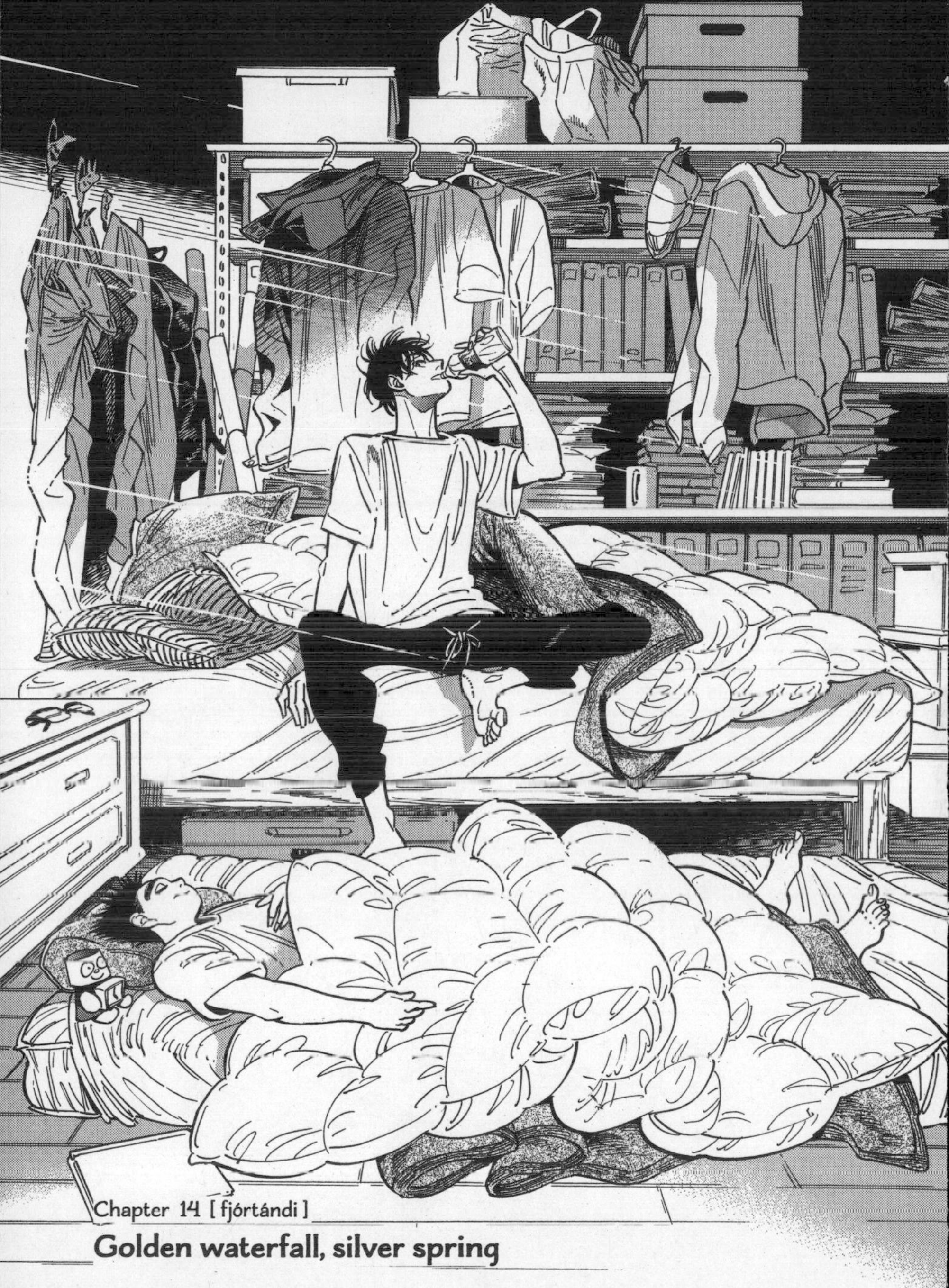

Chapter 14 [fjórtándi]

Golden waterfall, silver spring

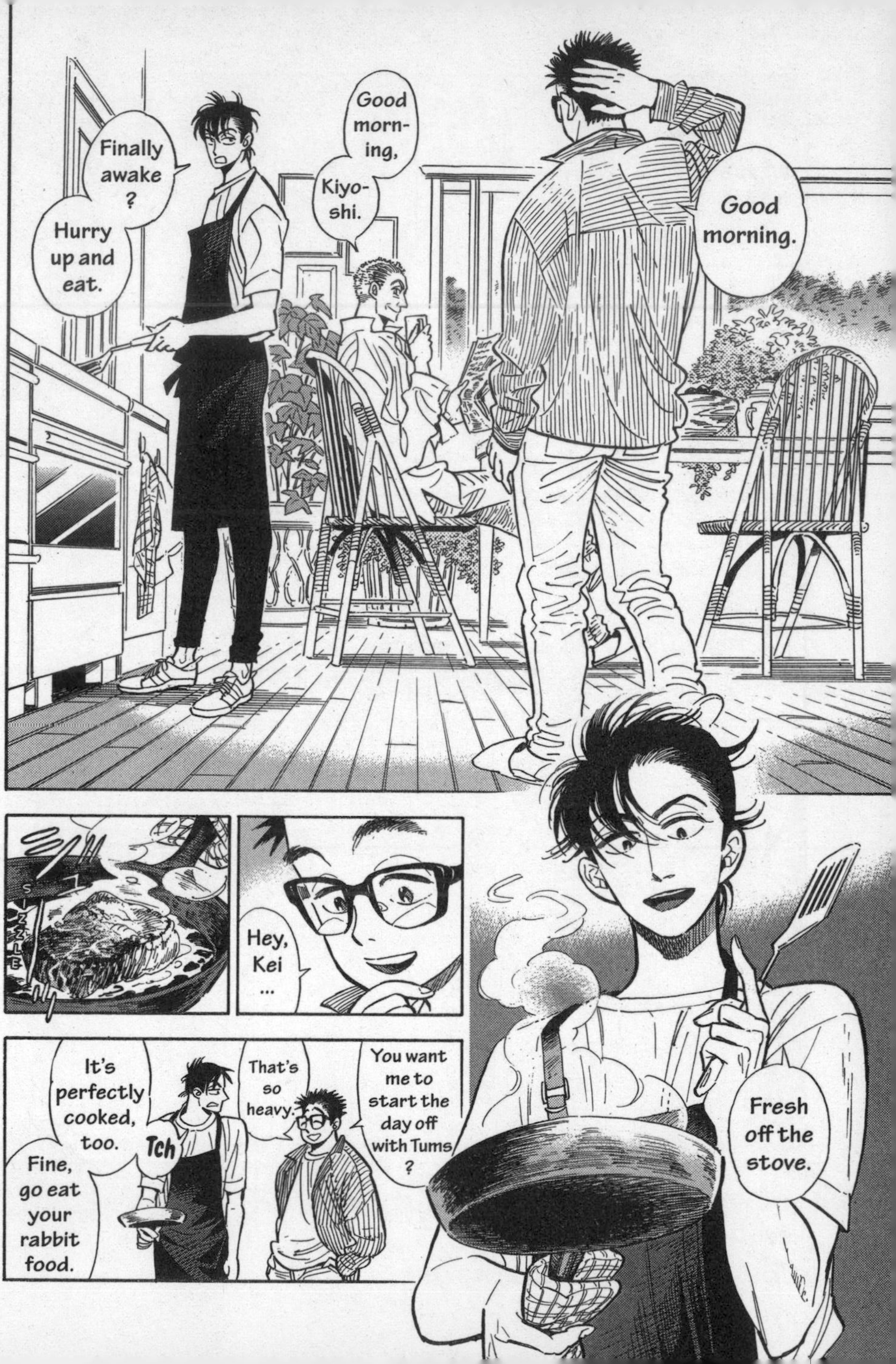
Good morning.
Good morning, Kiyoshi.
Finally awake?
Hurry up and eat.
Fresh off the stove.
Hey, Kei ...
SIZZLE
You want me to start the day off with Tums?
That's so heavy.
It's perfectly cooked, too.
Tch
Fine, go eat your rabbit food.

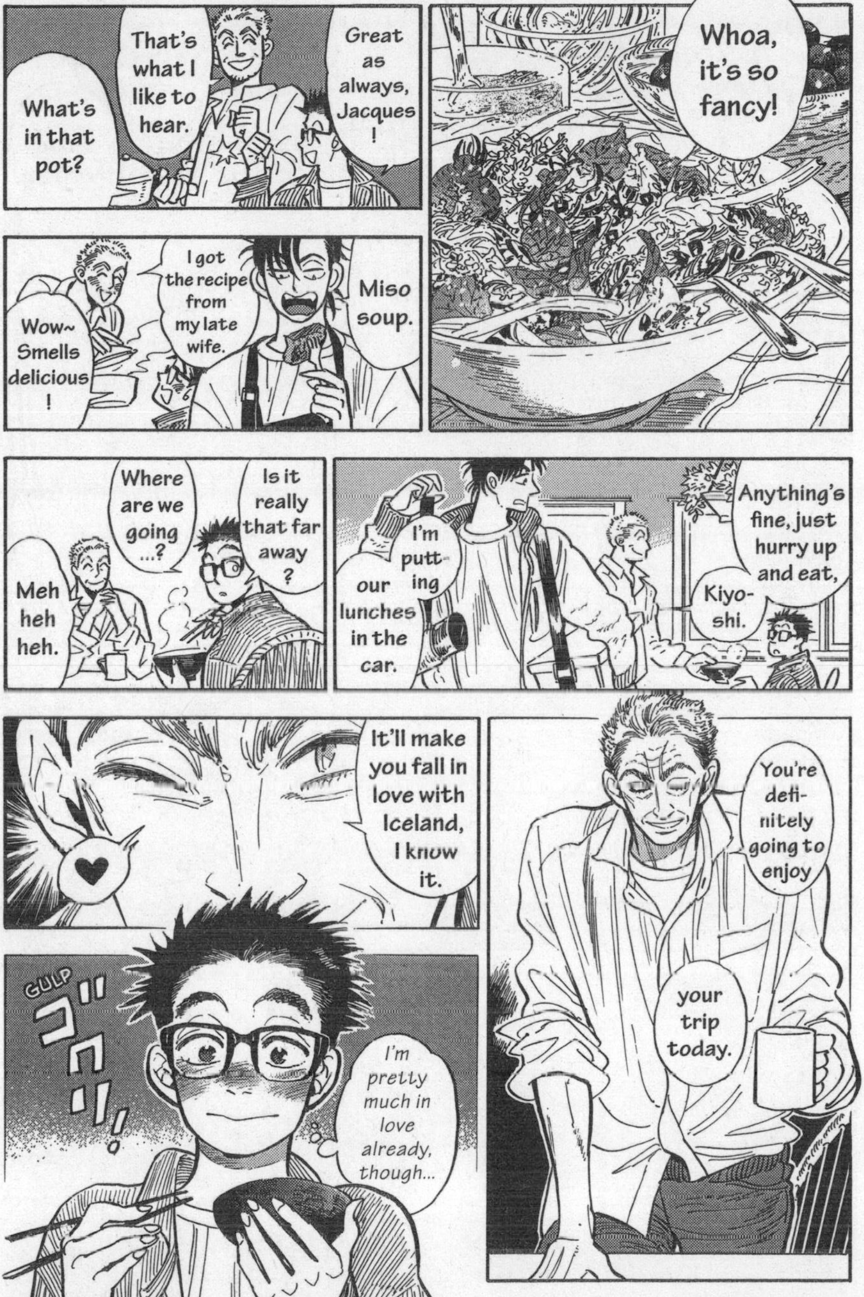
Whoa, it's so fancy!
Great as always, Jacques!
That's what I like to hear.
What's in that pot?
Miso soup.
I got the recipe from my late wife.
Wow~ Smells delicious!
Anything's fine, just hurry up and eat,
Kiyoshi.
I'm putting our lunches in the car.
Is it really that far away?
Where are we going...?
Meh heh heh.
You're definitely going to enjoy
your trip today.
It'll make you fall in love with Iceland, I know it.
GULP
ゴクリ!
I'm pretty much in love already, though...

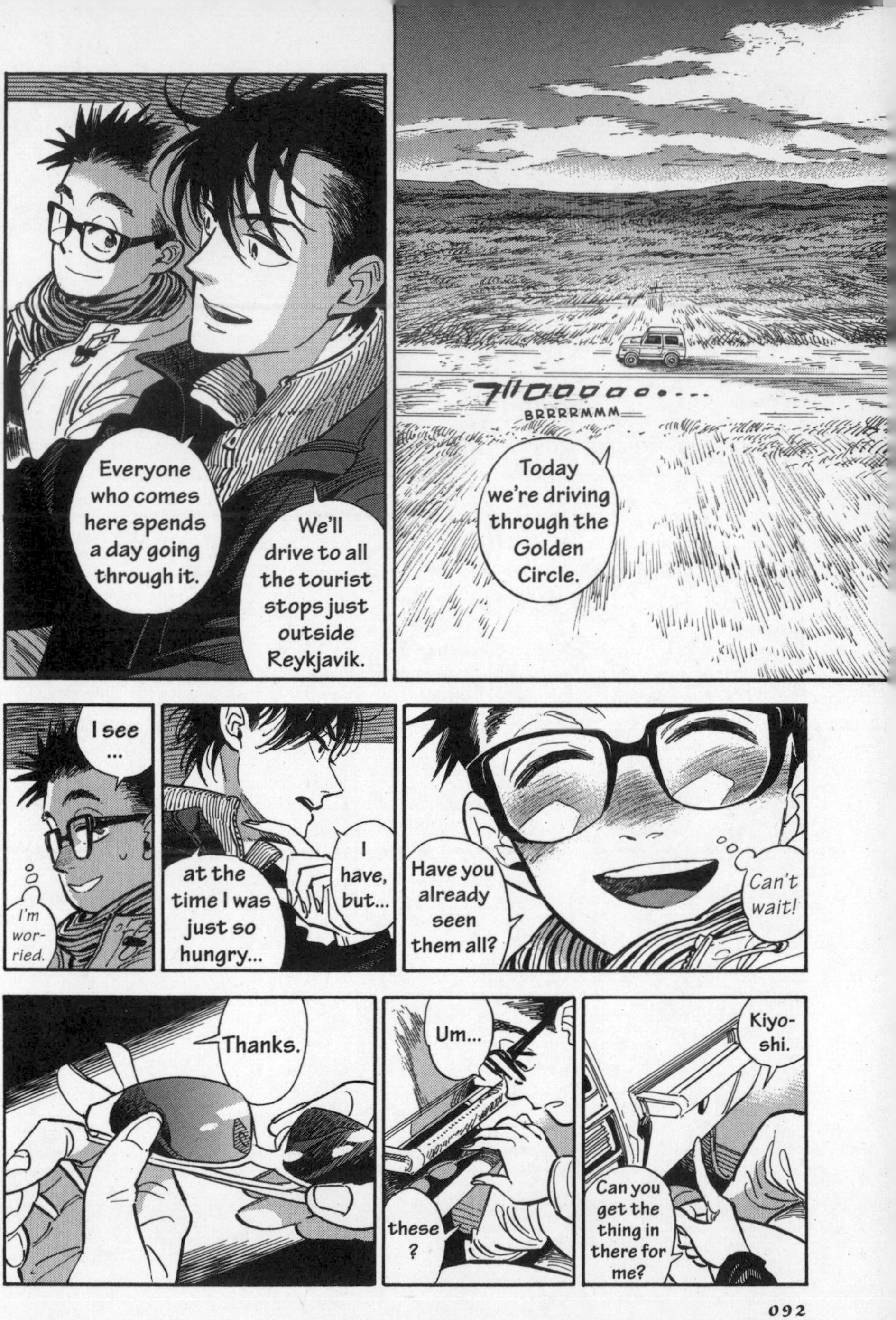
BRRRRMMM
Today we're driving through the Golden Circle.
We'll drive to all the tourist stops just outside Reykjavik.
Everyone who comes here spends a day going through it.
Can't wait!
Have you already seen them all?
I have, but...
at the time I was just so hungry...
I see ...
I'm wor-ried.
Kiyo-shi.
Can you get the thing in there for me?
Um...
these?
Thanks.

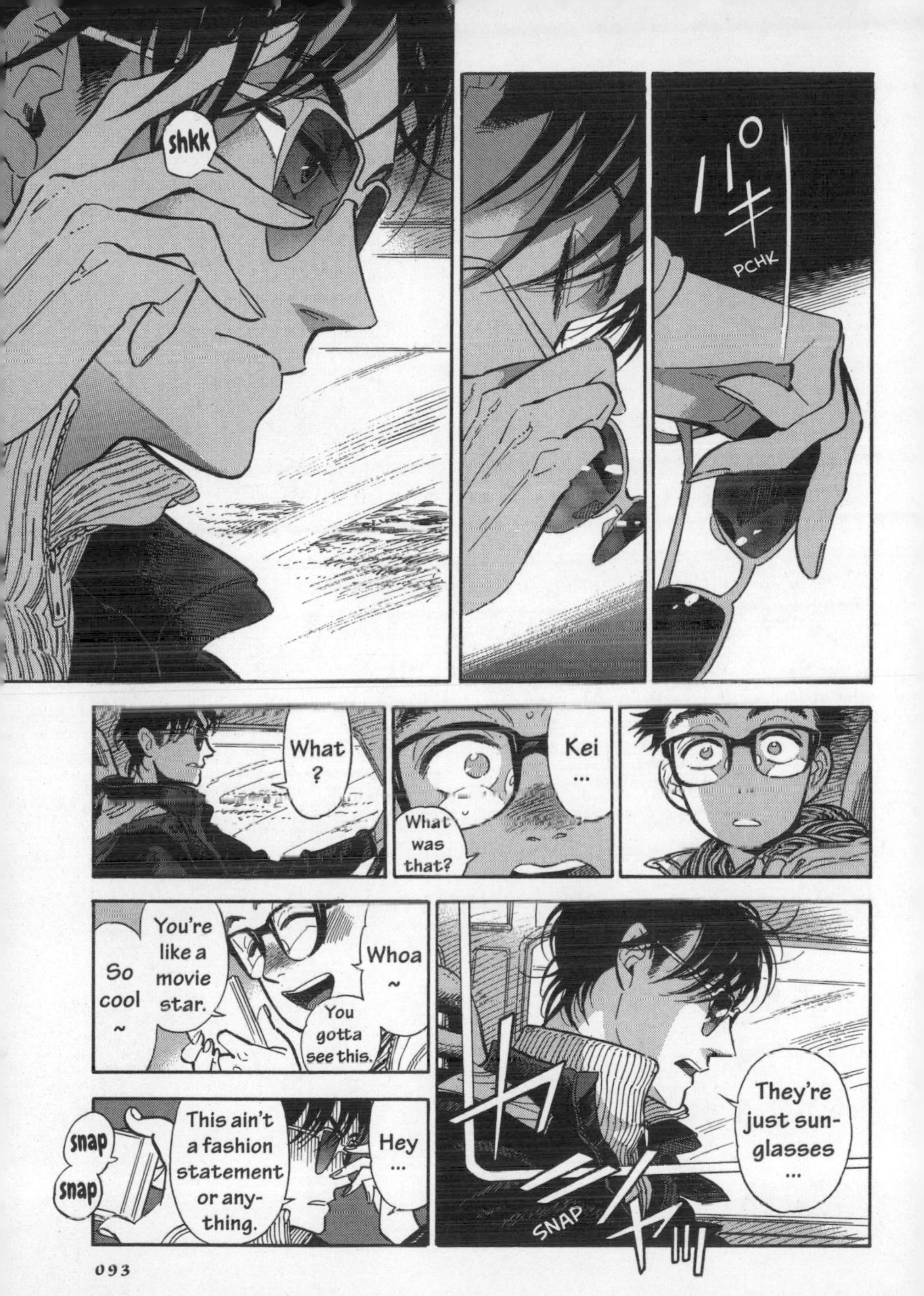

パキ
PCHK
shkk
Kei ...
What was that?
What ?
They're just sun-glasses ...
SNAP
Whoa ~
You're like a movie star.
So cool ~
You gotta see this.
Hey ...
This ain't a fashion statement or any-thing.
snap
snap

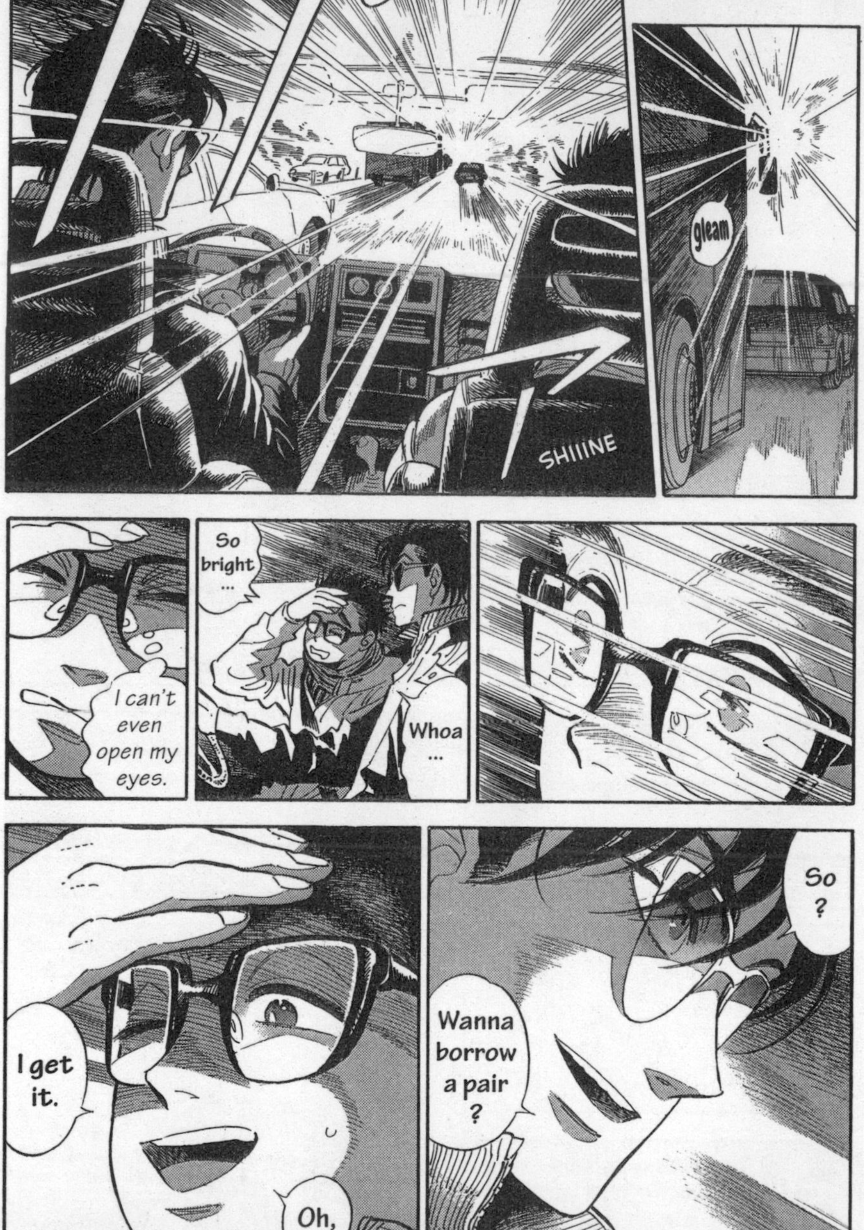
gleam
SHIIINE
So bright ...
Whoa ...
I can't even open my eyes.
So ?
Wanna borrow a pair ?
Oh,
I get it.

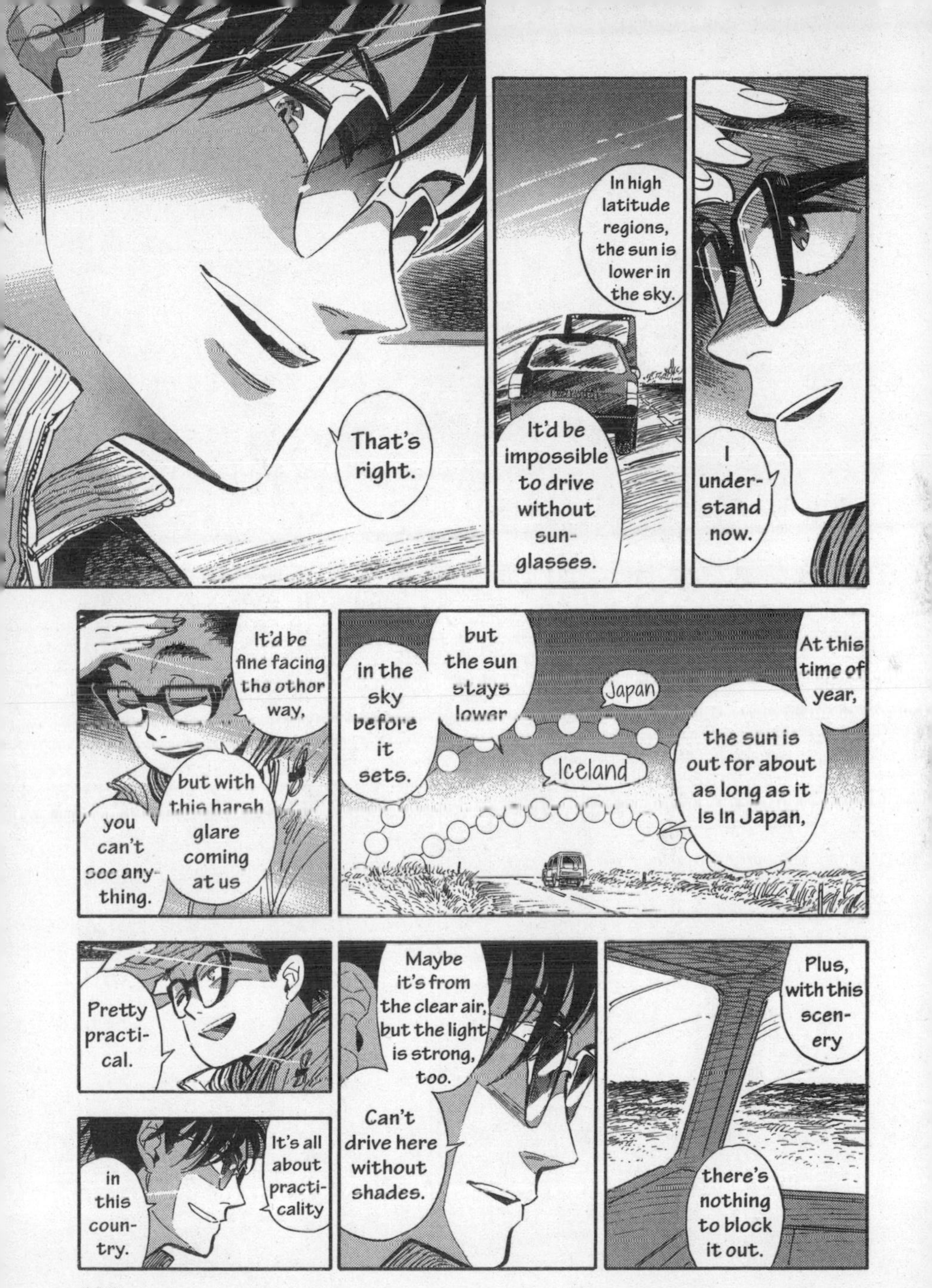
I understand now.
In high latitude regions, the sun is lower in the sky.
It'd be impossible to drive without sun-glasses.
That's right.
At this time of year,
the sun is out for about as long as it is in Japan,
Japan
Iceland
but the sun stays lower
in the sky before it sets.
It'd be fine facing the other way,
but with this harsh glare coming at us
you can't see any-thing.
Plus, with this scen-ery
there's nothing to block it out.
Maybe it's from the clear air, but the light is strong, too.
Can't drive here without shades.
Pretty practi-cal.
It's all about practi-cality
in this coun-try.

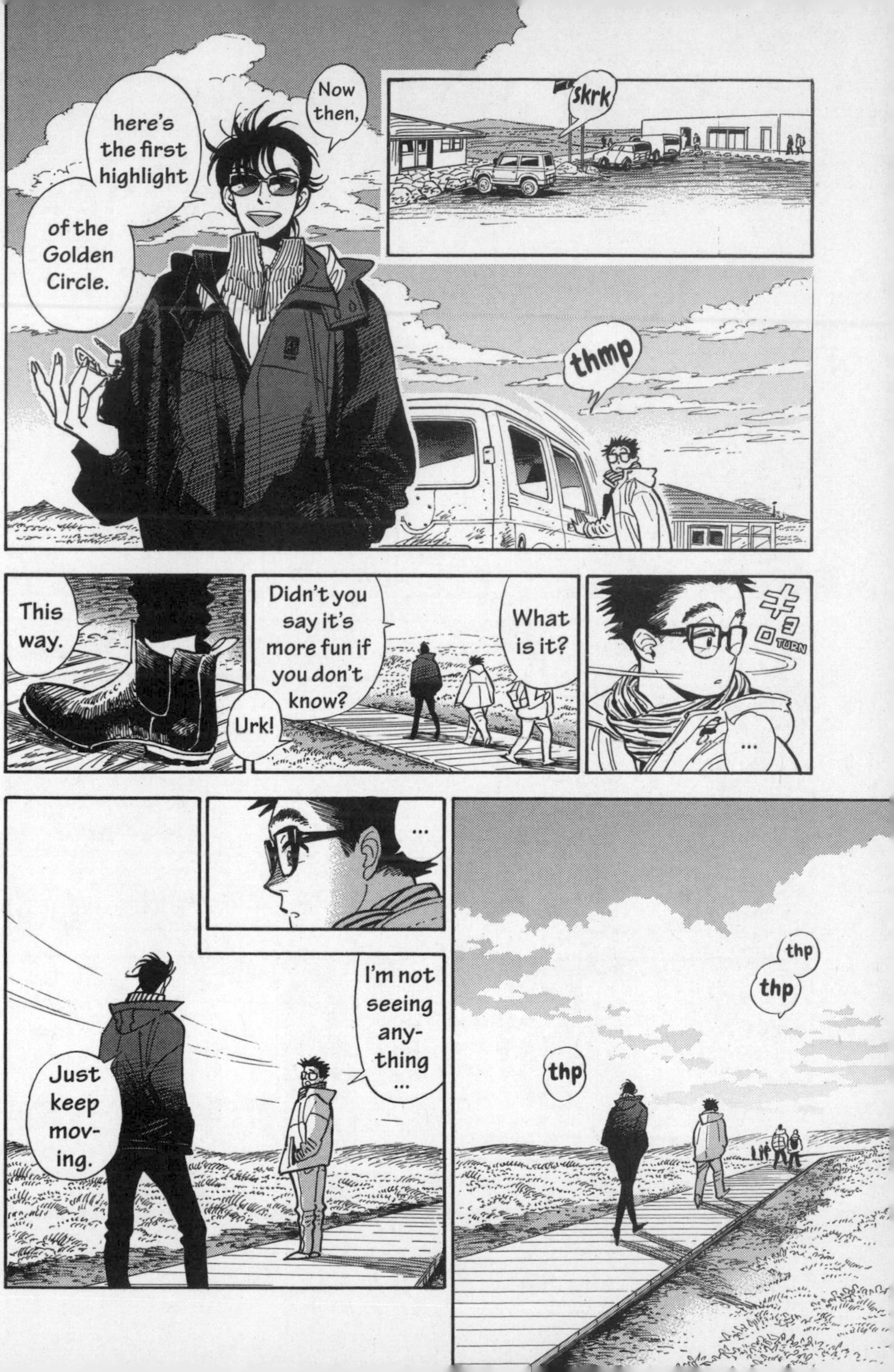
skrk
thmp
Now then,
here's the first highlight
of the Golden Circle.
キョロ TURN
...
What is it?
Didn't you say it's more fun if you don't know?
Urk!
This way.
thp
thp
thp
...
I'm not seeing any-thing ...
Just keep mov-ing.

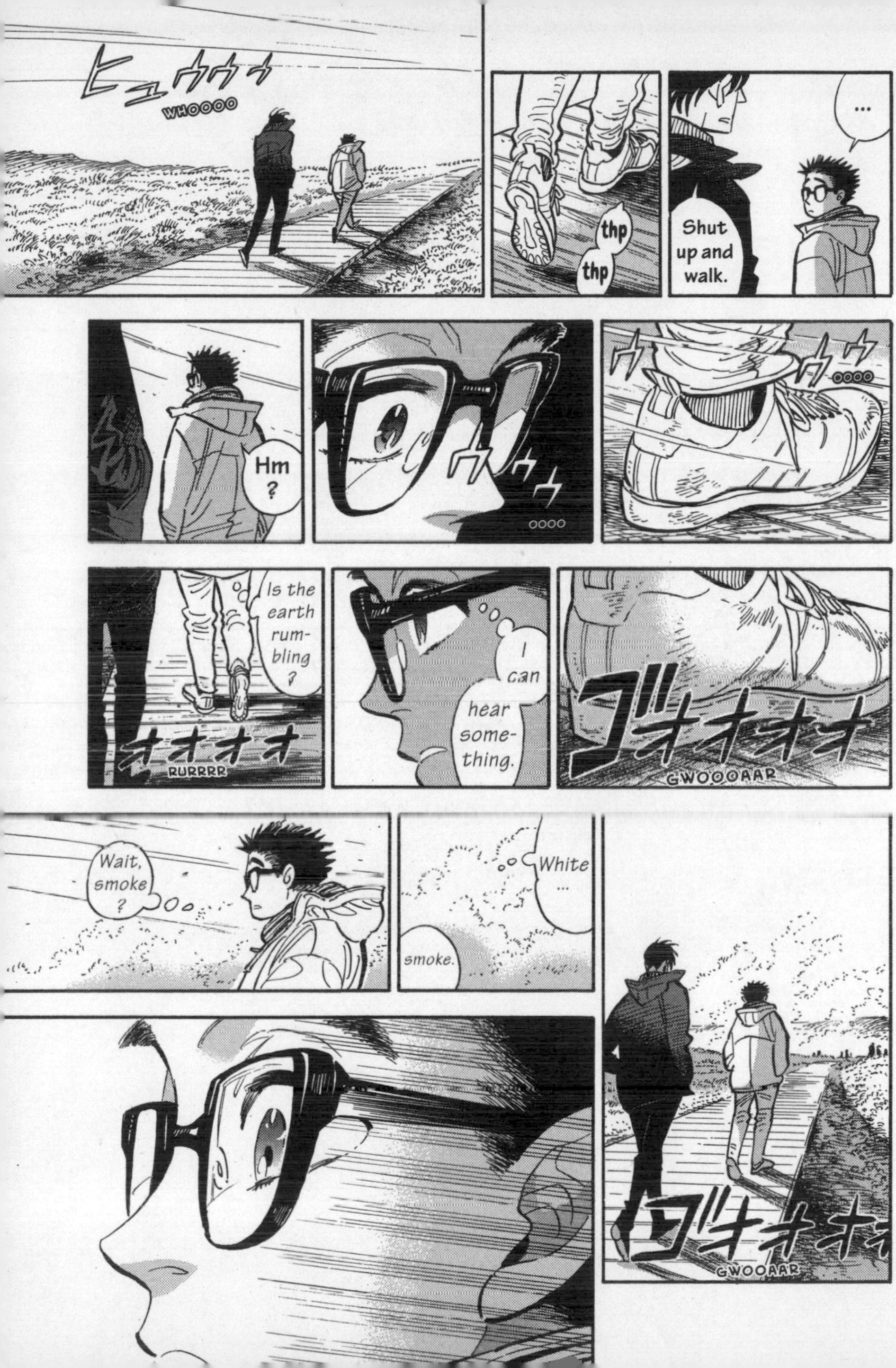
...
Shut up and walk.
thp
thp
ヒュウウウ
WHOOOO
ウウウ
oooo
ウウウ
oooo
Hm?
ゴオオオオ
GWOOOOAAR
I can hear something.
Is the earth rumbling?
オオオオ
RURRRR
ゴオオオ
GWOOAAR
White...
smoke.
Wait, smoke?

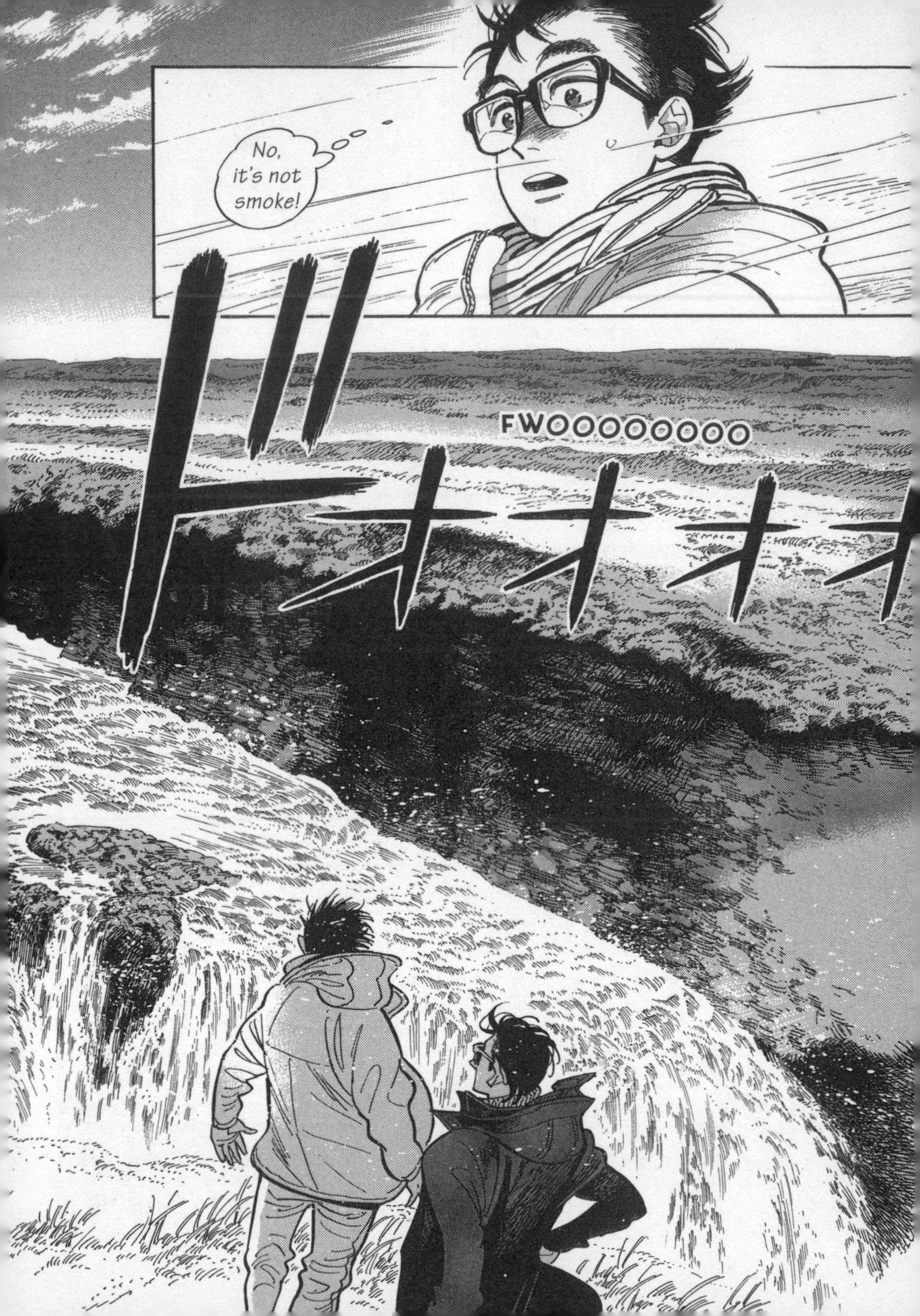
No, it's not smoke!
ドオオオオ
FWOOOOOOOOO

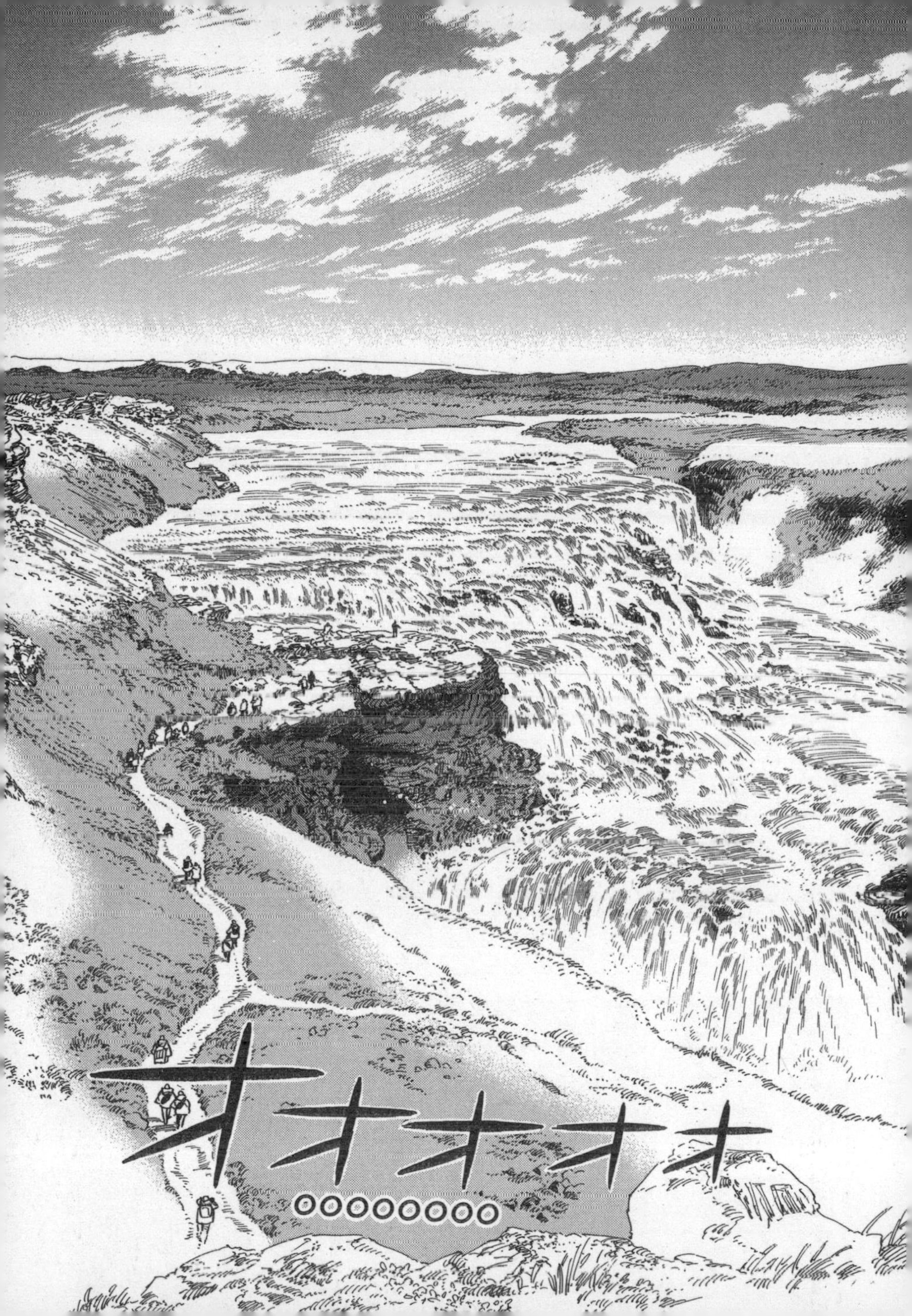
オオオオオ

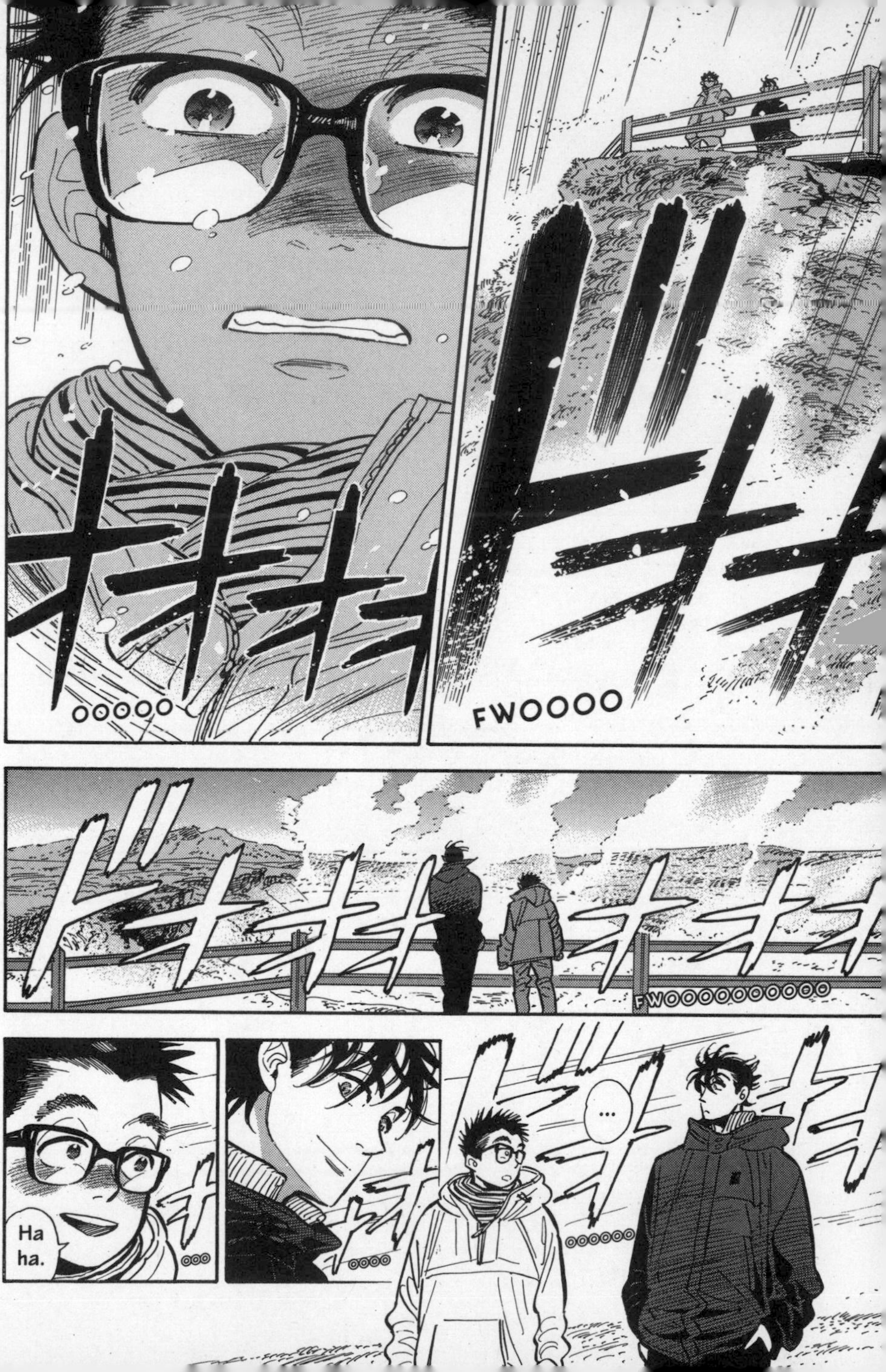
FWOOOO
OOOOO
FWOOOOOOOOOOO
...
OOOOOO
OOOO
Ha ha.
OOO

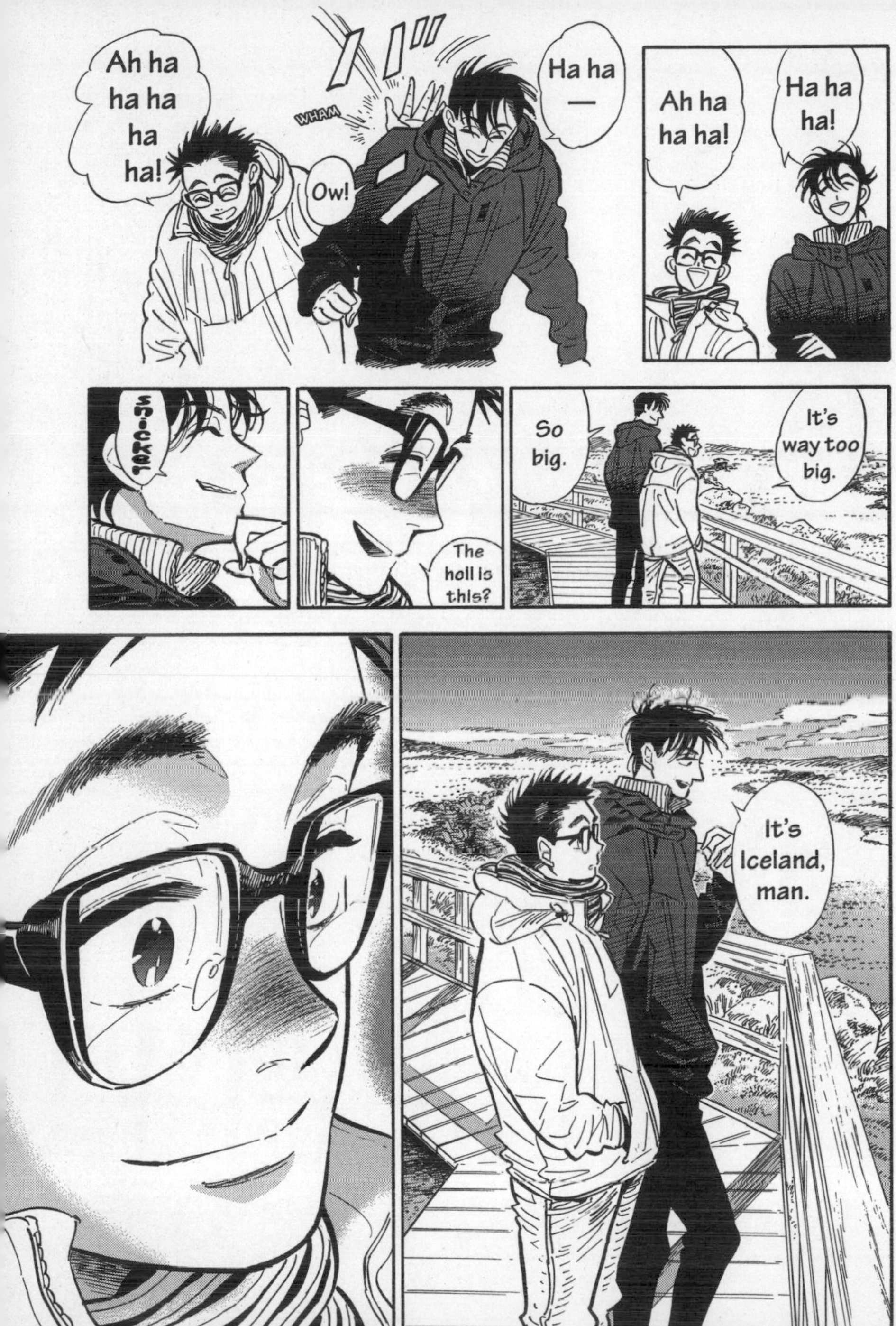
Ha ha ha!
Ah ha ha ha!
Ha ha —
WHAM
Ah ha ha ha ha ha!
Ow!
It's way too big.
So big.
The hell is this?
snicker
It's Iceland, man.

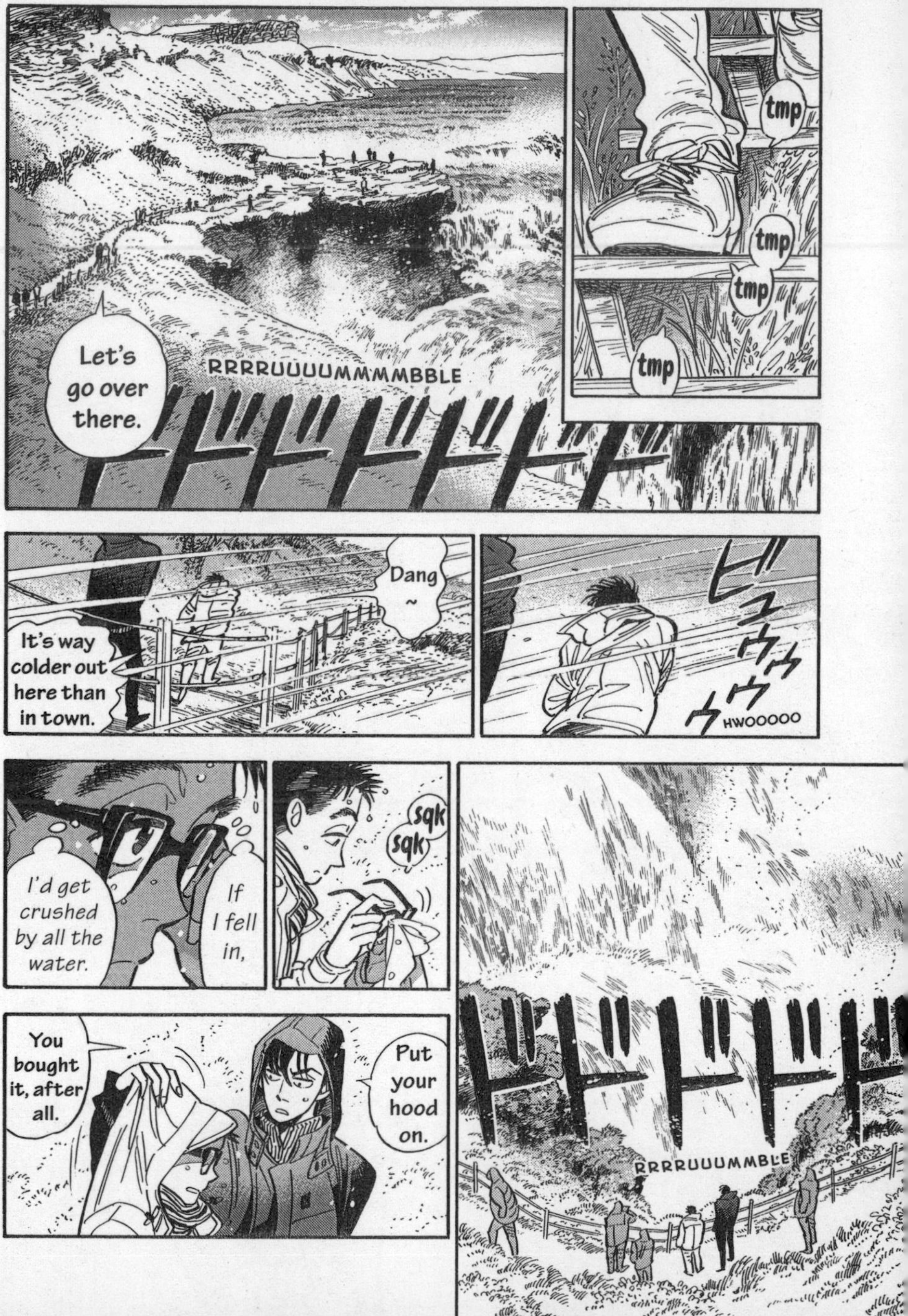
tmp
tmp
tmp
tmp
Let's go over there.
RRRRUUUUMMMMBBLE
HWOOOOO
Dang ~
It's way colder out here than in town.
RRRRUUUMMBLE
sqk
sqk
If I fell in,
I'd get crushed by all the water.
Put your hood on.
You bought it, after all.

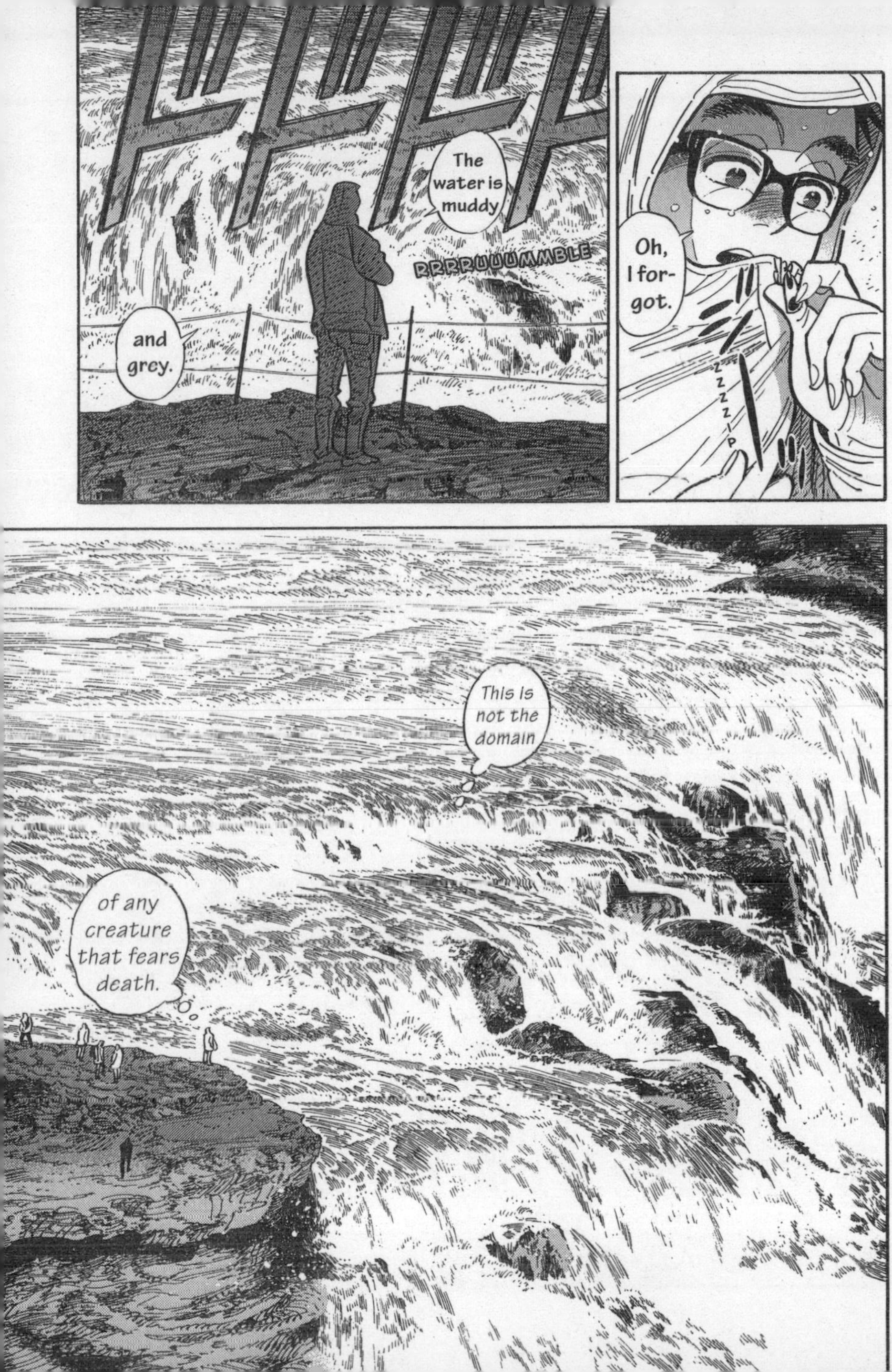
Oh, I for-got.
ZZZZIP
The water is muddy
RRRRUUUMMBLE
and grey.
This is not the domain
of any creature that fears death.

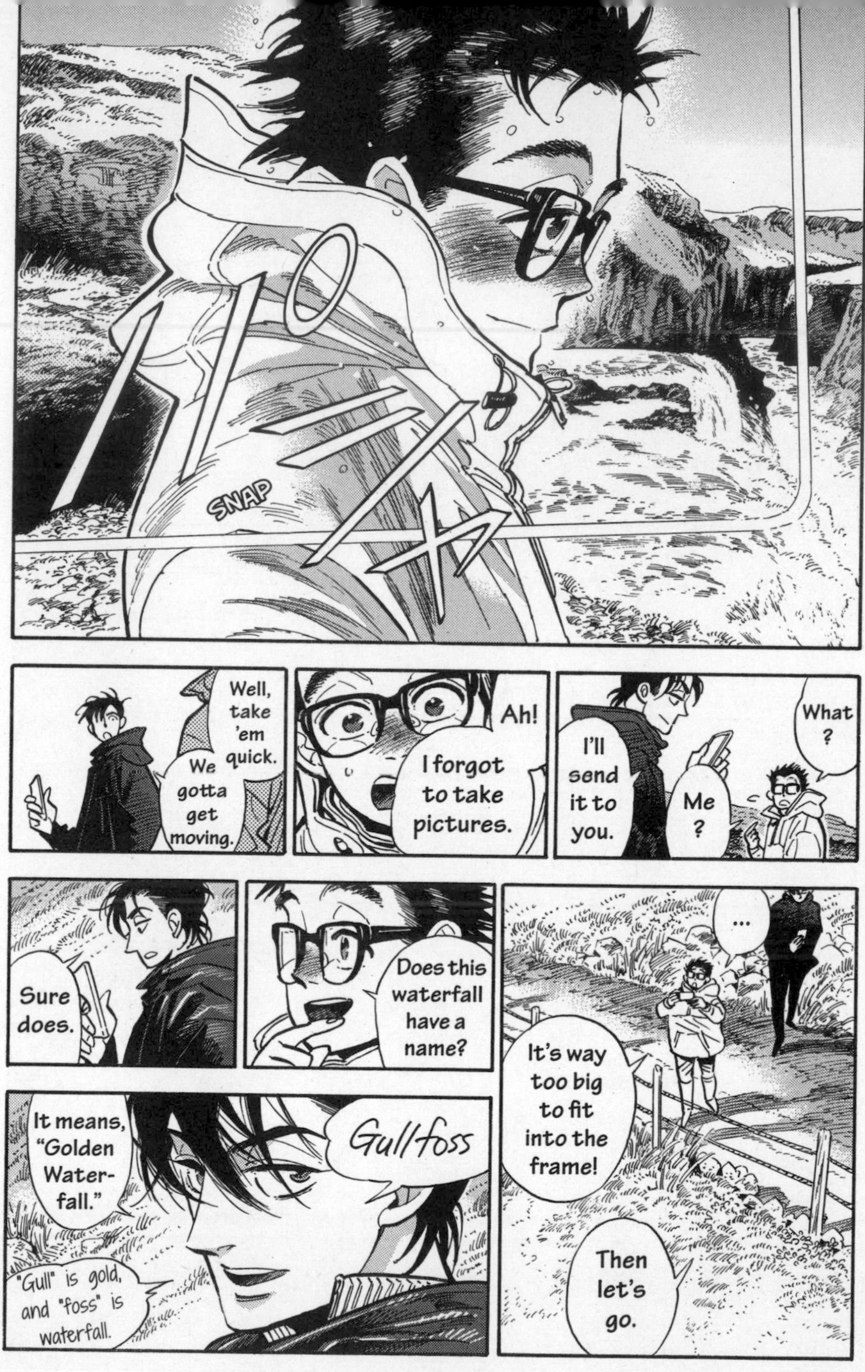
SNAP
What?
Me?
I'll send it to you.
Ah!
I forgot to take pictures.
Well, take 'em quick.
We gotta get moving.
...
It's way too big to fit into the frame!
Then let's go.
Does this waterfall have a name?
Sure does.
Gullfoss
It means, "Golden Waterfall."
"Gull" is gold, and "foss" is waterfall.

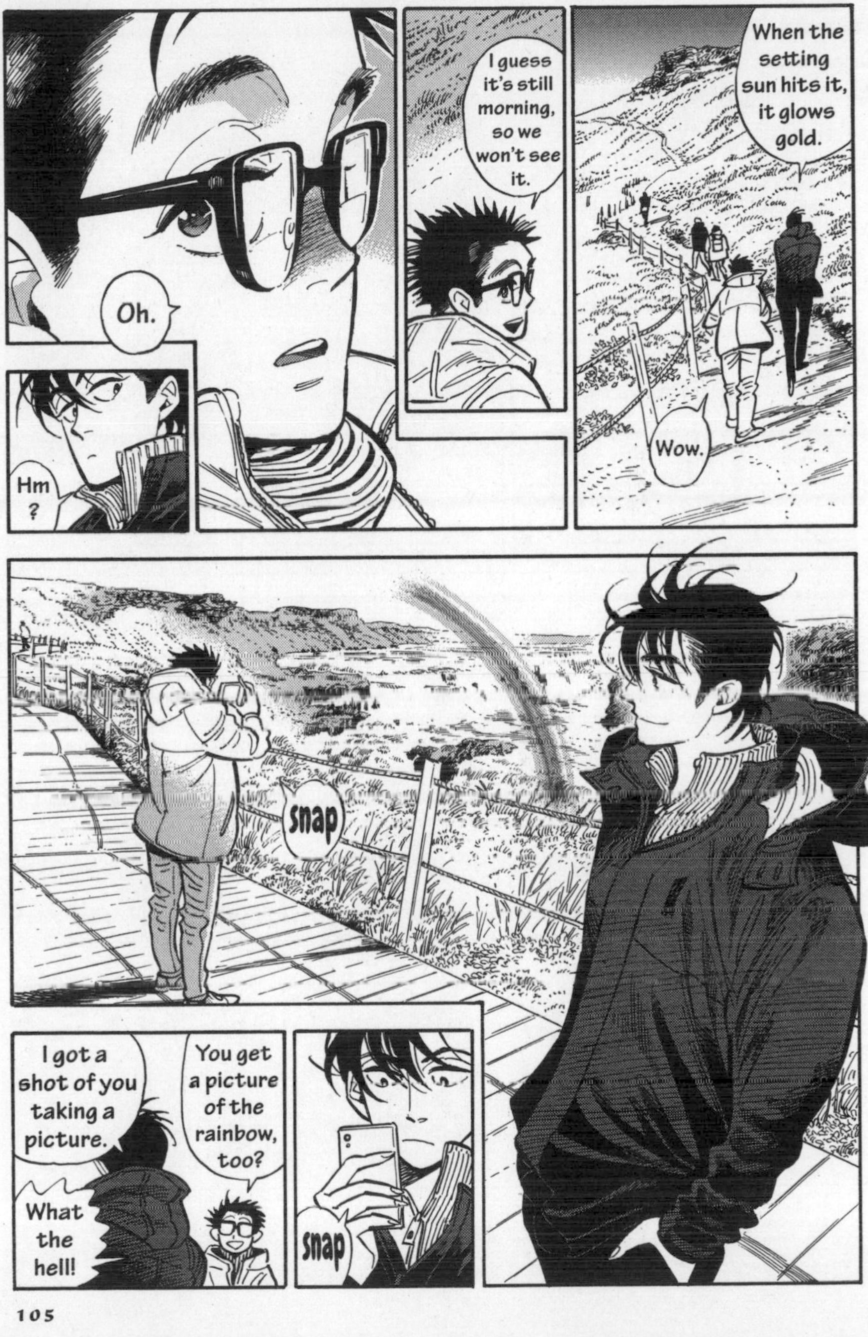
When the setting sun hits it, it glows gold.
Wow.
I guess it's still morning, so we won't see it.
Oh.
Hm?
snap
snap
You get a picture of the rainbow, too?
I got a shot of you taking a picture.
What the hell!

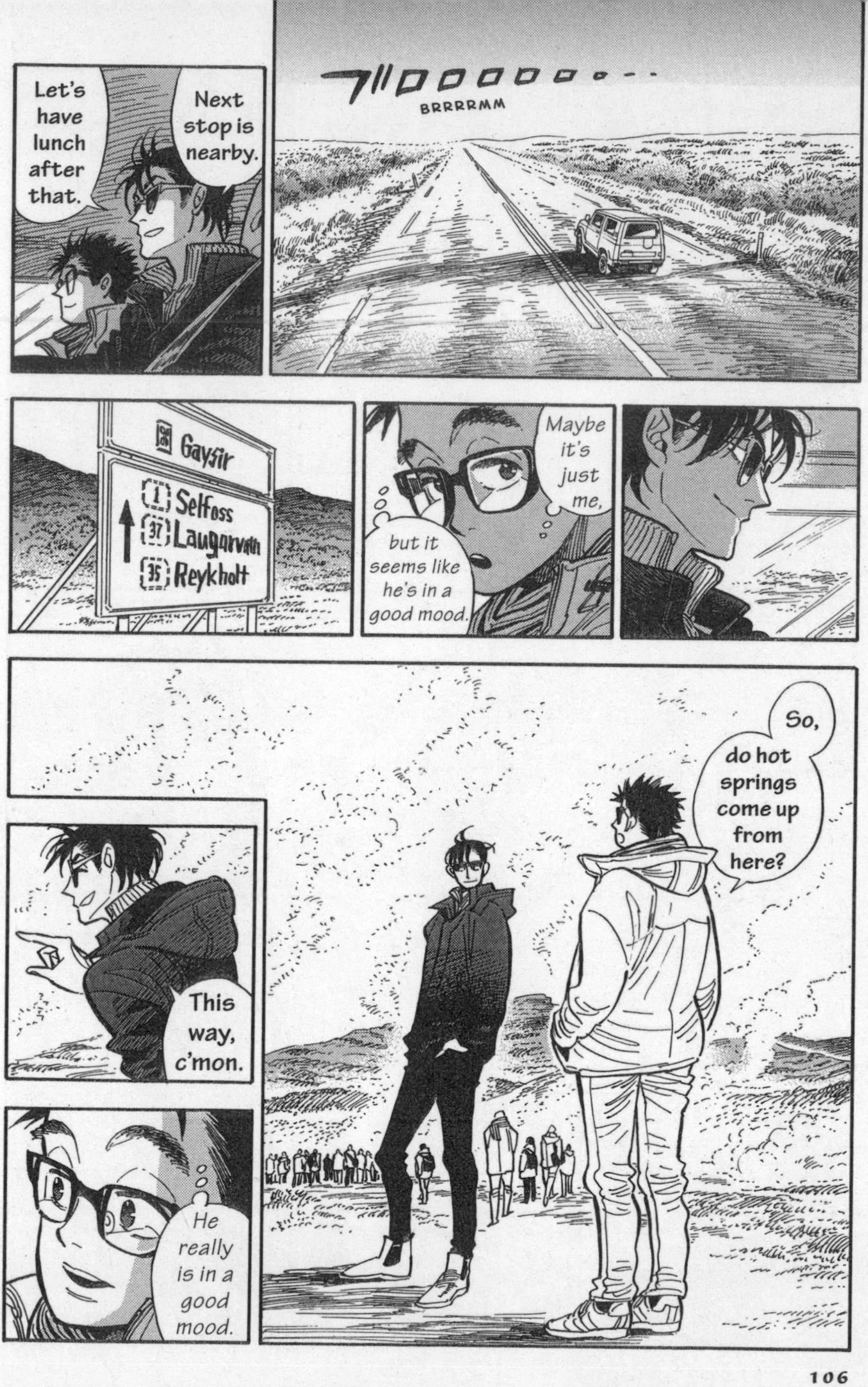
BRRRRMM
Next stop is nearby.
Let's have lunch after that.
Maybe it's just me,
but it seems like he's in a good mood.
Gaysir
1 Selfoss
37 Laugarvatn
35 Reykholt
So, do hot springs come up from here?
This way, c'mon.
He really is in a good mood.

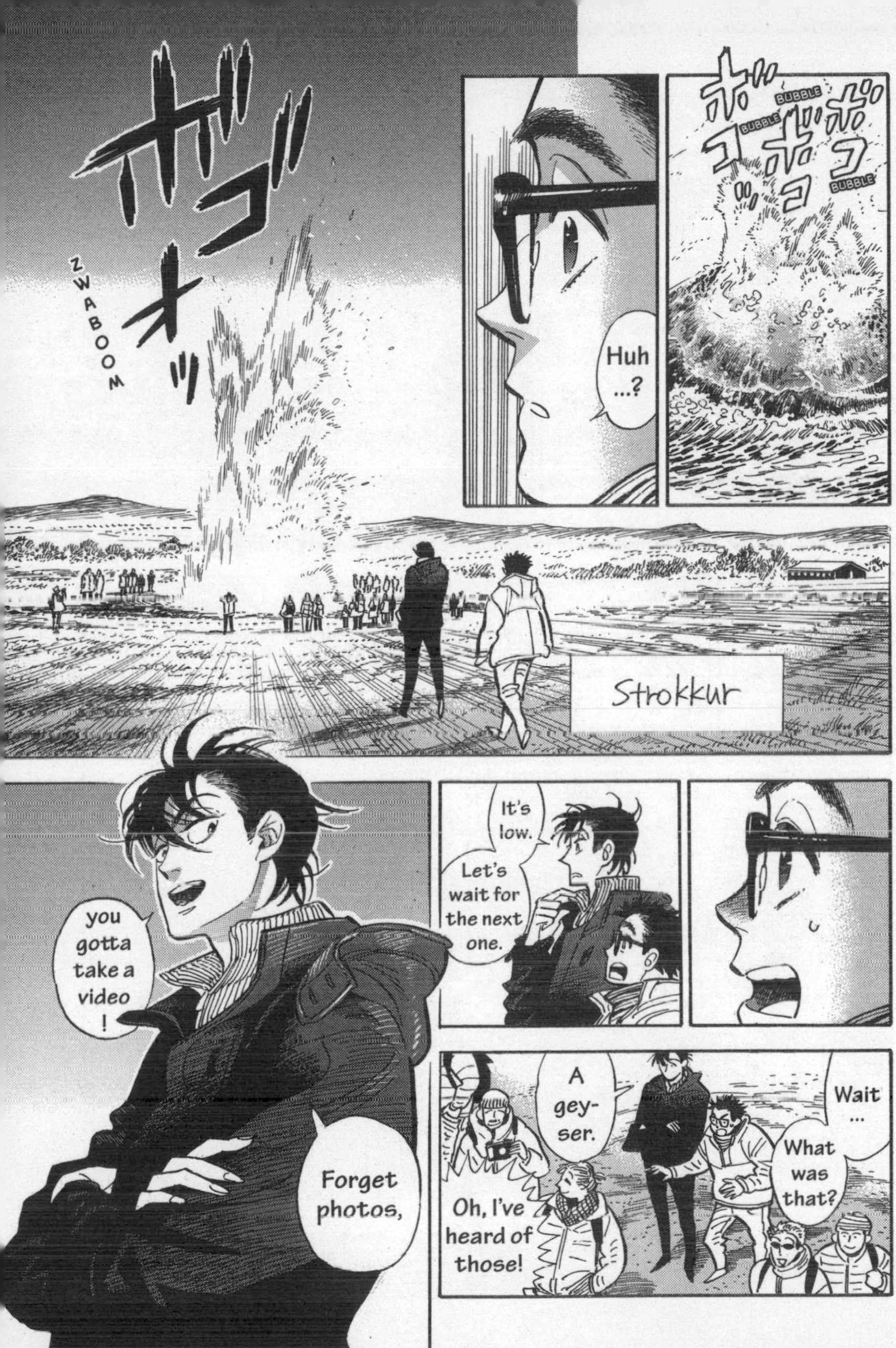
BUBBLE
BUBBLE
BUBBLE
Huh ...?
ZWABOOM
Strokkur
It's low.
Let's wait for the next one.
Wait ...
What was that?
A gey-ser.
Oh, I've heard of those!
Forget photos,
you gotta take a video!

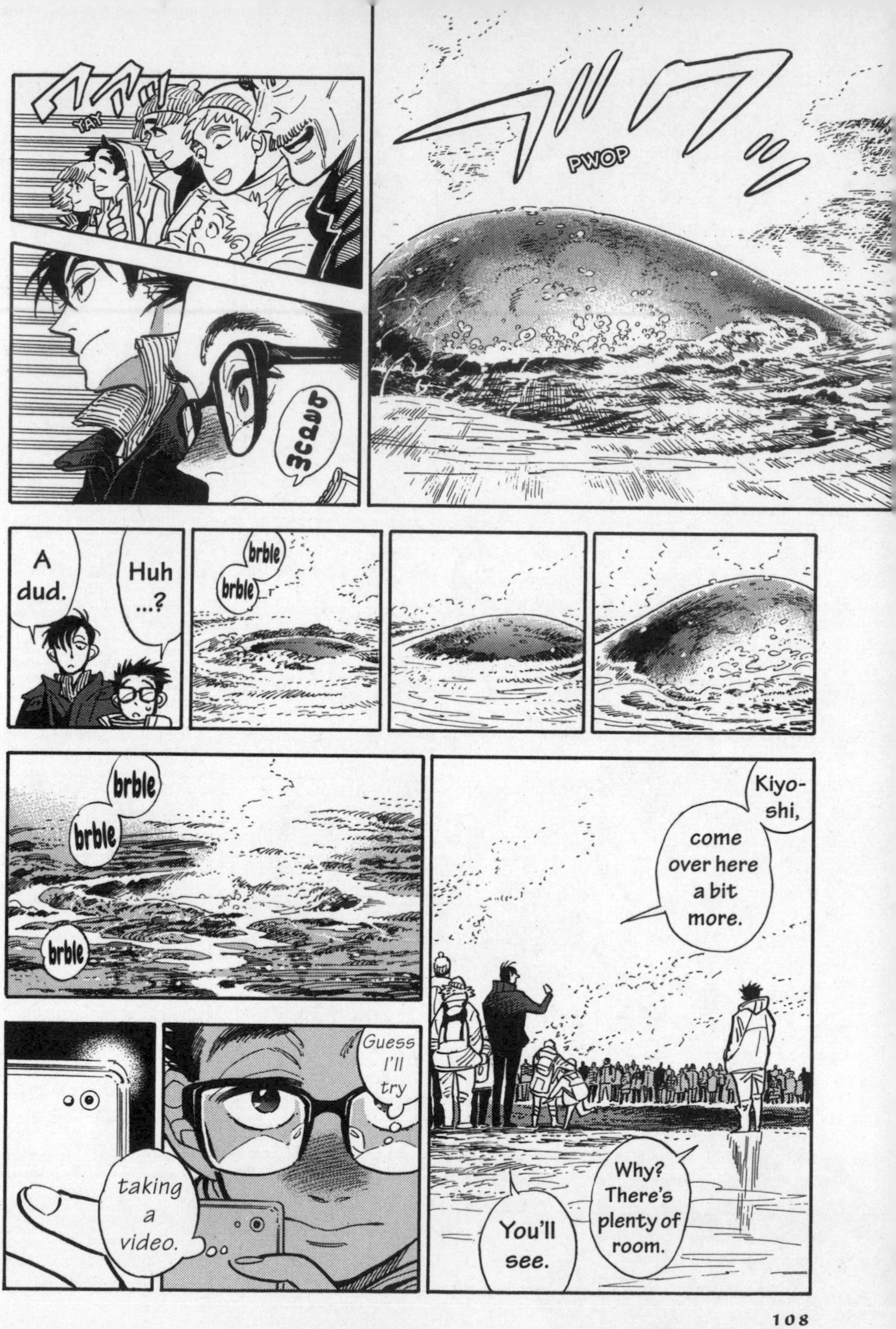
PWOP
YAY
A dud.
Huh ...?
brble
brble
brble
brble
brble
Kiyo-shi, come over here a bit more.
Why? There's plenty of room.
You'll see.
Guess I'll try
taking a video.

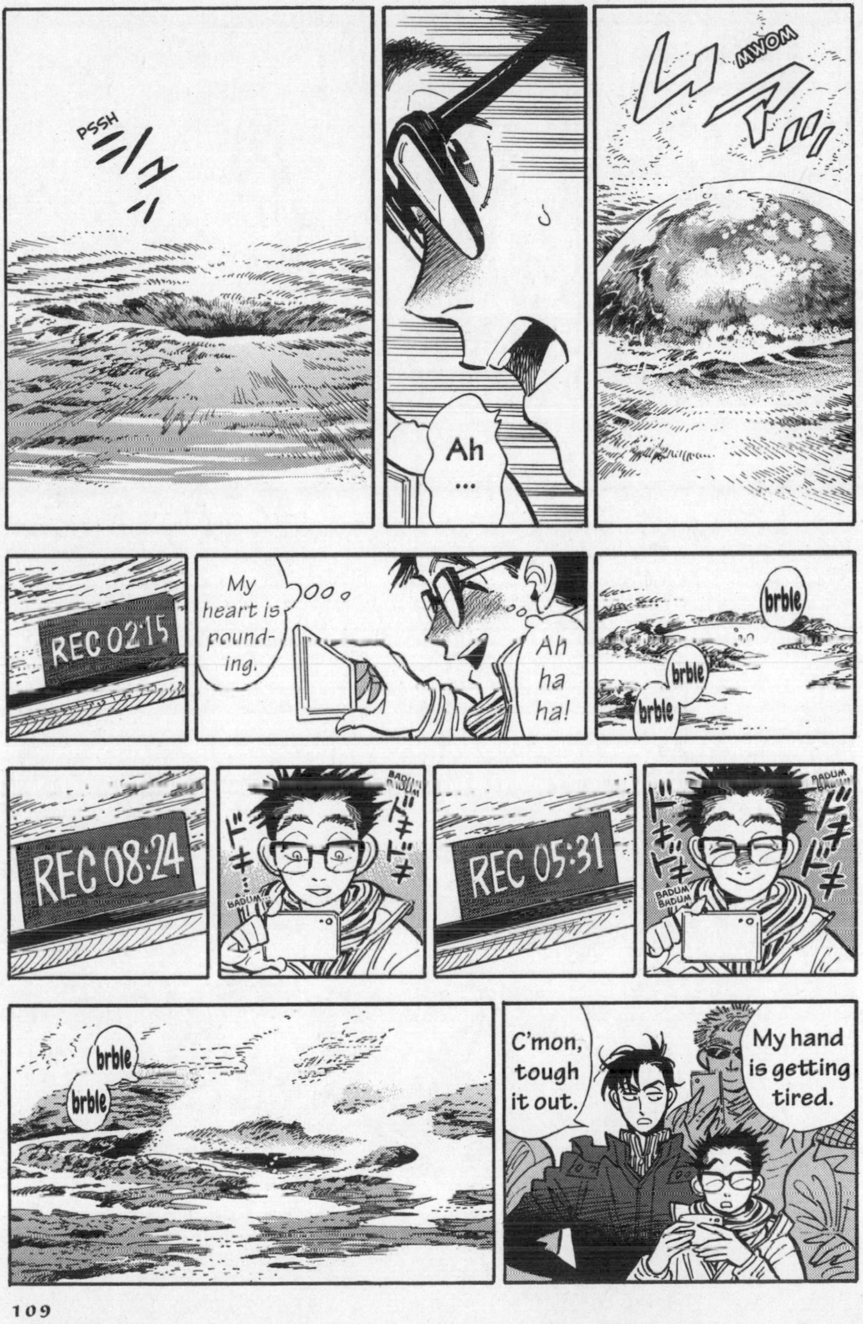
WWOM
Ah …
PSSH
brble
brble
brble
Ah ha ha!
My heart is pounding.
REC 02:15
BADUM BADUM
ドキドキ
ドキドキ
BADUM BADUM
REC 05:31
BADUM BADUM
ドキドキ
REC 08:24
My hand is getting tired.
C'mon, tough it out.
brble
brble

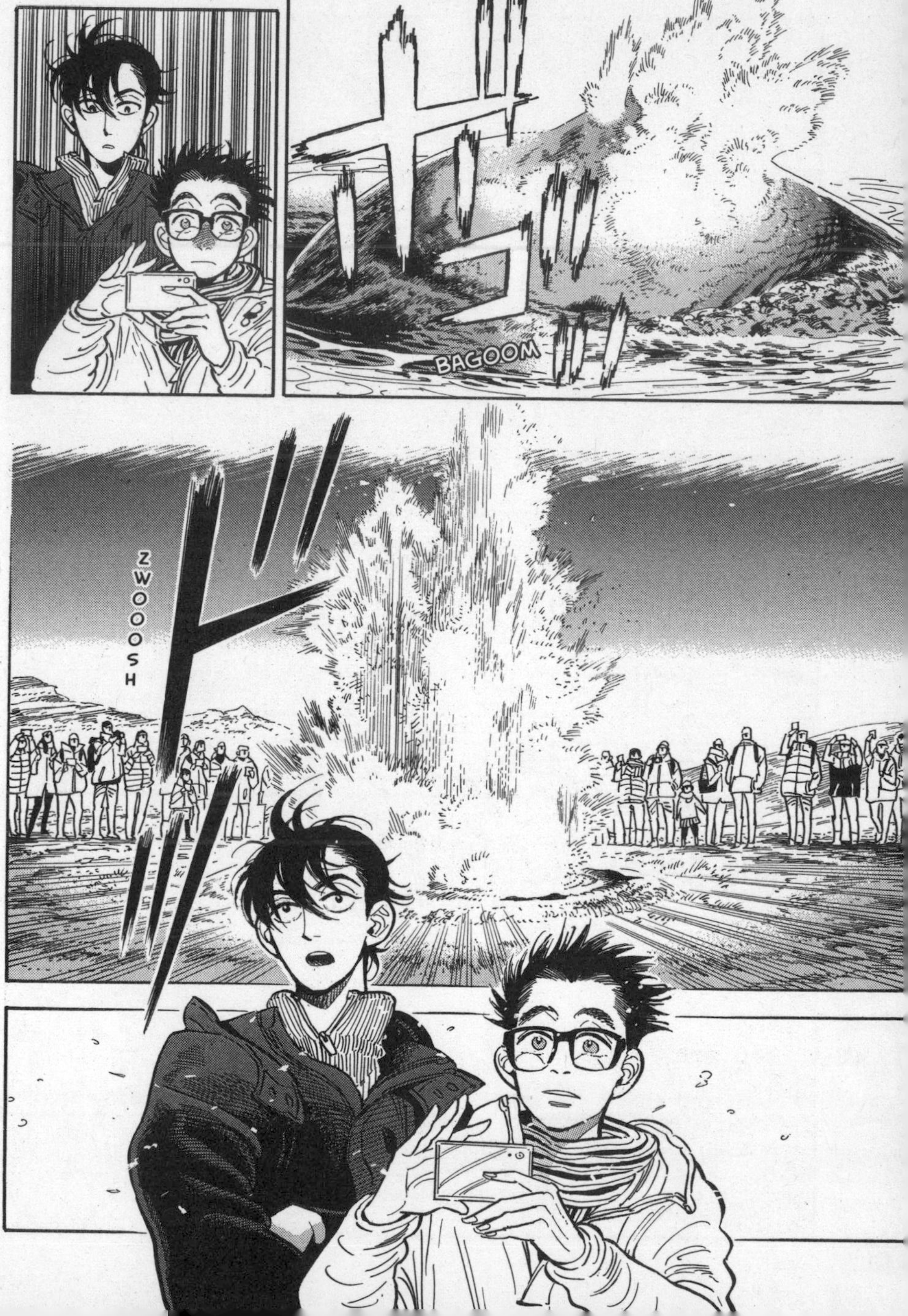
BAGOOM
ZWOOOOSH

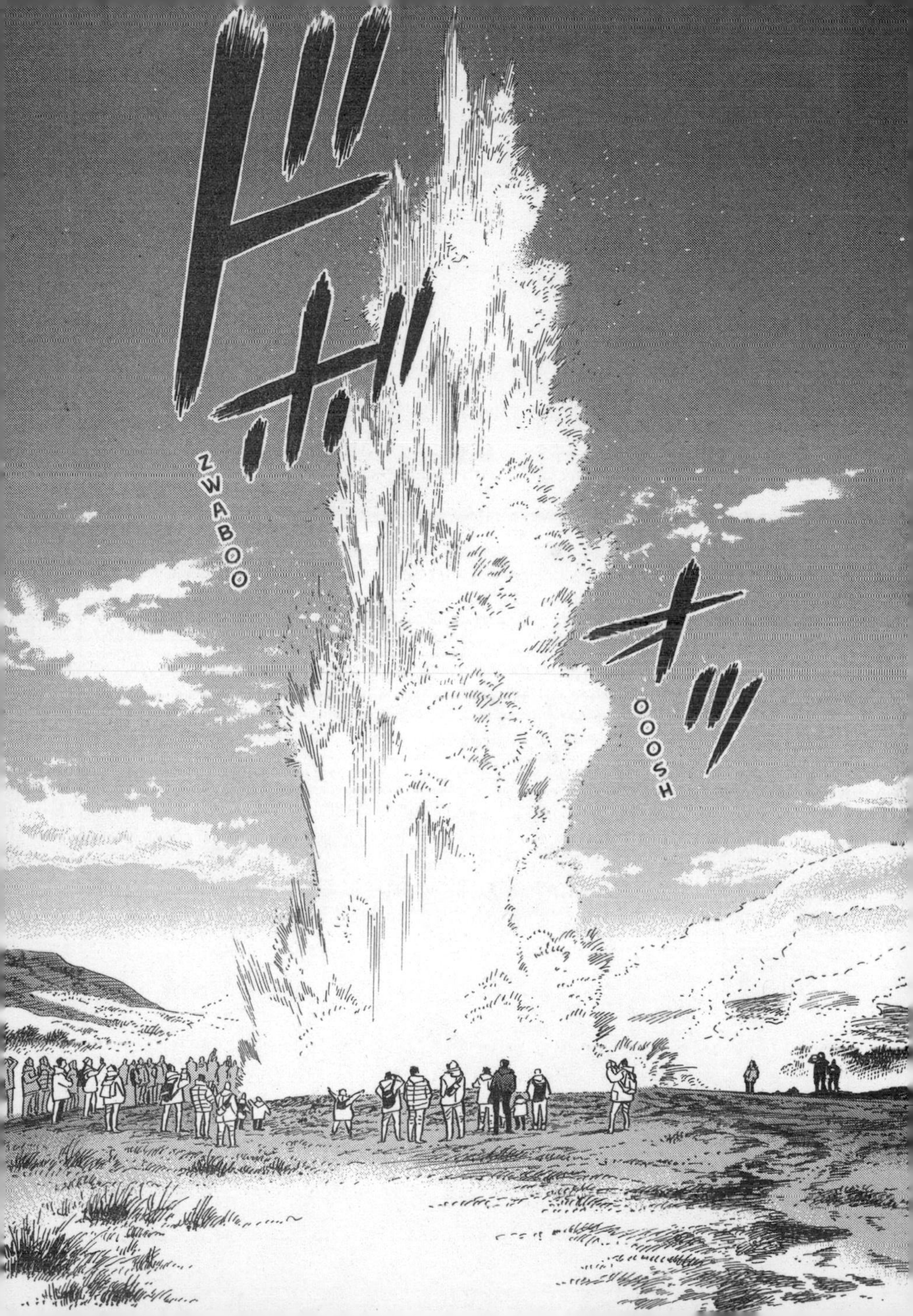
ドザッ
ZWABOO
オッ
OOOSH

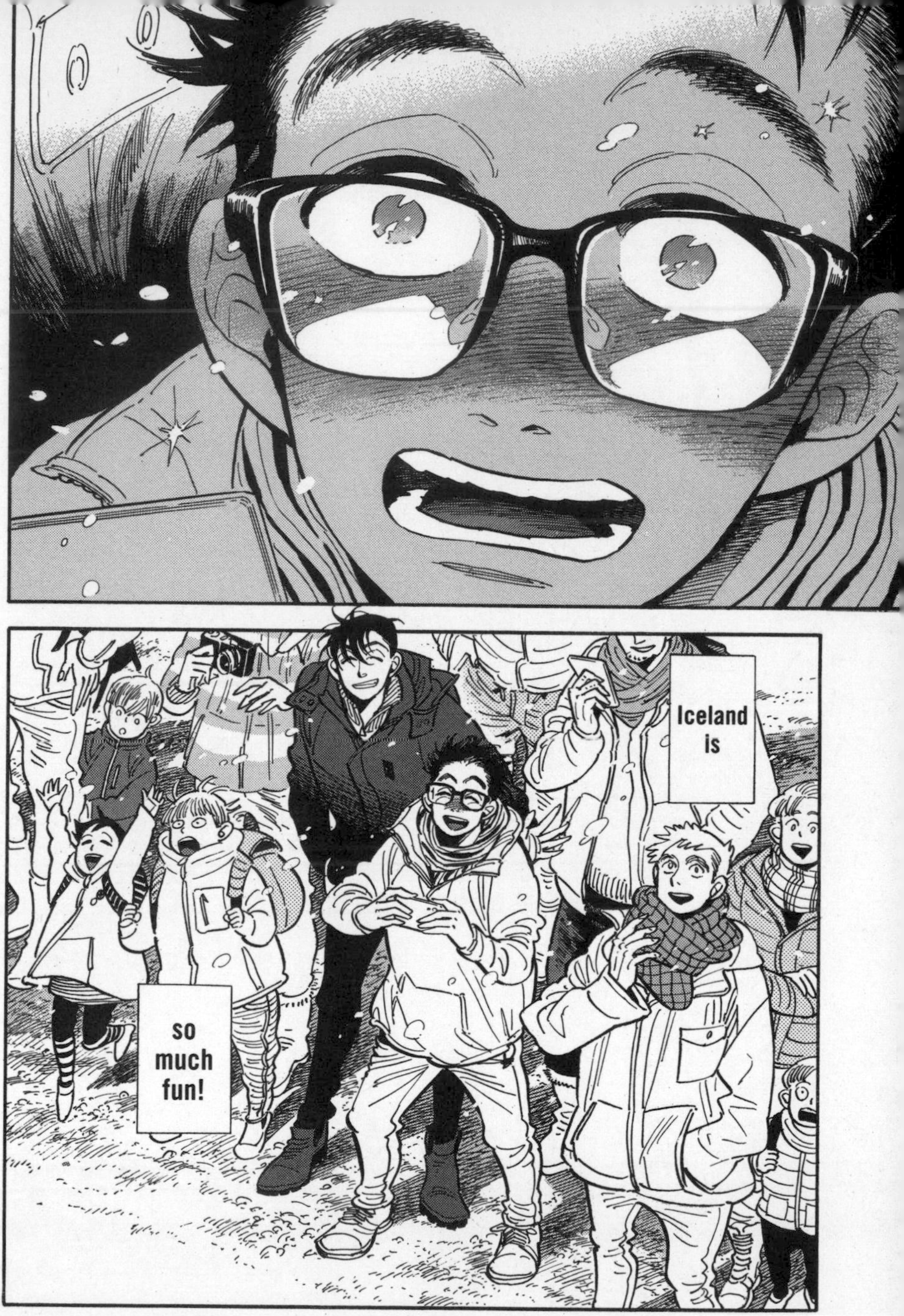
Iceland is
so much fun!

Chapter 14 – End

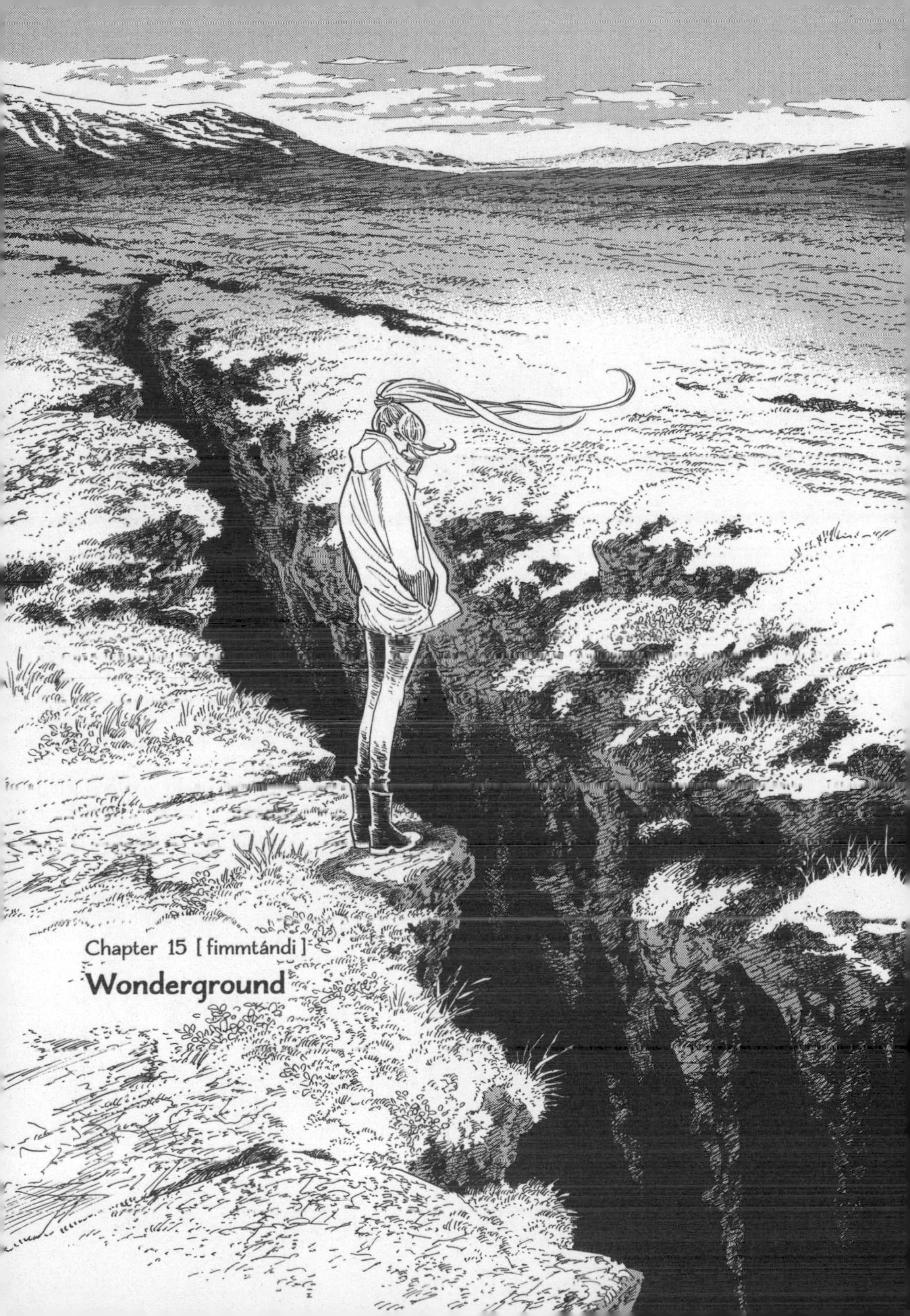
Chapter 15 [fimmtándi]
Wonderground

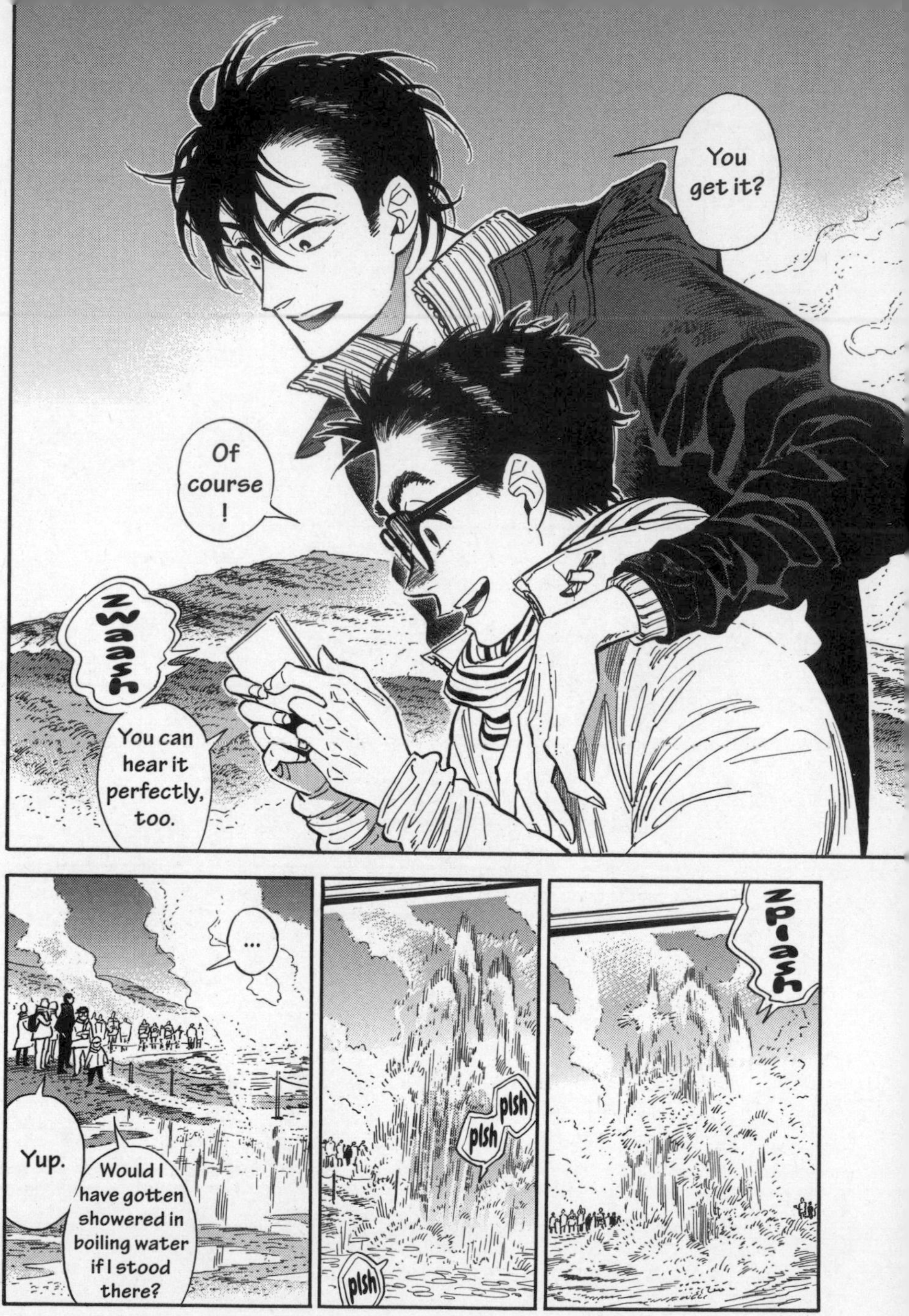
You get it?
Of course!
Zwaash
You can hear it perfectly, too.
Zplash
plsh
plsh
plsh
...
Would I have gotten showered in boiling water if I stood there?
Yup.

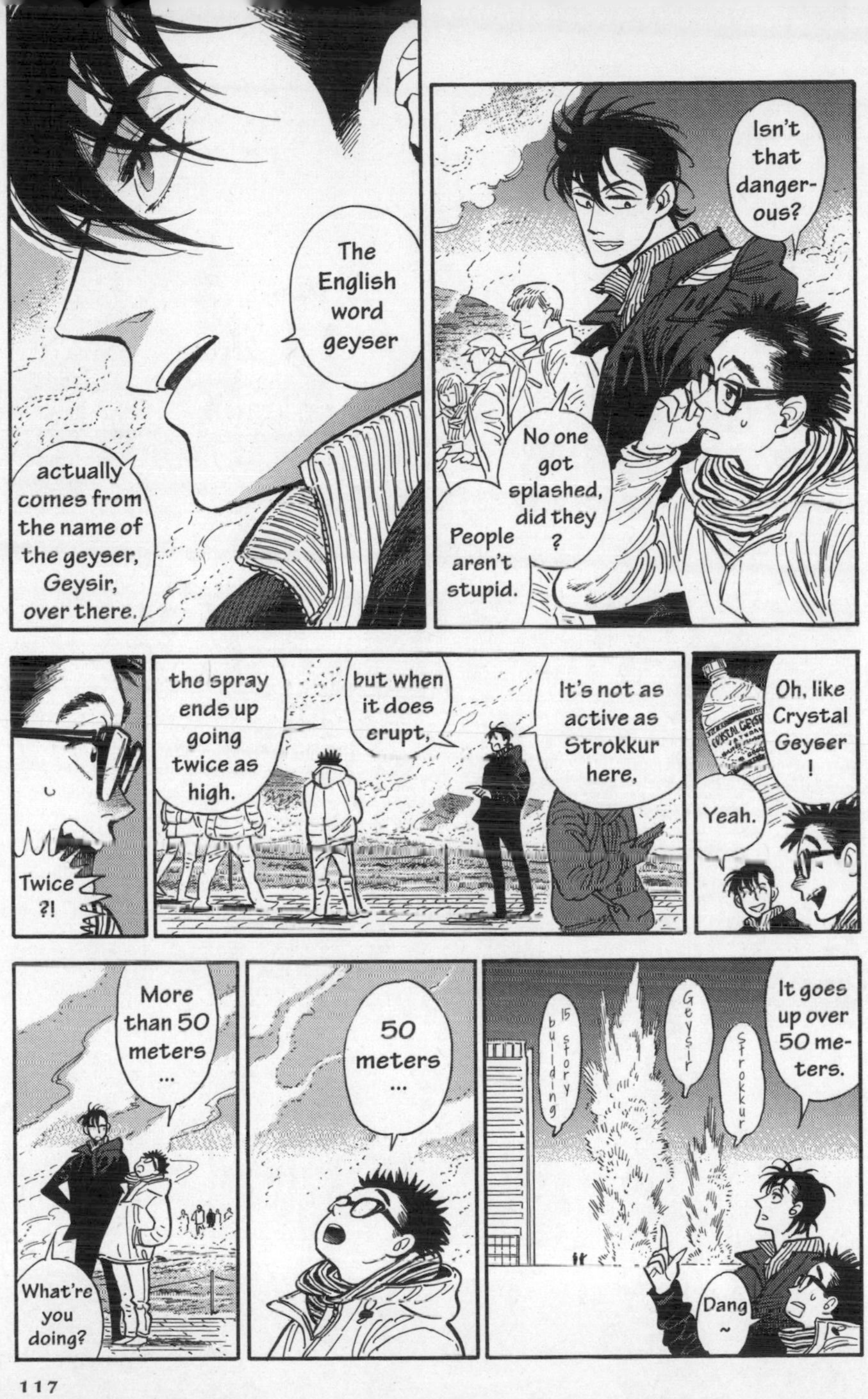
Isn't that danger-ous?
No one got splashed, did they?
People aren't stupid.
The English word geyser
actually comes from the name of the geyser, Geysir, over there.
Oh, like Crystal Geyser!
Yeah.
It's not as active as Strokkur here,
but when it does erupt,
the spray ends up going twice as high.
Twice?!
It goes up over 50 me-ters.
Strokkur
Geysir
15 story building
Dang~
50 meters...
More than 50 meters...
What're you doing?

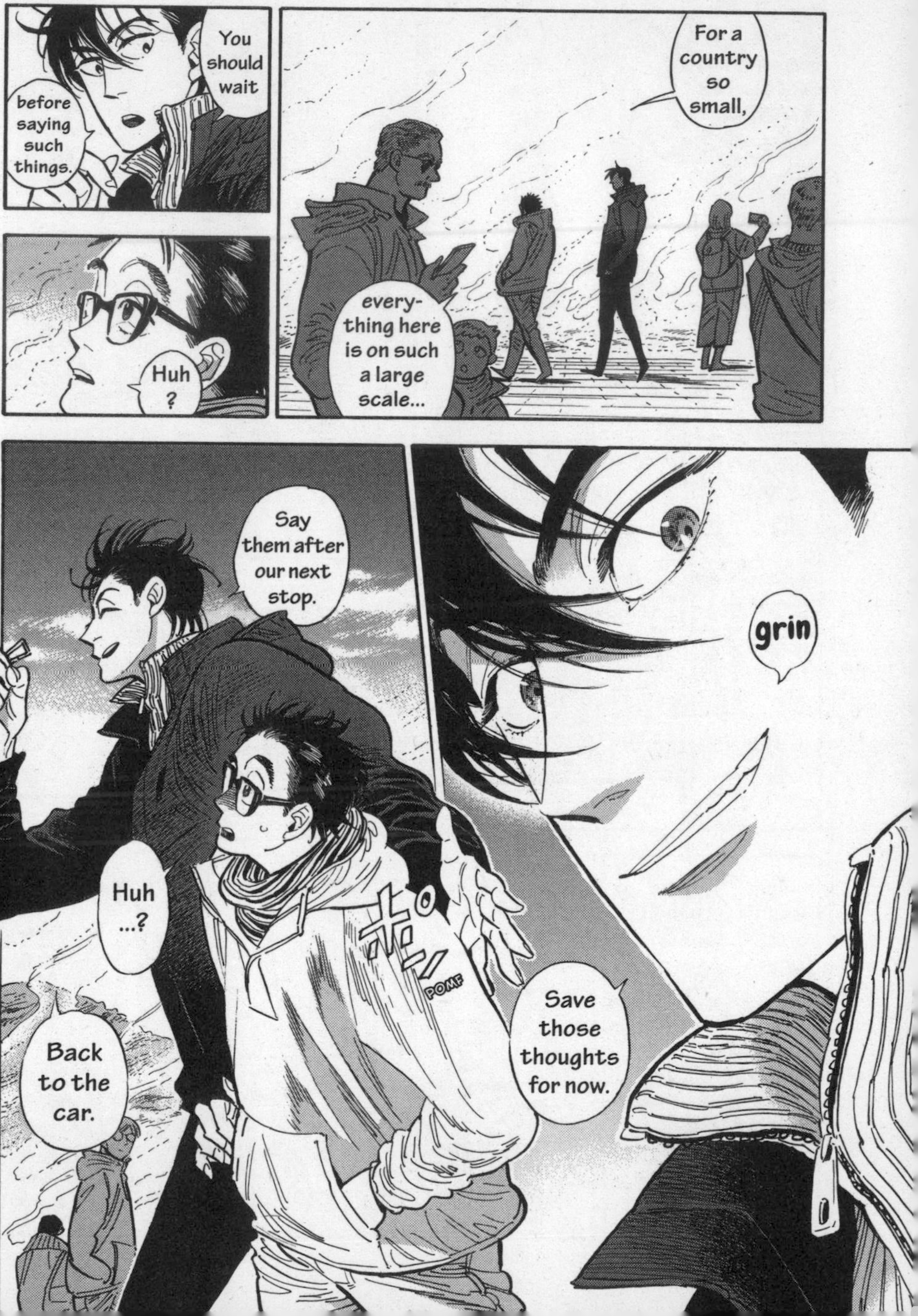
For a country so small,
everything here is on such a large scale...
You should wait before saying such things.
Huh?
grin
Save those thoughts for now.
Say them after our next stop.
Huh ...?
POMF
Back to the car.

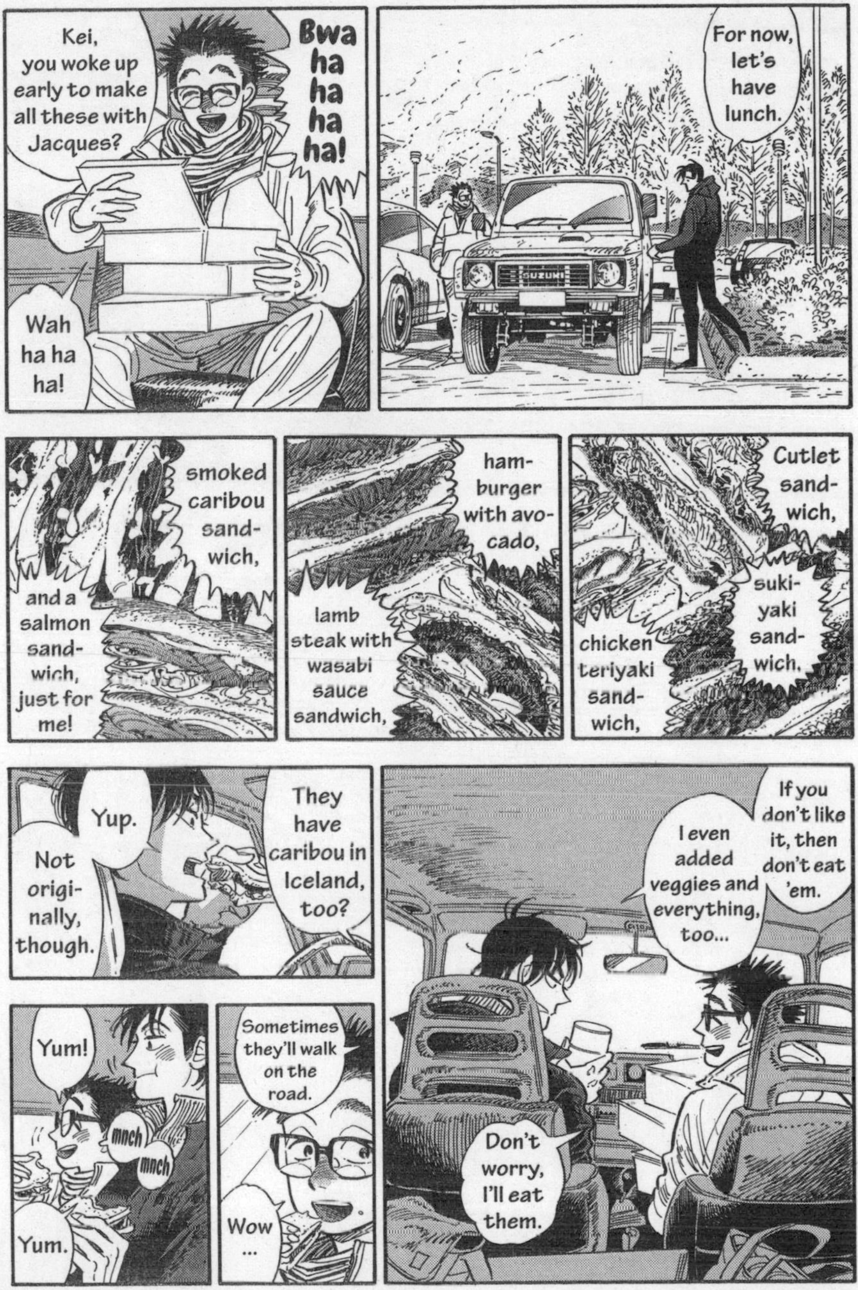
For now, let's have lunch.
Bwa ha ha ha ha!
Kei, you woke up early to make all these with Jacques?
Wah ha ha ha!
Cutlet sand-wich,
suki-yaki sand-wich,
chicken teriyaki sand-wich,
ham-burger with avo-cado,
lamb steak with wasabi sauce sandwich,
smoked caribou sand-wich,
and a salmon sand-wich, just for me!
If you don't like it, then don't eat 'em.
I even added veggies and everything, too...
Don't worry, I'll eat them.
They have caribou in Iceland, too?
Yup.
Not origi-nally, though.
Sometimes they'll walk on the road.
Wow ...
Yum!
mnch
mnch
Yum.

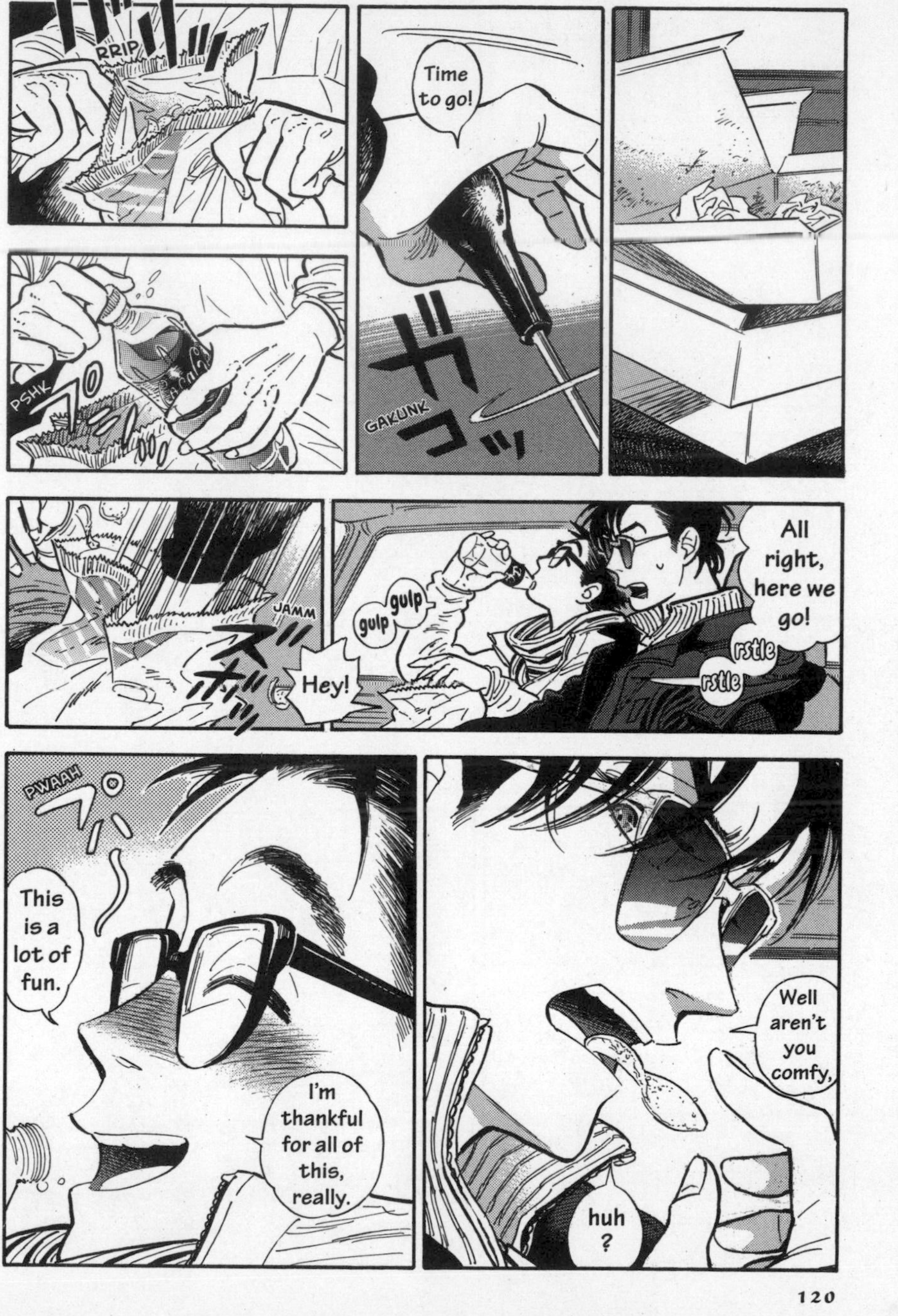
Time to go!
GAKUNK
RRIP
PSHK
All right, here we go!
gulp
gulp
rstle
rstle
Hey!
JAMM
Well aren't you comfy,
huh?
PWAAH
This is a lot of fun.
I'm thankful for all of this, really.

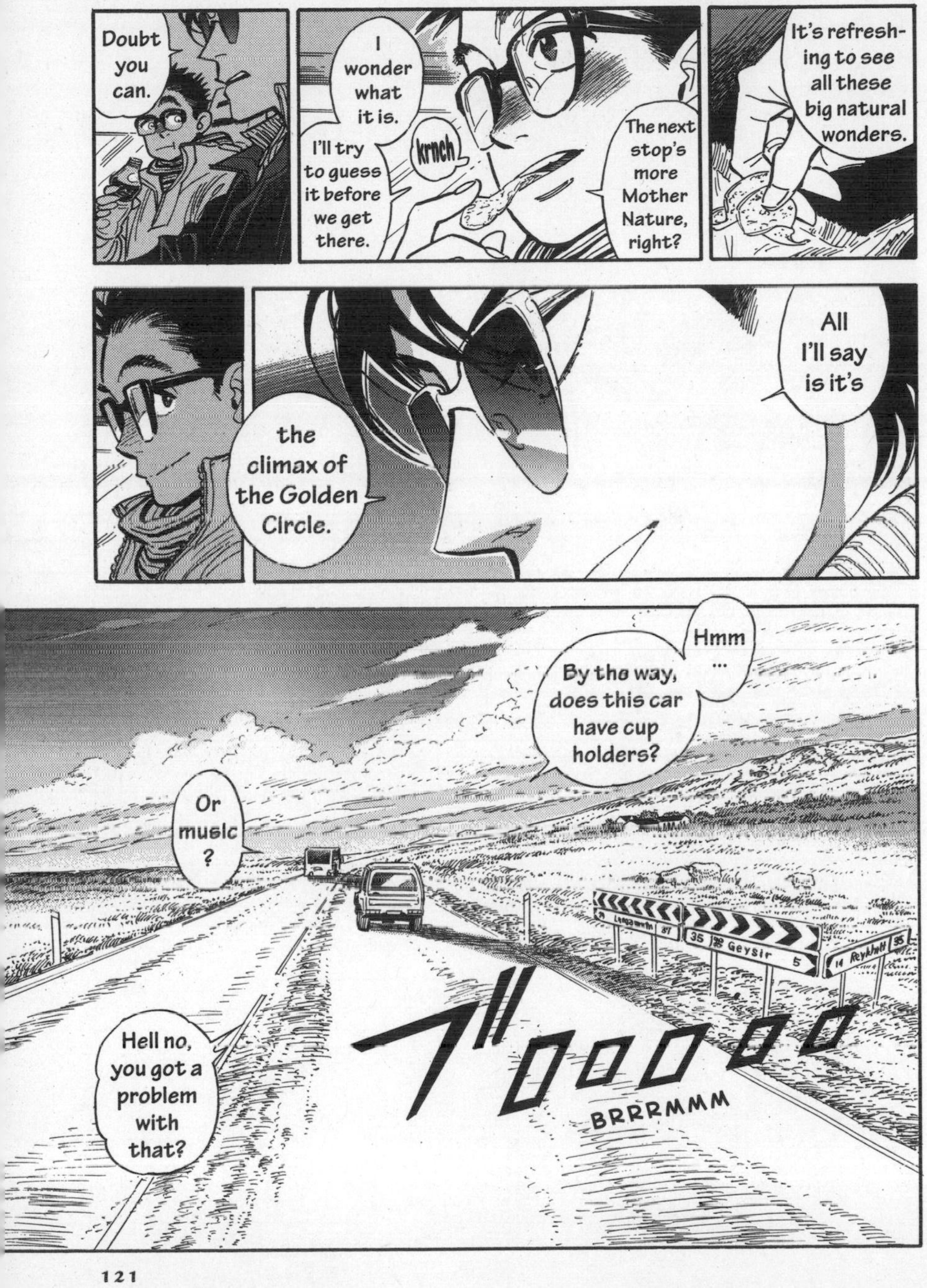
It's refreshing to see all these big natural wonders.
The next stop's more Mother Nature, right?
krnch
I wonder what it is.
I'll try to guess it before we get there.
Doubt you can.
All I'll say is it's
the climax of the Golden Circle.
Hmm ...
By the way, does this car have cup holders?
Or music?
Geysir
BRRRMMM
Hell no, you got a problem with that?

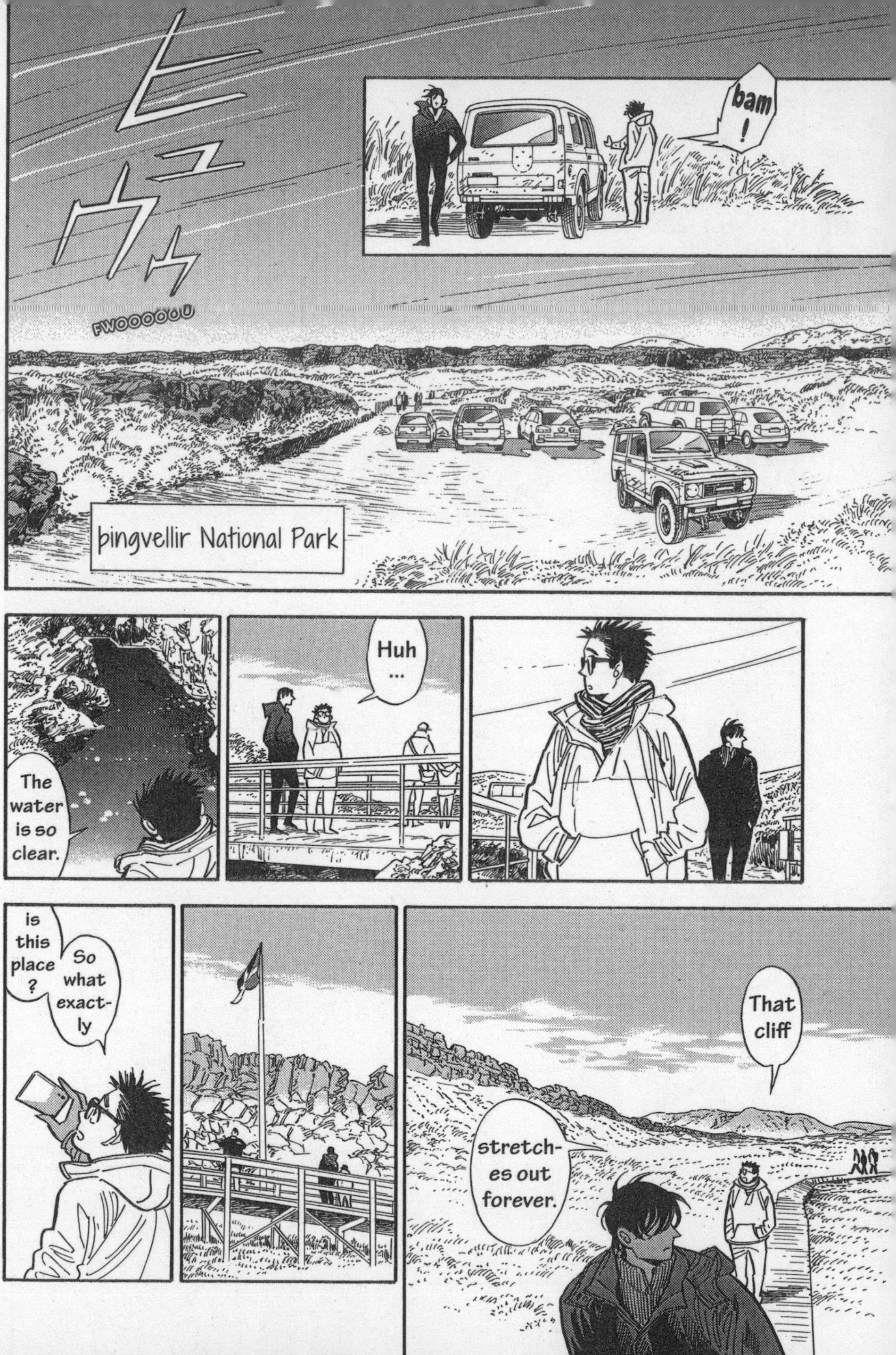
bam !
ヒュウゥ
FWOOOOOU
þingvellir National Park
Huh ...
The water is so clear.
That cliff
stretches out forever.
So what exactly
is this place ?

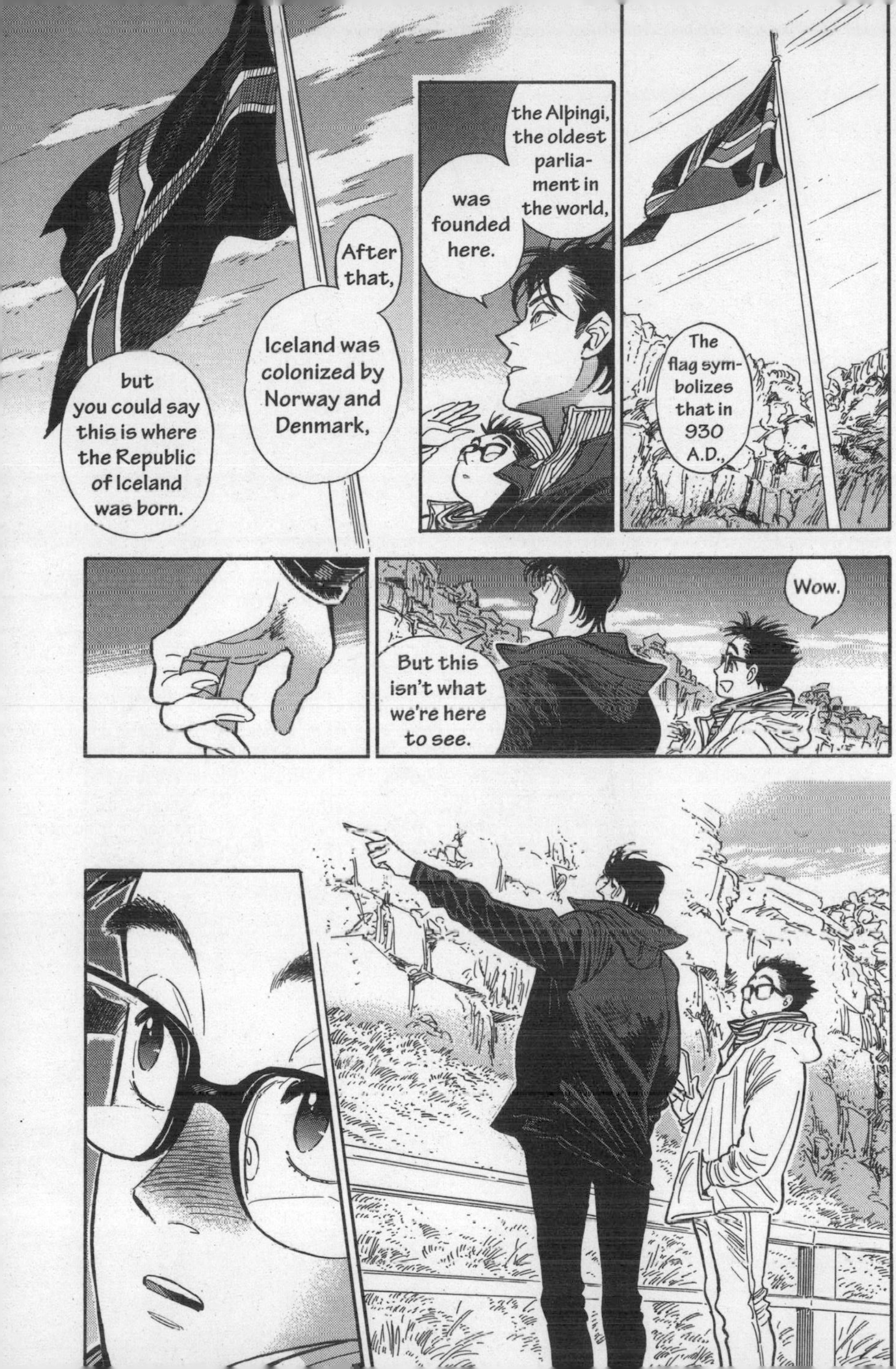
The flag symbolizes that in 930 A.D.,
the Alþingi, the oldest parliament in the world,
was founded here.
After that,
Iceland was colonized by Norway and Denmark,
but you could say this is where the Republic of Iceland was born.
Wow.
But this isn't what we're here to see.

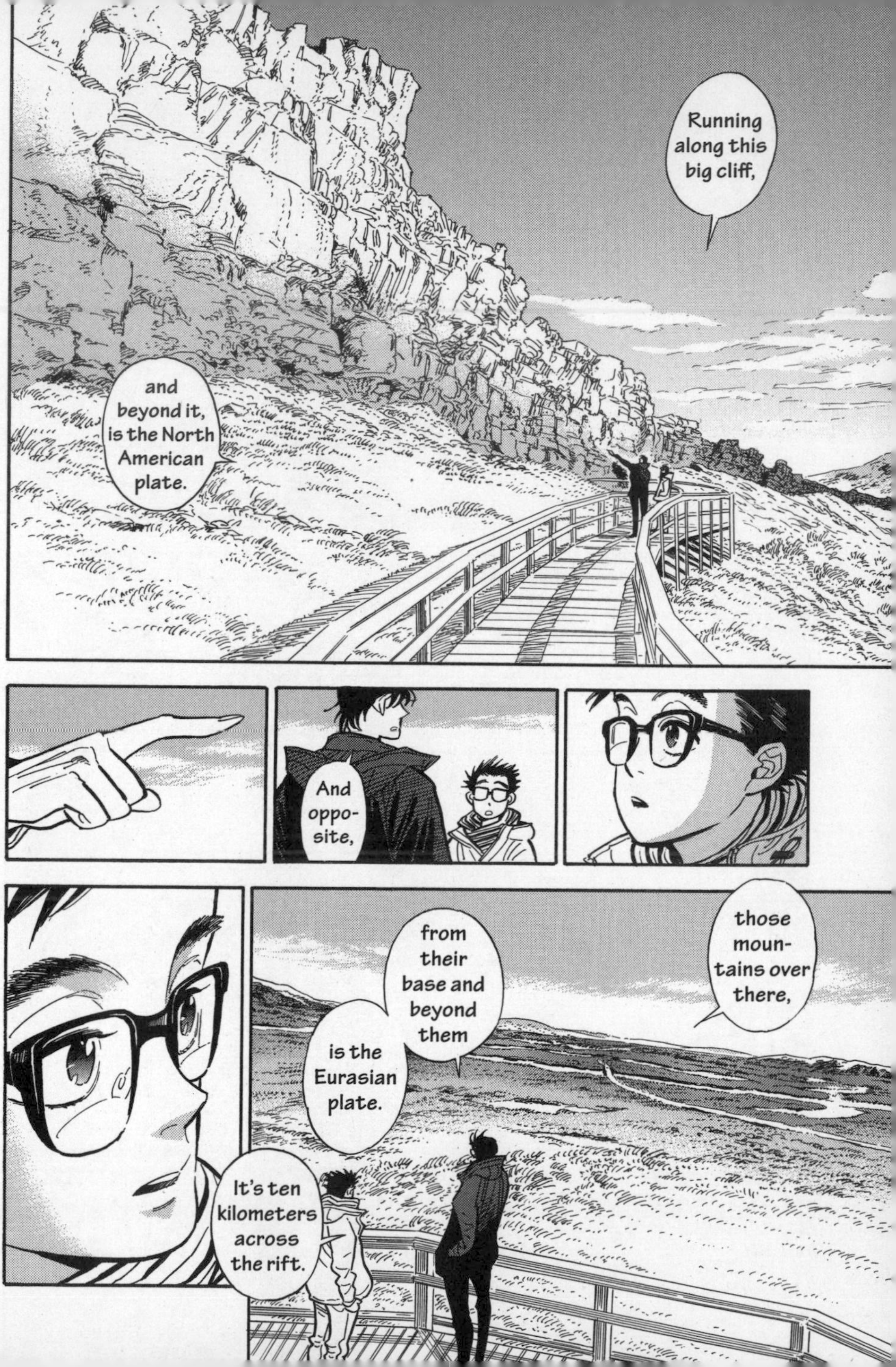
Running along this big cliff,
and beyond it, is the North American plate.
And oppo-site,
those moun-tains over there,
from their base and beyond them
is the Eurasian plate.
It's ten kilometers across the rift.

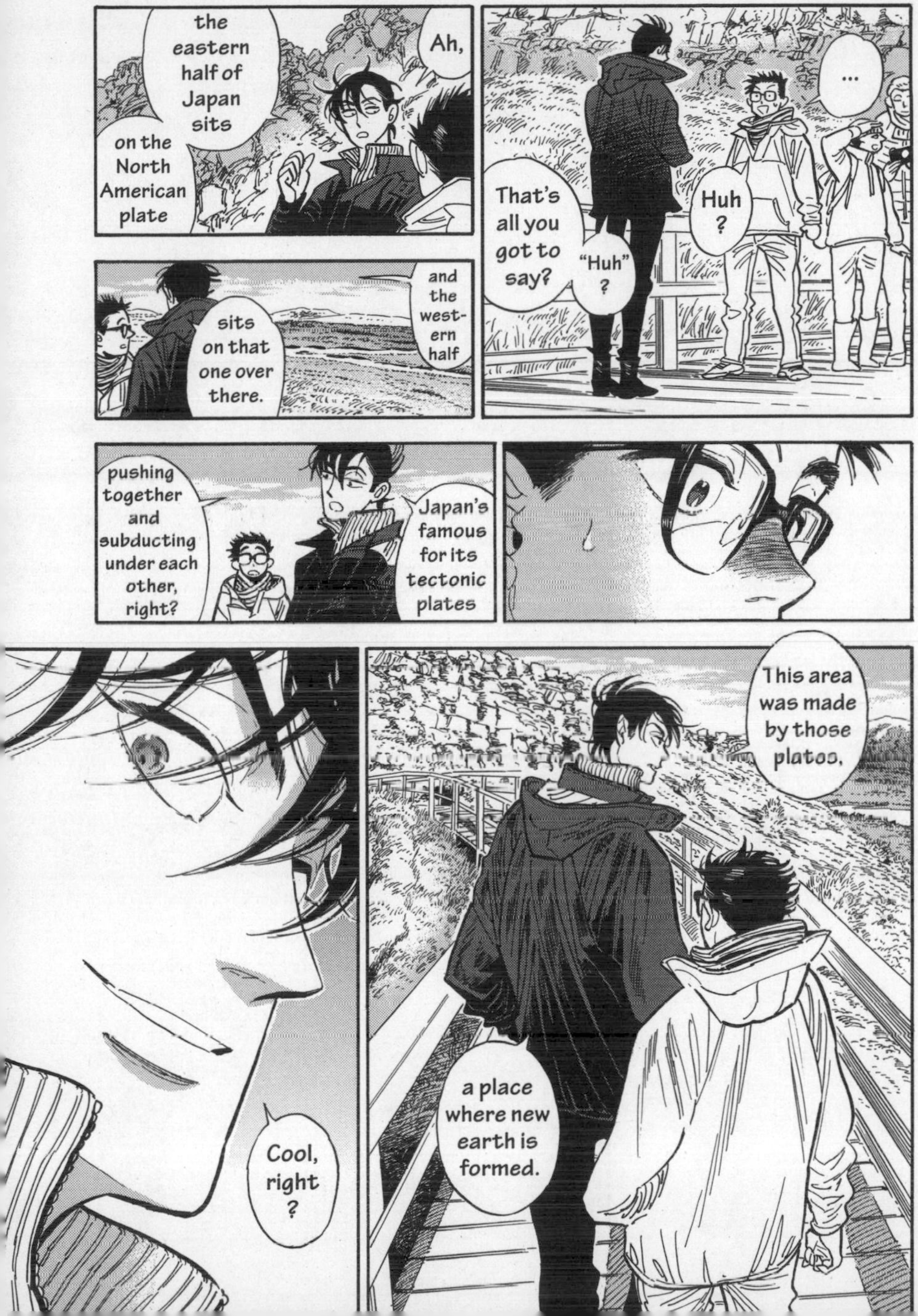
Ah,
the eastern half of Japan sits
on the North American plate
and the western half
sits on that one over there.
...
Huh?
That's all you got to say?
"Huh"?
Japan's famous for its tectonic plates
pushing together and subducting under each other, right?
This area was made by those platos,
a place where new earth is formed.
Cool, right?

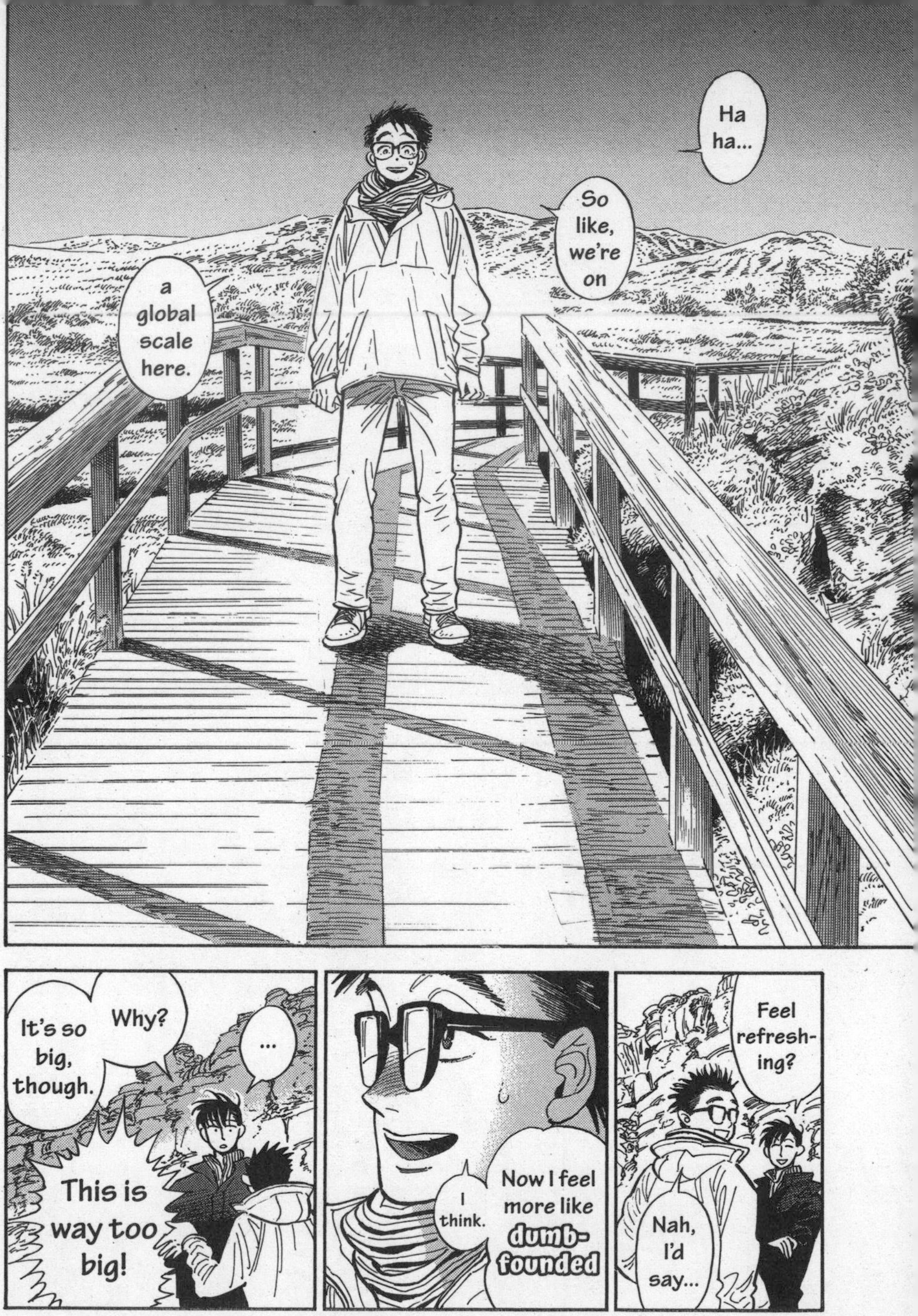
Ha ha...
So like, we're on
a global scale here.
Feel refresh-ing?
Nah, I'd say...
Now I feel more like dumb-founded
I think.
Why?
...
It's so big, though.
This is way too big!

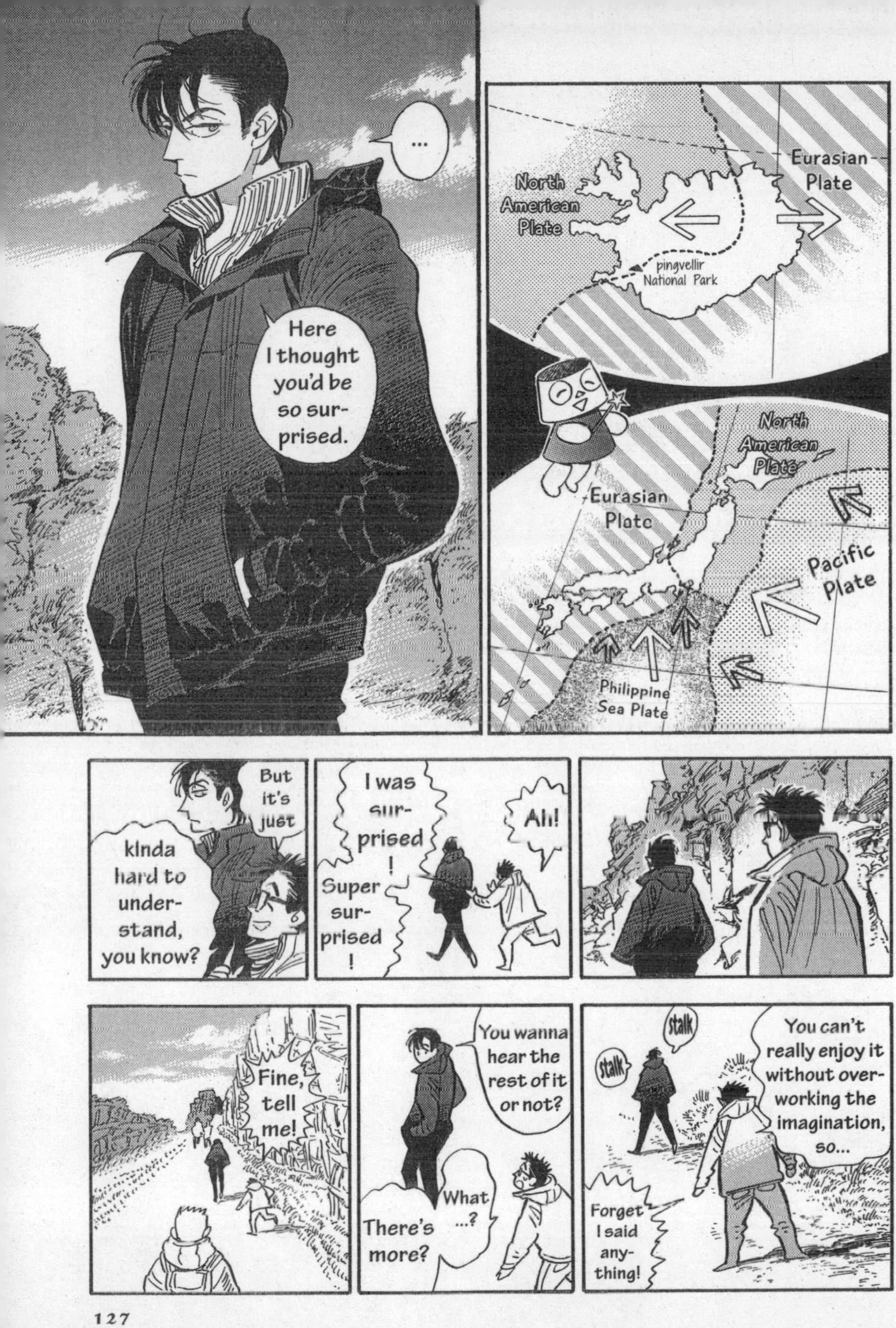
North American Plate
Eurasian Plate
þingvellir National Park
North American Plate
Eurasian Plate
Pacific Plate
Philippine Sea Plate
...
Here I thought you'd be so surprised.
Ah!
I was surprised!
Super surprised!
But it's just
kinda hard to understand, you know?
stalk
stalk
You can't really enjoy it without over-working the imagination, so...
Forget I said anything!
You wanna hear the rest of it or not?
What ...?
There's more?
Fine, tell me!

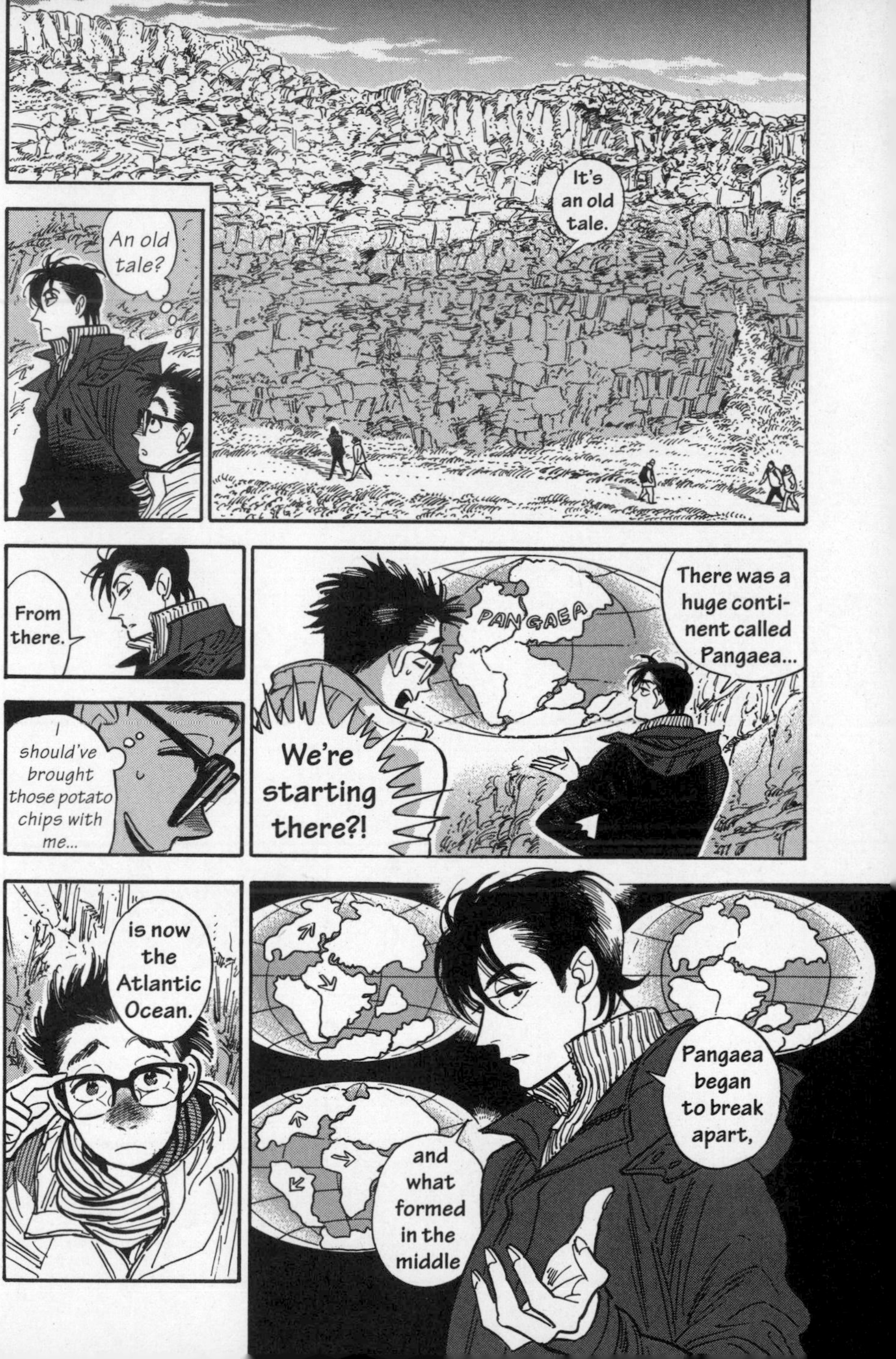
It's an old tale.
An old tale?
There was a huge conti-nent called Pangaea...
PANGAEA
We're starting there?!
From there.
I should've brought those potato chips with me...
Pangaea began to break apart,
and what formed in the middle
is now the Atlantic Ocean.

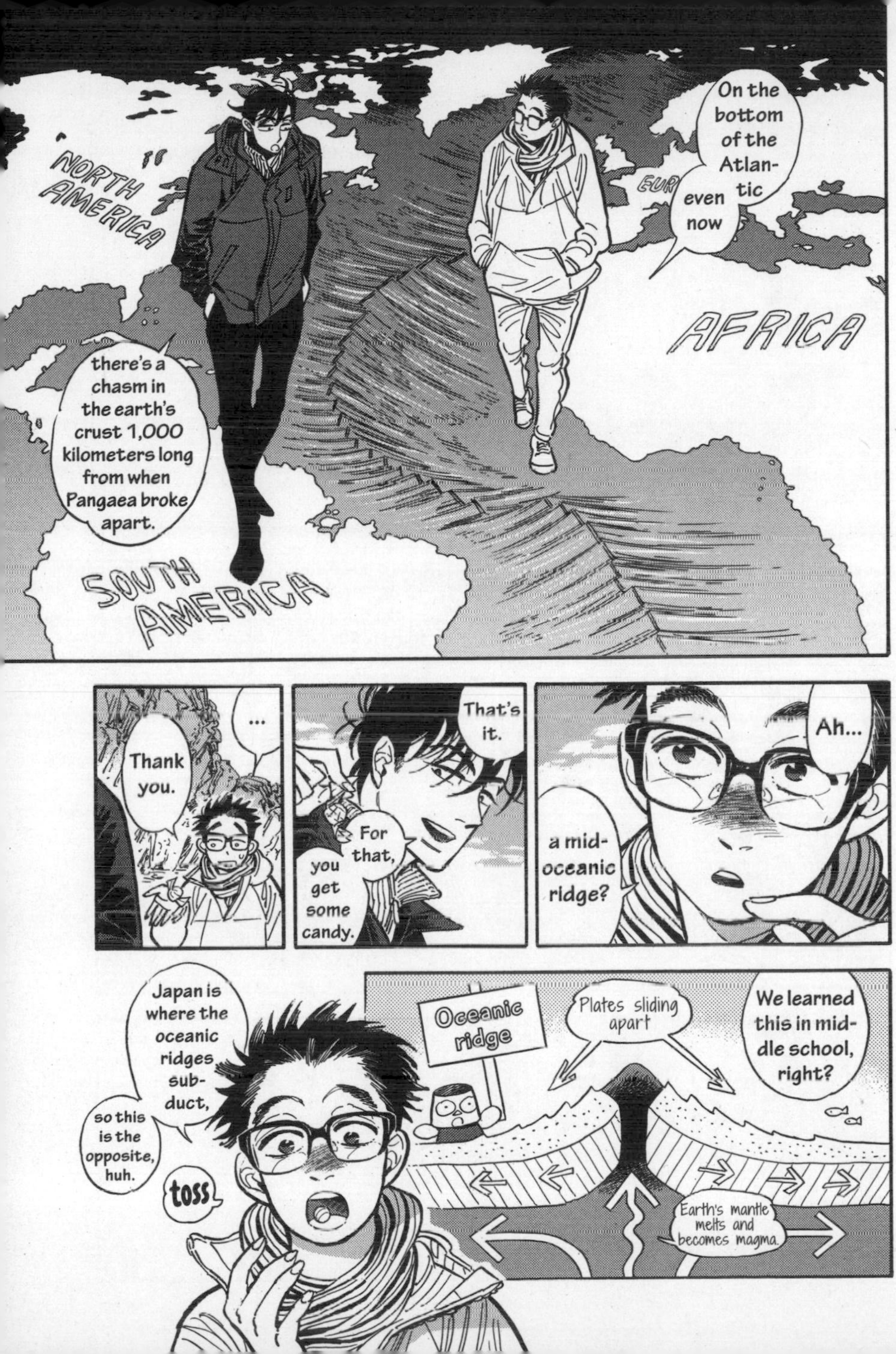
NORTH AMERICA
EUR
AFRICA
SOUTH AMERICA
On the bottom of the Atlantic
even now
there's a chasm in the earth's crust 1,000 kilometers long from when Pangaea broke apart.
Ah...
a mid-oceanic ridge?
That's it.
For that,
you get some candy.
...
Thank you.
We learned this in middle school, right?
Plates sliding apart
Oceanic ridge
Earth's mantle melts and becomes magma.
Japan is where the oceanic ridges subduct,
so this is the opposite, huh.
toss

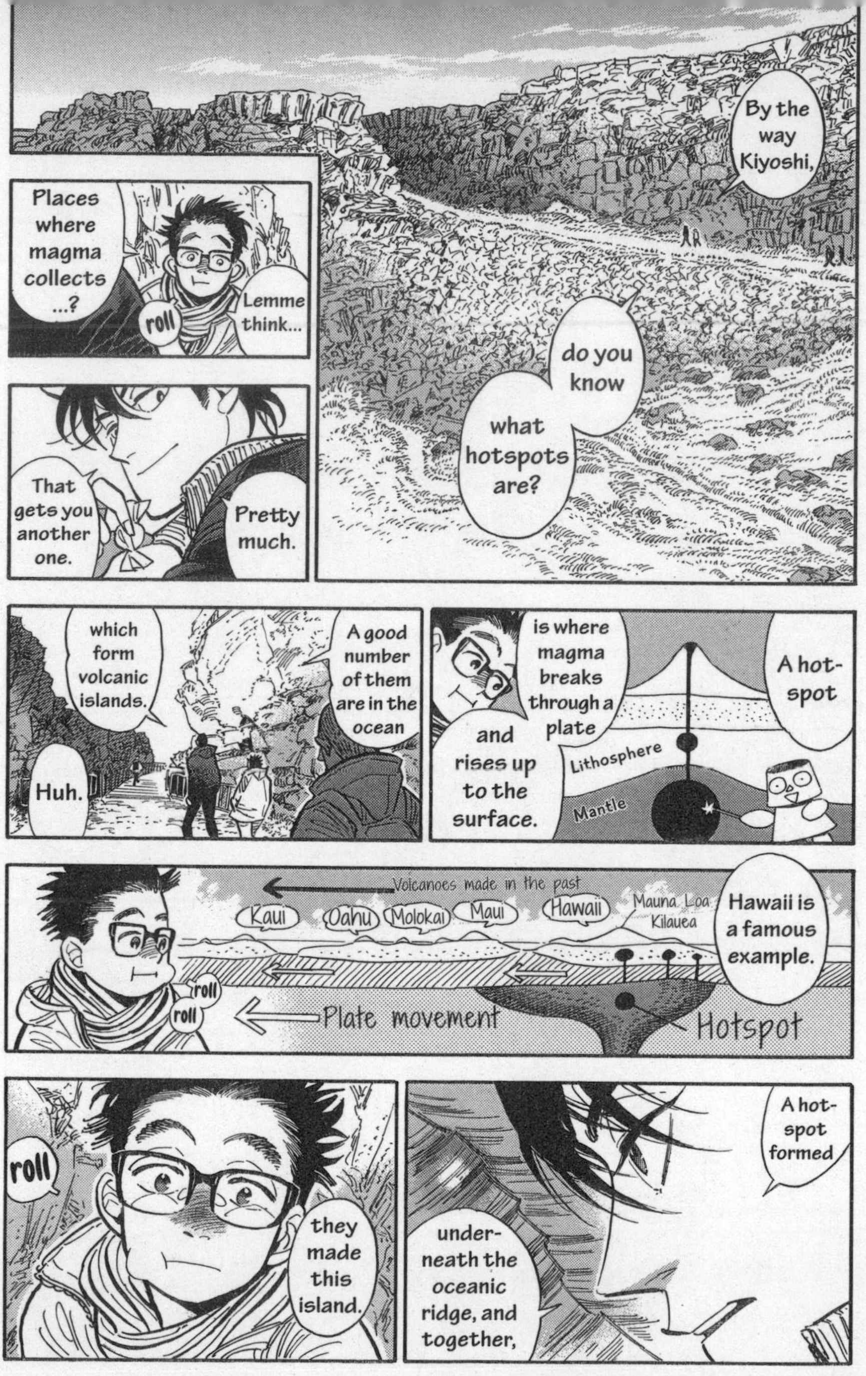
By the way Kiyoshi,
do you know
what hotspots are?
Lemme think...
roll
Places where magma collects ...?
Pretty much.
That gets you another one.
A hot-spot
is where magma breaks through a plate
and rises up to the surface.
Lithosphere
Mantle
A good number of them are in the ocean
which form volcanic islands.
Huh.
Hawaii is a famous example.
Volcanoes made in the past
Kaui
Oahu
Molokai
Maui
Hawaii
Mauna Loa
Kilauea
Hotspot
Plate movement
roll
roll
A hot-spot formed
under-neath the oceanic ridge, and together,
they made this island.
roll

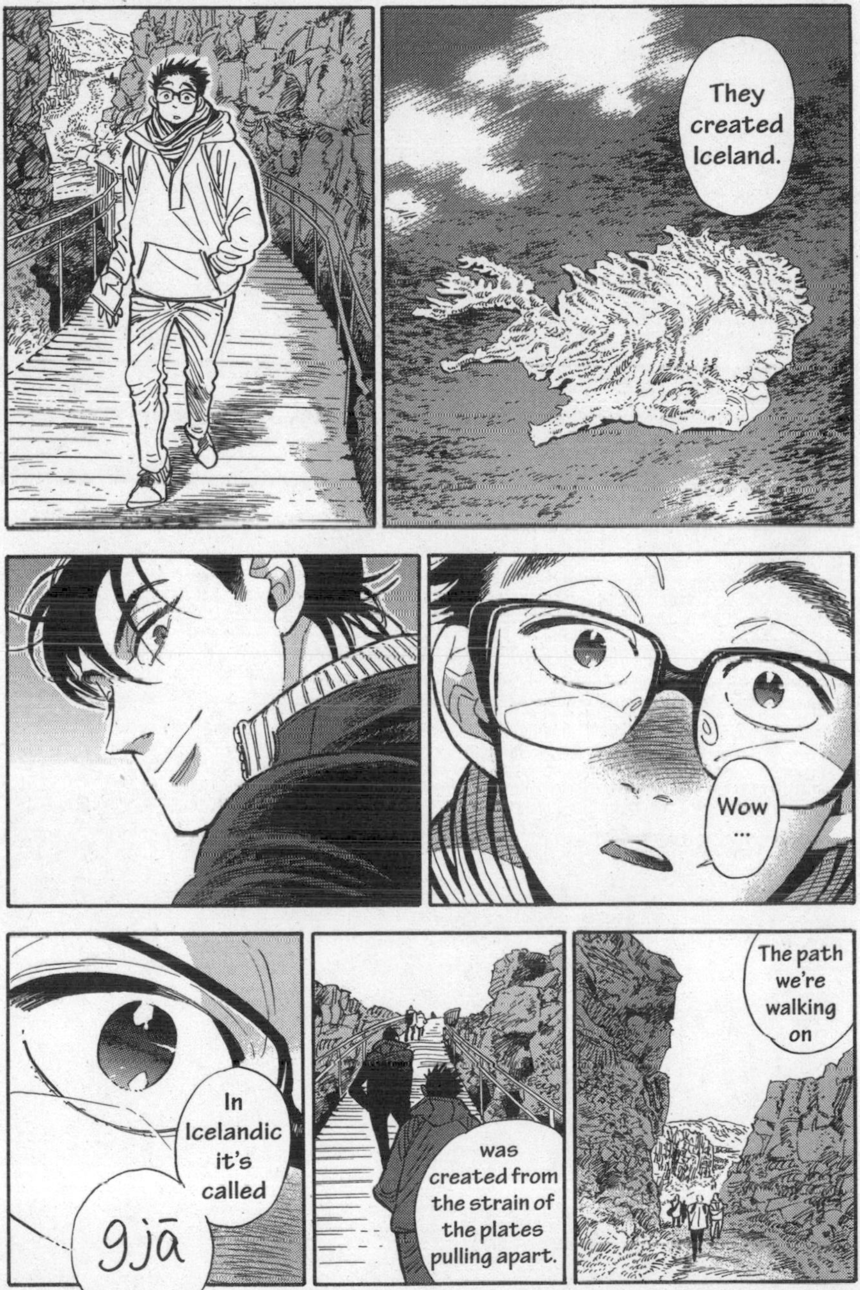
They created Iceland.
Wow ...
The path we're walking on
was created from the strain of the plates pulling apart.
In Icelandic it's called
gjā

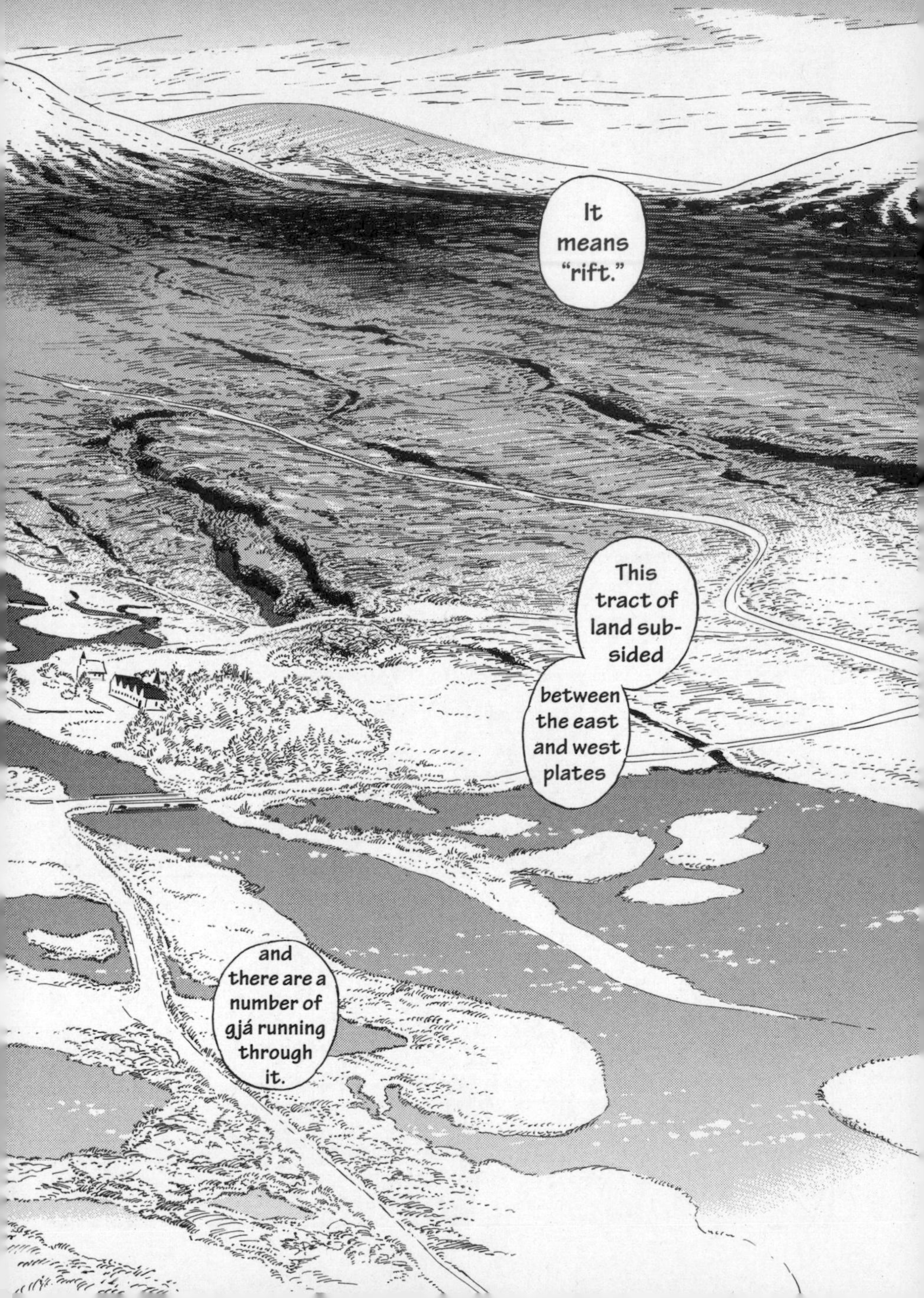
It means "rift."
This tract of land sub-sided
between the east and west plates
and there are a number of gjá running through it.

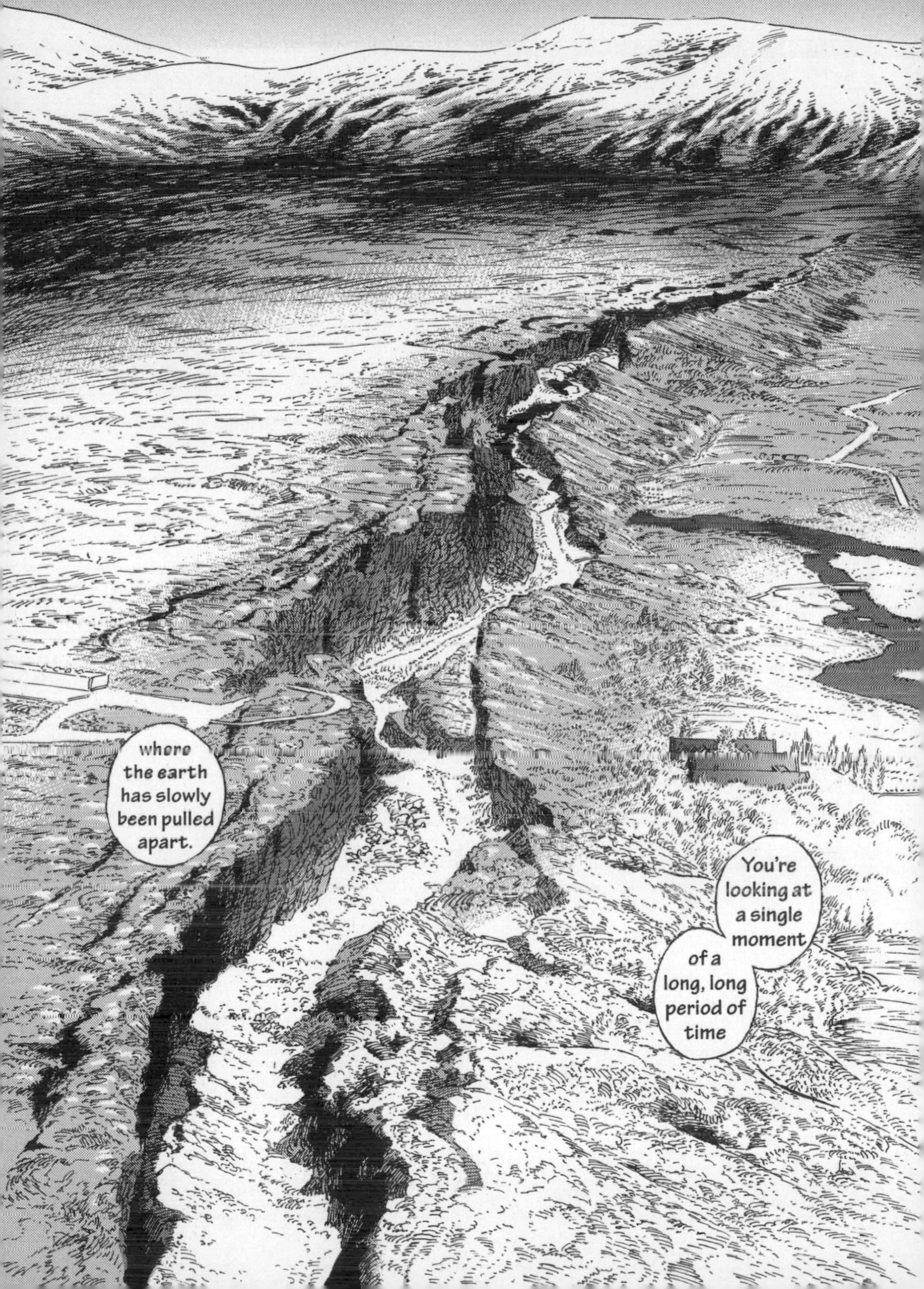
You're looking at a single moment
of a long, long period of time
where the earth has slowly been pulled apart.

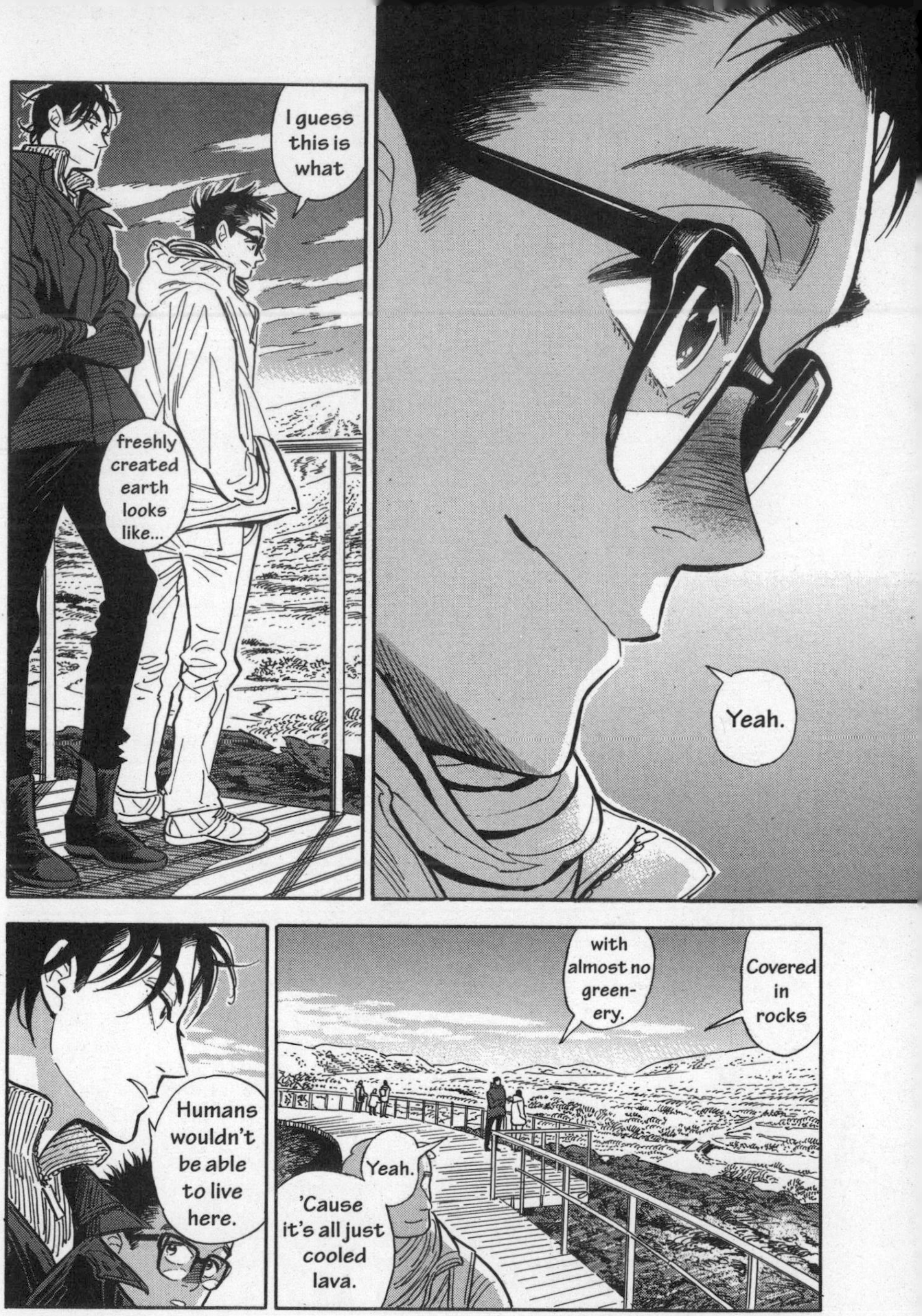
Yeah.
I guess this is what
freshly created earth looks like...
Covered in rocks
with almost no greenery.
Yeah.
'Cause it's all just cooled lava.
Humans wouldn't be able to live here.

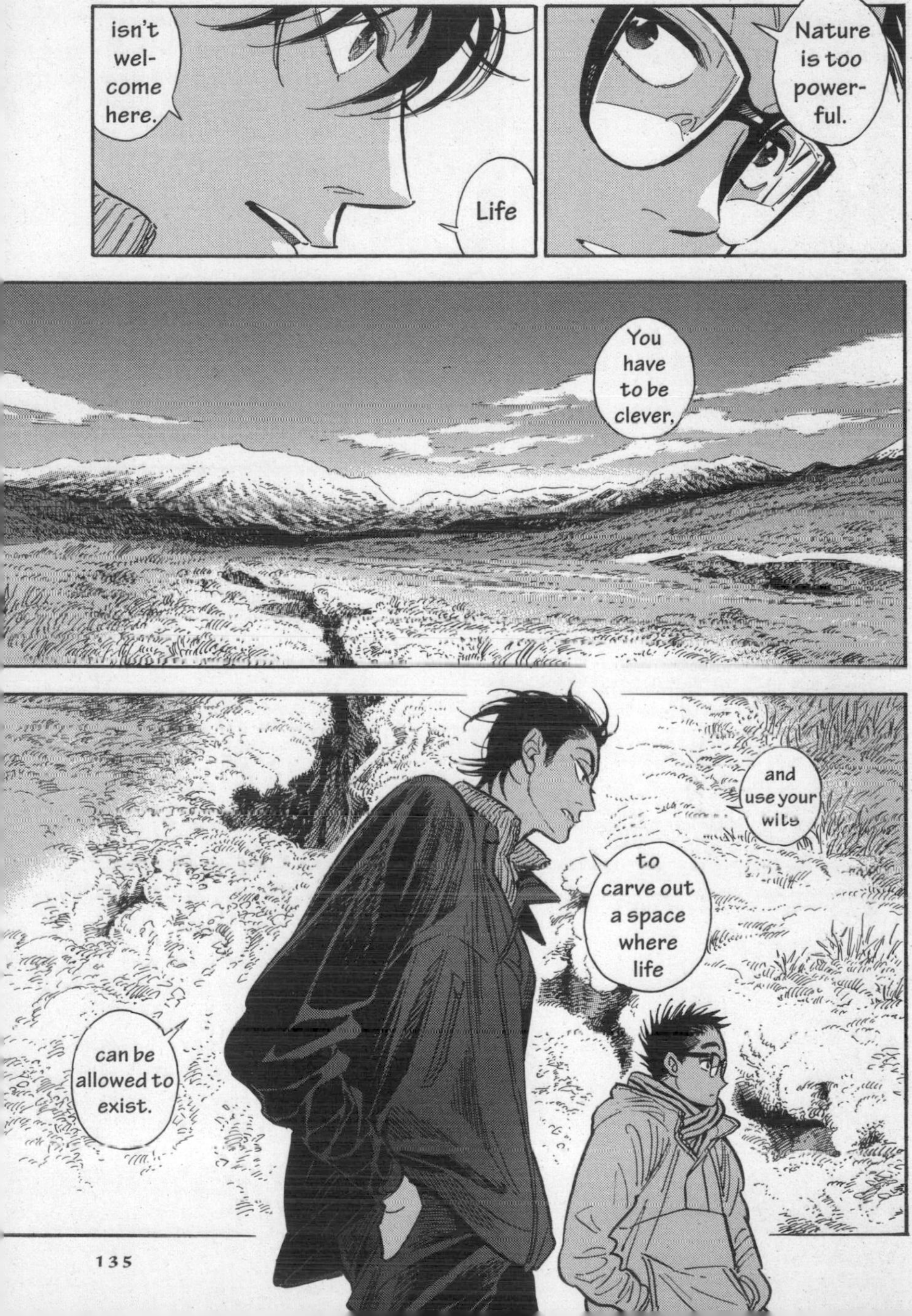
Nature is too power-ful.
Life
isn't wel-come here.
You have to be clever,
and use your wits
to carve out a space where life
can be allowed to exist.

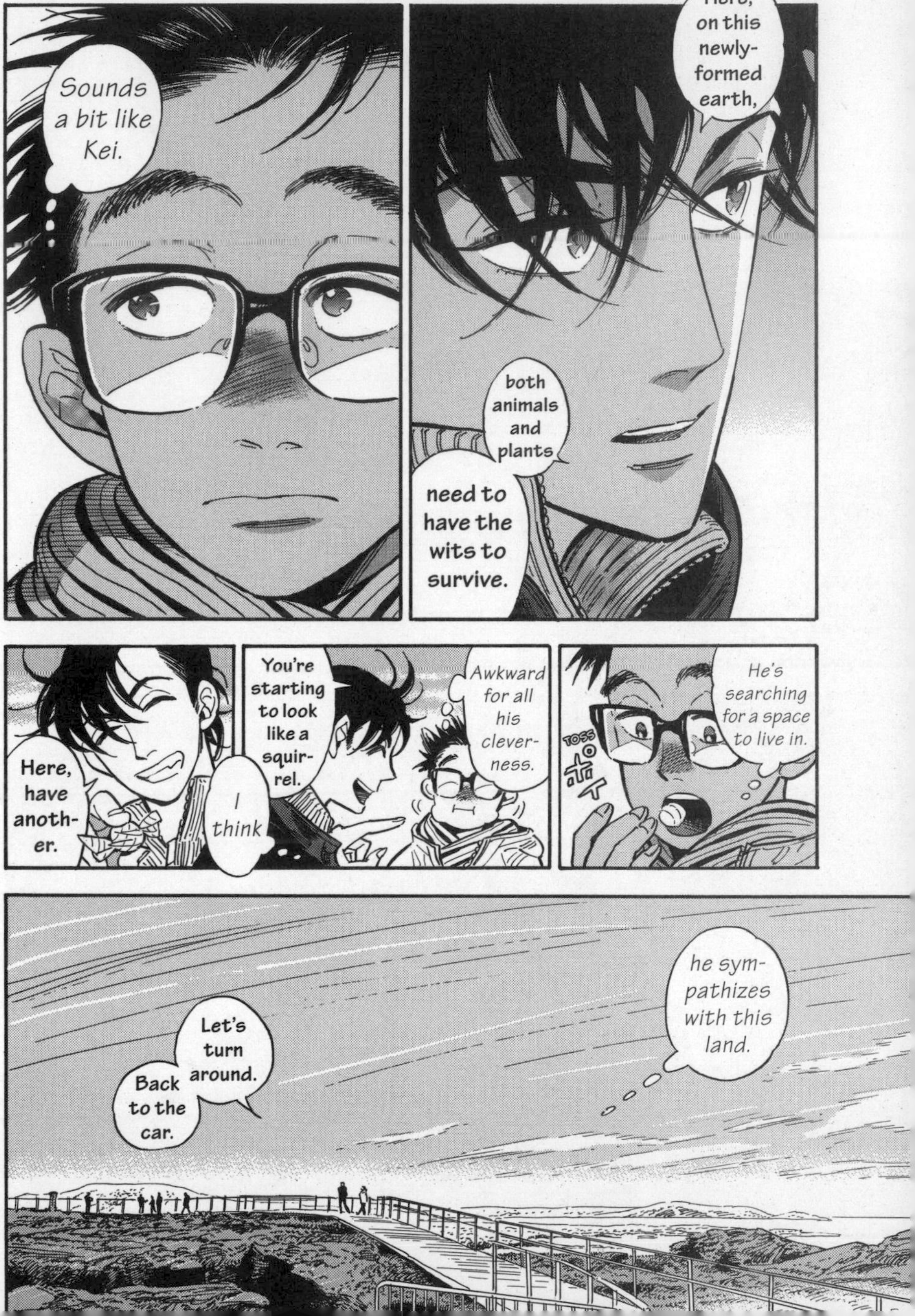
Here, on this newly-formed earth,
both animals and plants
need to have the wits to survive.
Sounds a bit like Kei.
TOSS
ポイ
He's searching for a space to live in.
Awkward for all his cleverness.
You're starting to look like a squirrel.
I think
Here, have another.
he sympathizes with this land.
Let's turn around.
Back to the car.

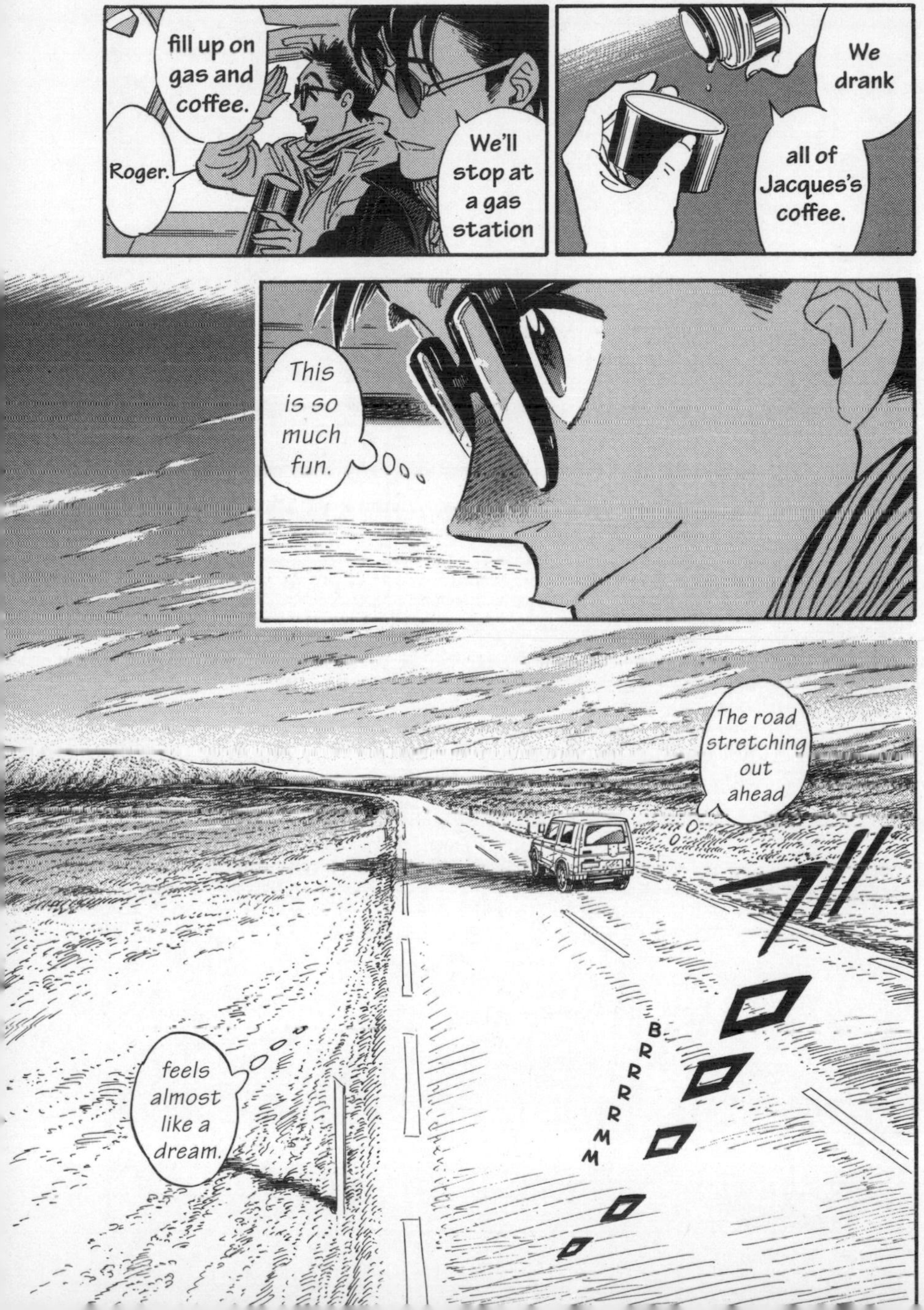
We drank
all of Jacques's coffee.
We'll stop at a gas station
fill up on gas and coffee.
Roger.
This is so much fun.
The road stretching out ahead
feels almost like a dream.
BRRRRMM

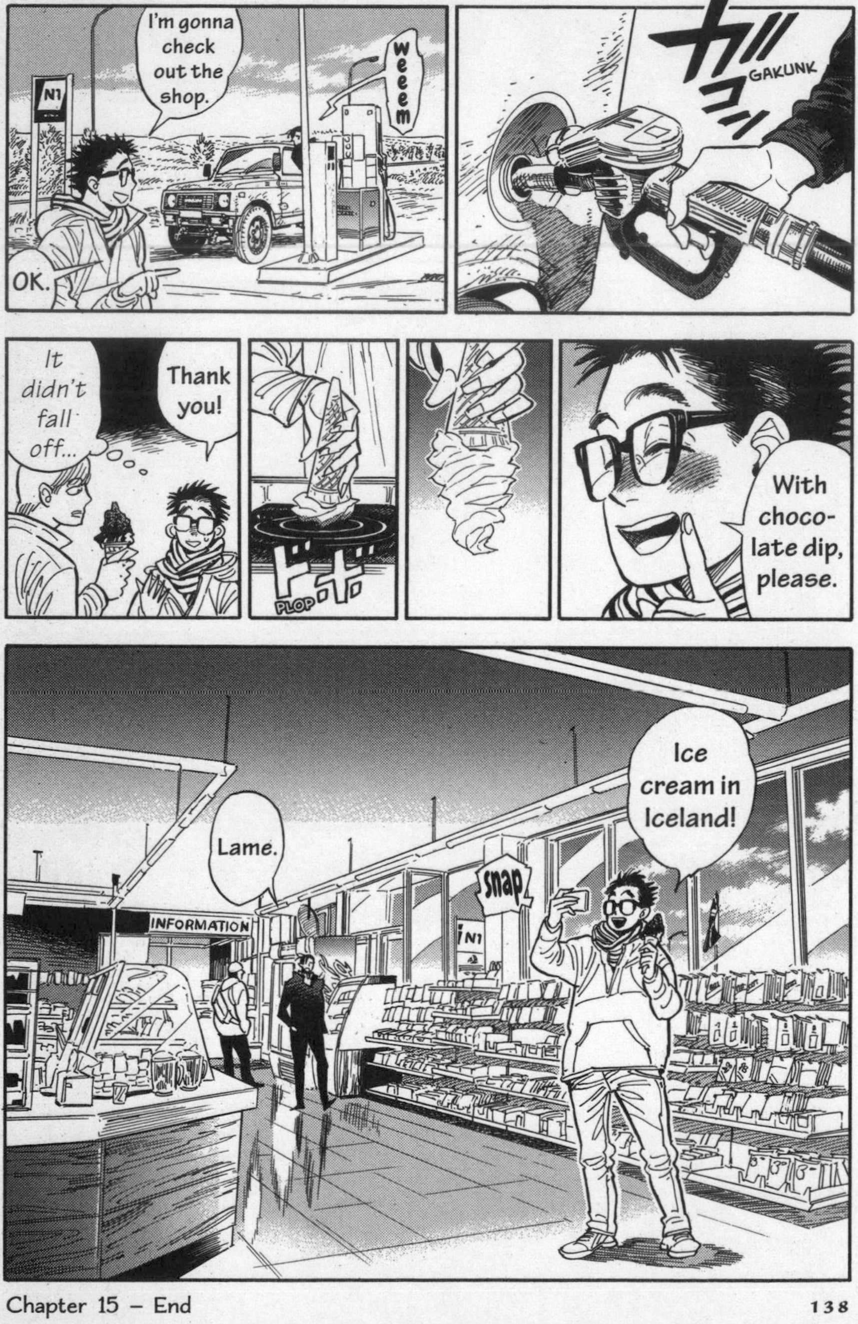
GAKUNK
I'm gonna check out the shop.
weeeem
N1
OK.
With chocolate dip, please.
PLOP
Thank you!
It didn't fall off...
Ice cream in Iceland!
snap
N1
Lame.
INFORMATION

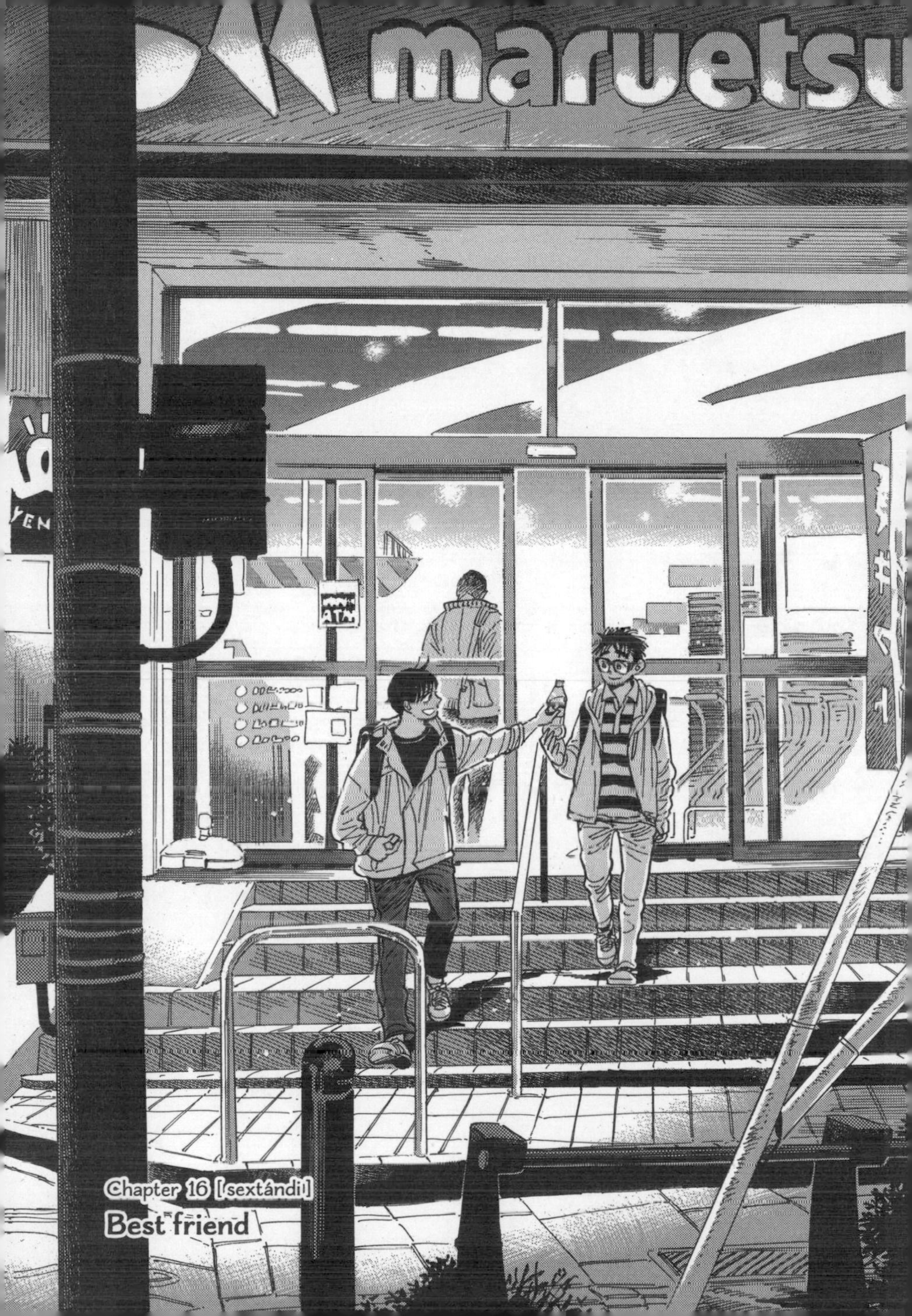
maruetsu
ATM

Chapter 16 [sextándi]
Best friend

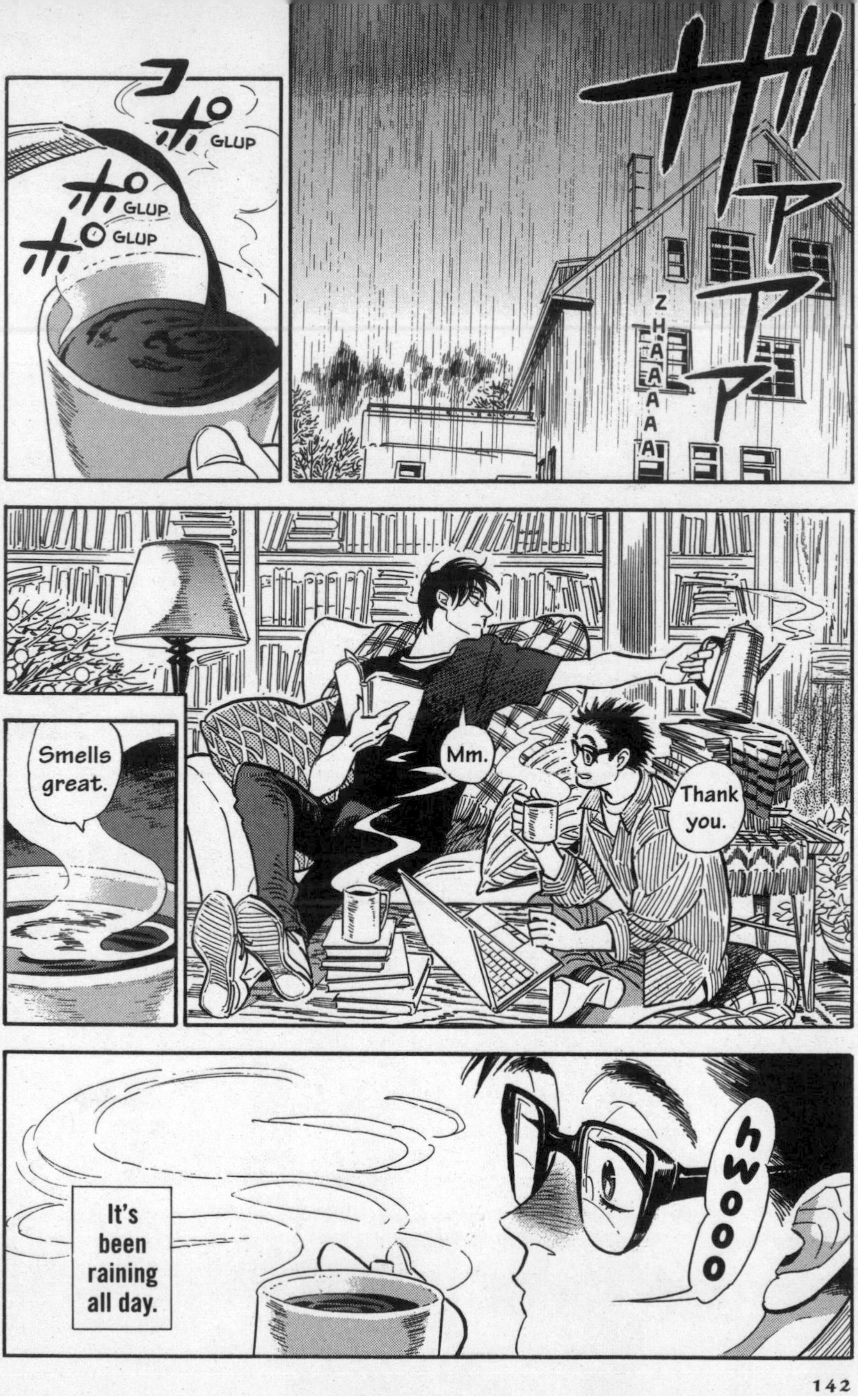
ZHAAAAA
GLUP
GLUP
GLUP
Thank you.
Mm.
Smells great.
hwooo
It's been raining all day.

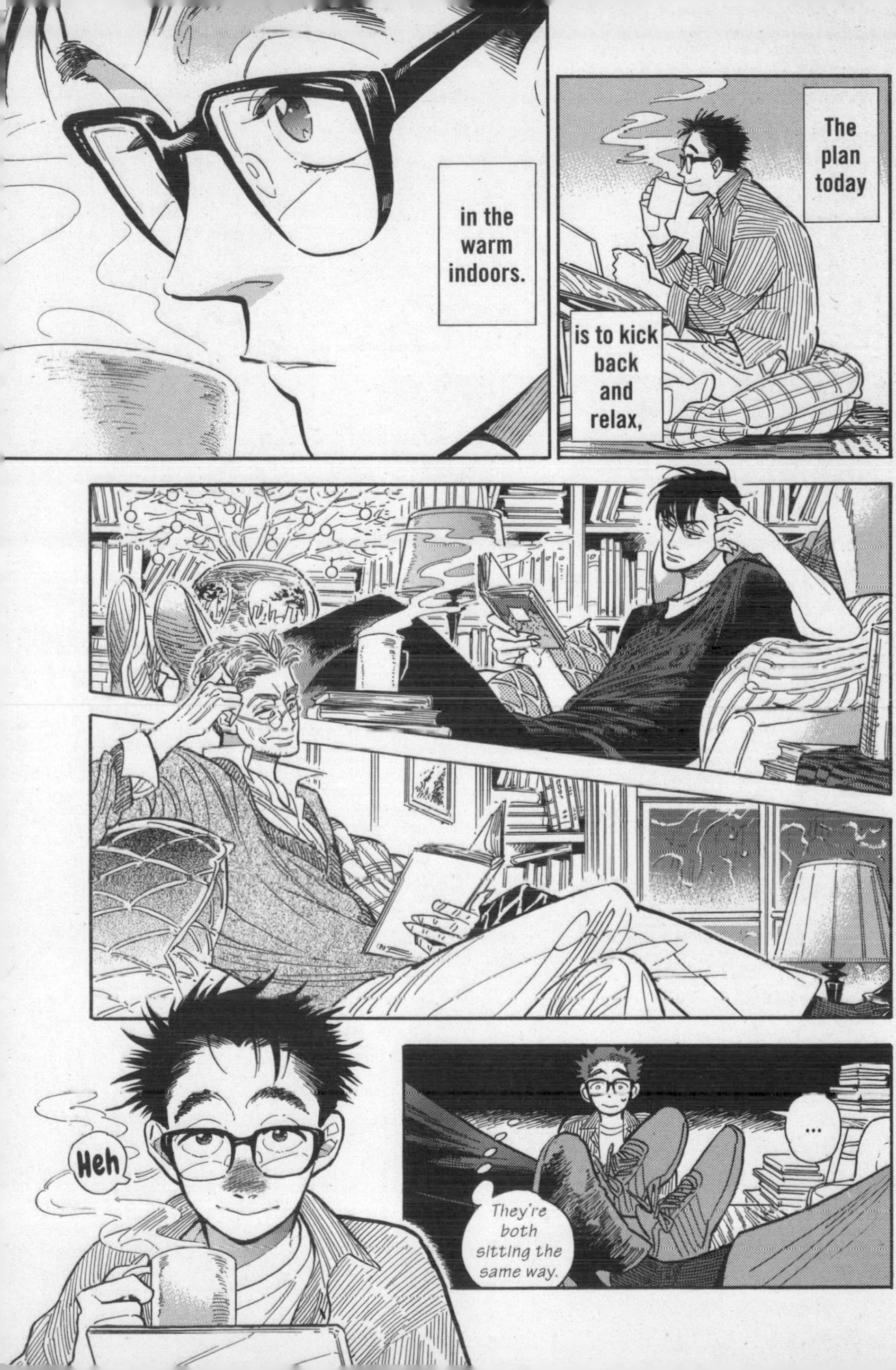
The plan today
is to kick back and relax,
in the warm indoors.
...
They're both sitting the same way.
Heh

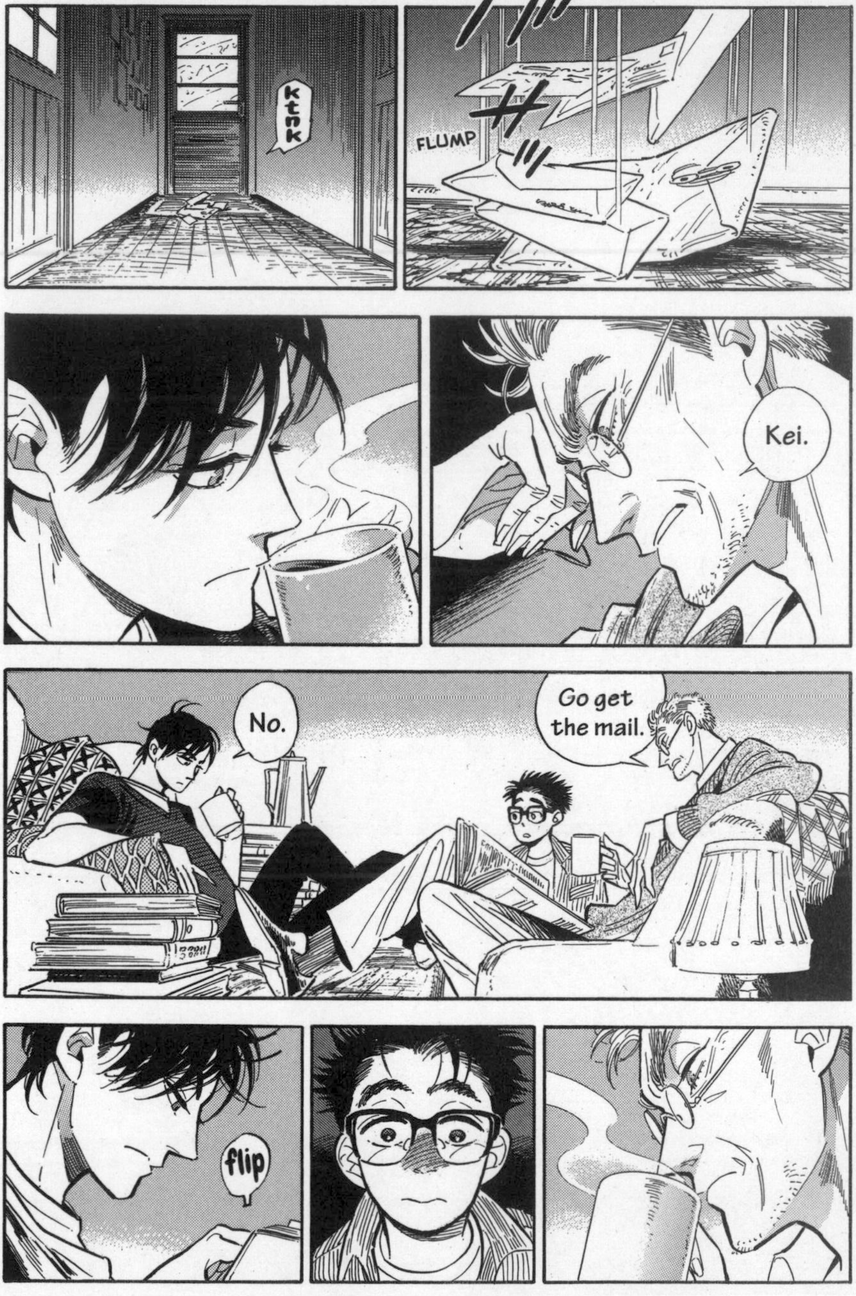
FLUMP
ktnk
Kei.
Go get the mail.
No.
flip

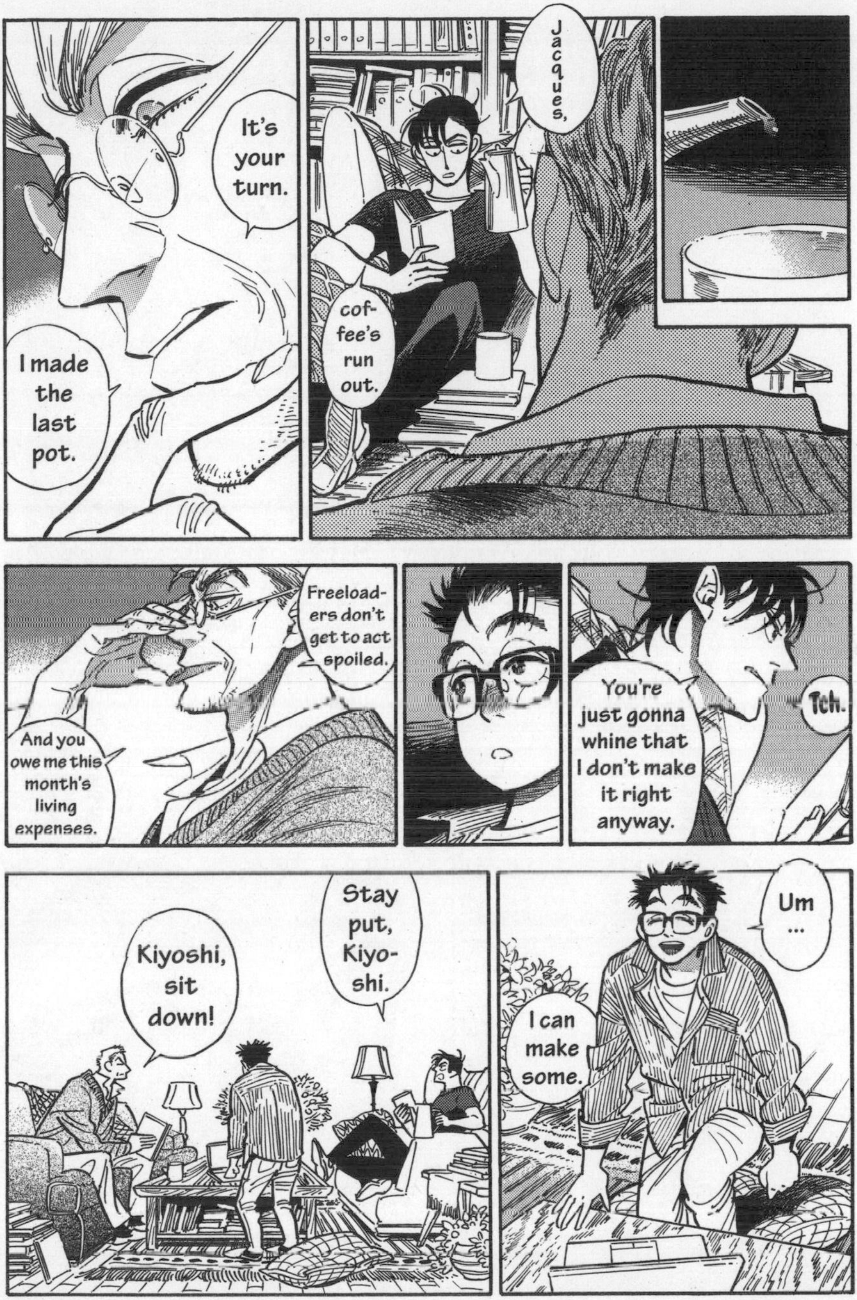
Jacques,
coffee's run out.
It's your turn.
I made the last pot.
Tch.
You're just gonna whine that I don't make it right anyway.
Freeloaders don't get to act spoiled.
And you owe me this month's living expenses.
Um ...
I can make some.
Stay put, Kiyoshi.
Kiyoshi, sit down!

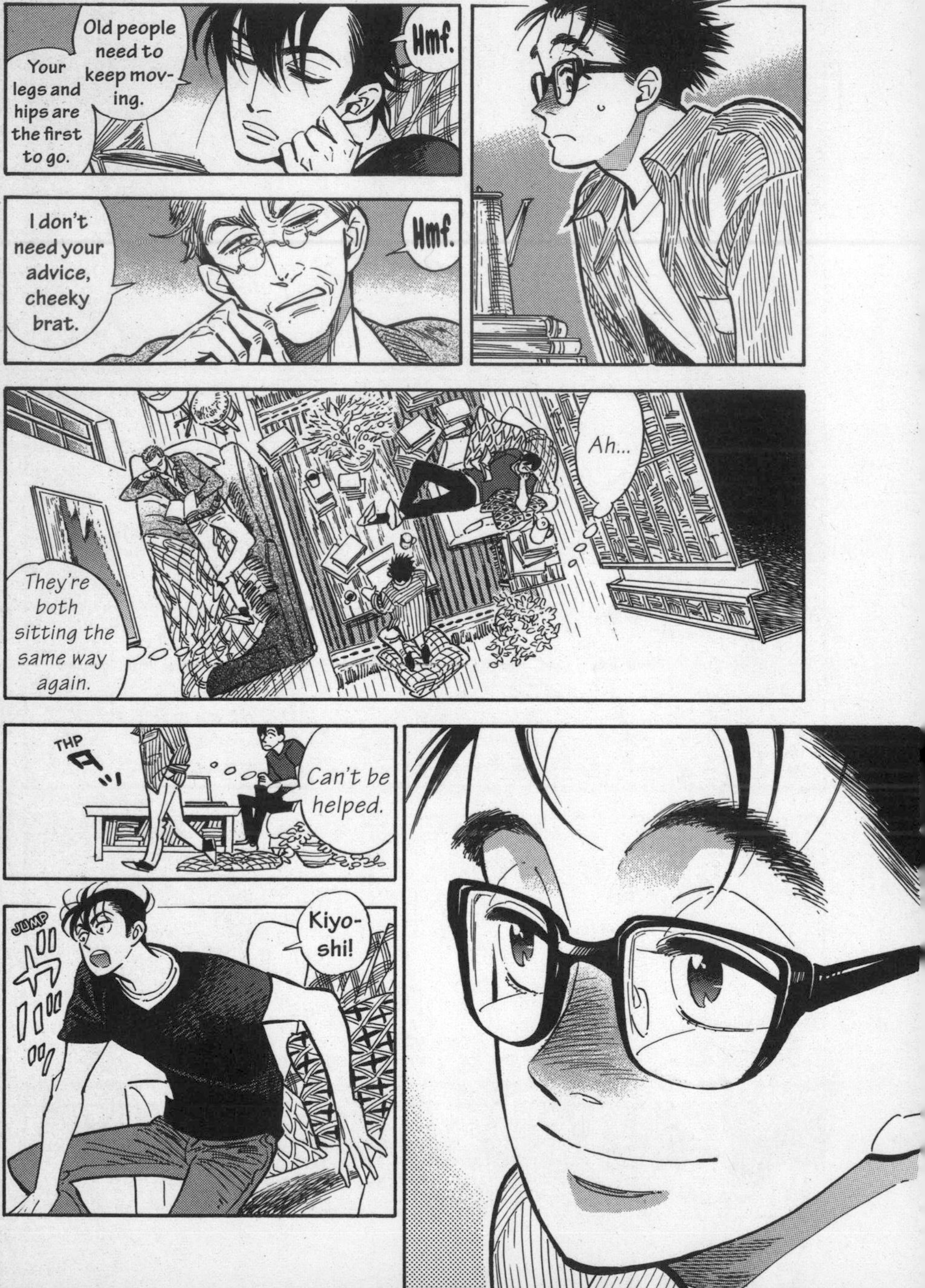
Hmf.
Old people need to keep mov-ing.
Your legs and hips are the first to go.
Hmf.
I don't need your advice, cheeky brat.
Ah...
They're both sitting the same way again.
Can't be helped.
THP
Kiyo-shi!
JUMP

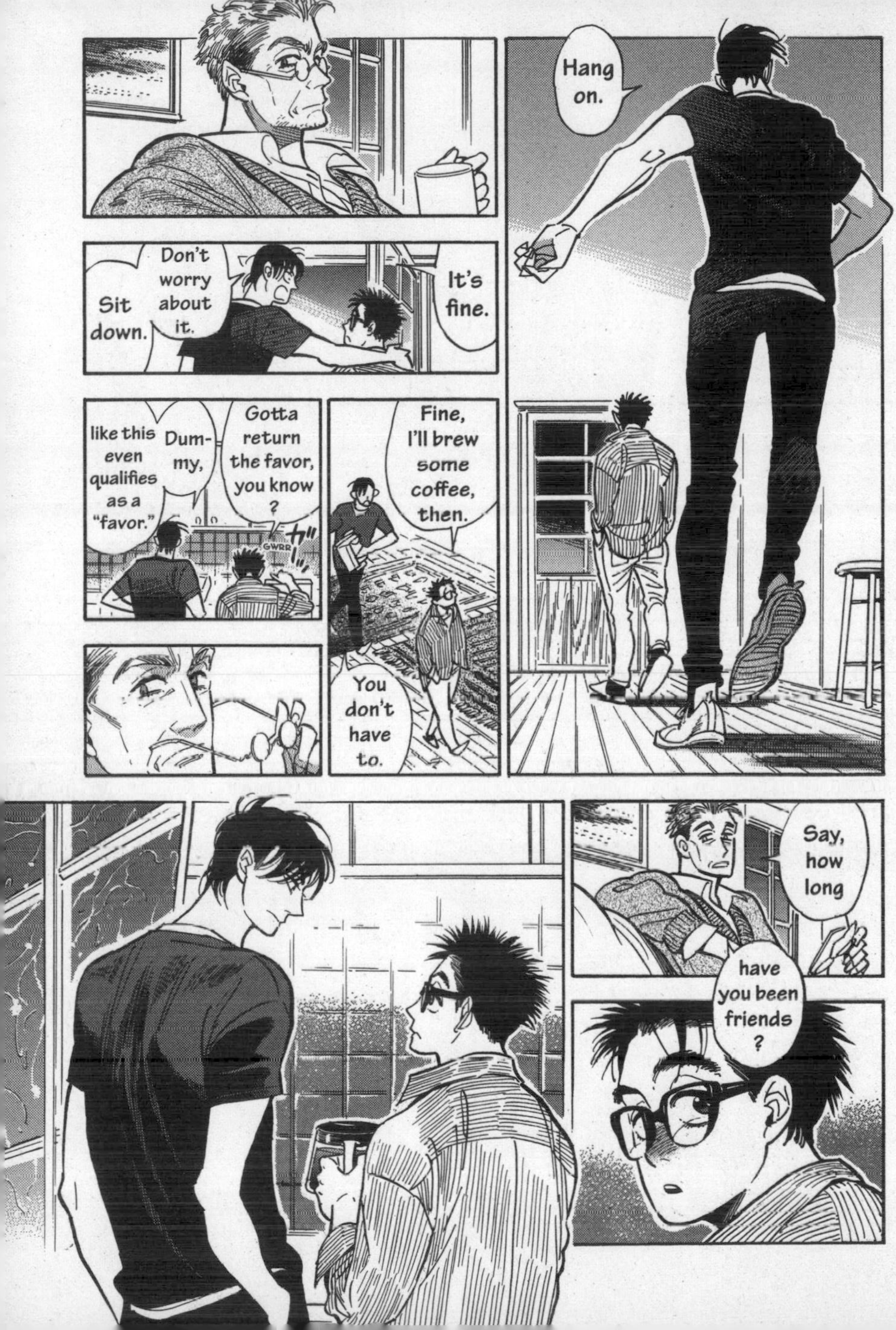
Hang on.
It's fine.
Don't worry about it.
Sit down.
Fine, I'll brew some coffee, then.
You don't have to.
Gotta return the favor, you know?
GWRR
Dum-my,
like this even qualifies as a "favor."
Say, how long
have you been friends?

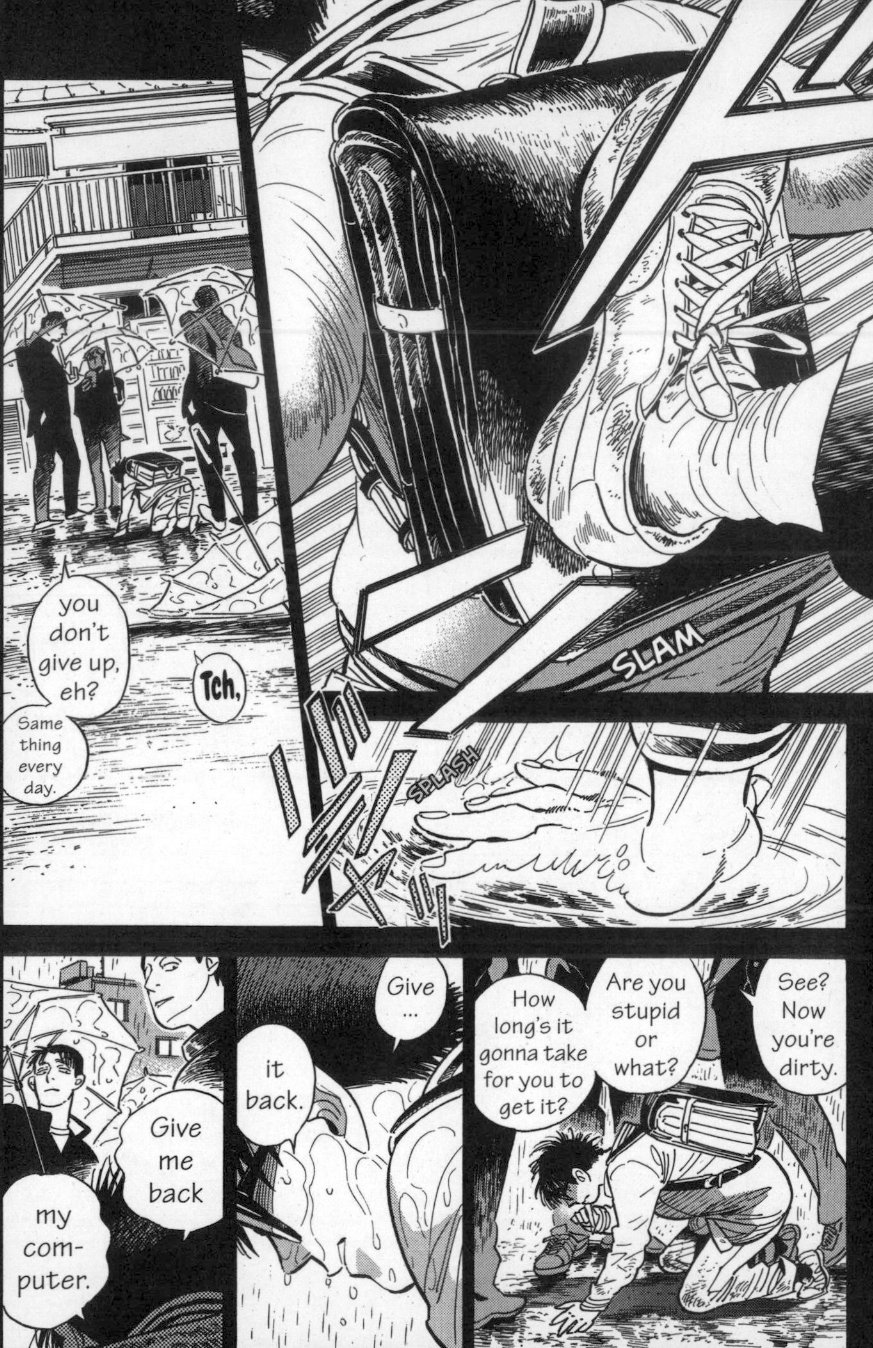
SLAM
SPLASH
Tch,
you don't give up, eh?
Same thing every day.
See? Now you're dirty.
Are you stupid or what?
How long's it gonna take for you to get it?
Give ...
it back.
Give me back
my com-puter.

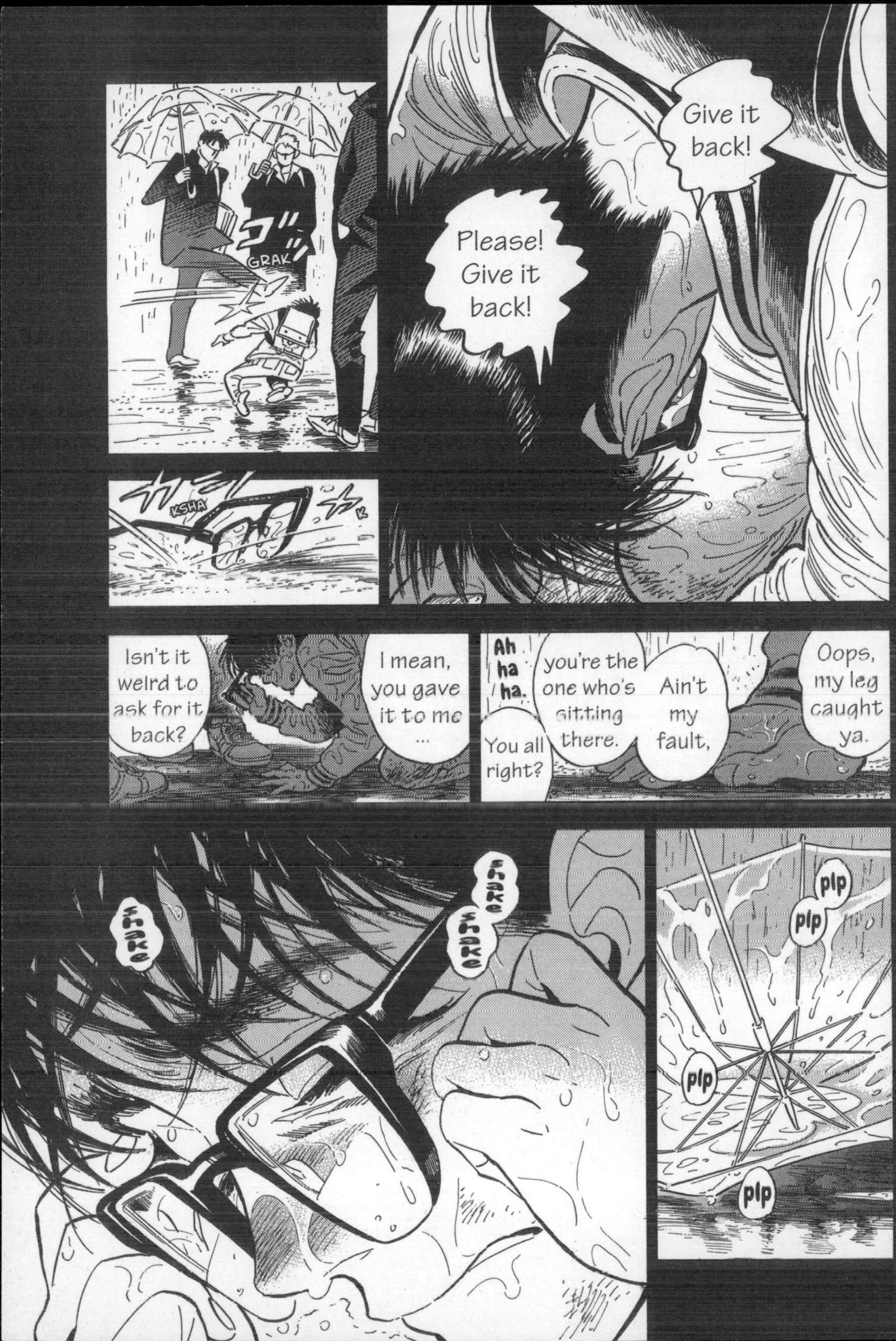
Give it back!
Please! Give it back!
GRAK
KSHA
K
Oops, my leg caught ya.
Ain't my fault,
you're the one who's sitting there.
Ah ha ha.
You all right?
I mean, you gave it to me ...
Isn't it weird to ask for it back?
plp
plp
plp
plp
shake
shake
shake

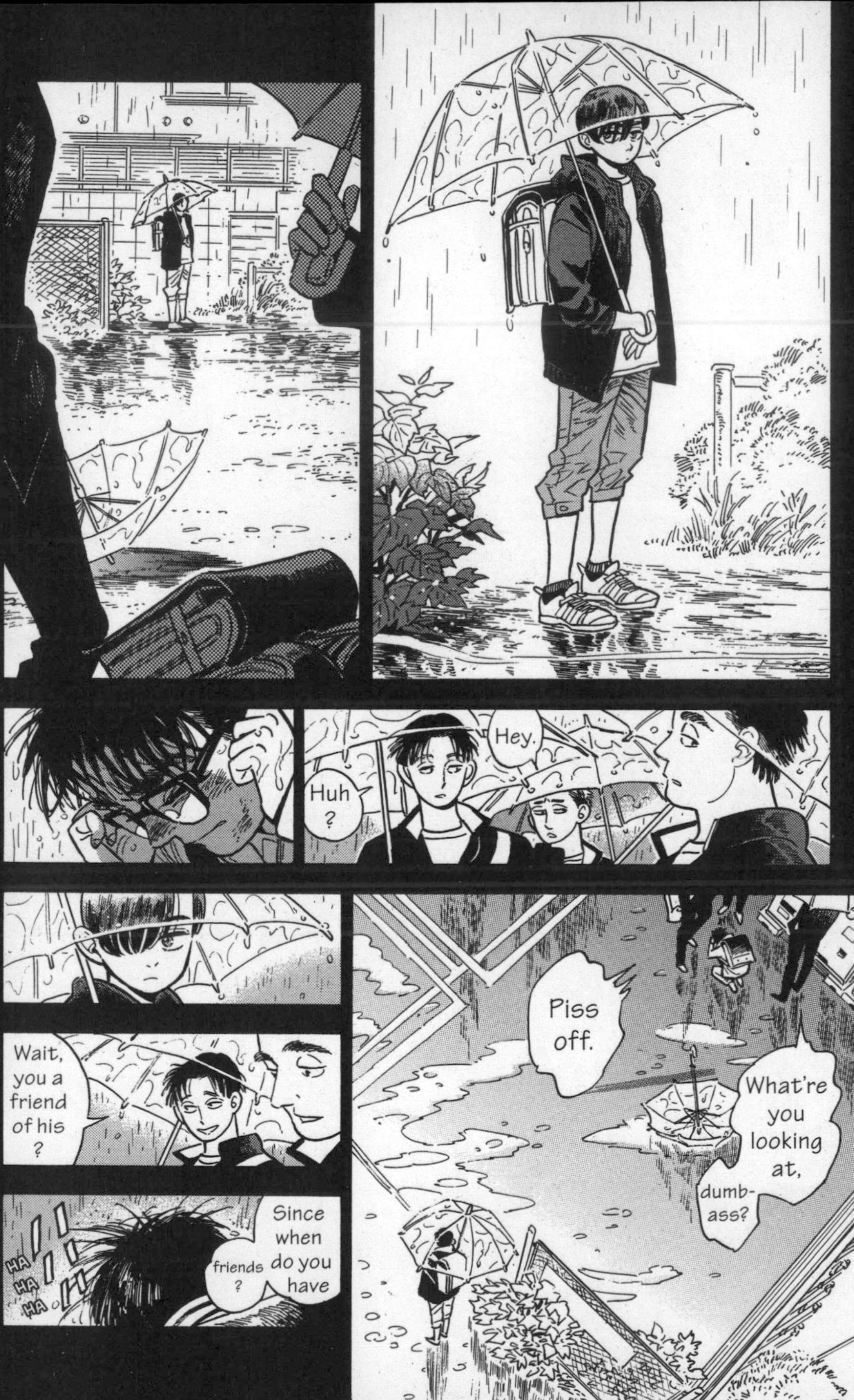

Hey.
Huh?
Piss off.
What're you looking at, dumb-ass?
Wait, you a friend of his?
Since when do you have friends?
HA HA HA

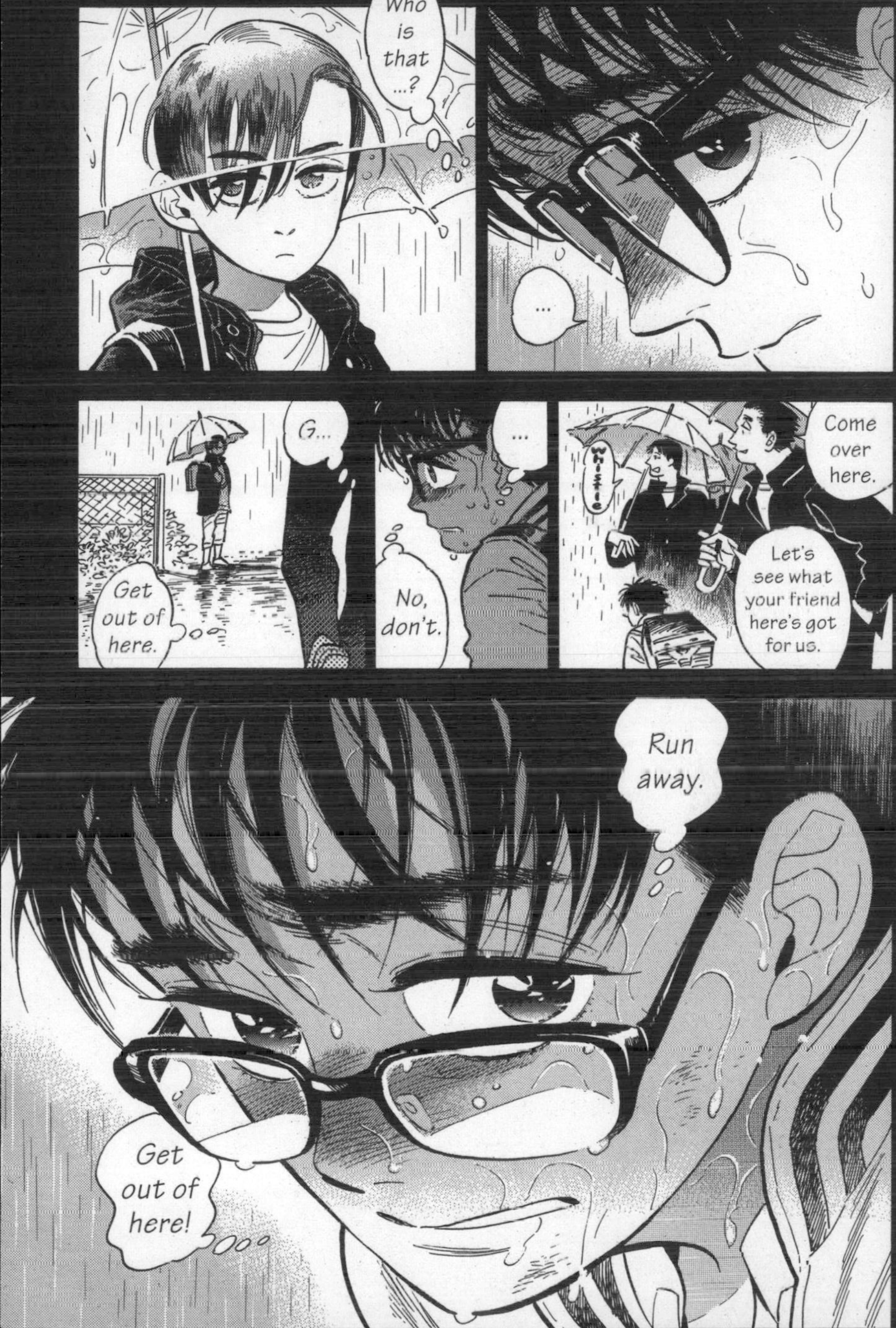
...
Who is that ...?
Come over here.
Whistle
Let's see what your friend here's got for us.
...
No, don't.
G...
Get out of here.
Run away.
Get out of here!

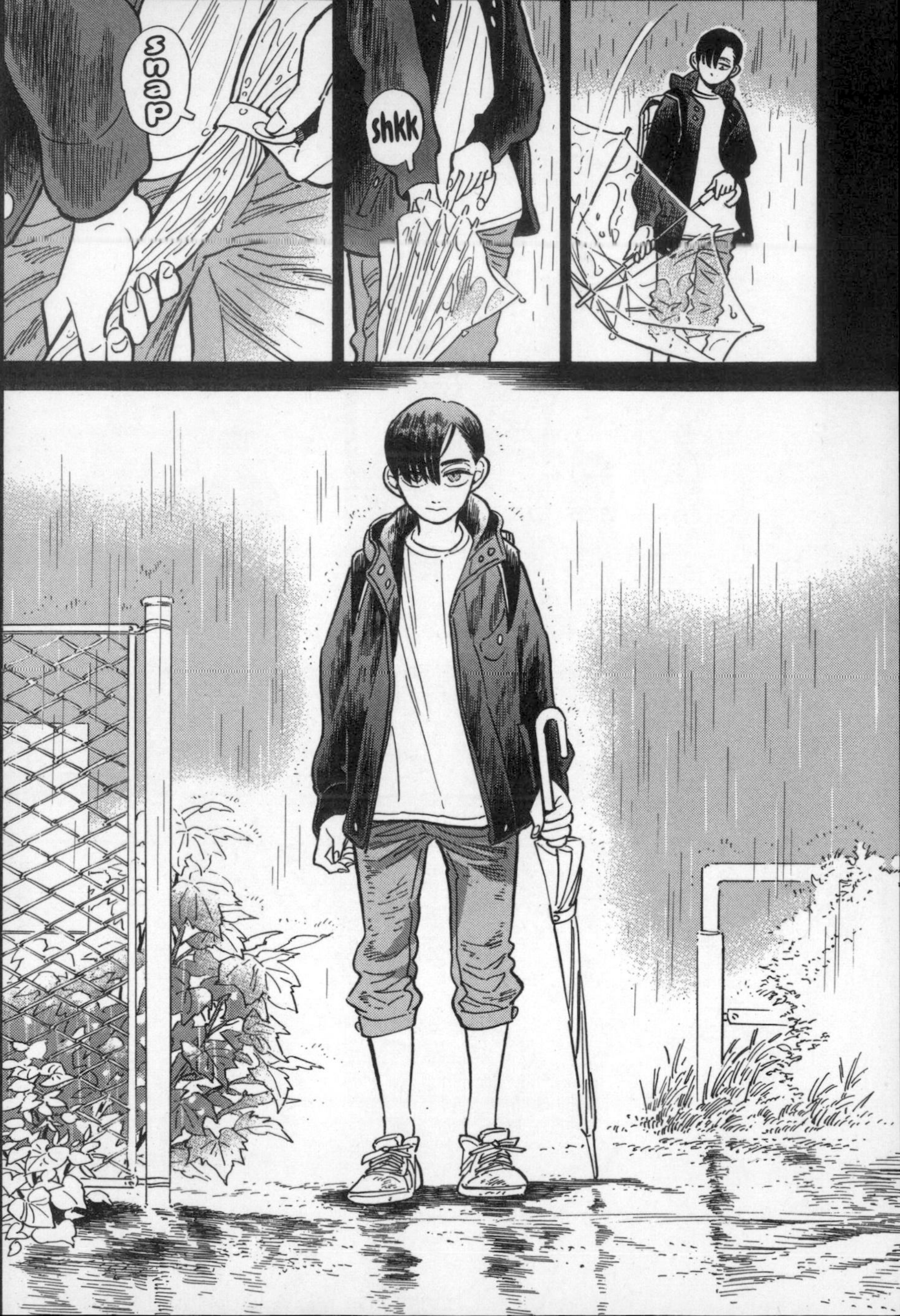
shkk
snap

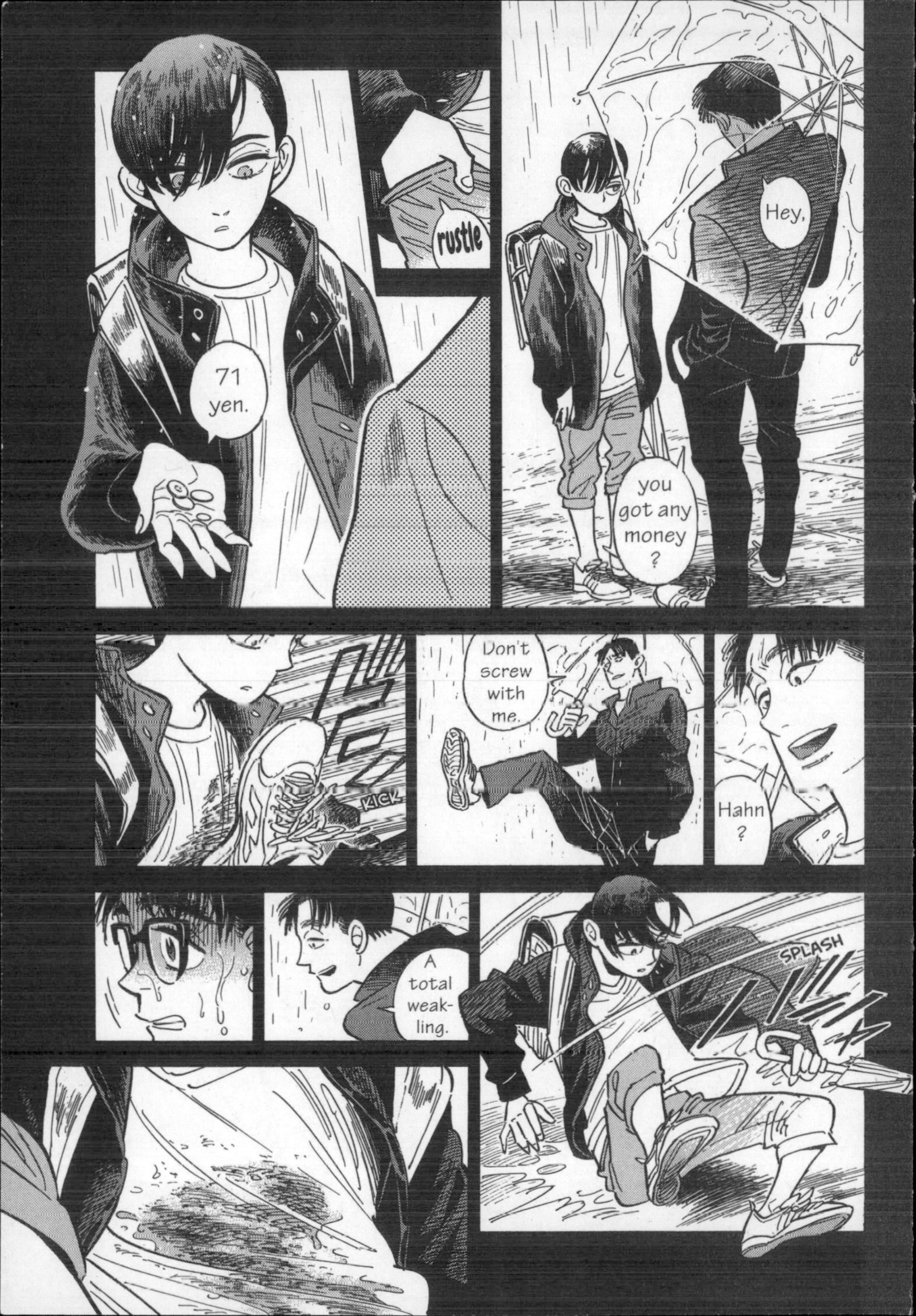
Hey,
you got any money ?
rustle
71 yen.
Hahn ?
Don't screw with me.
KICK
SPLASH
A total weak-ling.

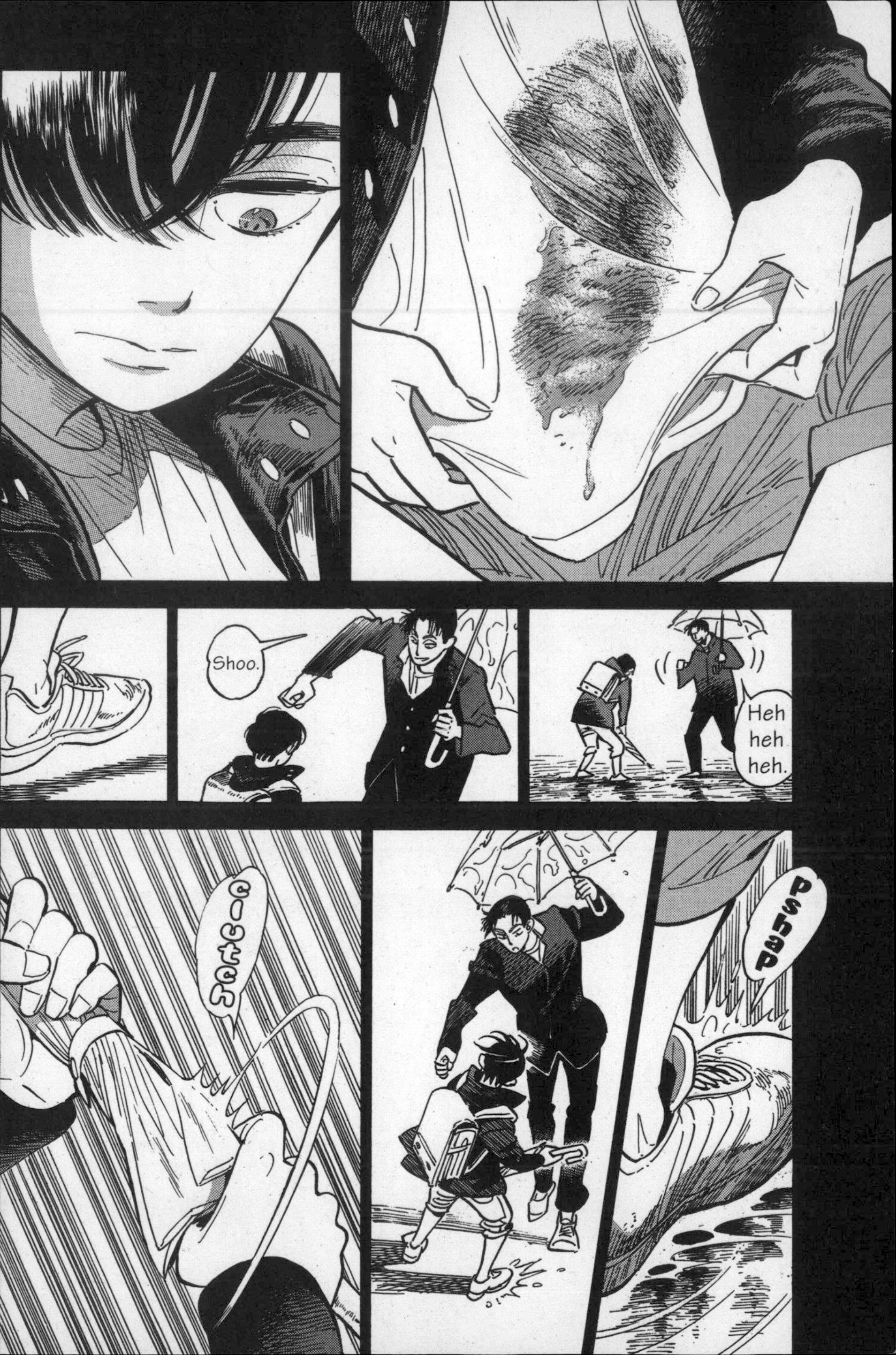
Heh heh heh.
Shoo.
pshap
clutch

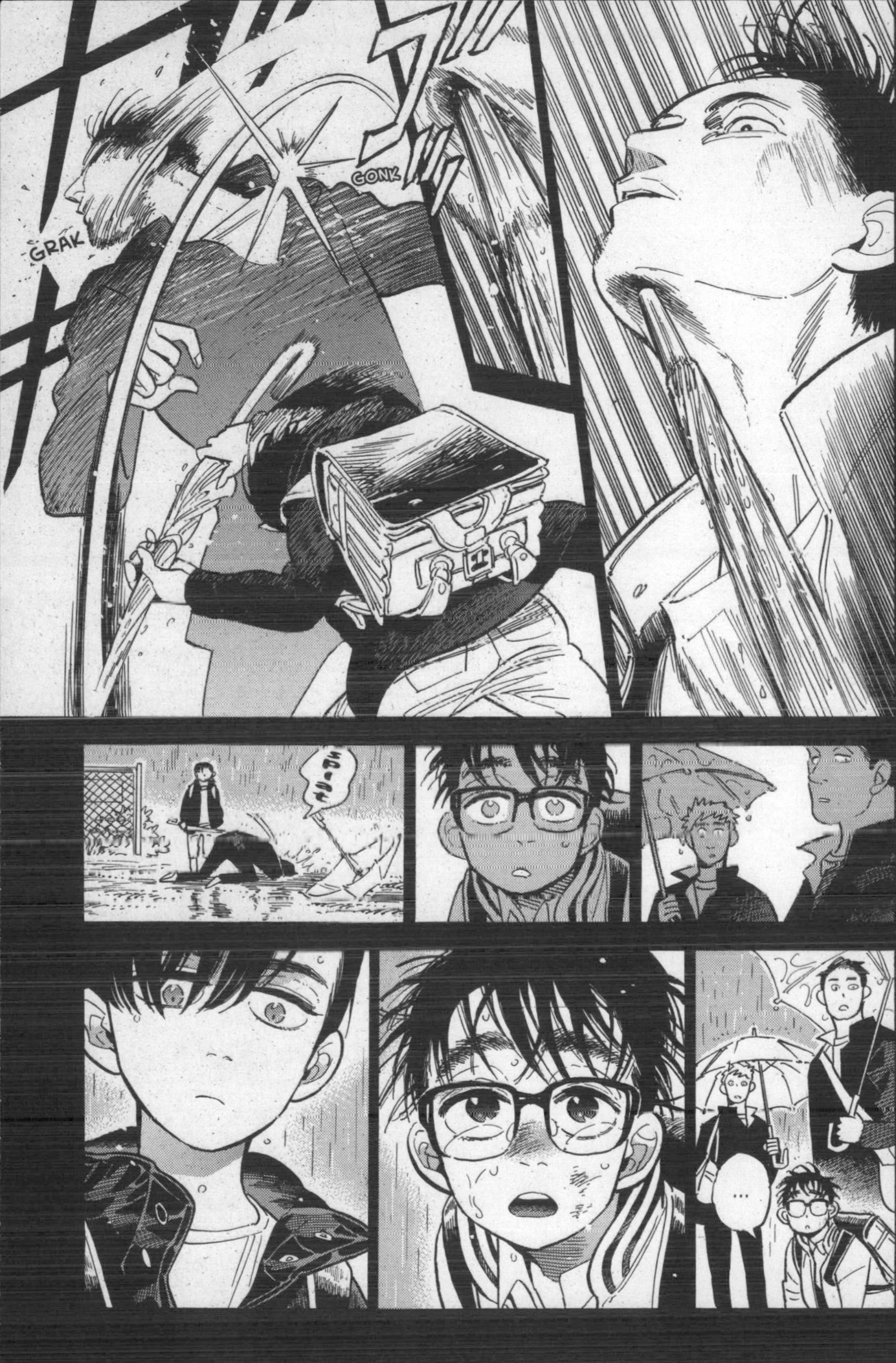
GONK
GRAK
...

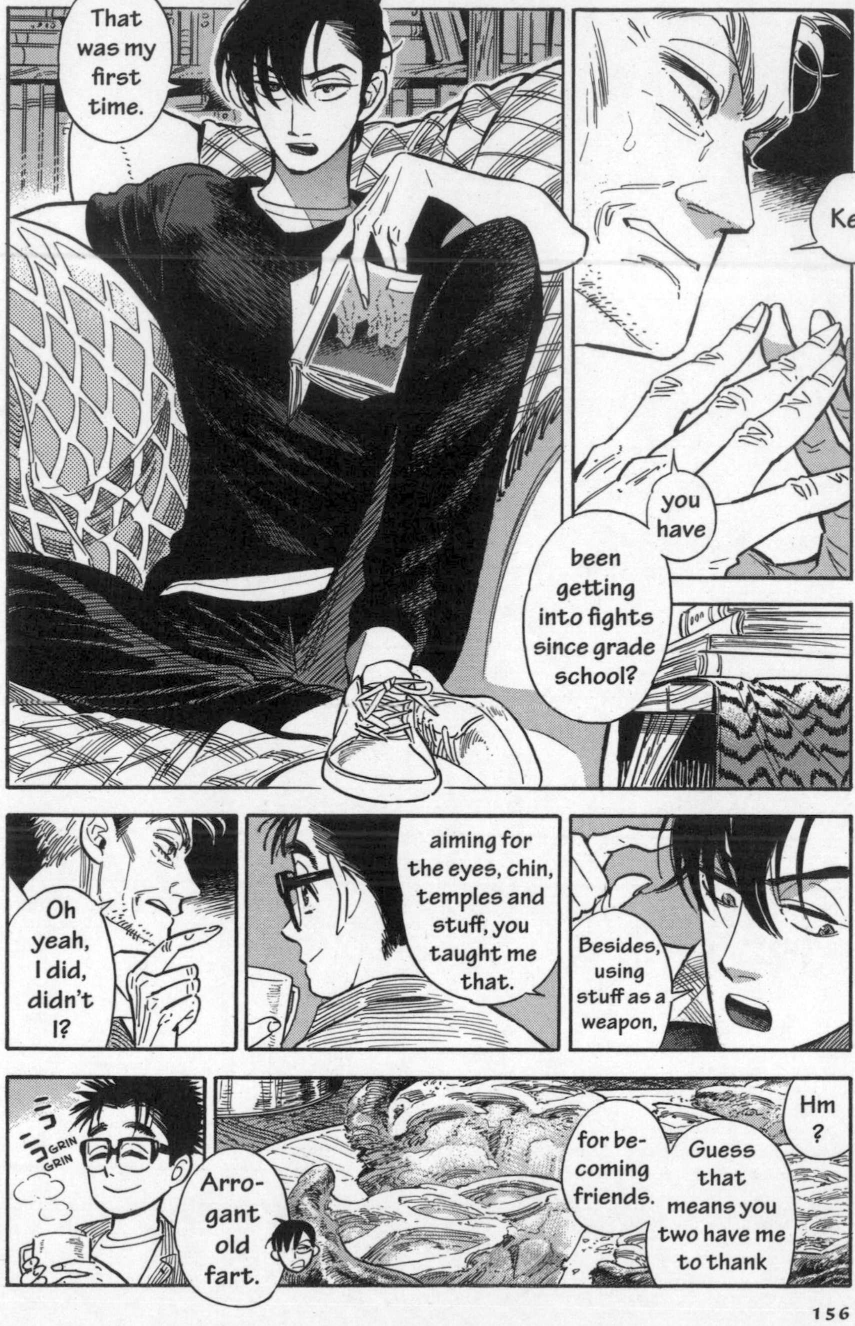

Kei,
you have
been getting into fights since grade school?
That was my first time.
Besides, using stuff as a weapon,
aiming for the eyes, chin, temples and stuff, you taught me that.
Oh yeah, I did, didn't I?
Hm?
Guess that means you two have me to thank
for be-coming friends.
GRIN GRIN
Arro-gant old fart.

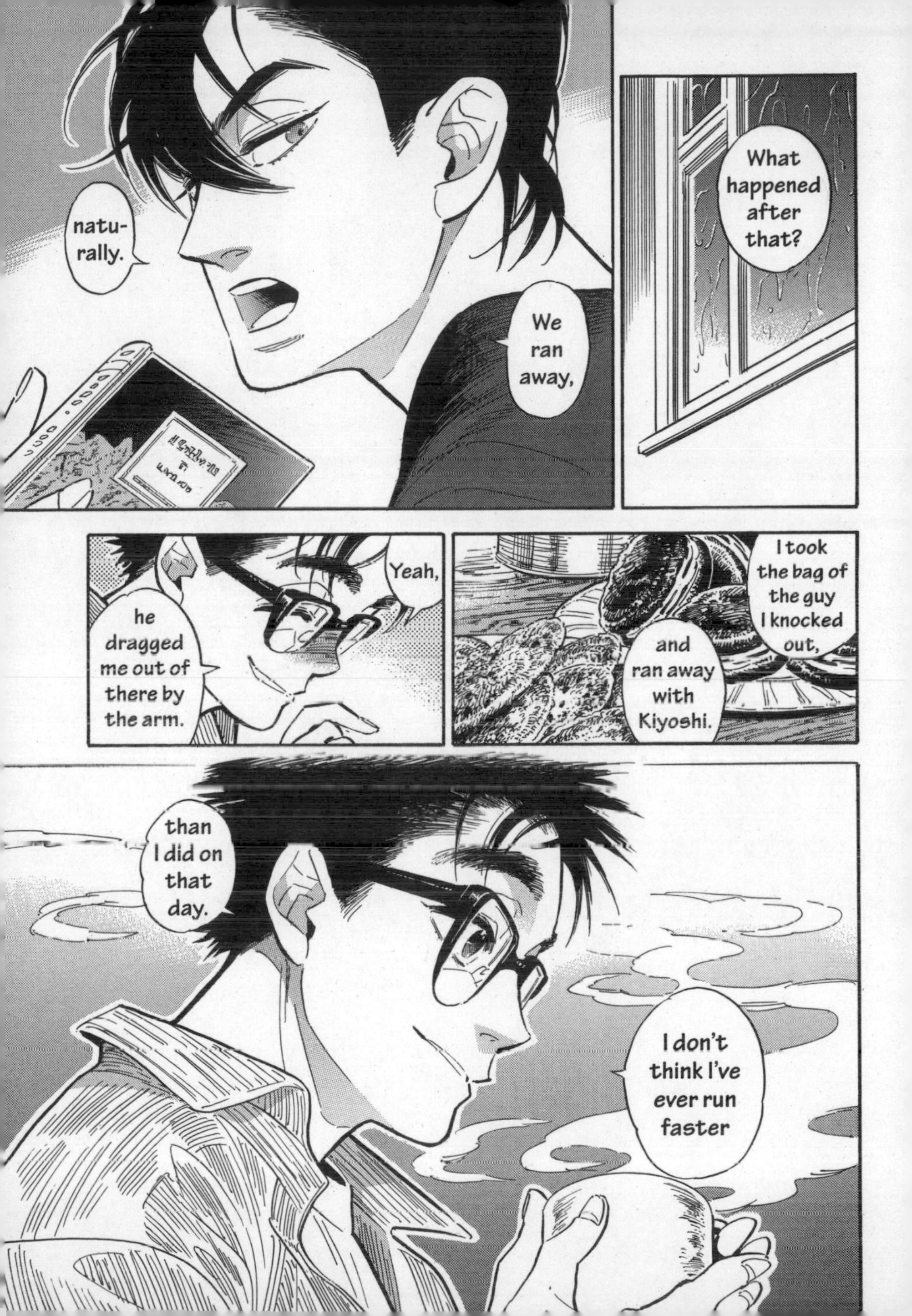
What happened after that?
We ran away,
naturally.
I took the bag of the guy I knocked out,
and ran away with Kiyoshi.
Yeah,
he dragged me out of there by the arm.
I don't think I've ever run faster
than I did on that day.

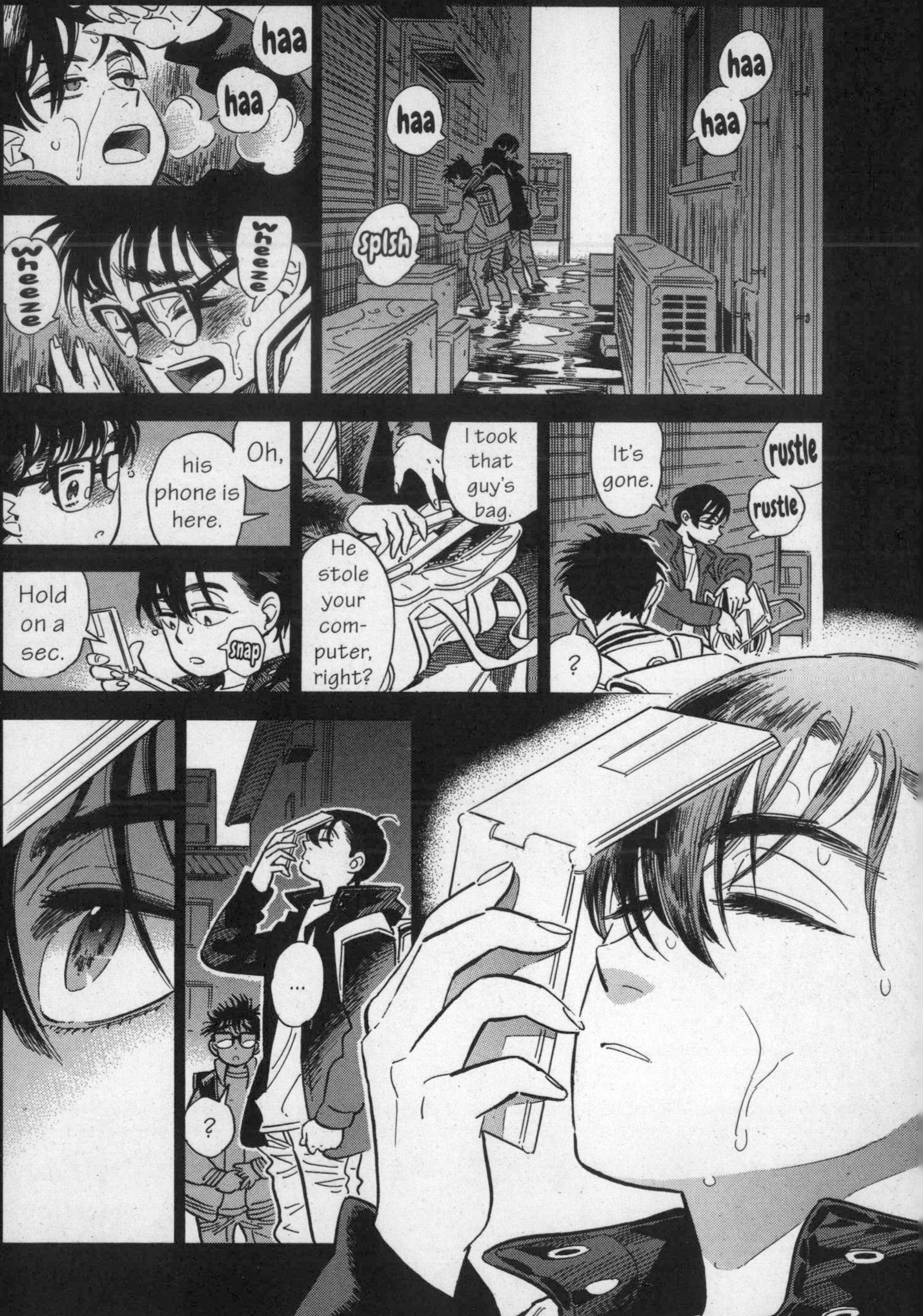
haa
haa
haa
splsh
haa
haa
Wheeze
Wheeze
rustle
rustle
It's gone.
?
I took that guy's bag.
He stole your computer, right?
Oh, his phone is here.
snap
Hold on a sec.
...
?

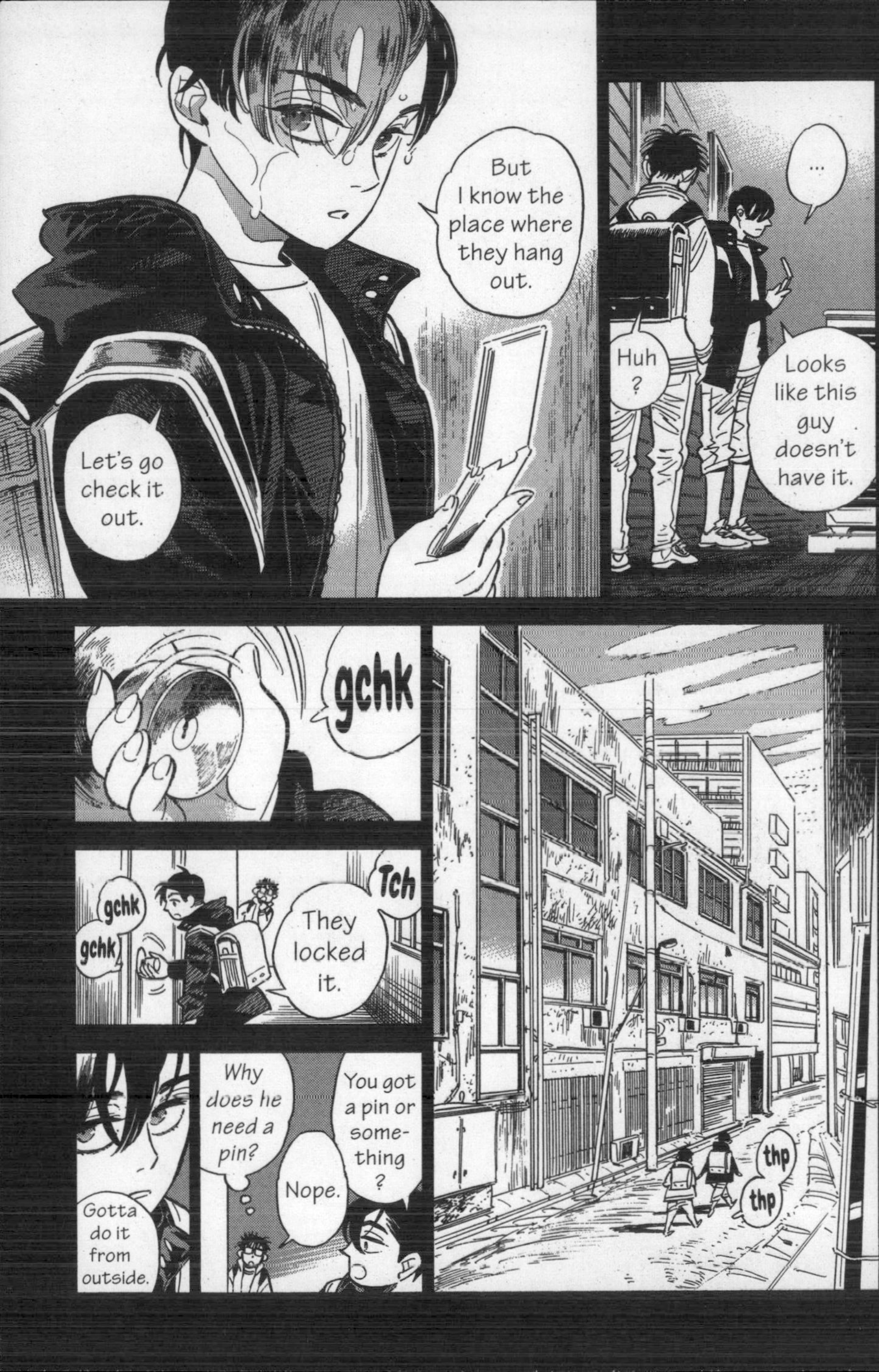
...
Looks like this guy doesn't have it.
Huh?
But I know the place where they hang out.
Let's go check it out.
thp
thp
gchk
Tch
They locked it.
gchk
gchk
You got a pin or something?
Why does he need a pin?
Nope.
Gotta do it from outside.

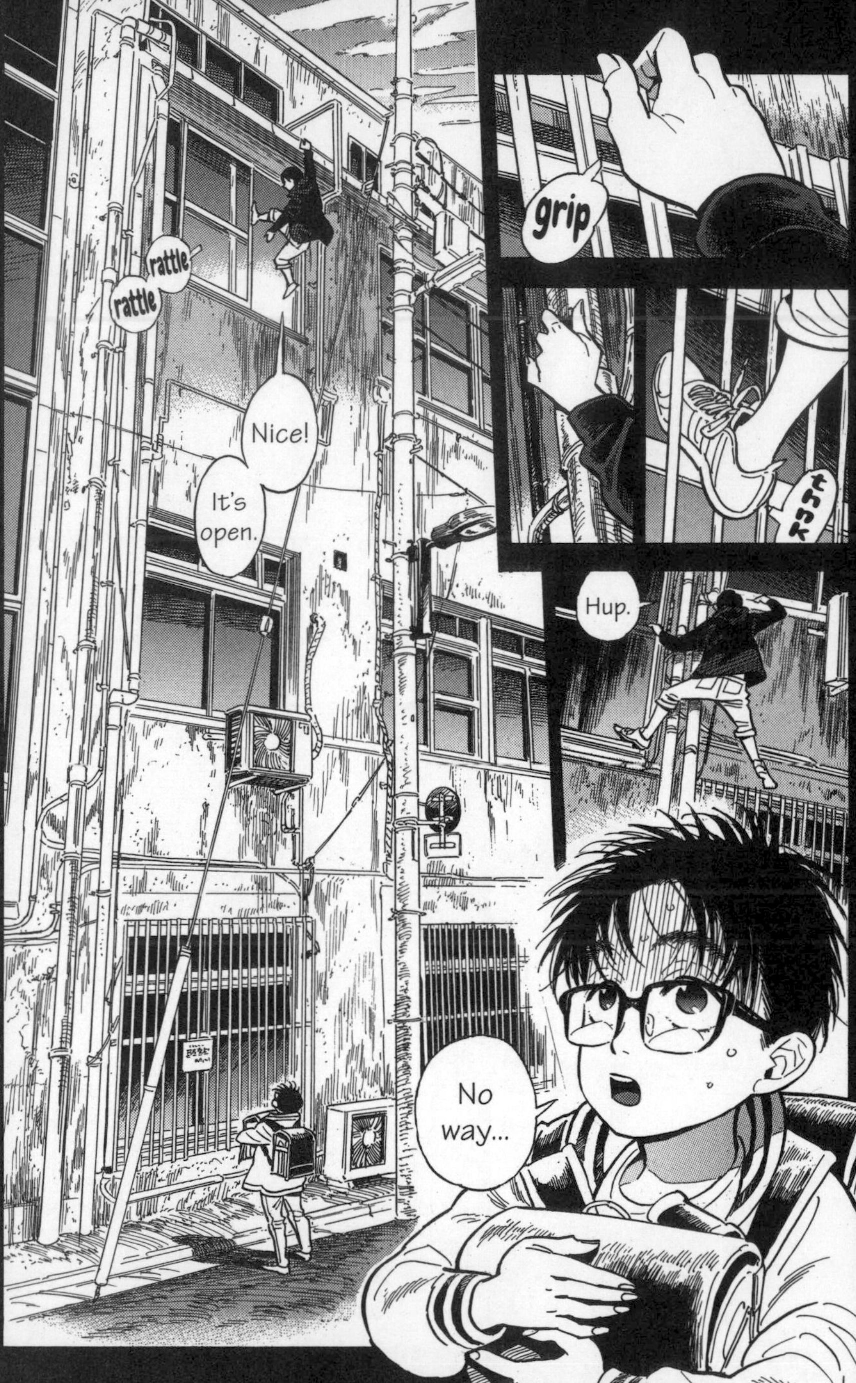
grip
thnk
Hup.
rattle
rattle
Nice!
It's open.
No way...

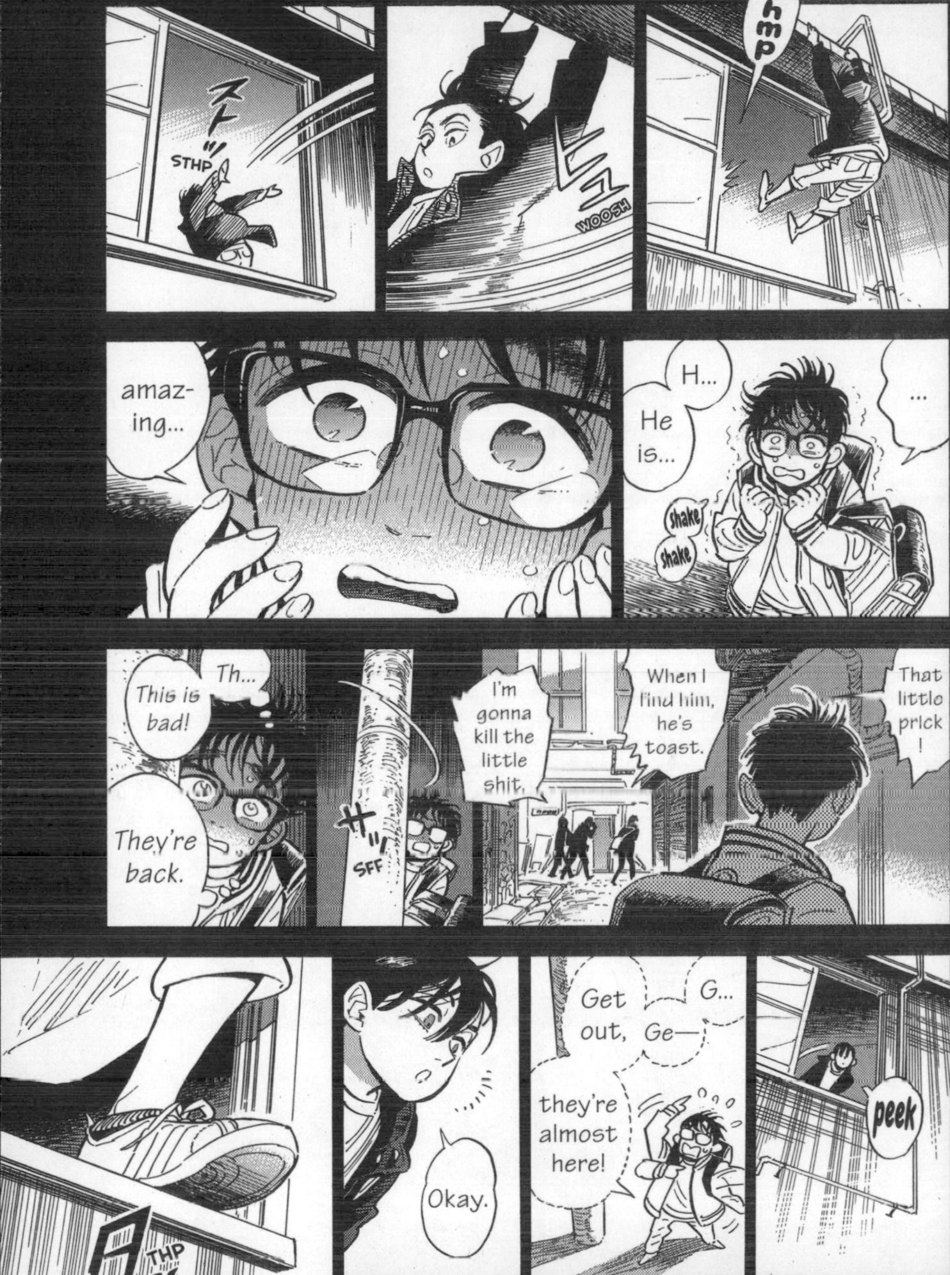
thmp
WOOSH
STHP
H...
He is...
...
shake
shake
amaz-ing...
That little prick!
When I find him, he's toast.
I'm gonna kill the little shit.
SFF
Th...
This is bad!
They're back.
peek
G...
Ge—
Get out,
they're almost here!
...
Okay.
THP

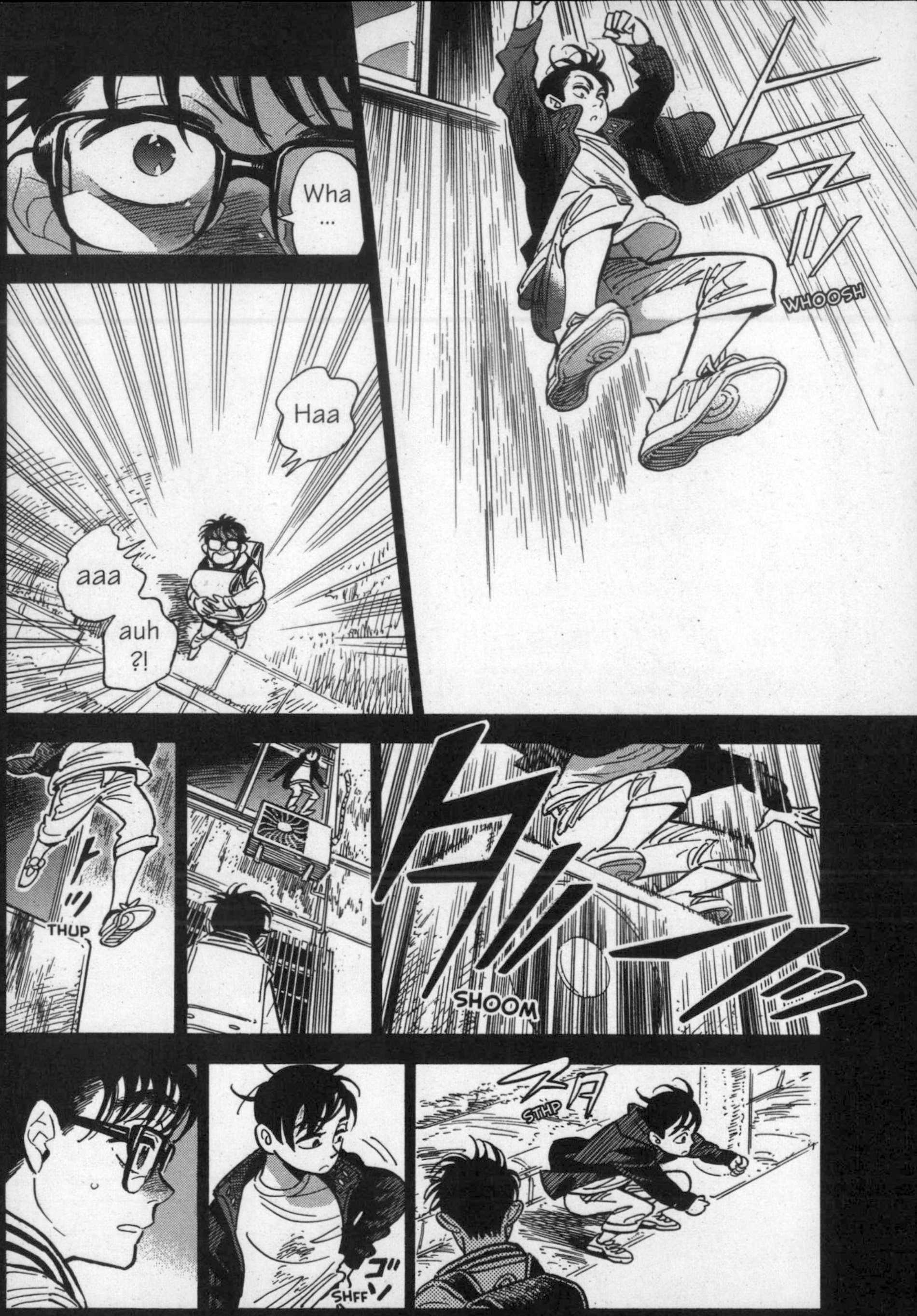

WHOOSH
Wha ...
Haa
aaa auh ?!
SHOOM
THUP
STHP
SHFF

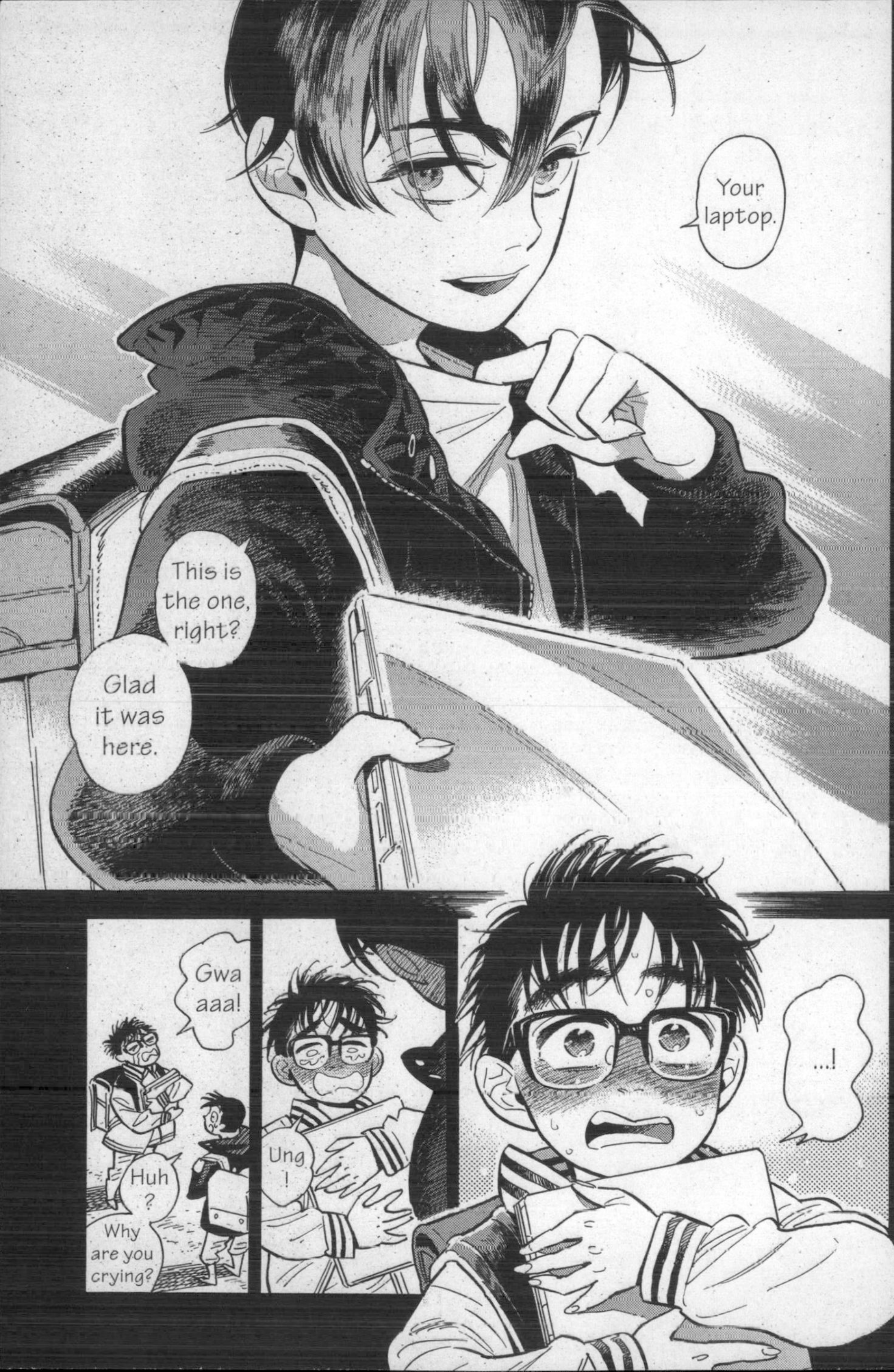
Your laptop.
This is the one, right?
Glad it was here.
...!
Ung !
Gwa aaa!
Huh ?
Why are you crying?

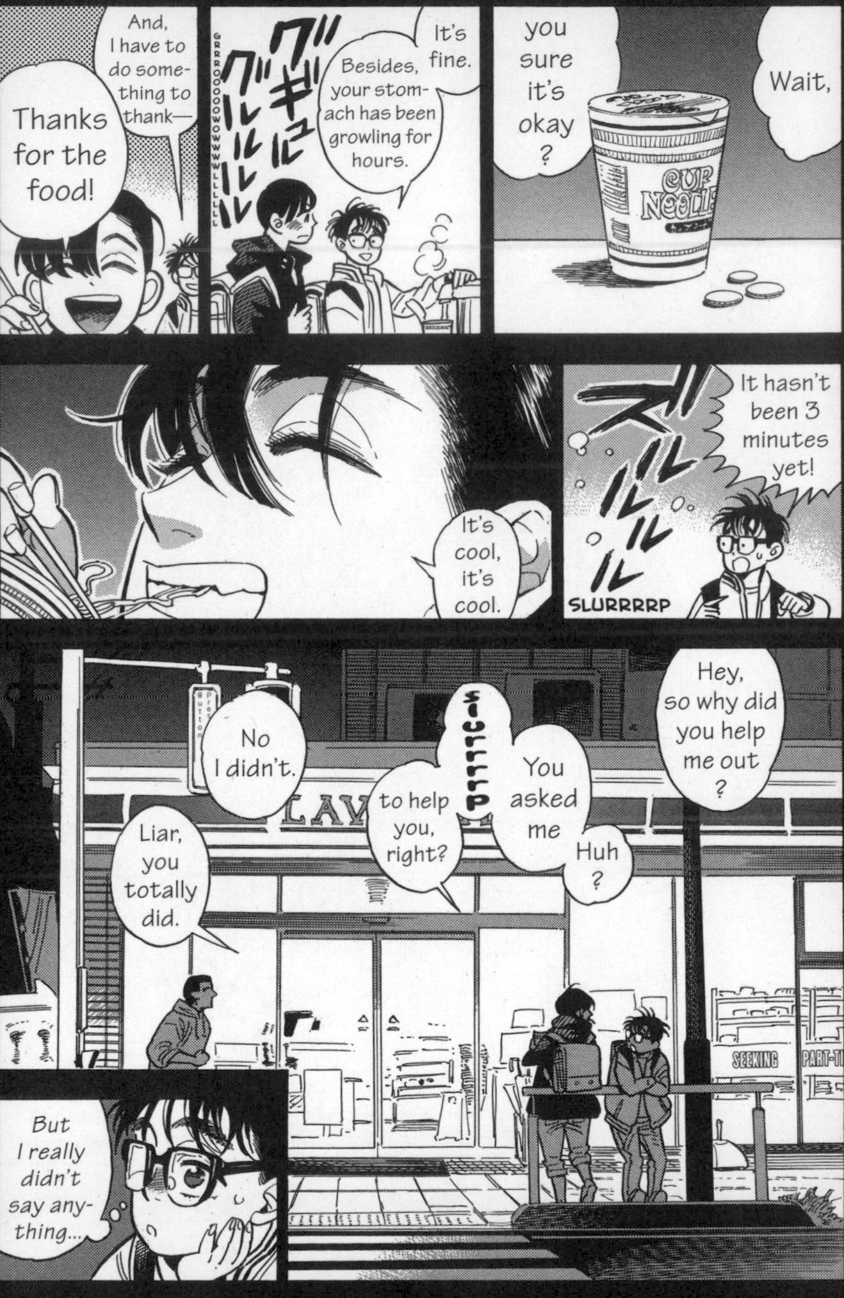
Wait,
you sure it's okay?
It's fine.
Besides, your stomach has been growling for hours.
GRRROOOOOWWWWLLLLLL
And, I have to do something to thank—
Thanks for the food!
It hasn't been 3 minutes yet!
SLURRRRP
It's cool, it's cool.
Hey, so why did you help me out?
Huh?
You asked me
to help you, right?
SLURRRRP
No I didn't.
Liar, you totally did.
SEEKING PART-TI
But I really didn't say anything...

Chapter 16 – End

Chapter 17 [sautjándi]

The valley where clouds rise

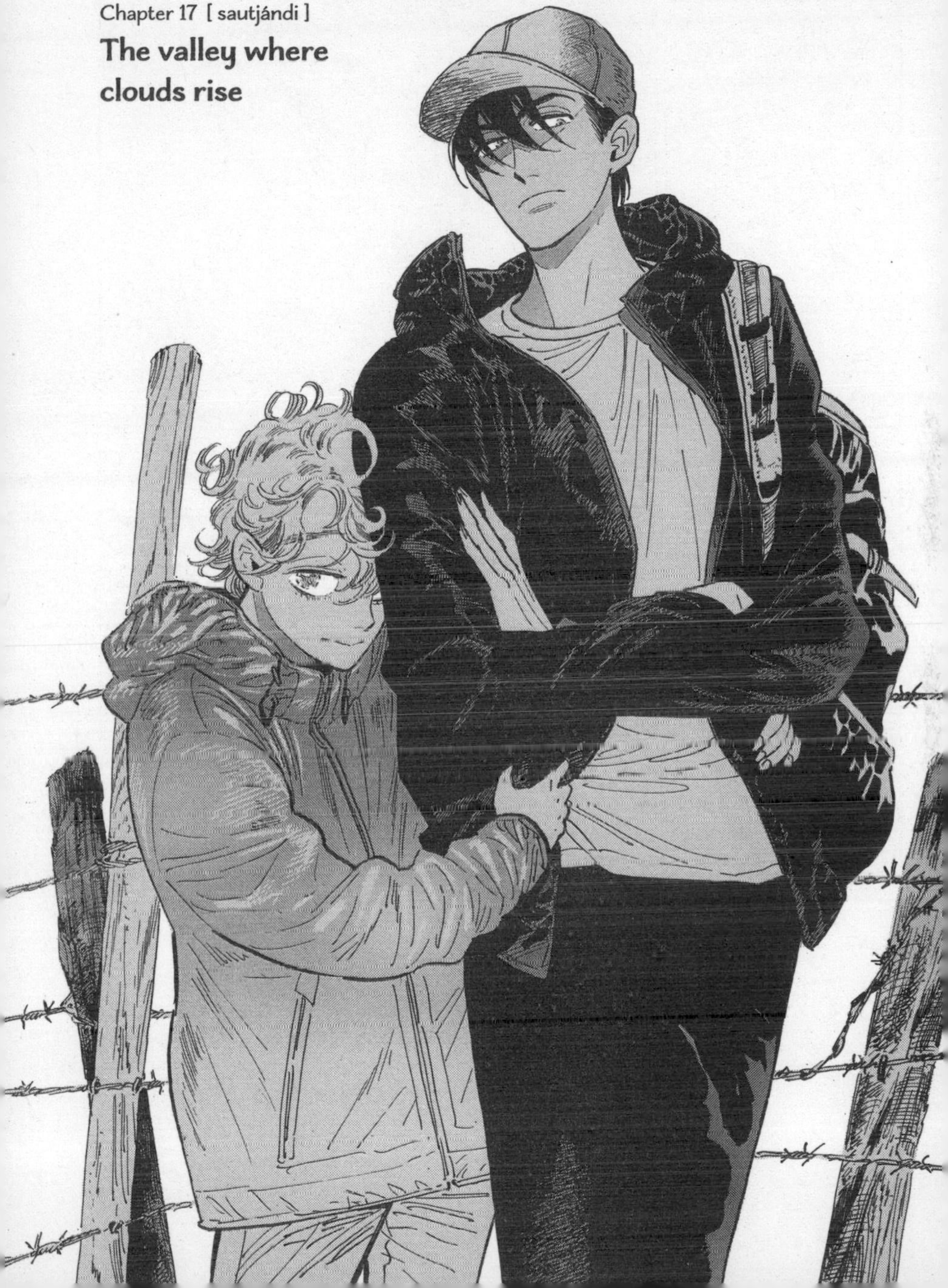

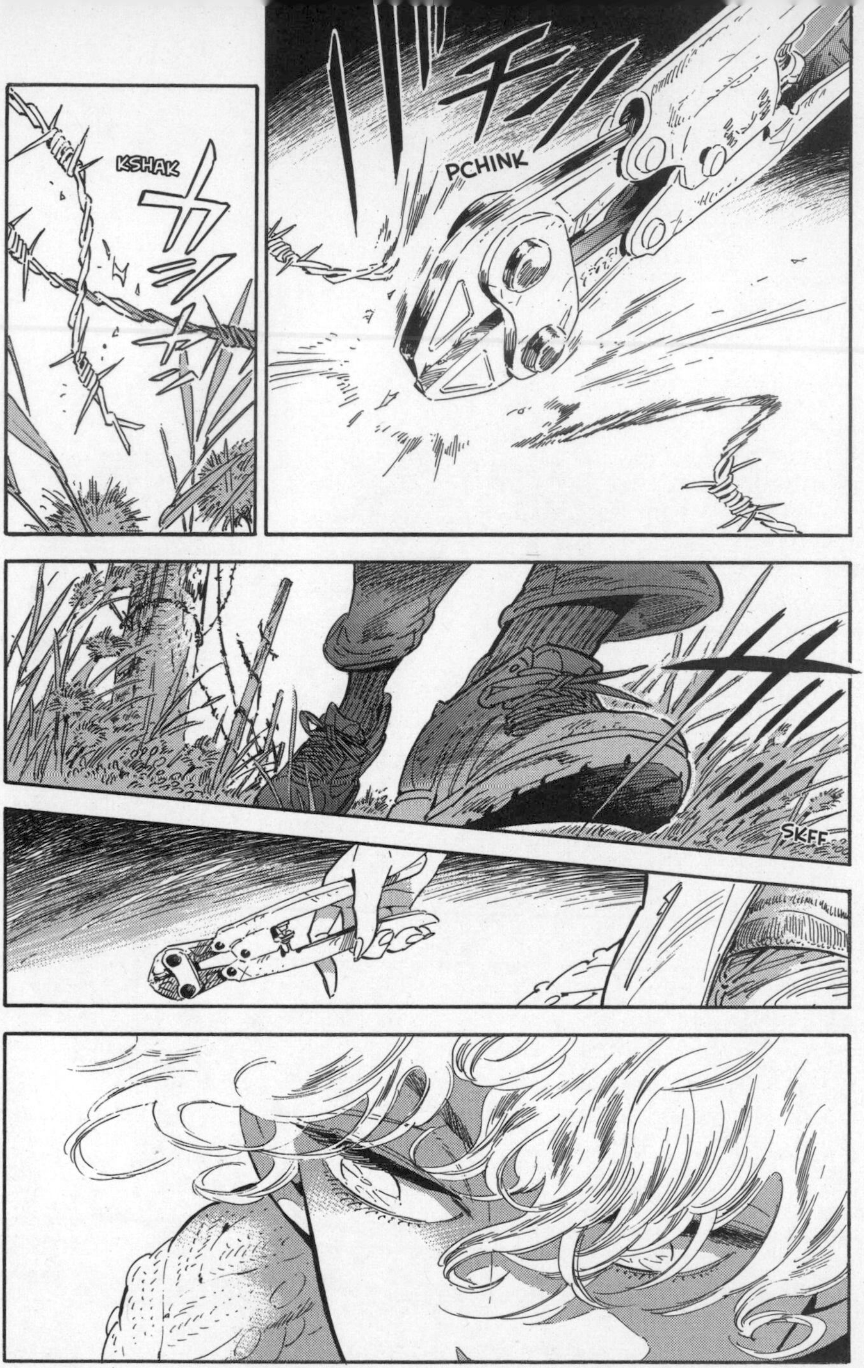
PCHINK
KSHAK
SKFF

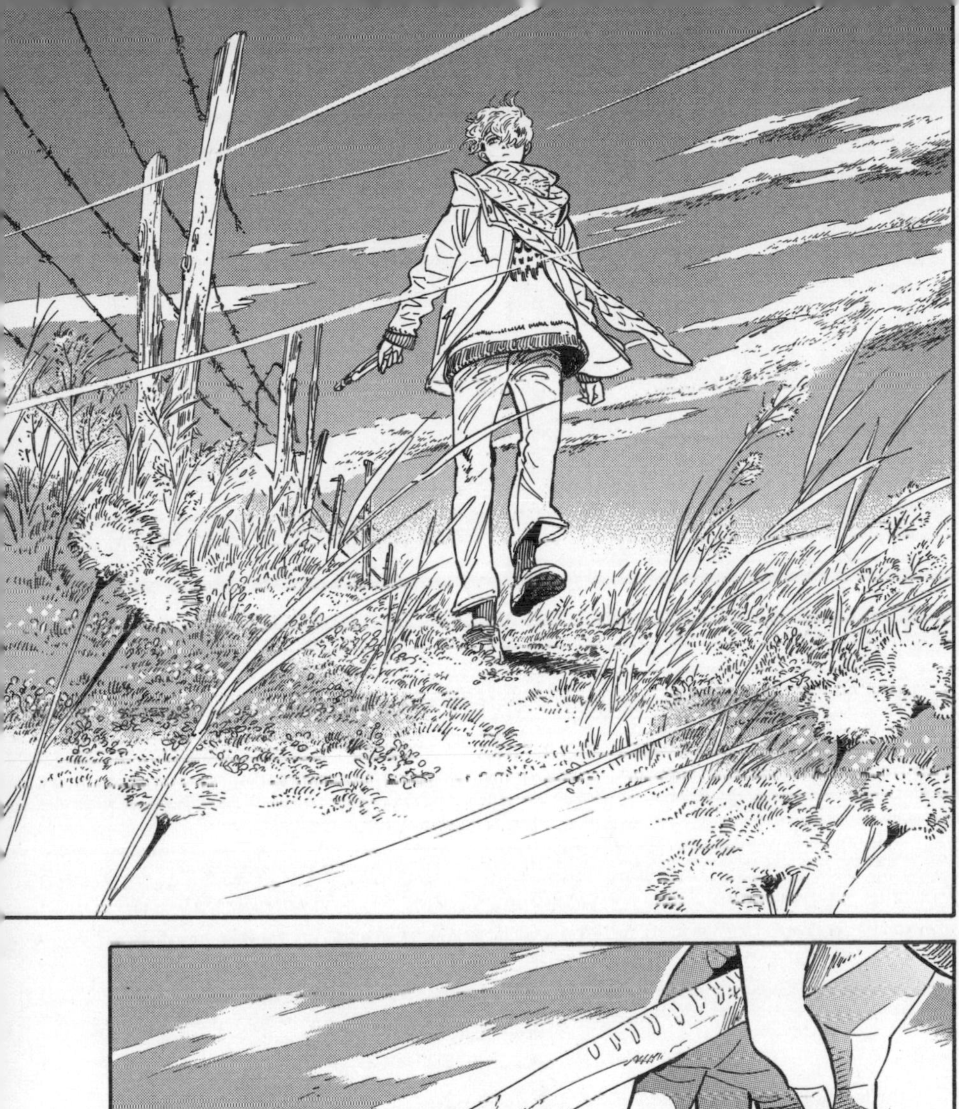
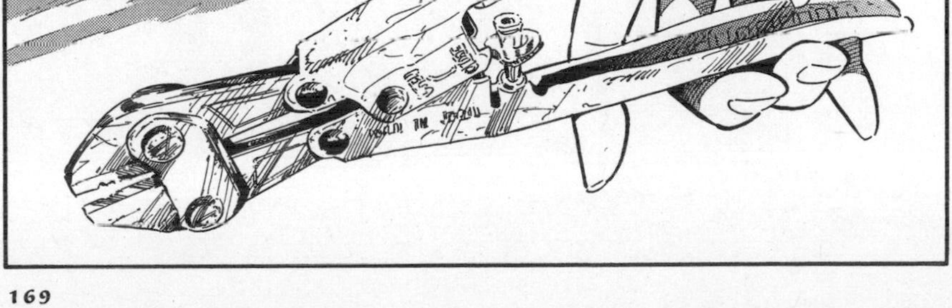

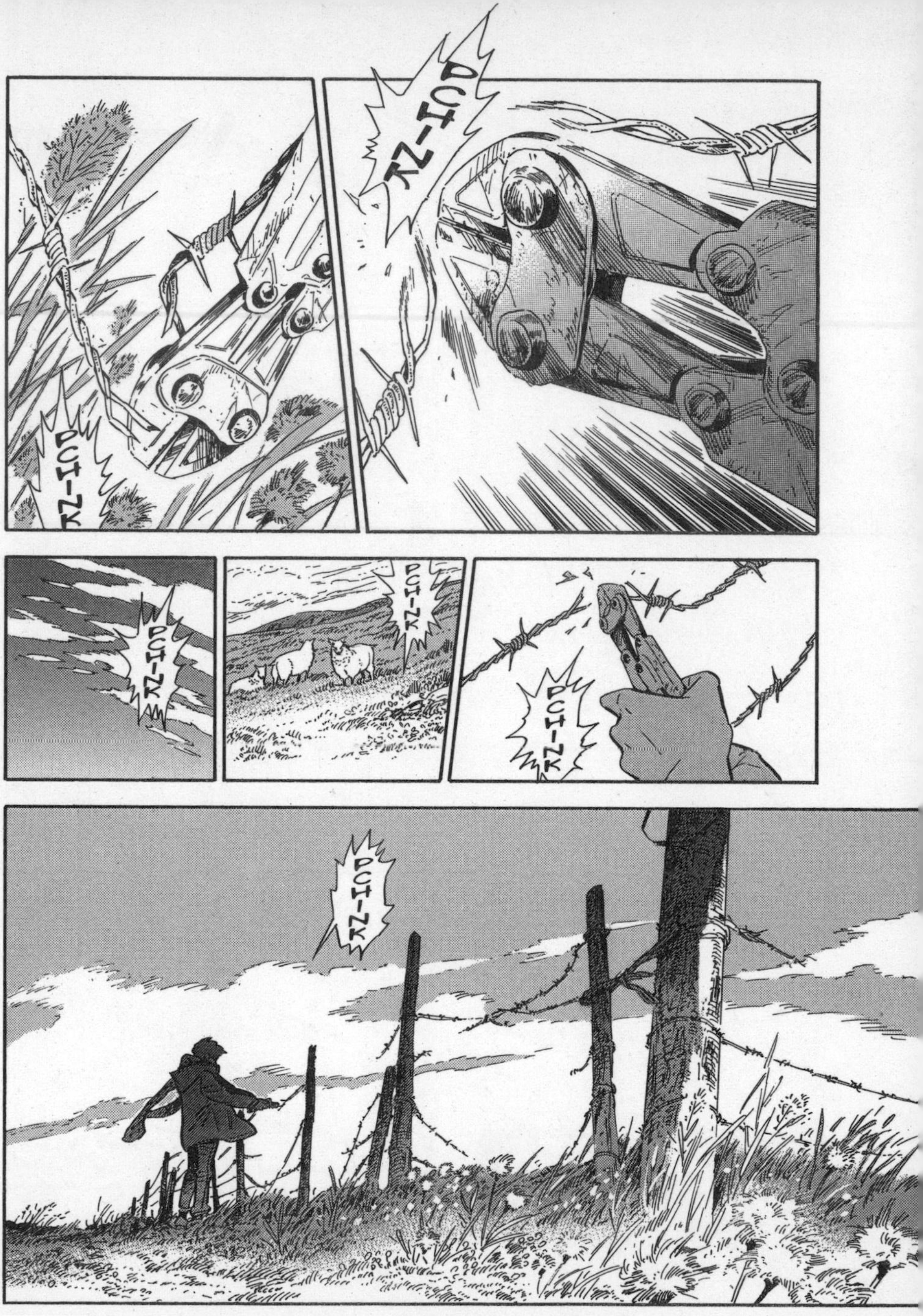
PCHINK
PCHINK
PCHINK
PCHINK
PCHINK
PCHINK

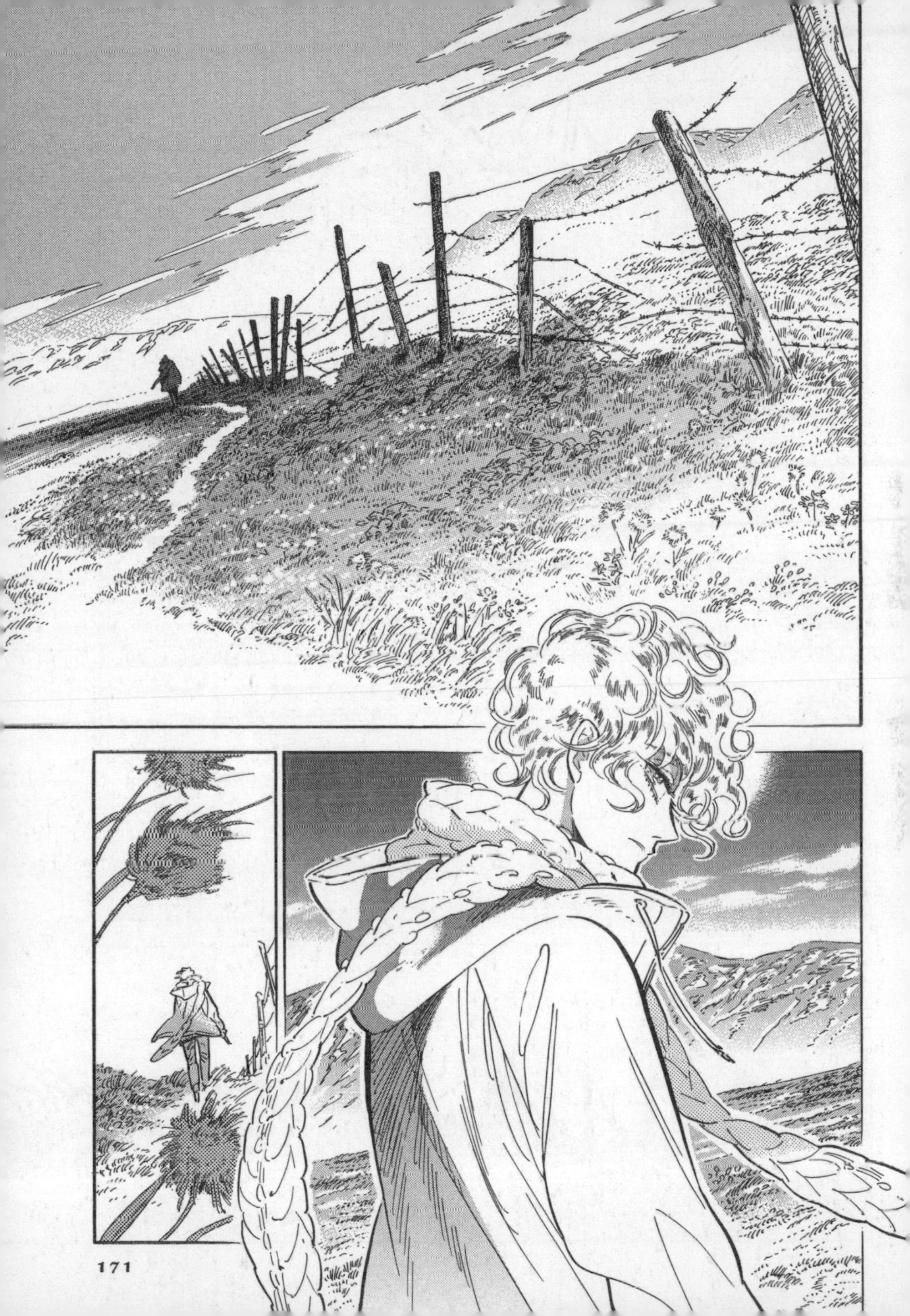

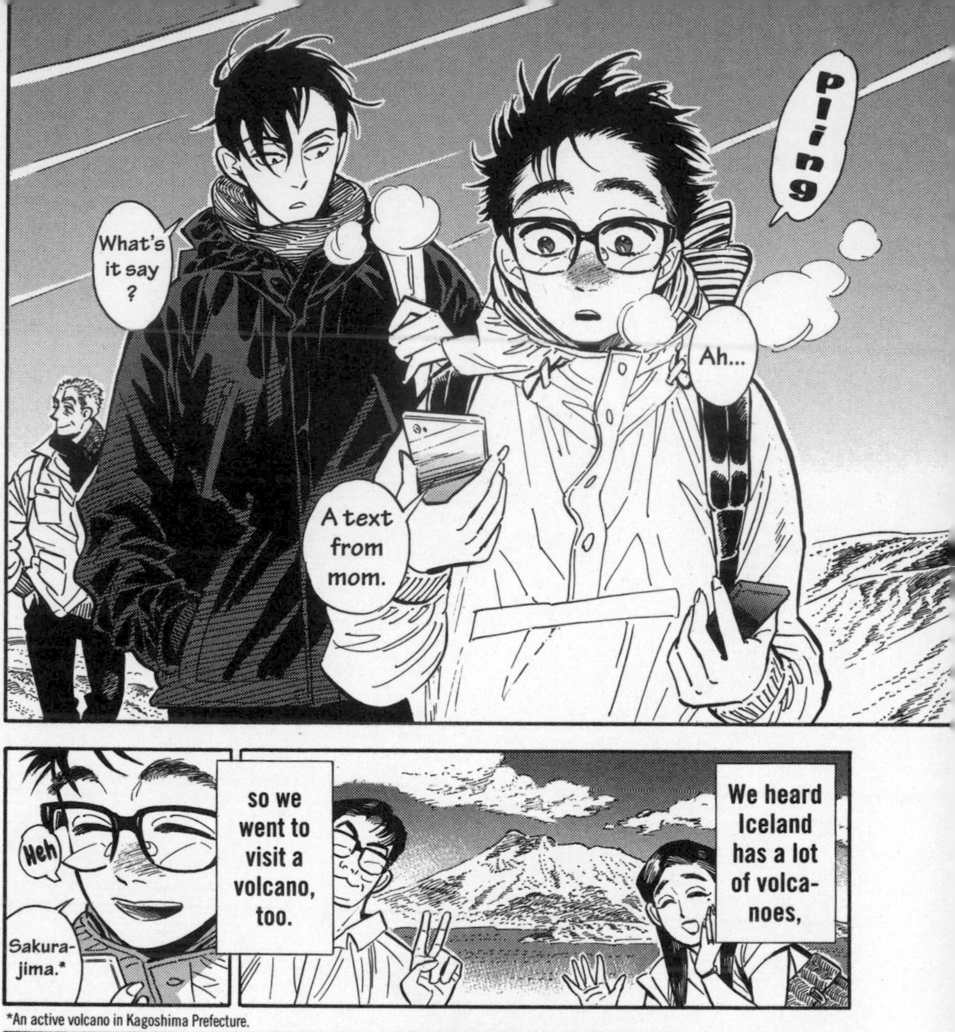
Pling
Ah...
What's it say?
A text from mom.
We heard Iceland has a lot of volca-noes,
so we went to visit a volcano, too.
Heh
Sakura-jima.*

*An active volcano in Kagoshima Prefecture.

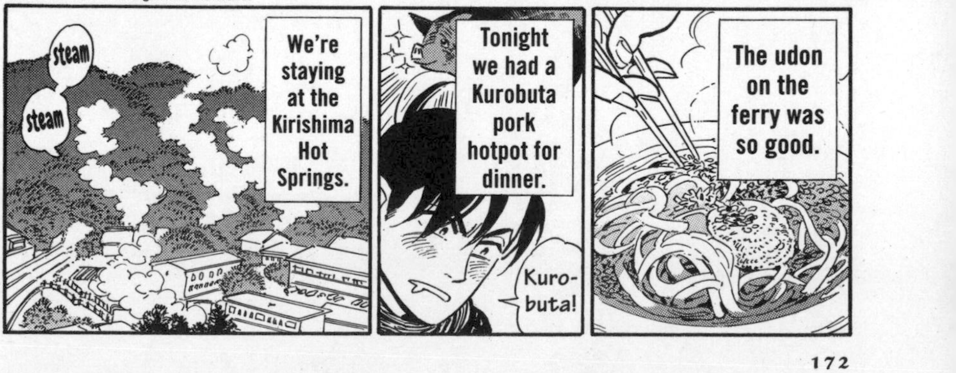
The udon on the ferry was so good.
Tonight we had a Kurobuta pork hotpot for dinner.
Kuro-buta!
We're staying at the Kirishima Hot Springs.
steam
steam

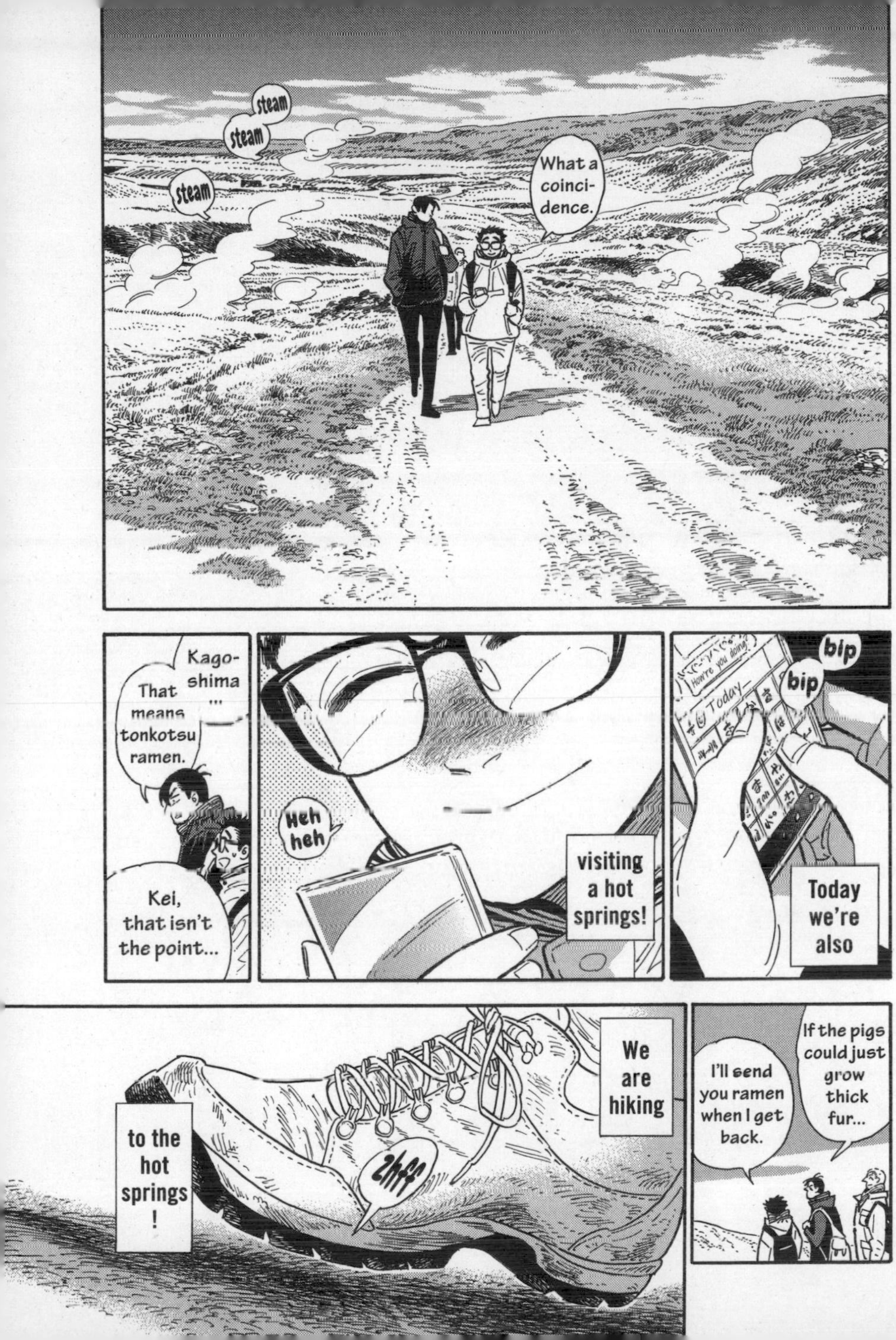
What a coincidence.
steam
steam
steam
bip
bip
How're you doing?
Today
Today we're also
visiting a hot springs!
Heh heh
Kagoshima...
That means tonkotsu ramen.
Kei, that isn't the point...
If the pigs could just grow thick fur...
I'll send you ramen when I get back.
We are hiking
zhff
to the hot springs!

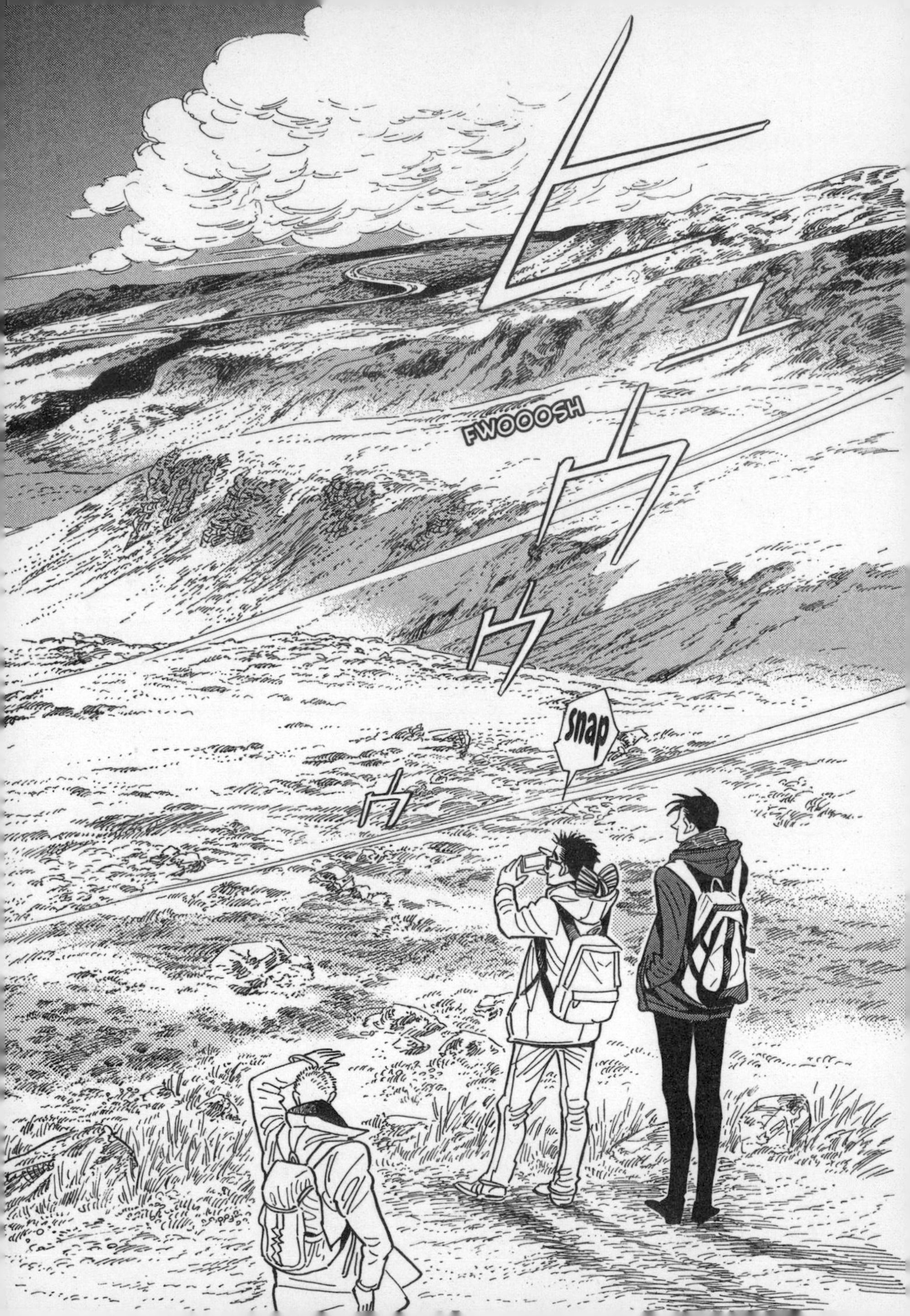
FWOOOSH
snap

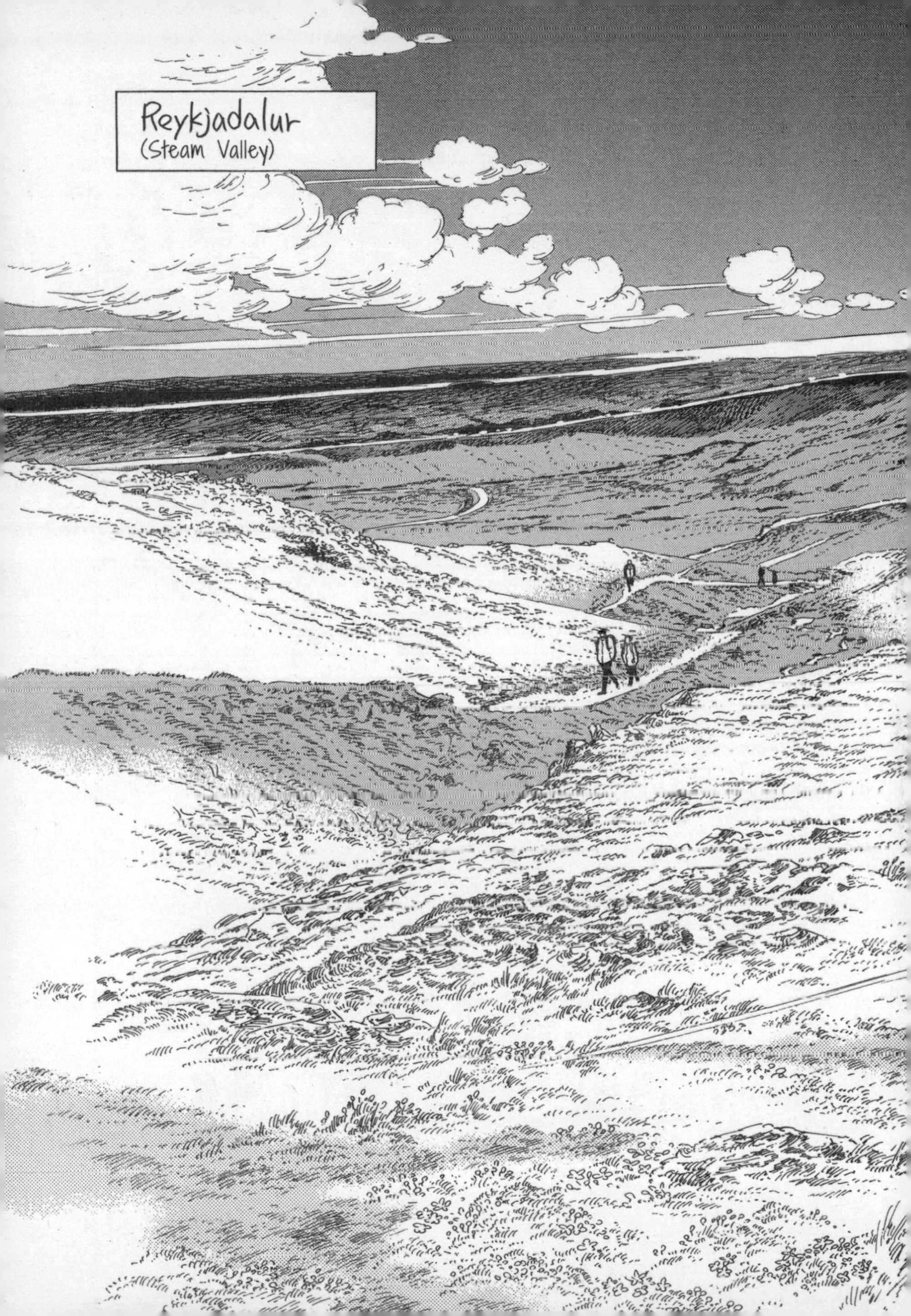
Reykjadalur
(Steam Valley)

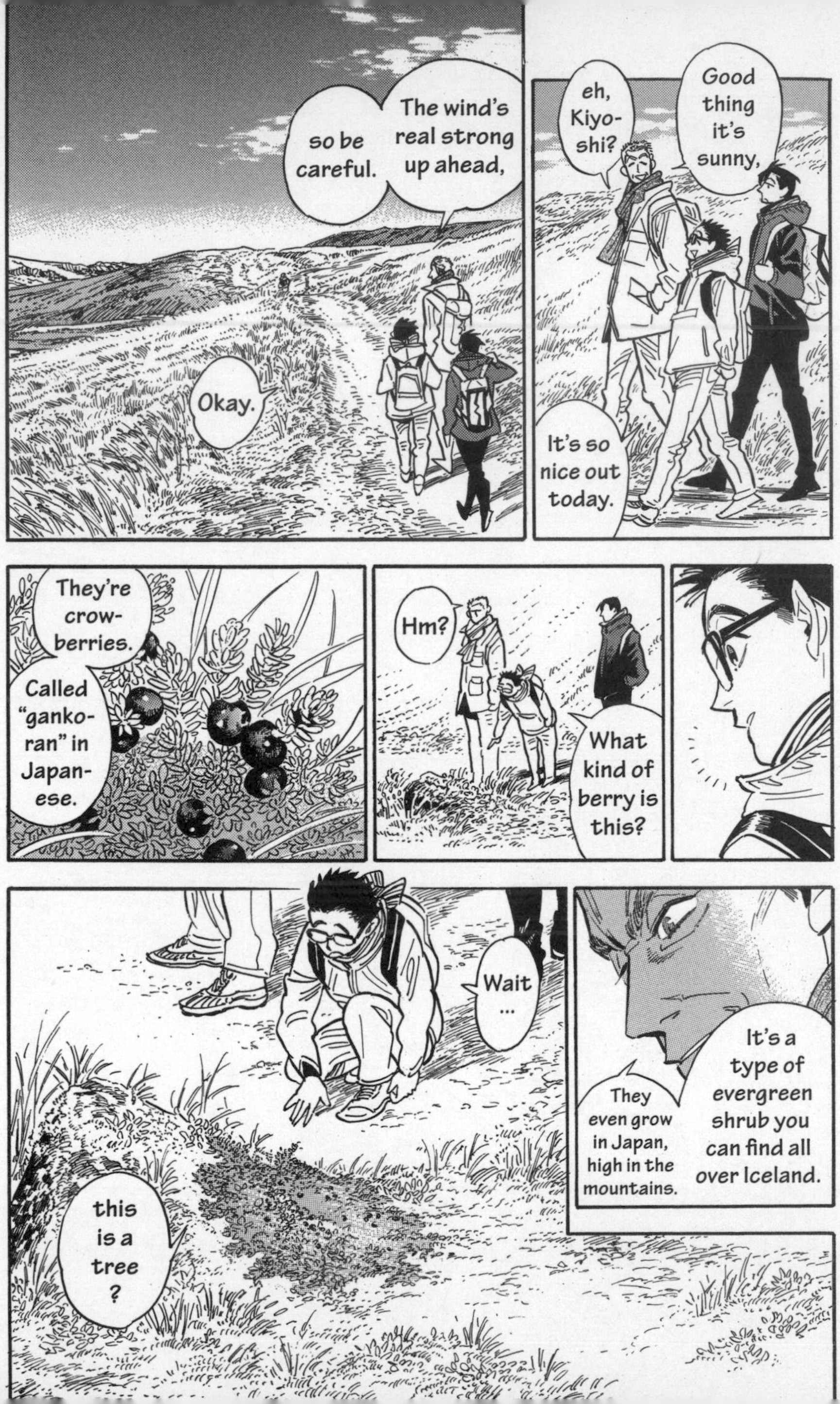
Good thing it's sunny,
eh, Kiyoshi?
It's so nice out today.
The wind's real strong up ahead,
so be careful.
Okay.
Hm?
What kind of berry is this?
They're crowberries.
Called "gankoran" in Japanese.
It's a type of evergreen shrub you can find all over Iceland.
They even grow in Japan, high in the mountains.
Wait ...
this is a tree?

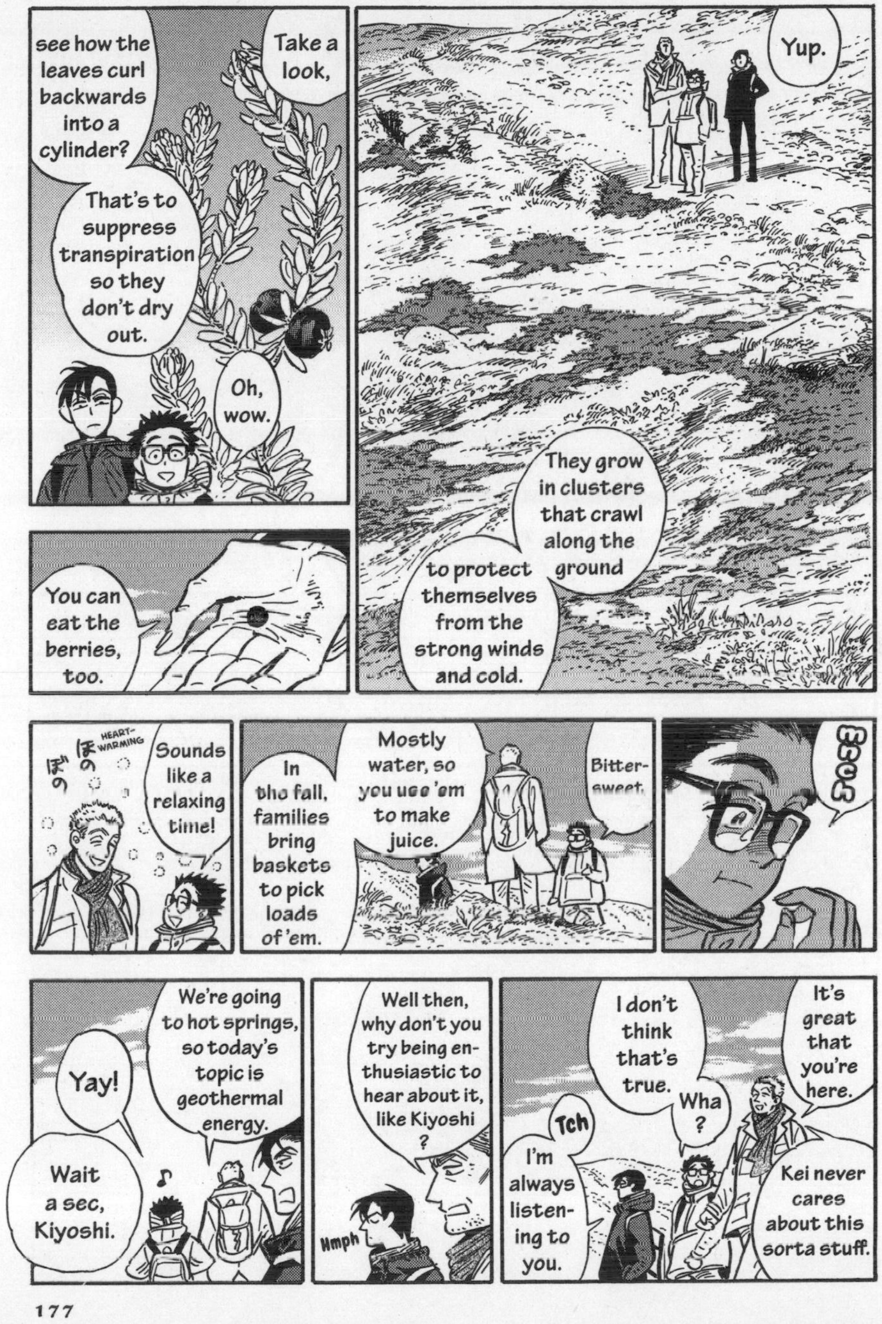
Take a look,
see how the leaves curl backwards into a cylinder?
That's to suppress transpiration so they don't dry out.
Oh, wow.
You can eat the berries, too.
Yup.
They grow in clusters that crawl along the ground
to protect themselves from the strong winds and cold.
HEART-WARMING
ほのぼの
Sounds like a relaxing time!
In the fall, families bring baskets to pick loads of 'em.
Mostly water, so you use 'em to make juice.
Bitter-sweet.
Munch
We're going to hot springs, so today's topic is geothermal energy.
Yay!
Wait a sec, Kiyoshi.
Well then, why don't you try being enthusiastic to hear about it, like Kiyoshi?
Hmph
I don't think that's true.
Wha?
Tch
I'm always listening to you.
It's great that you're here.
Kei never cares about this sorta stuff.

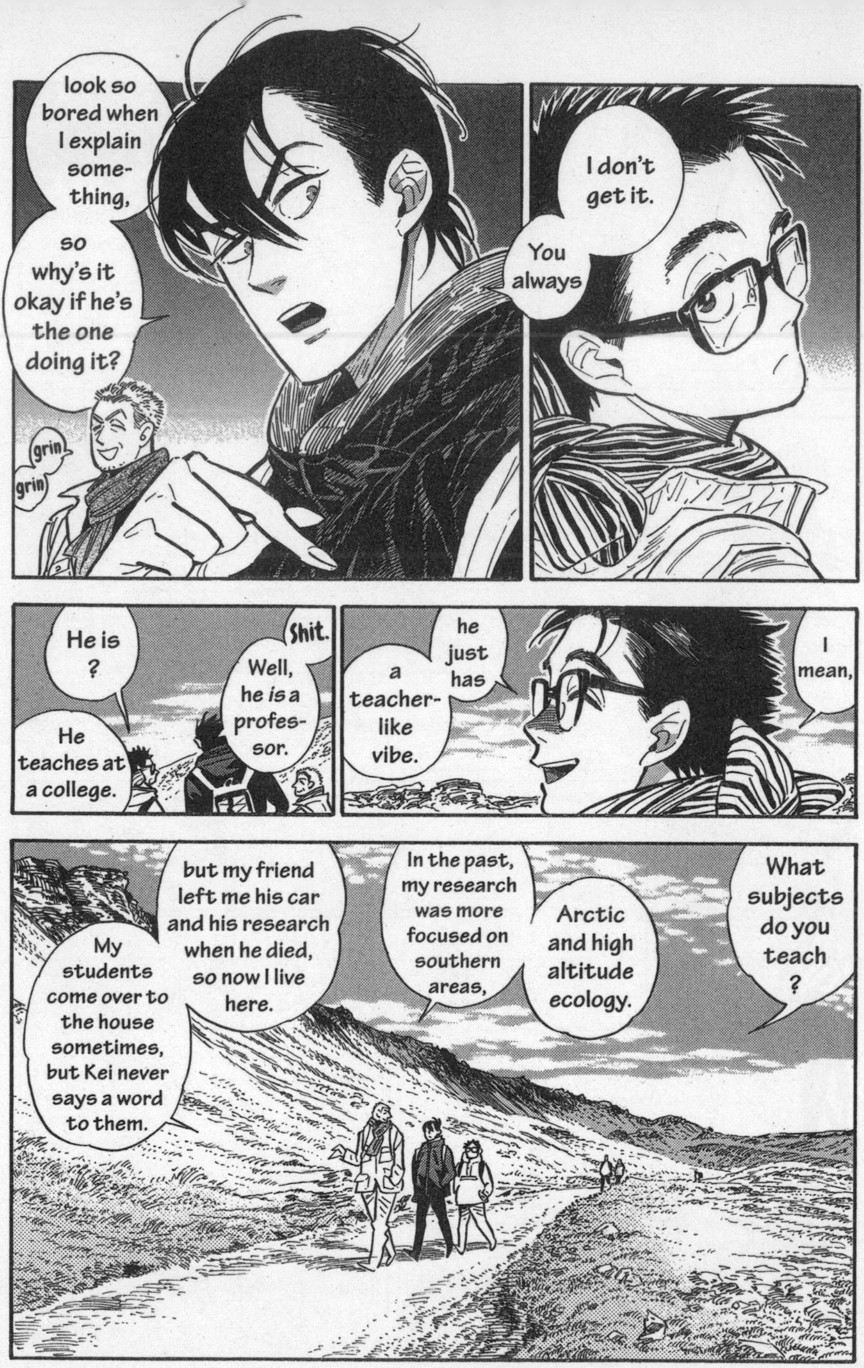
I don't get it.
You always
look so bored when I explain some-thing,
so why's it okay if he's the one doing it?
grin
grin
I mean,
he just has
a teacher-like vibe.
Shit.
Well, he *is* a profes-sor.
He is?
He teaches at a college.
What subjects do you teach?
Arctic and high altitude ecology.
In the past, my research was more focused on southern areas,
but my friend left me his car and his research when he died, so now I live here.
My students come over to the house sometimes, but Kei never says a word to them.

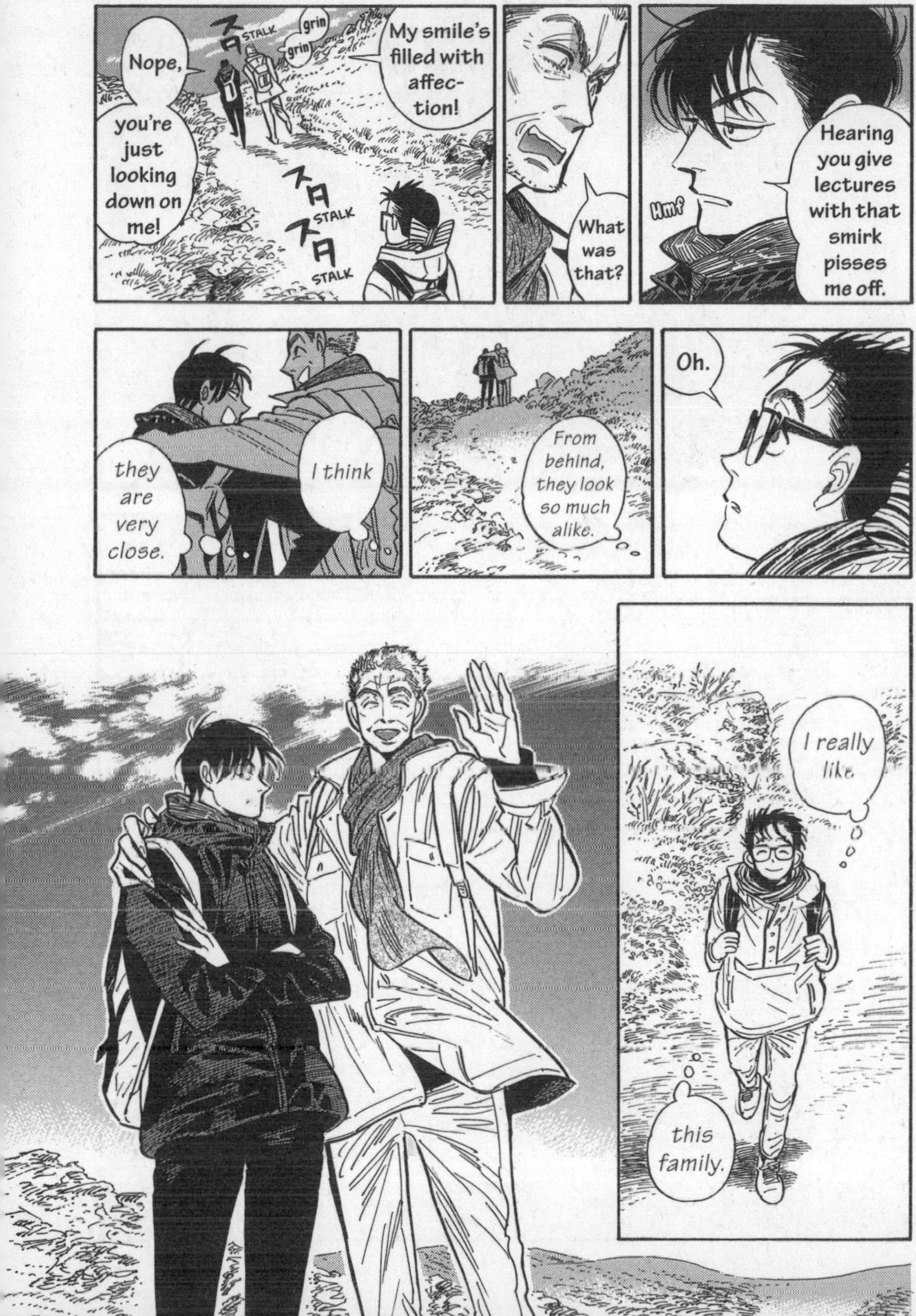
Hearing you give lectures with that smirk pisses me off.
Hmf
What was that?
My smile's filled with affec-tion!
grin
grin
スタ STALK
Nope, you're just looking down on me!
スタ STALK
スタ STALK
Oh.
From behind, they look so much alike.
I think
they are very close.
I really like
this family.

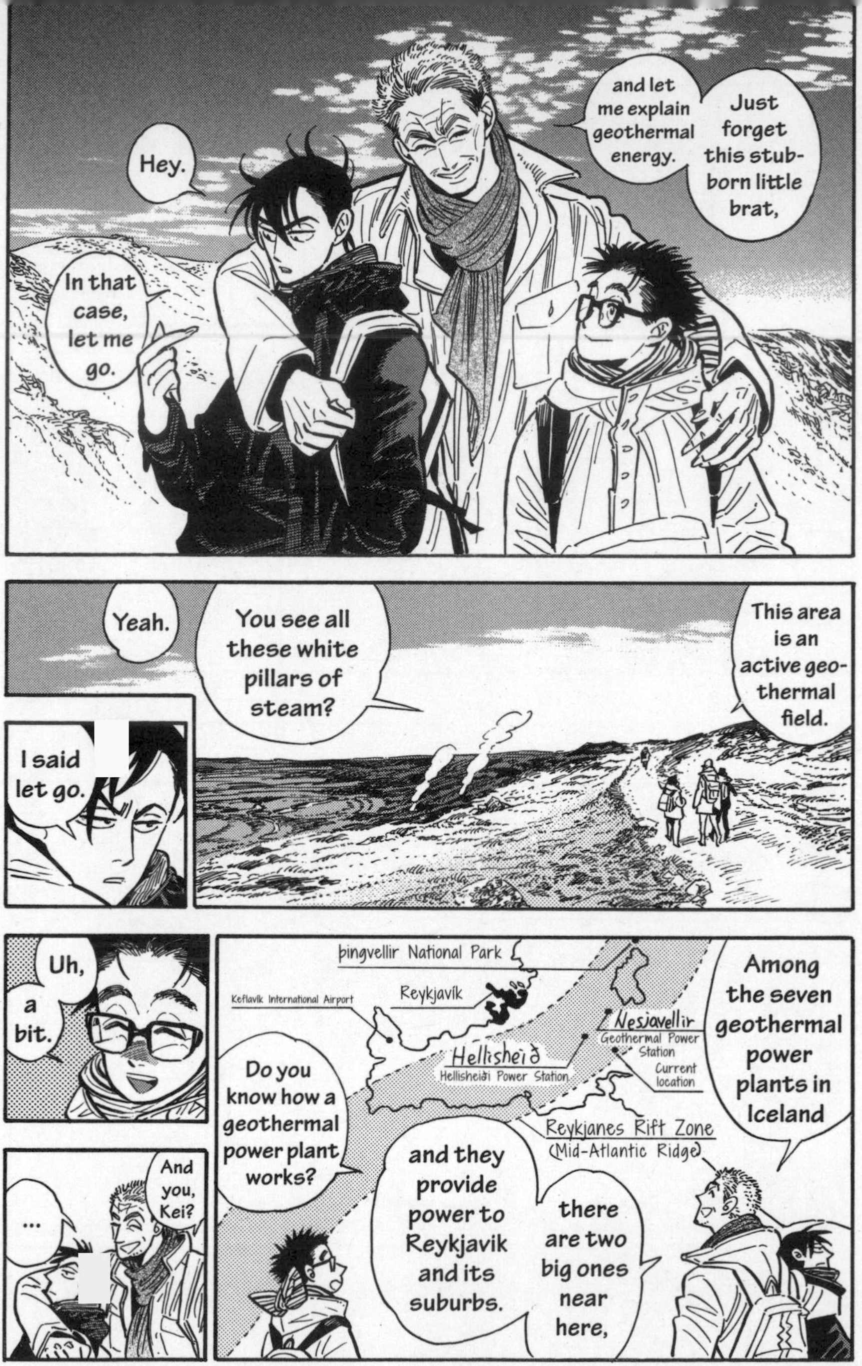
Just forget this stub-born little brat,
and let me explain geothermal energy.
Hey.
In that case, let me go.
This area is an active geo-thermal field.
You see all these white pillars of steam?
Yeah.
I said let go.
Among the seven geothermal power plants in Iceland
there are two big ones near here,
and they provide power to Reykjavik and its suburbs.
Do you know how a geothermal power plant works?
þingvellir National Park
Keflavík International Airport
Reykjavík
Nesjavellir
Geothermal Power Station
Hellisheið
Hellisheiði Power Station
Current location
Reykjanes Rift Zone
(Mid-Atlantic Ridge)
Uh, a bit.
And you, Kei?
...

You don't?
What am I gonna do with you?
All right, I'll tell you.
I've heard this like ten times already!
You just wanna hear yourself talk!
In areas where geo-thermal power is possible,
there is a layer of water under-ground that's
warmed by pock-ets of magma.
Underground water reservoir
Natural boiler
That's where they dig a well.
squip
Under-ground, the water reaches temps far above 100°C.
When you bring that up to the surface, the water explodes into steam.
You under-stand so far?
You took a trip to Geysir, right?
Yeah, yeah.
That steam moves the turbine and creates elec-tricity.
Steam
Hot water
The vapor turns into rain and falls back to earth and
the cooled water goes back under-ground.
And then
it gets warmed by the magma again, and rises to the surface.

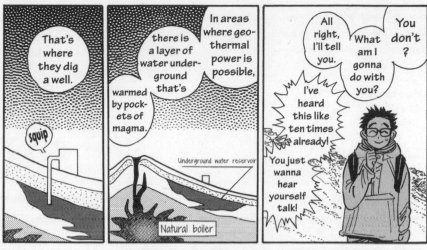

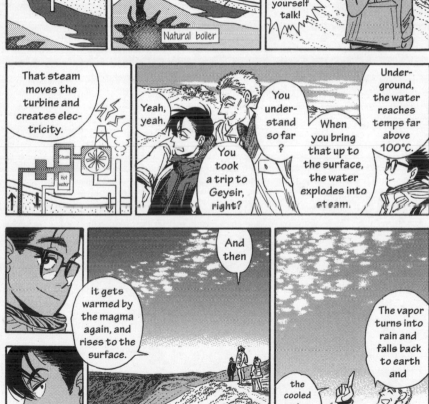

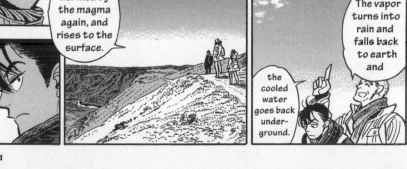

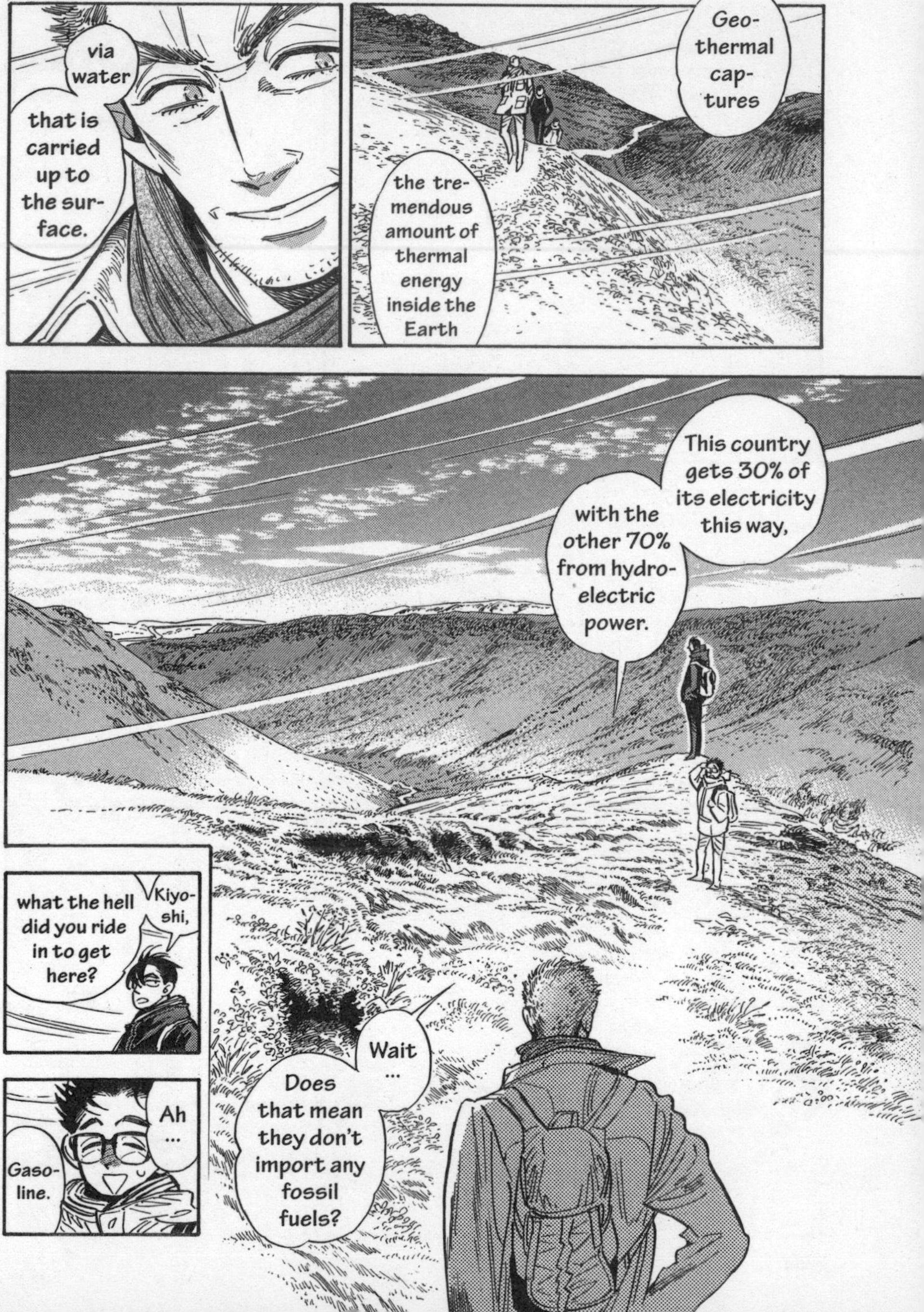

Geo- thermal cap- tures
the tre- mendous amount of thermal energy inside the Earth
via water
that is carried up to the sur- face.
This country gets 30% of its electricity this way,
with the other 70% from hydro- electric power.
Wait ...
Does that mean they don't import any fossil fuels?
Kiyo- shi,
what the hell did you ride in to get here?
Ah ...
Gaso- line.

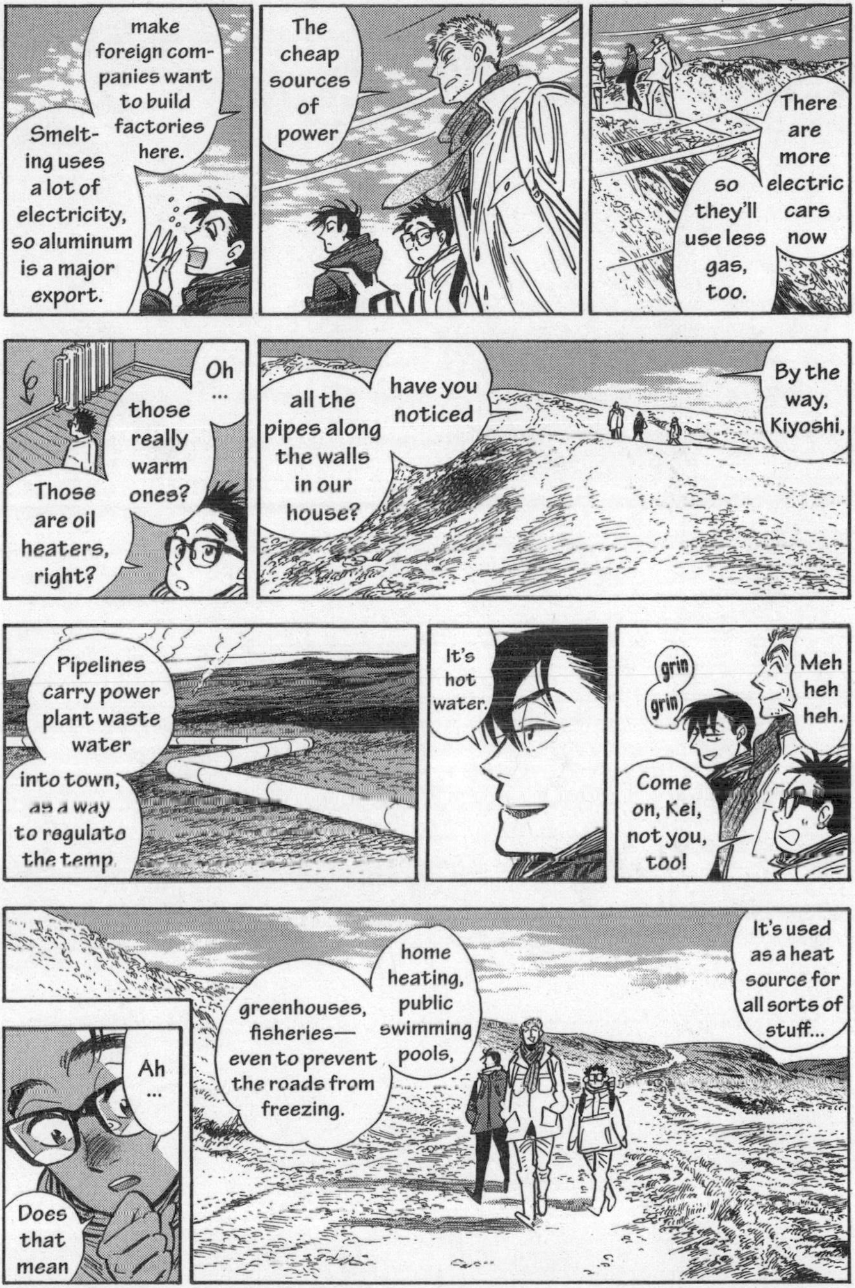
There are more electric cars now
so they'll use less gas, too.
The cheap sources of power
make foreign companies want to build factories here.
Smelting uses a lot of electricity, so aluminum is a major export.
By the way, Kiyoshi,
have you noticed
all the pipes along the walls in our house?
Oh ...
those really warm ones?
Those are oil heaters, right?
Meh heh heh.
grin
grin
Come on, Kei, not you, too!
It's hot water.
Pipelines carry power plant waste water
into town, as a way to regulate the temp.
It's used as a heat source for all sorts of stuff...
home heating, public swimming pools,
greenhouses, fisheries— even to prevent the roads from freezing.
Ah ...
Does that mean

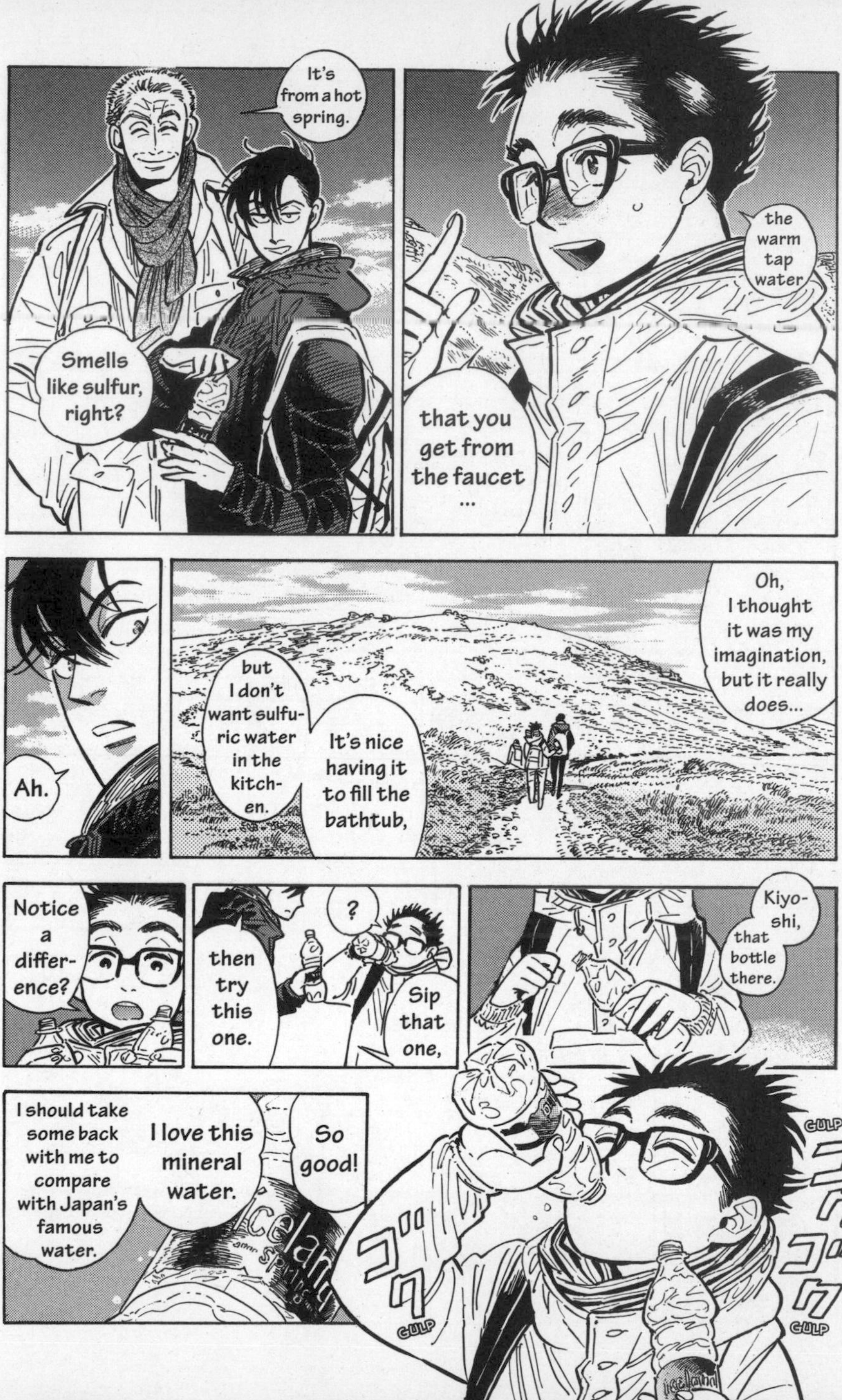
the warm tap water
that you get from the faucet ...
It's from a hot spring.
Smells like sulfur, right?
Oh, I thought it was my imagination, but it really does...
It's nice having it to fill the bathtub,
but I don't want sulfuric water in the kitchen.
Ah.
Kiyoshi, that bottle there.
?
Sip that one,
then try this one.
Notice a difference?
GULP
ゴクゴク
GULP
So good!
I love this mineral water.
I should take some back with me to compare with Japan's famous water.
ゴク
GULP

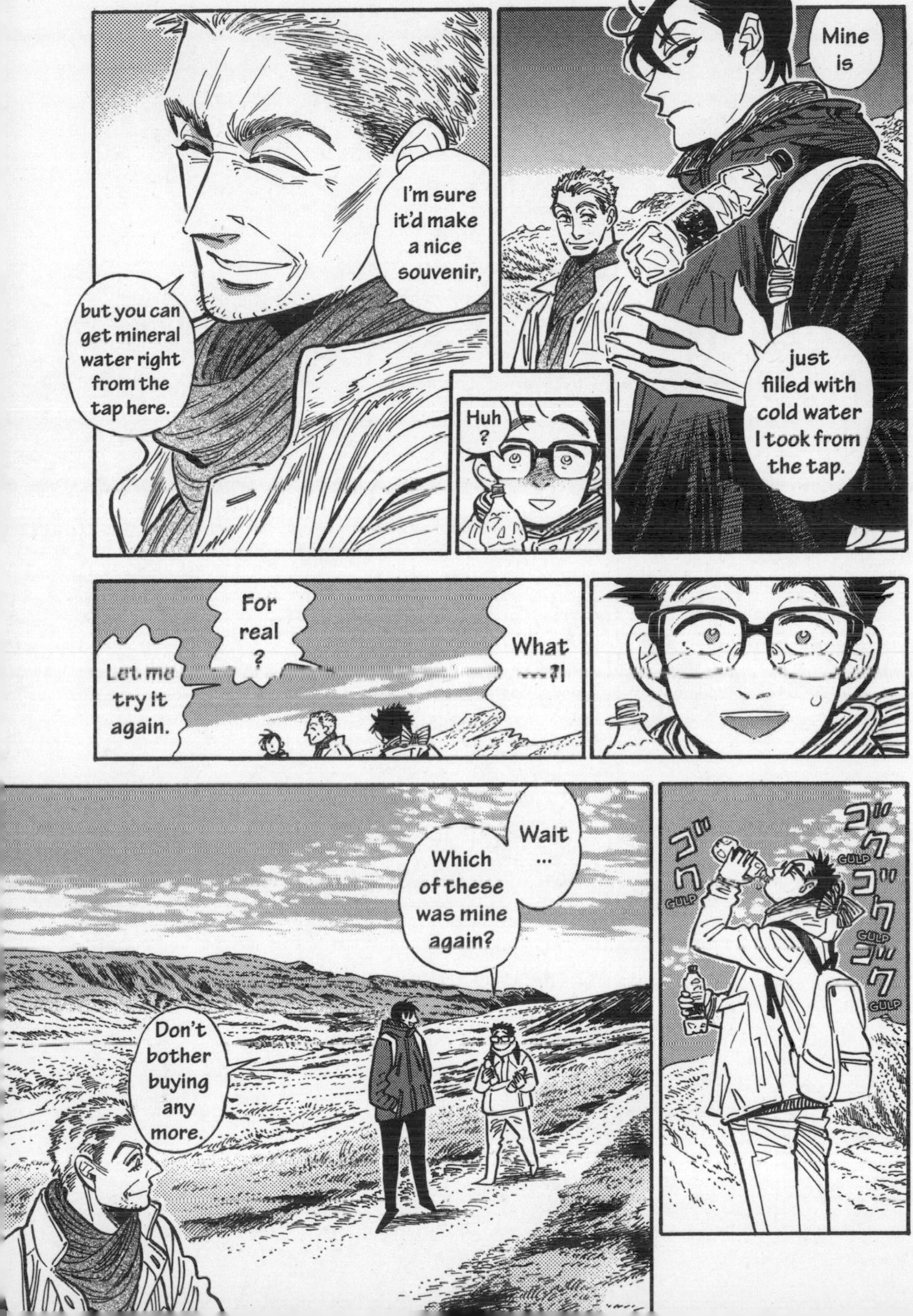
Mine is
just filled with cold water I took from the tap.
Huh?
I'm sure it'd make a nice souvenir,
but you can get mineral water right from the tap here.
What …?!
For real?
Let me try it again.
ゴク
GULP
ゴク
GULP
ゴク
GULP
ゴク
GULP
Wait …
Which of these was mine again?
Don't bother buying any more.

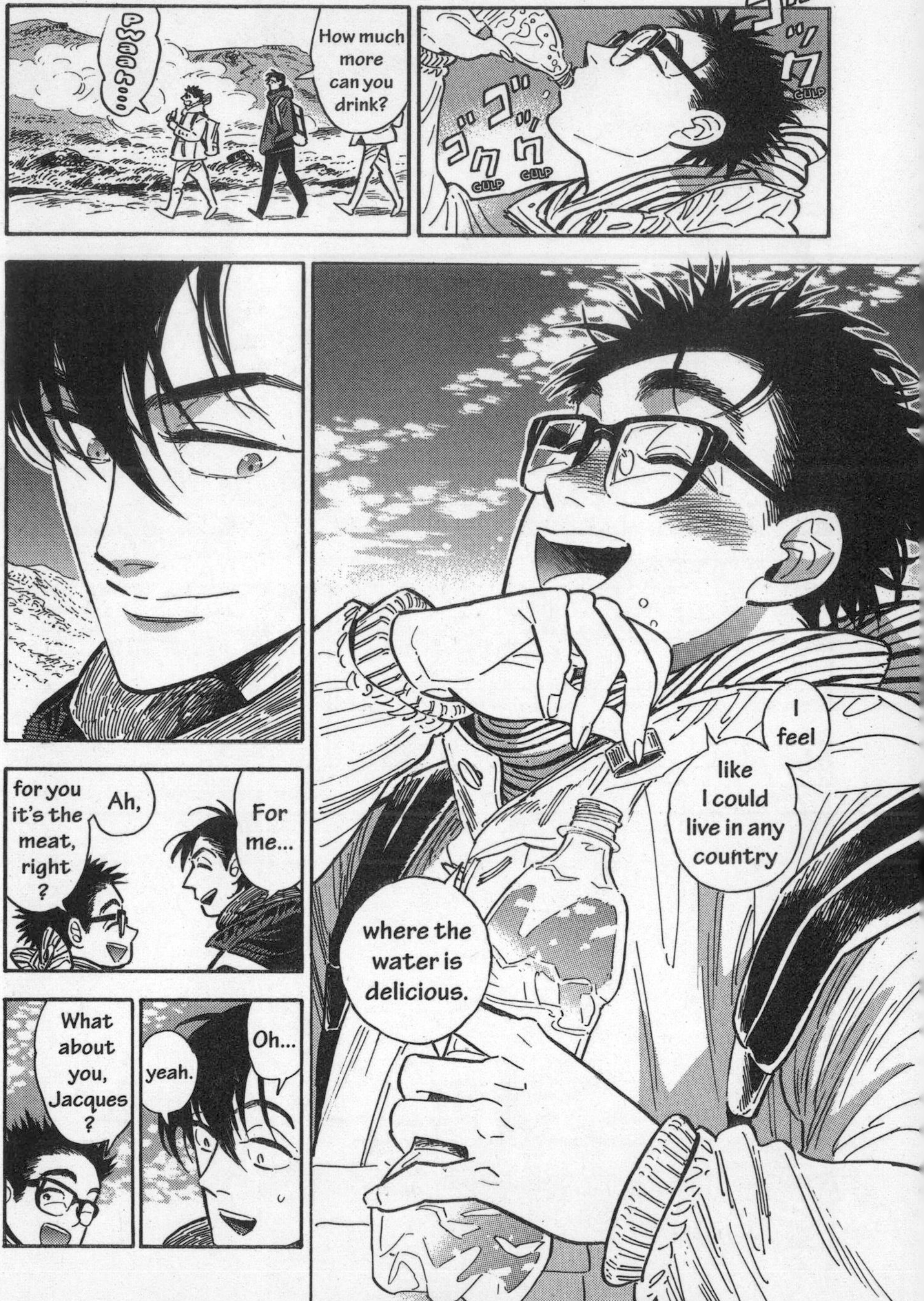
GULP
GULP
GULP
How much more can you drink?
Pwaah...
I feel like I could live in any country
where the water is delicious.
For me...
Ah,
for you it's the meat, right?
Oh...
yeah.
What about you, Jacques?

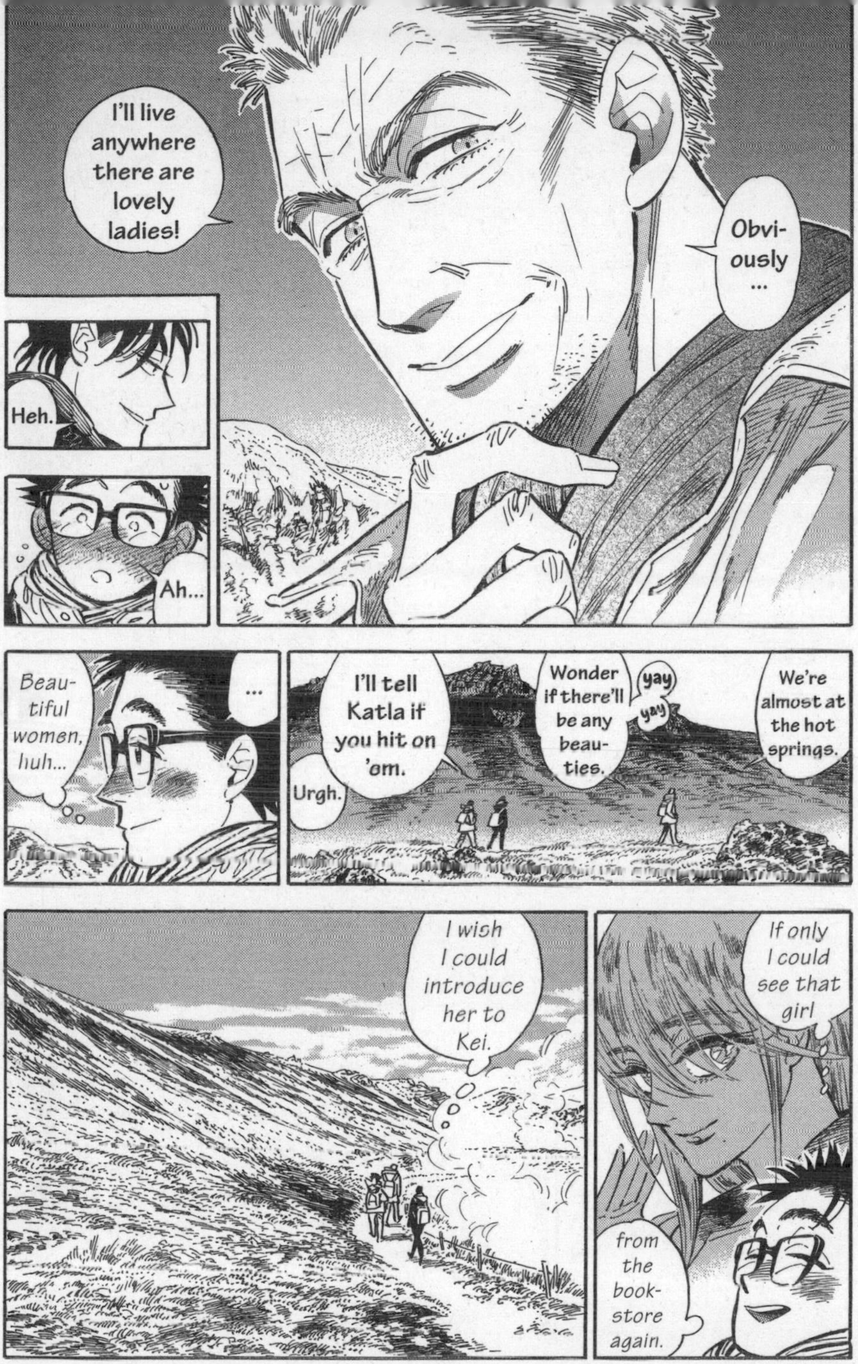

Obvi-ously...
I'll live anywhere there are lovely ladies!
Heh.
Ah...
We're almost at the hot springs.
yay
yay
Wonder if there'll be any beau-ties.
I'll tell Katla if you hit on 'em.
Urgh.
...
Beau-tiful women, huh...
If only I could see that girl
from the book-store again.
I wish I could introduce her to Kei.

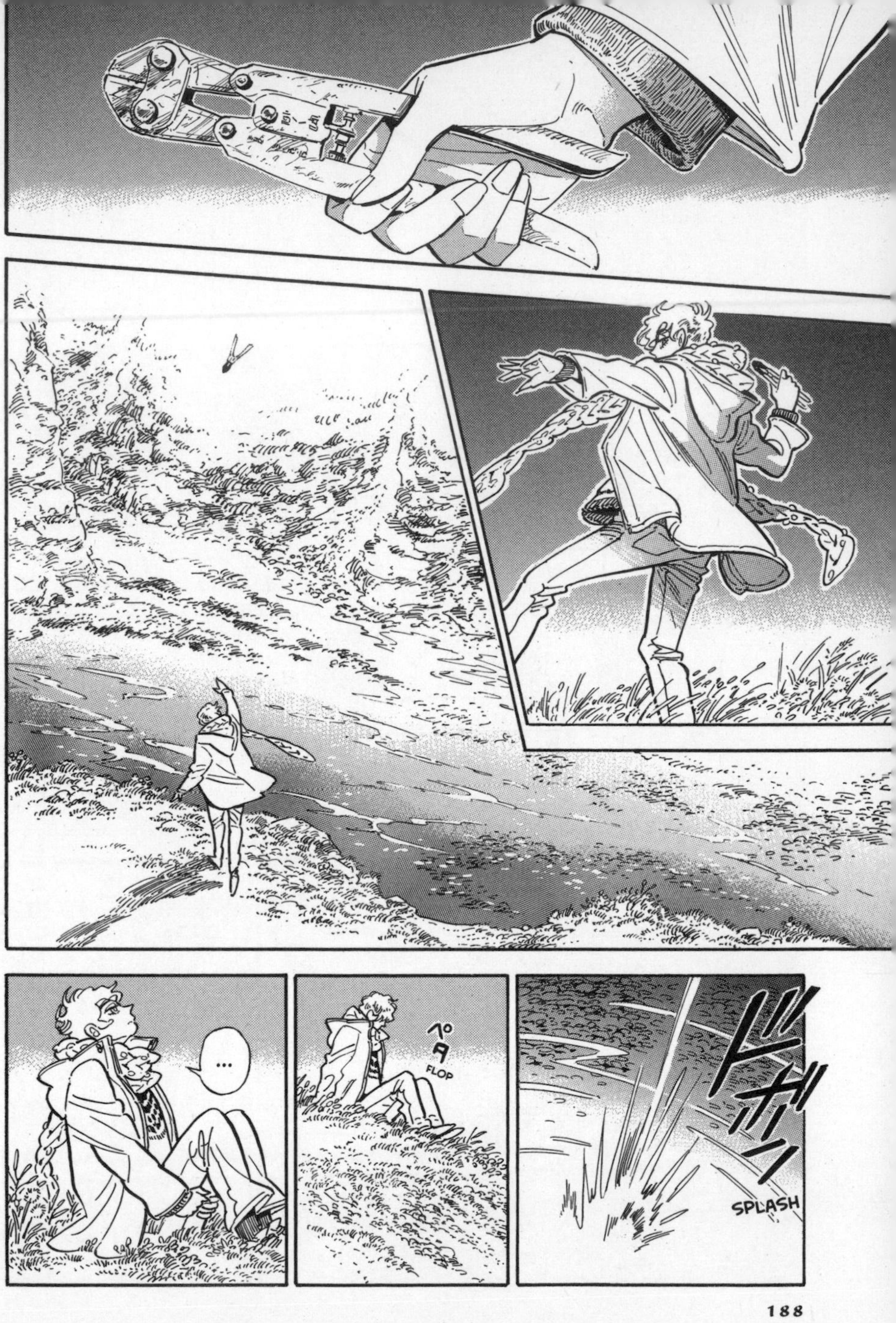
ドボン
SPLASH
ペタ
FLOP
...

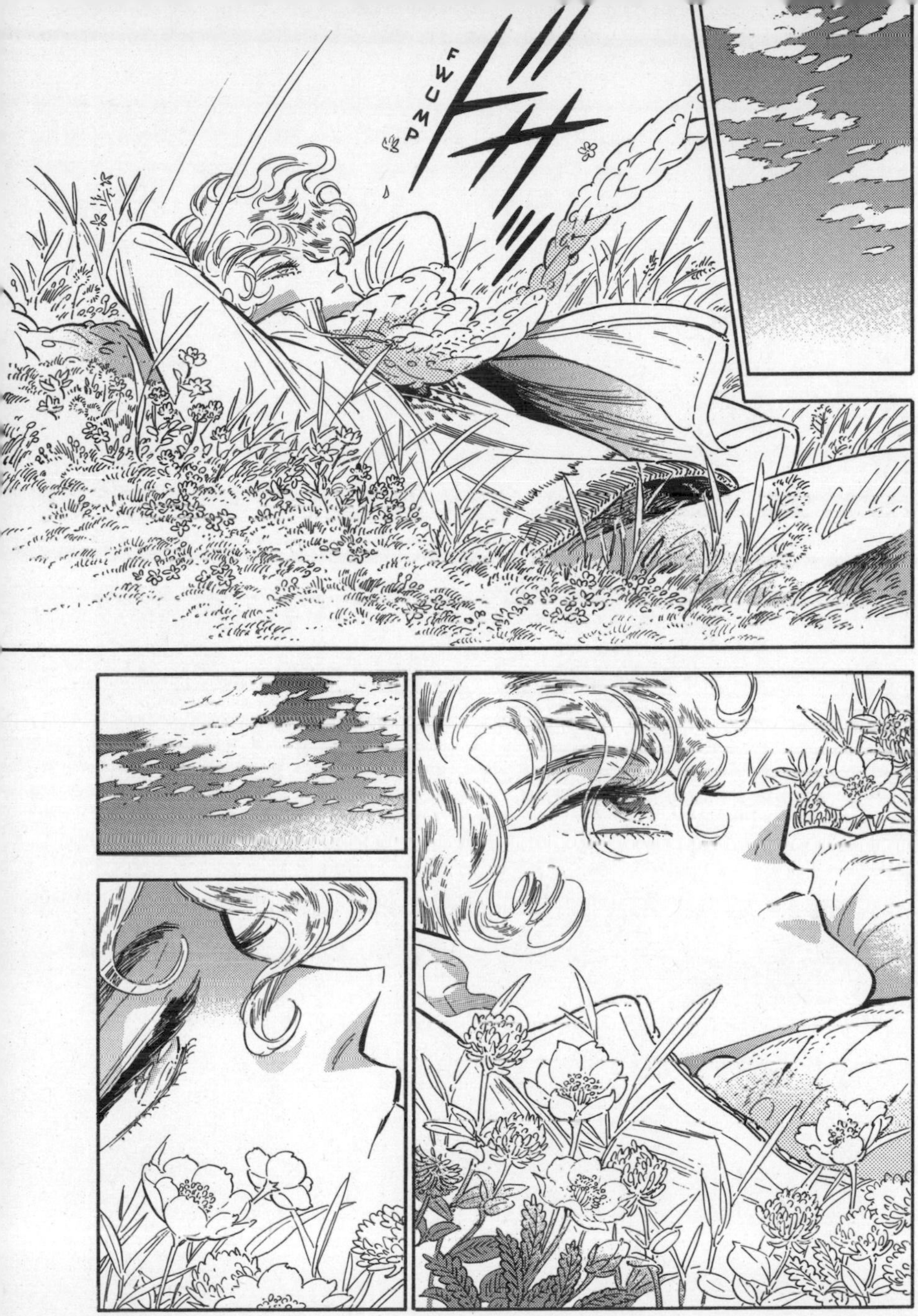
FWUMP

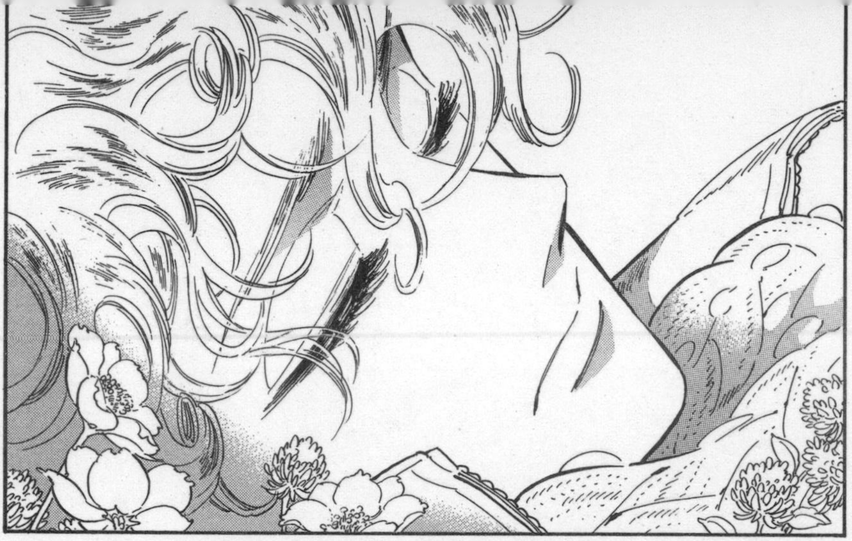

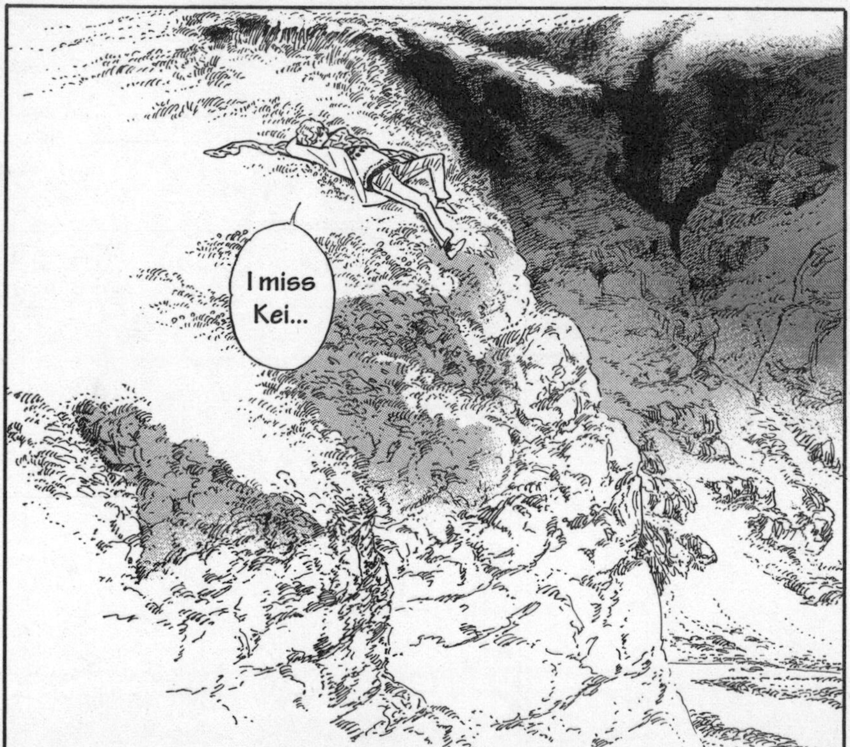
I miss Kei...

Chapter 17 – End

Chapter 18 [átjándi]

Fairies play in steam

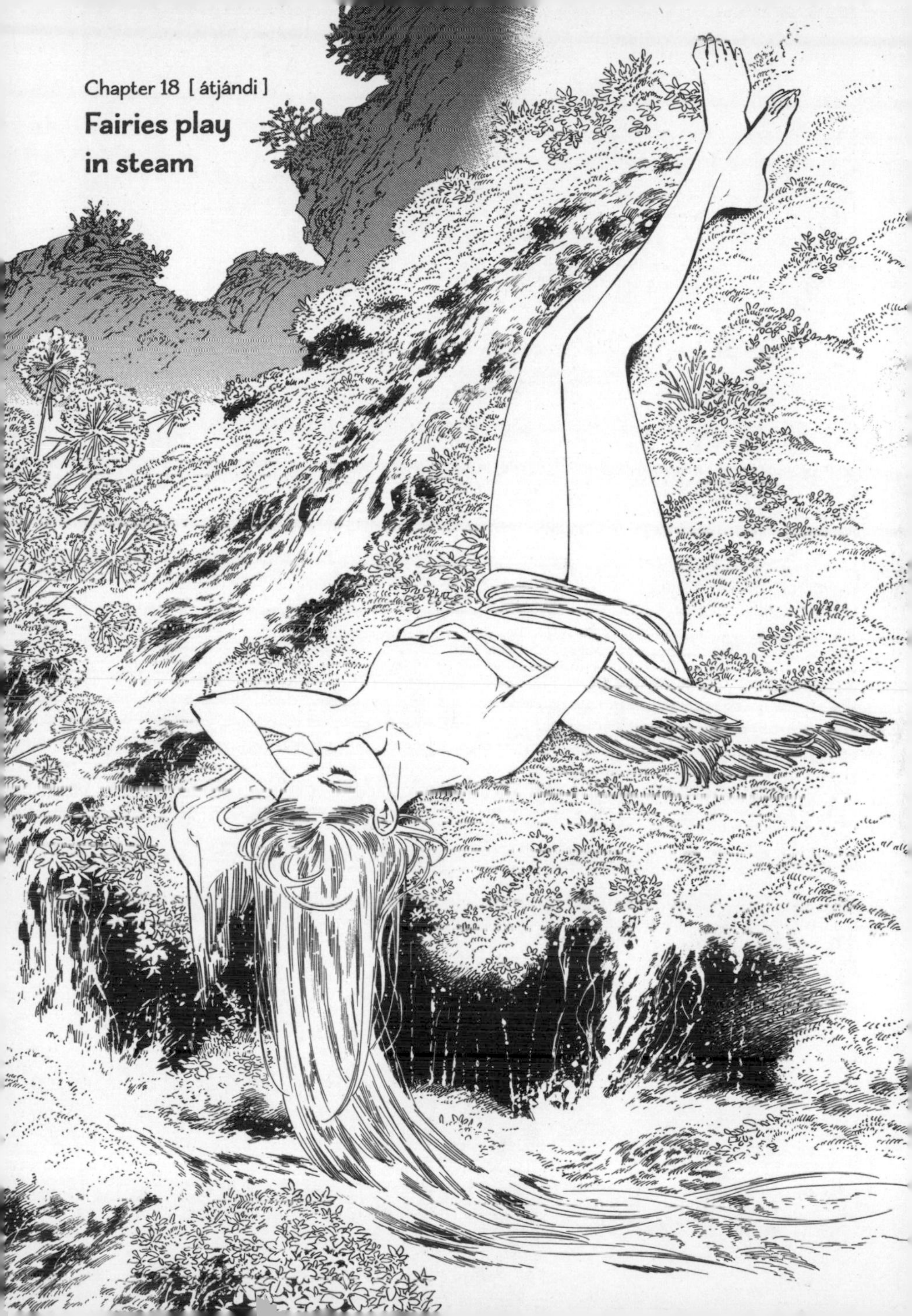

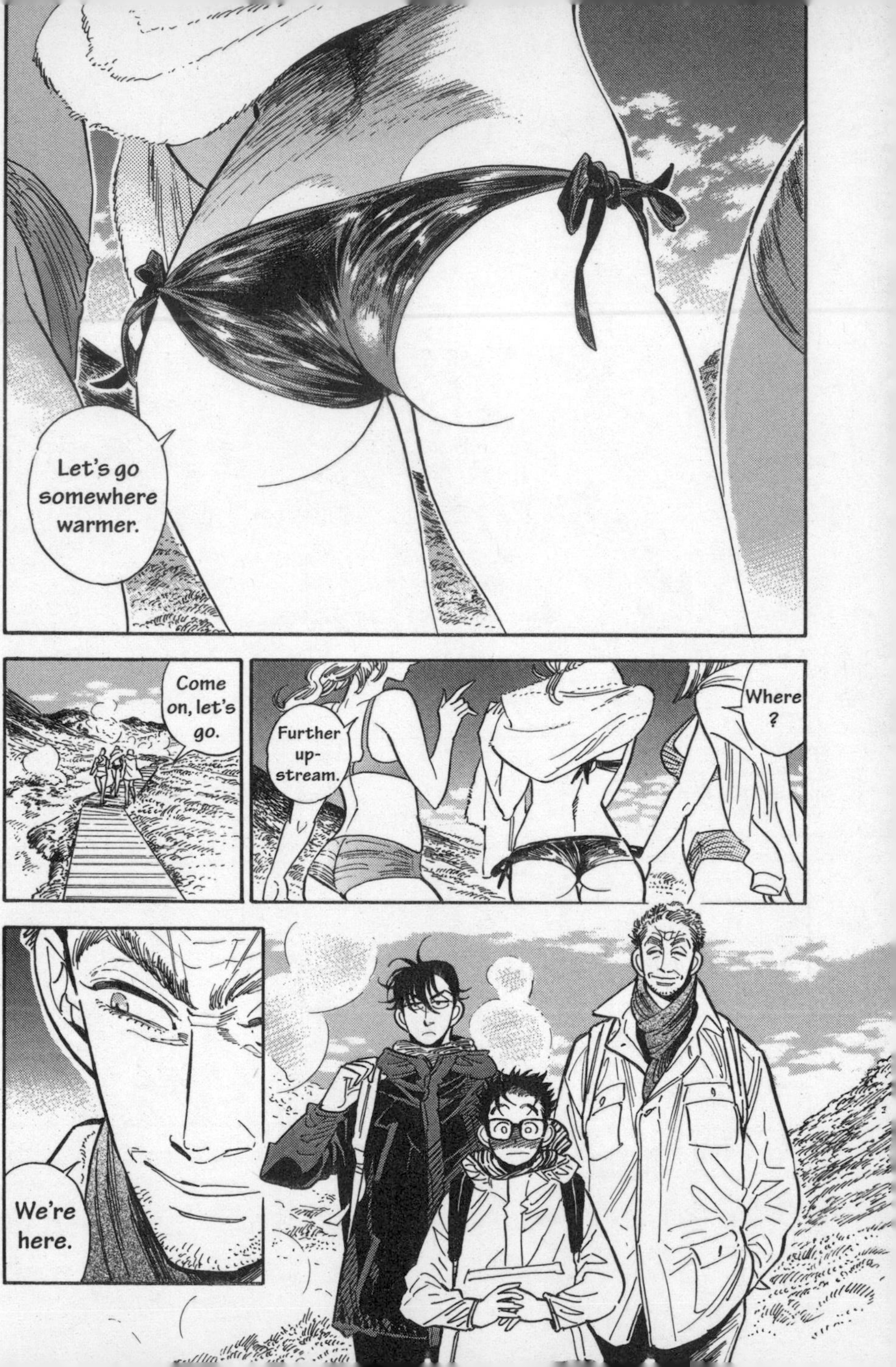
Let's go somewhere warmer.
Where ?
Further up-stream.
Come on, let's go.
We're here.

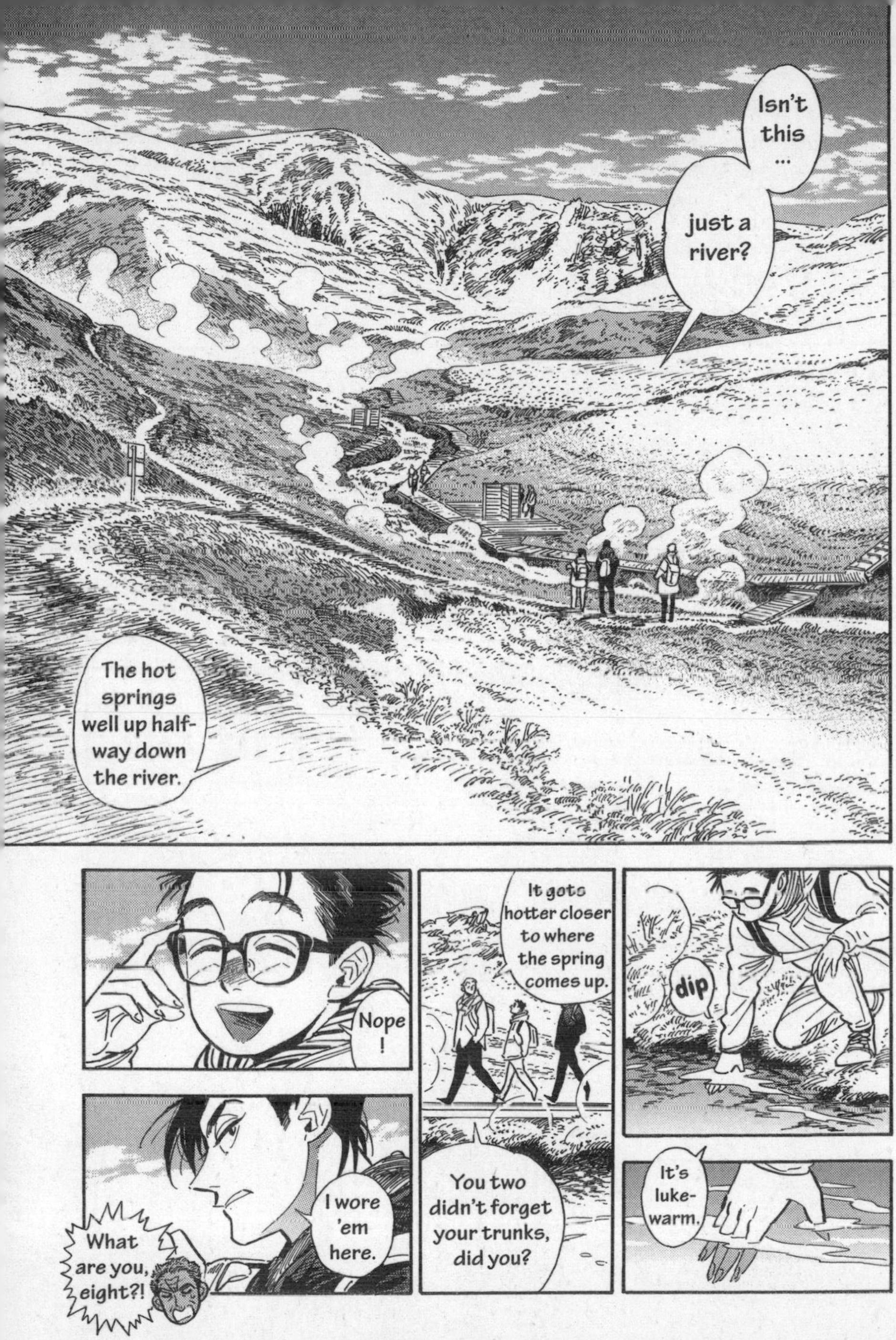
Isn't this ... just a river?
The hot springs well up half-way down the river.
dip
It's luke-warm.
It gets hotter closer to where the spring comes up.
You two didn't forget your trunks, did you?
Nope!
I wore 'em here.
What are you, eight?!

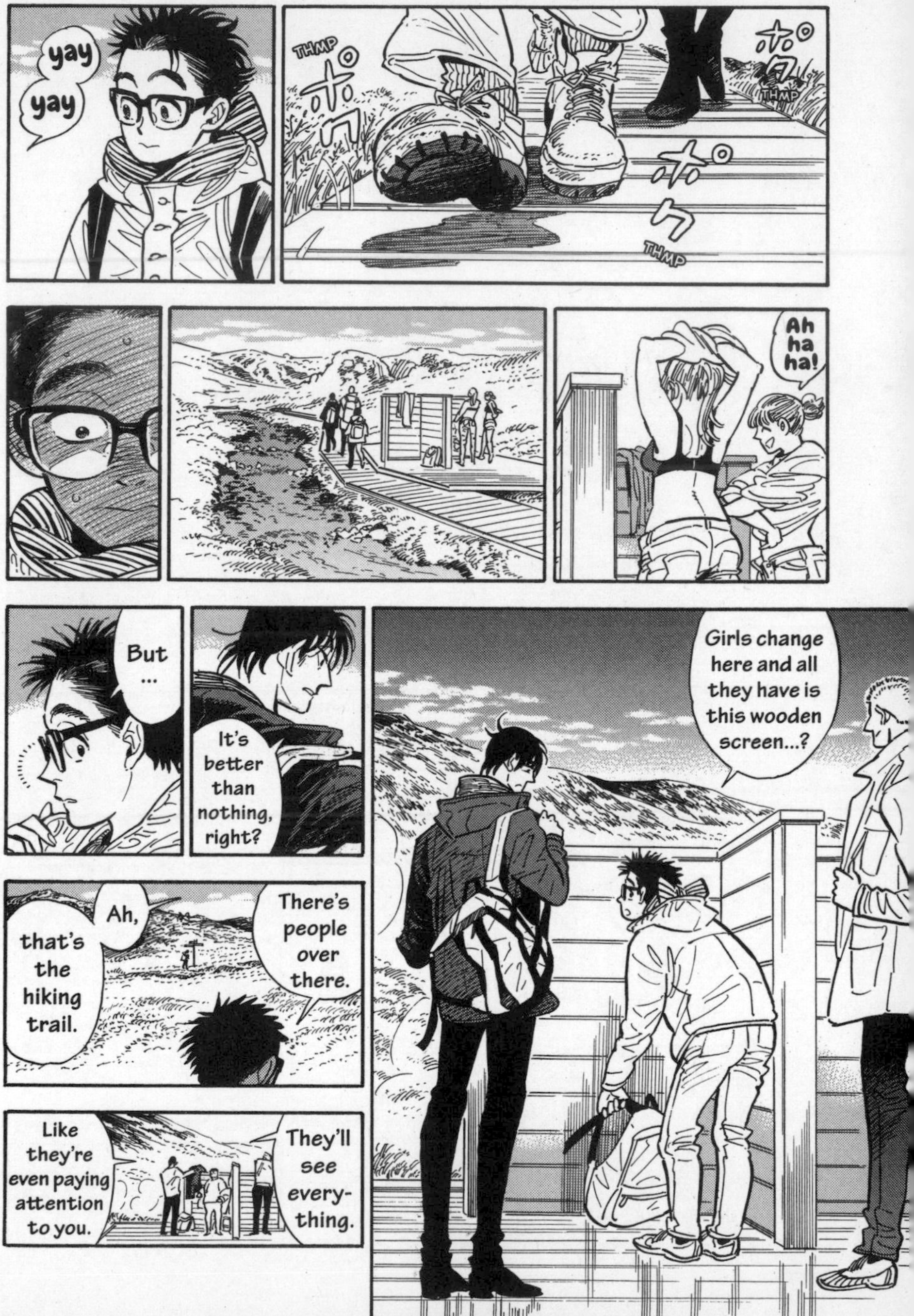
ポク
THMP
ポク
THMP
THMP
ポク
yay yay
Ah ha ha!
Girls change here and all they have is this wooden screen...?
It's better than nothing, right?
But ...
There's people over there.
Ah, that's the hiking trail.
They'll see everything.
Like they're even paying attention to you.

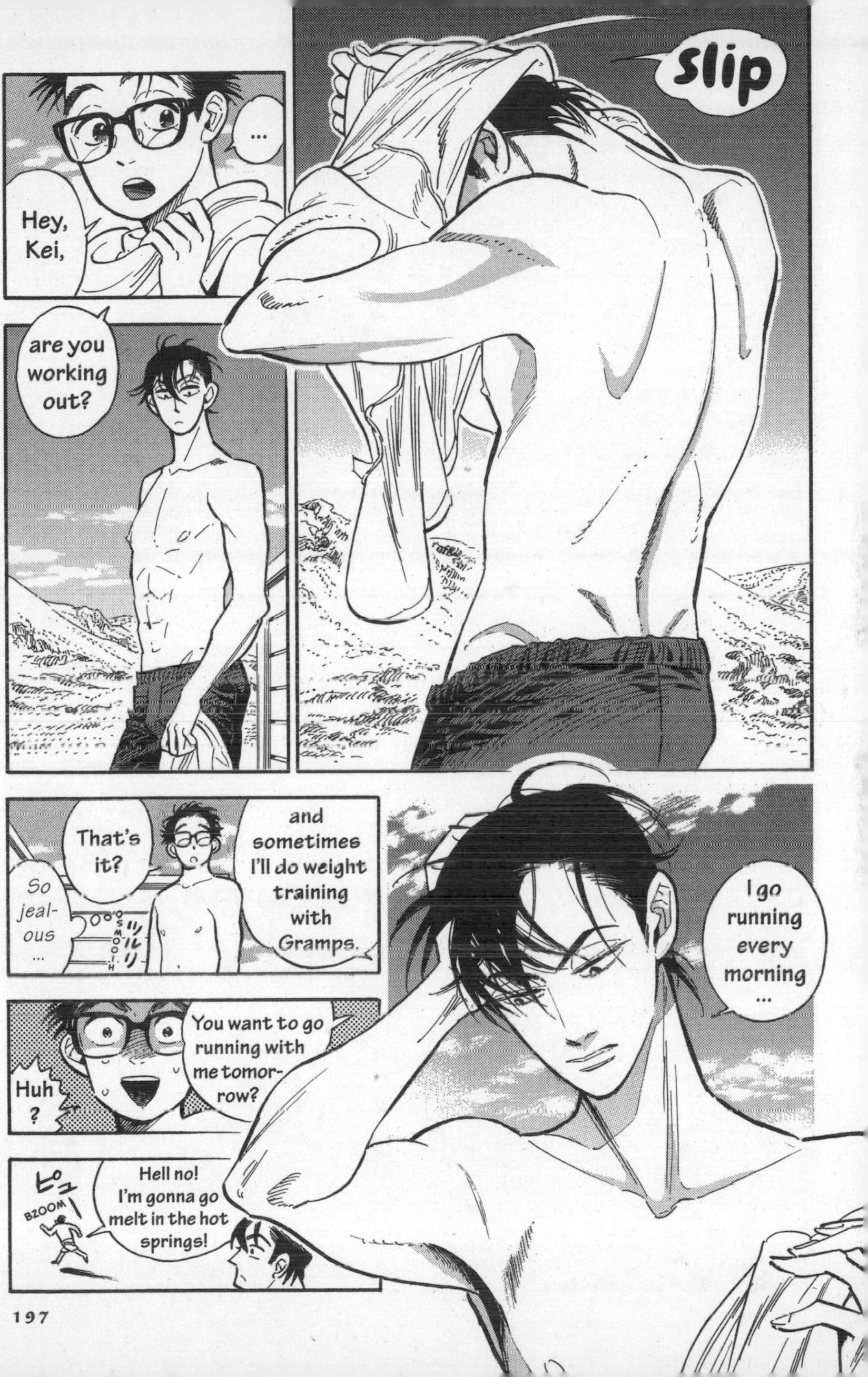
slip
...
Hey, Kei,
are you working out?
I go running every morning ...
and sometimes I'll do weight training with Gramps.
That's it?
So jeal-ous ...
SMOOTH
You want to go running with me tomor-row?
Huh?
Hell no! I'm gonna go melt in the hot springs!
BZOOM

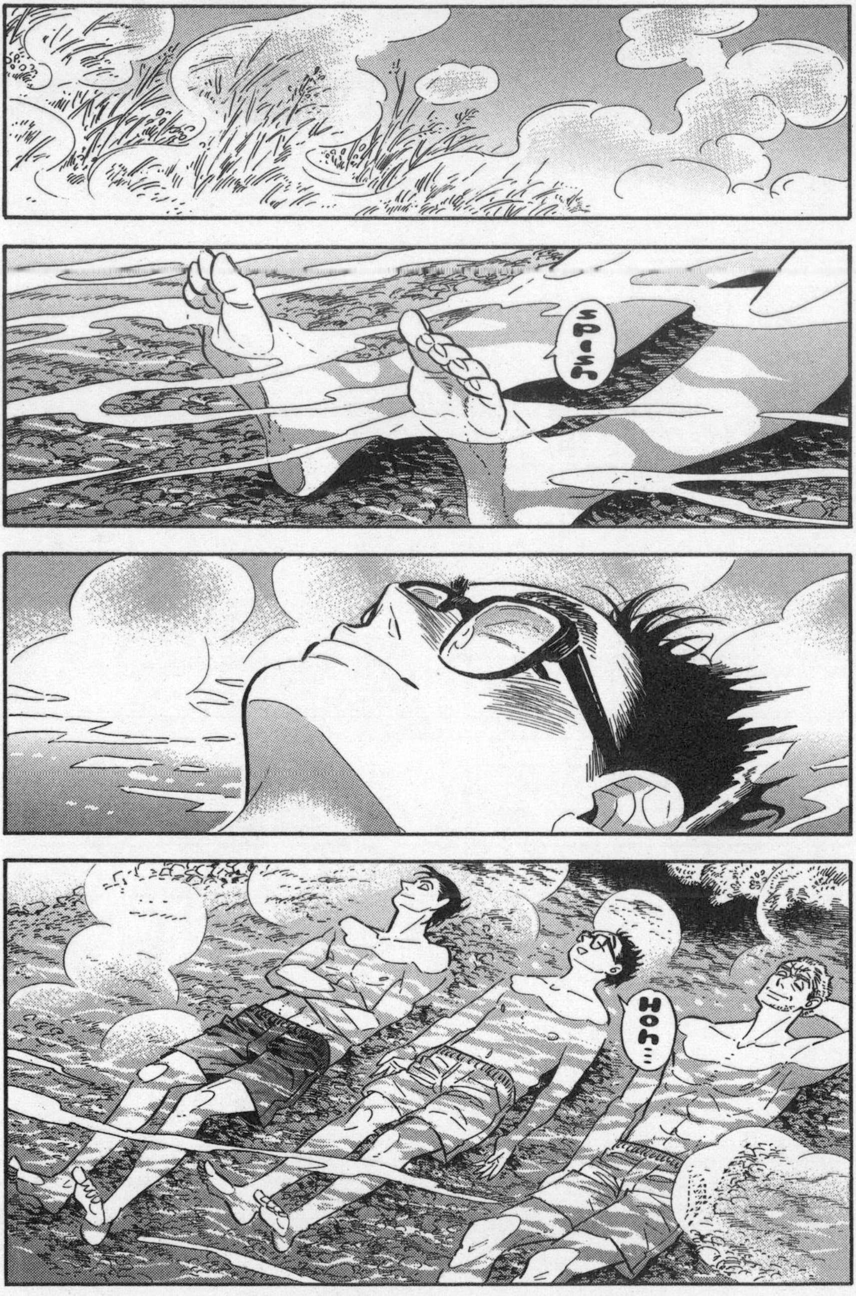
splish
...
Hoh...

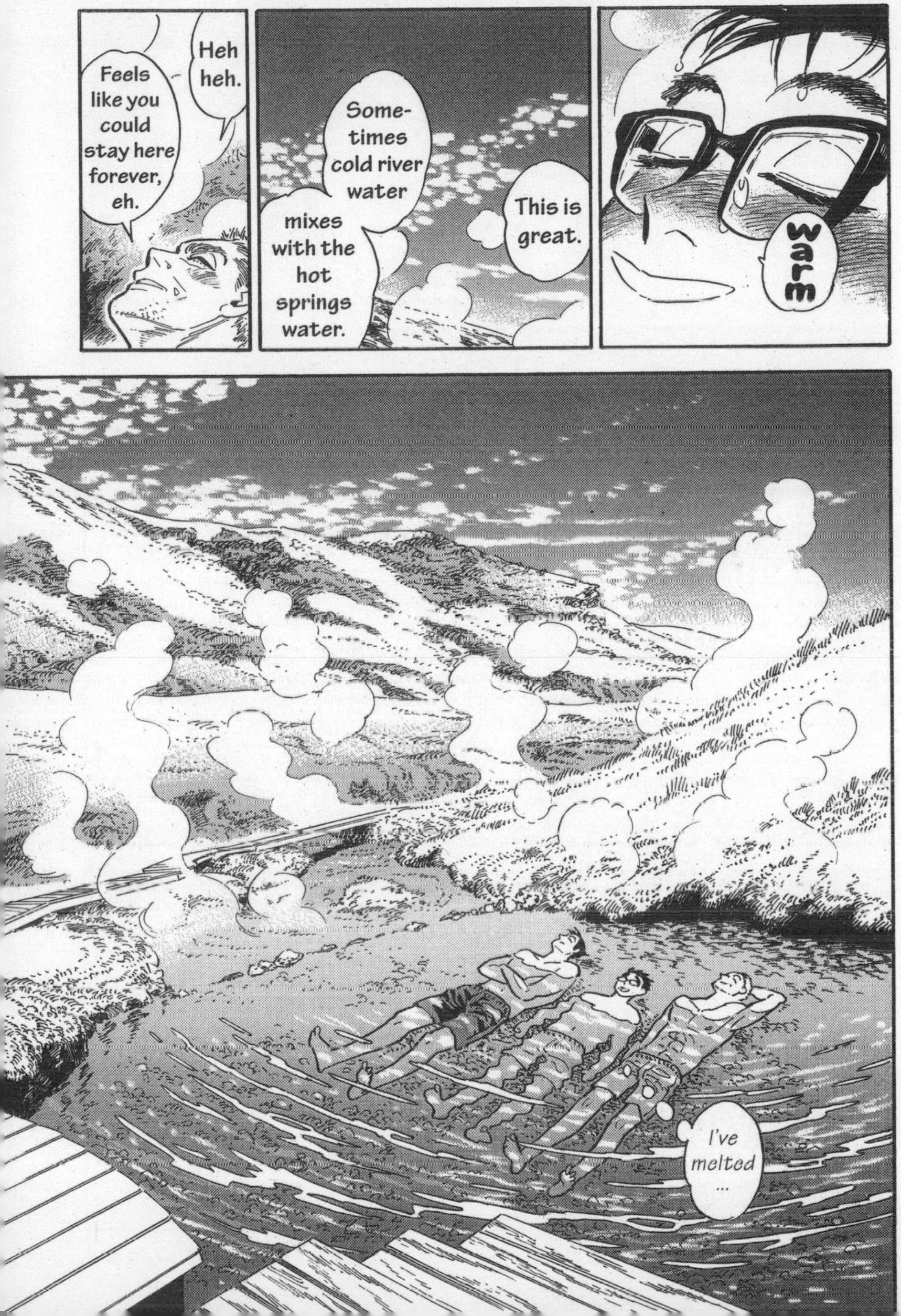
warm
This is great.
Some-times cold river water
mixes with the hot springs water.
Heh heh.
Feels like you could stay here forever, eh.
I've melted ...

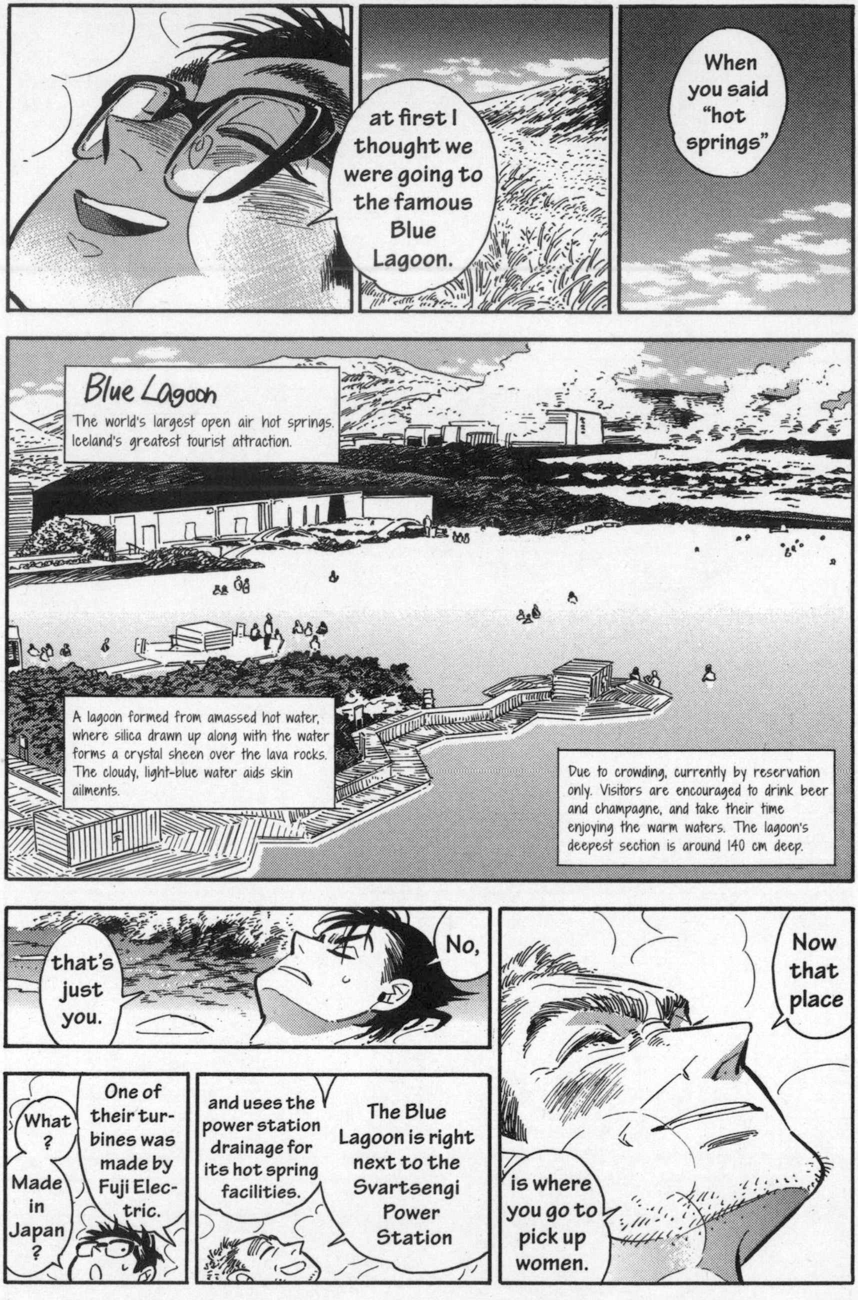
When you said "hot springs"
at first I thought we were going to the famous Blue Lagoon.
Blue Lagoon
The world's largest open air hot springs. Iceland's greatest tourist attraction.
A lagoon formed from amassed hot water, where silica drawn up along with the water forms a crystal sheen over the lava rocks. The cloudy, light-blue water aids skin ailments.
Due to crowding, currently by reservation only. Visitors are encouraged to drink beer and champagne, and take their time enjoying the warm waters. The lagoon's deepest section is around 140 cm deep.
Now that place
is where you go to pick up women.
No,
that's just you.
The Blue Lagoon is right next to the Svartsengi Power Station
and uses the power station drainage for its hot spring facilities.
One of their turbines was made by Fuji Electric.
What? Made in Japan?

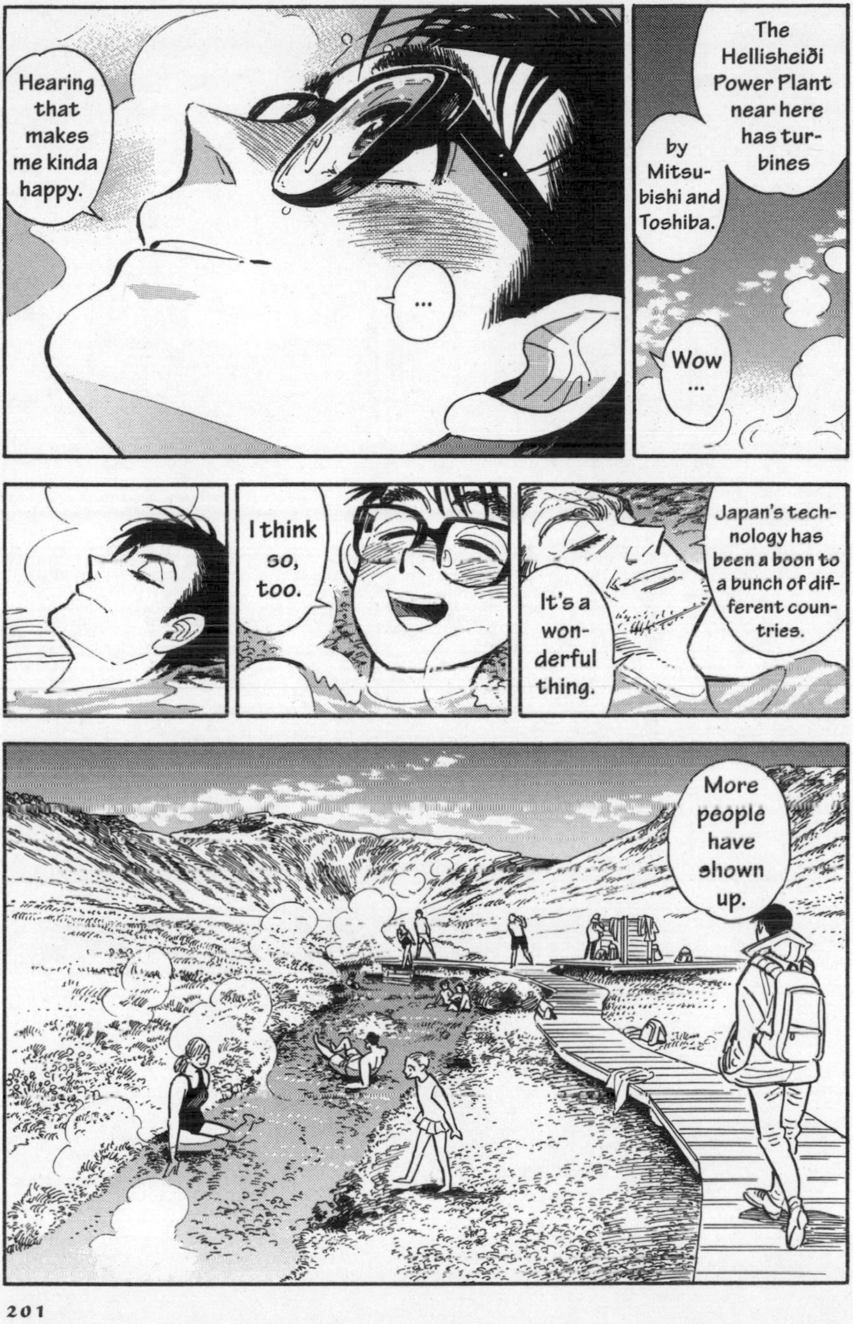
The Hellisheiði Power Plant near here has turbines
by Mitsubishi and Toshiba.
Wow ...
...
Hearing that makes me kinda happy.
Japan's technology has been a boon to a bunch of different countries.
It's a wonderful thing.
I think so, too.
More people have shown up.

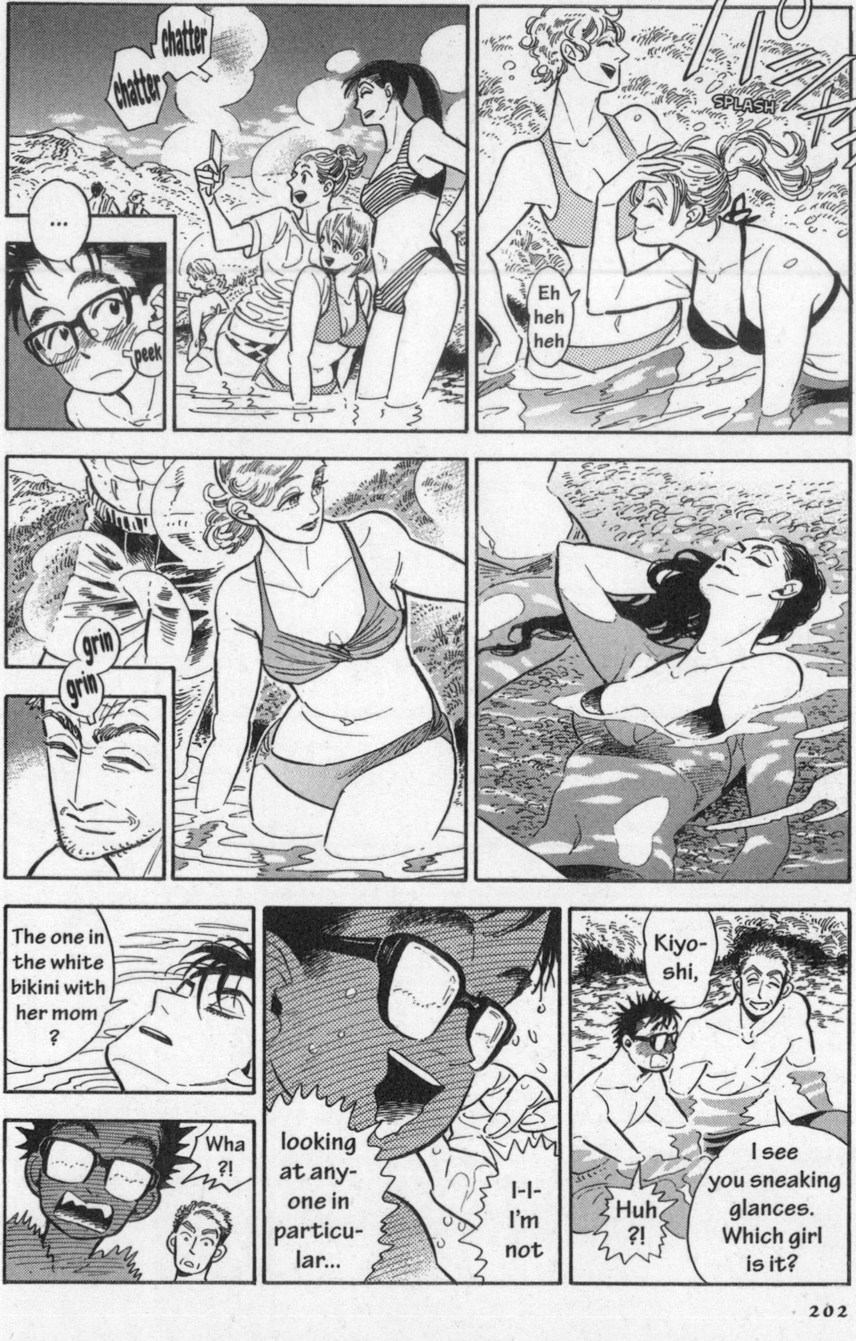

SPLASH
Eh heh heh
chatter
chatter
...
peek
...
grin
grin
Kiyo-shi,
I see you sneaking glances. Which girl is it?
Huh?!
I-I-I'm not
looking at any-one in particu-lar...
The one in the white bikini with her mom?
Wha?!

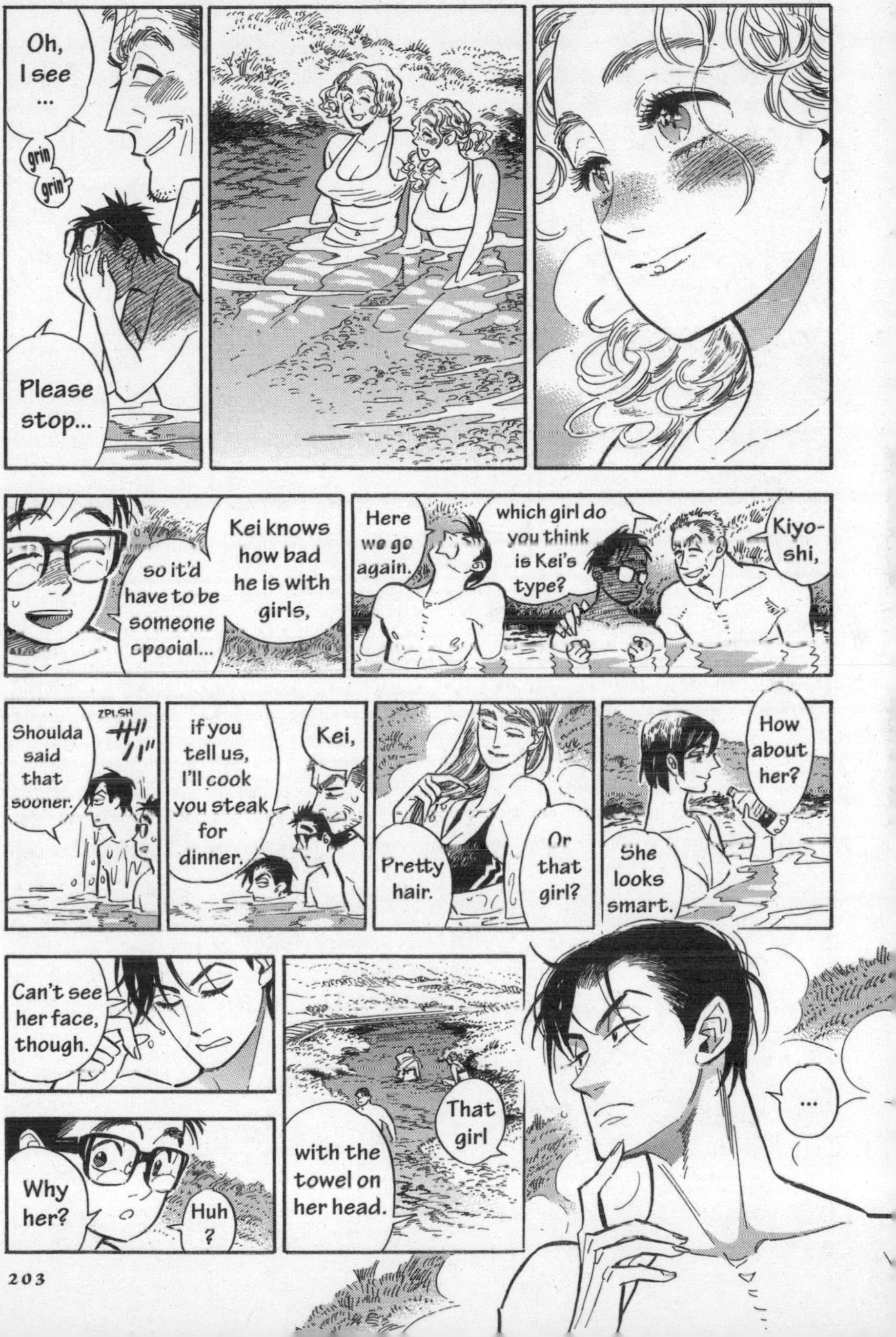

Oh, I see ...
grin
grin
Please stop...
Kiyo-shi,
which girl do you think is Kei's type?
Here we go again.
Kei knows how bad he is with girls,
so it'd have to be someone special...
How about her?
She looks smart.
Or that girl?
Pretty hair.
Kei,
if you tell us, I'll cook you steak for dinner.
ZPLSH
Shoulda said that sooner.
...
That girl
with the towel on her head.
Can't see her face, though.
Huh?
Why her?

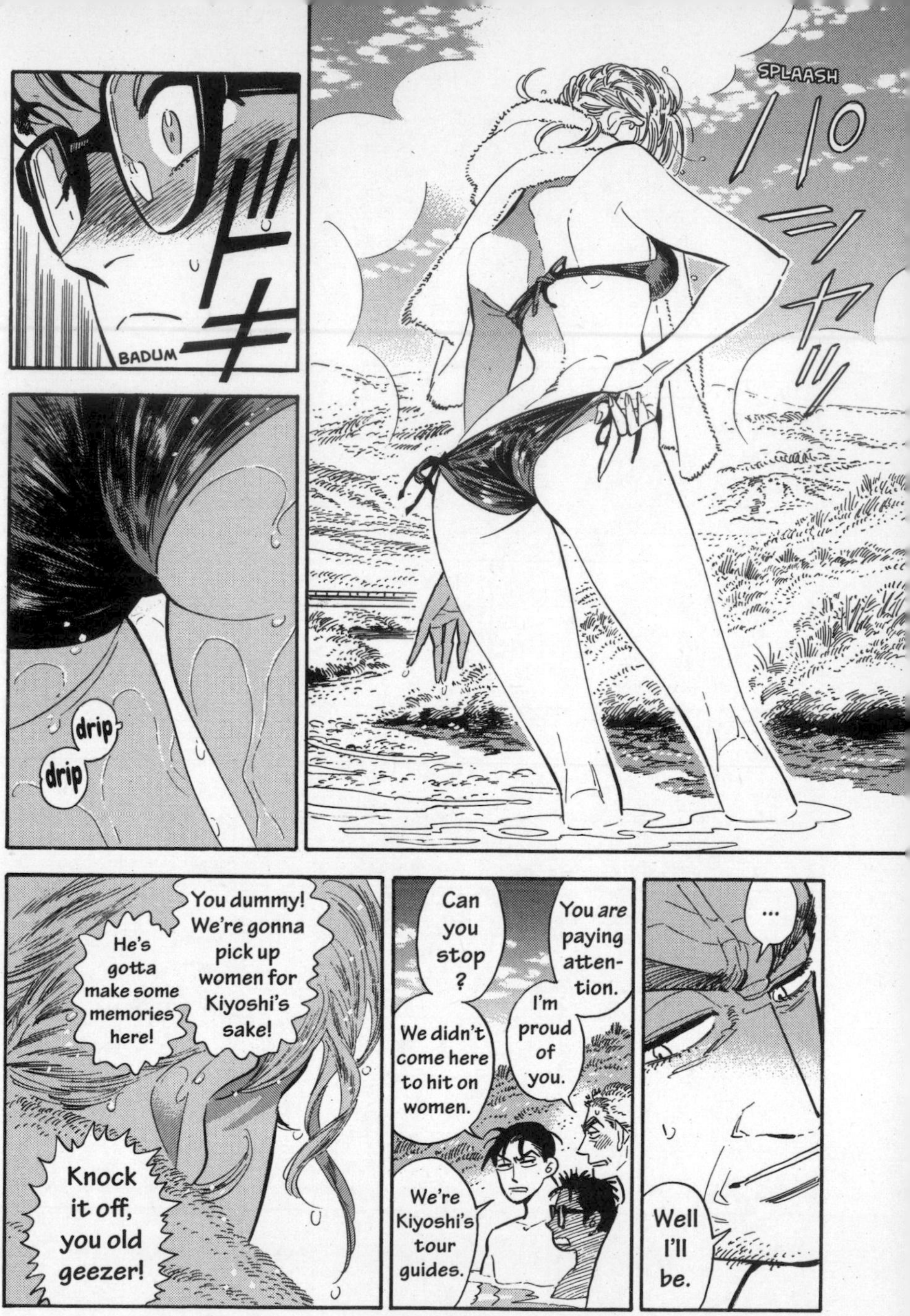
SPLAASH
BADUM
drip
drip
...
Well I'll be.
You *are* paying attention.
Can you stop?
I'm proud of you.
We didn't come here to hit on women.
We're Kiyoshi's tour guides.
You dummy! We're gonna pick up women for Kiyoshi's sake!
He's gotta make some memories here!
Knock it off, you old geezer!

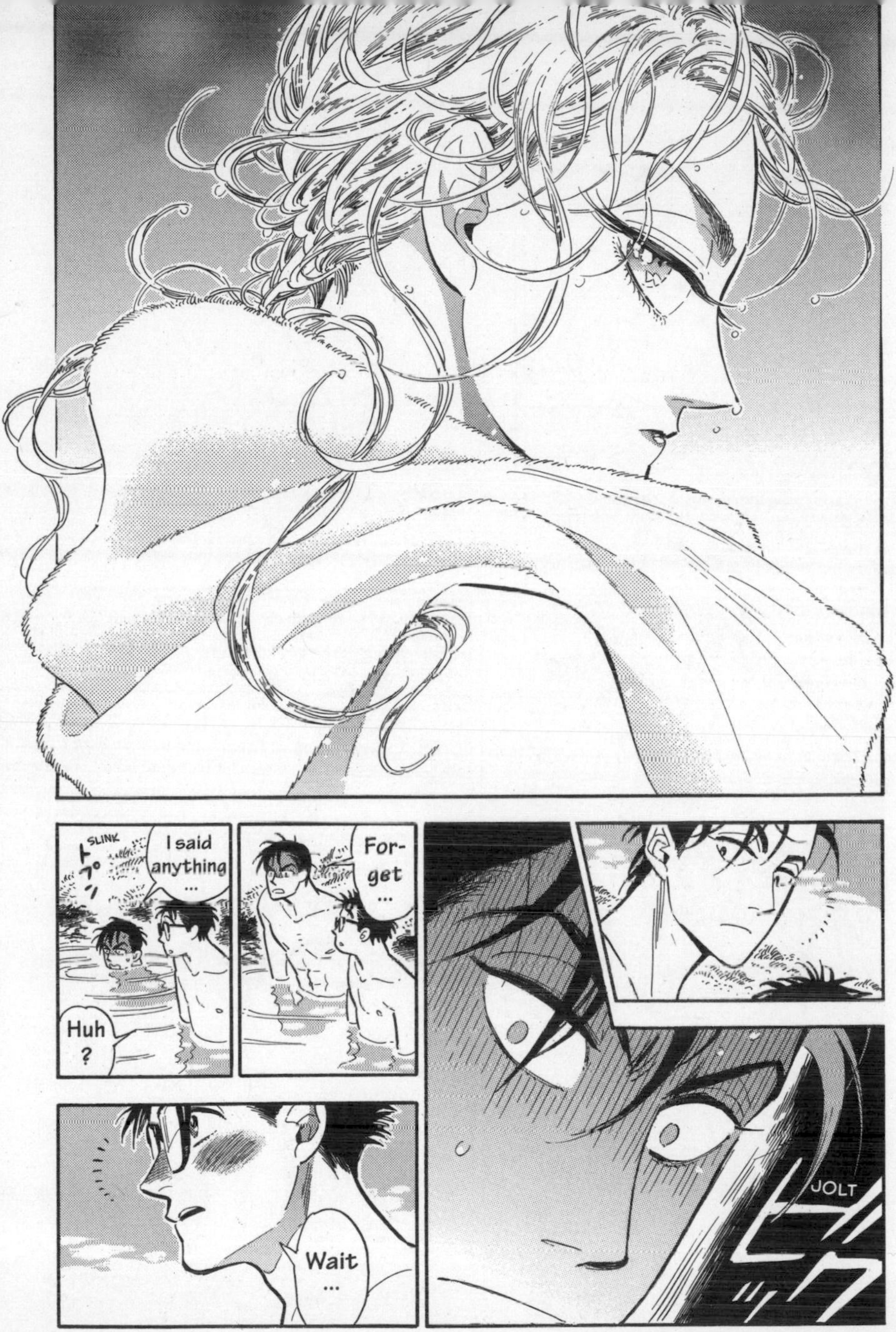
JOLT
For-get ...
SLINK
I said anything ...
Huh?
Wait ...

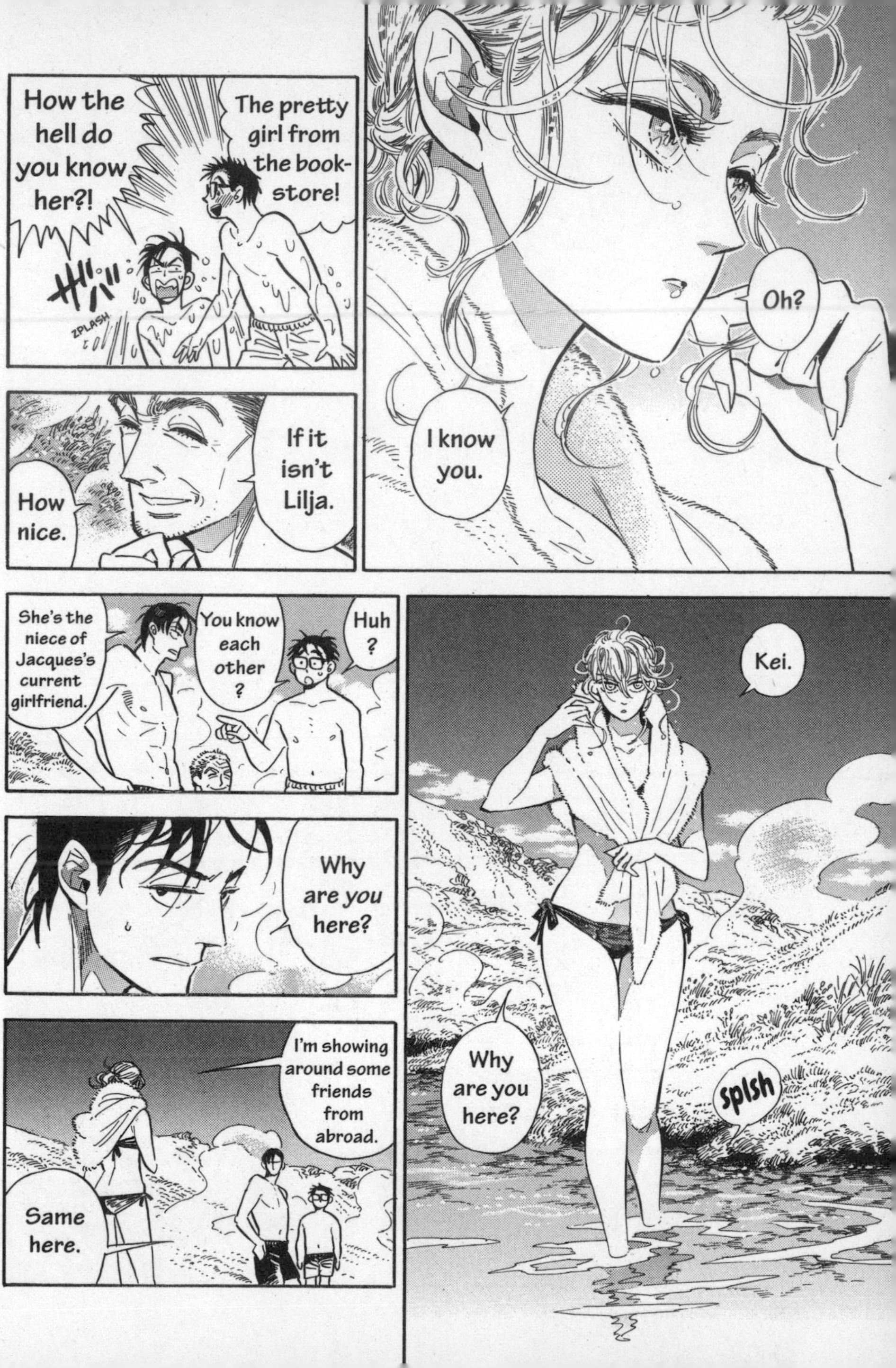
Oh?
I know you.
The pretty girl from the book-store!
How the hell do you know her?!
ZPLASH
If it isn't Lilja.
How nice.
Kei.
Why are you here?
splsh
Huh?
You know each other?
She's the niece of Jacques's current girlfriend.
Why are you here?
I'm showing around some friends from abroad.
Same here.

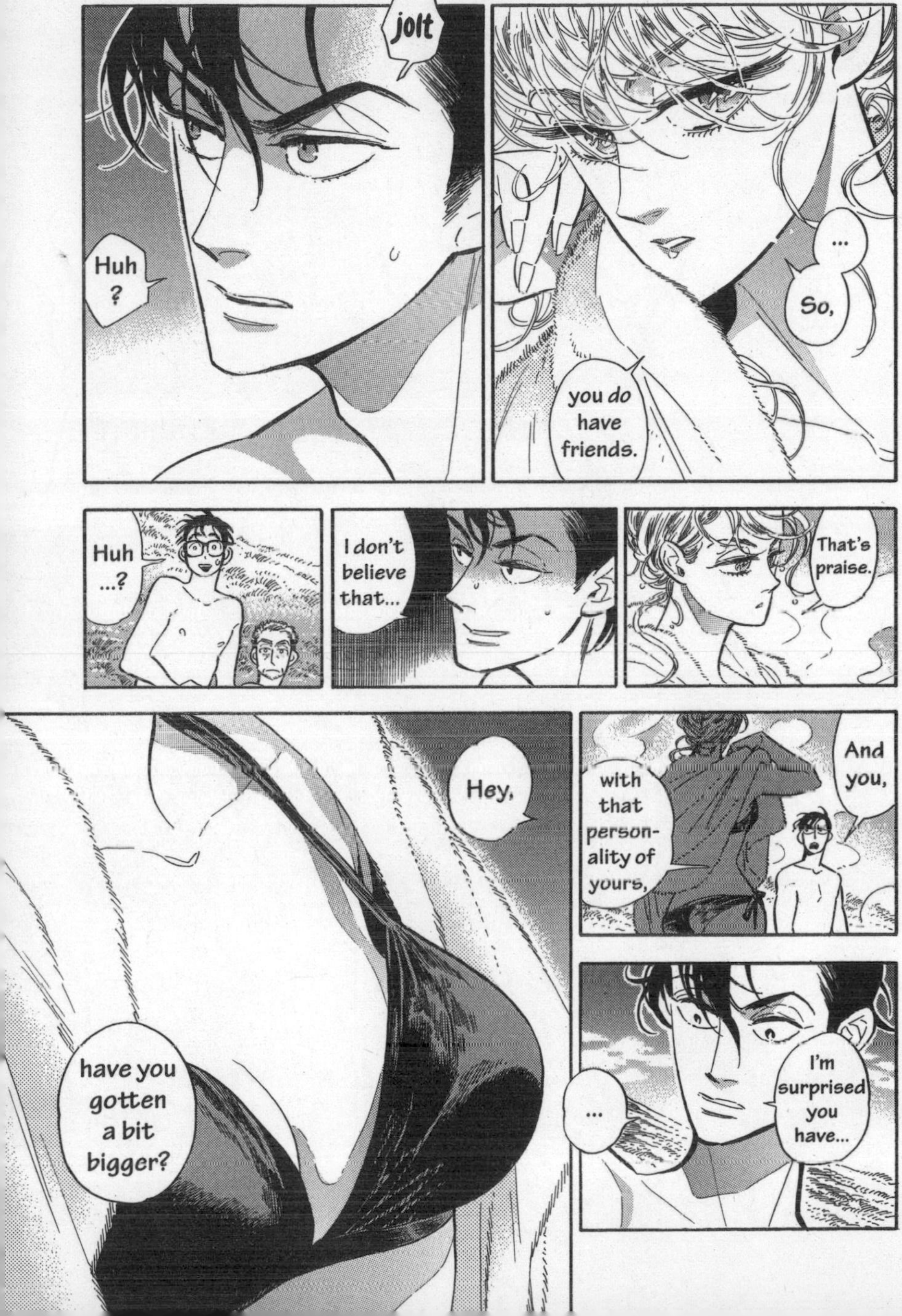
...
So,
you do have friends.
jolt
Huh?
That's praise.
I don't believe that...
Huh ...?
And you,
with that personality of yours,
I'm surprised you have...
...
Hey,
have you gotten a bit bigger?

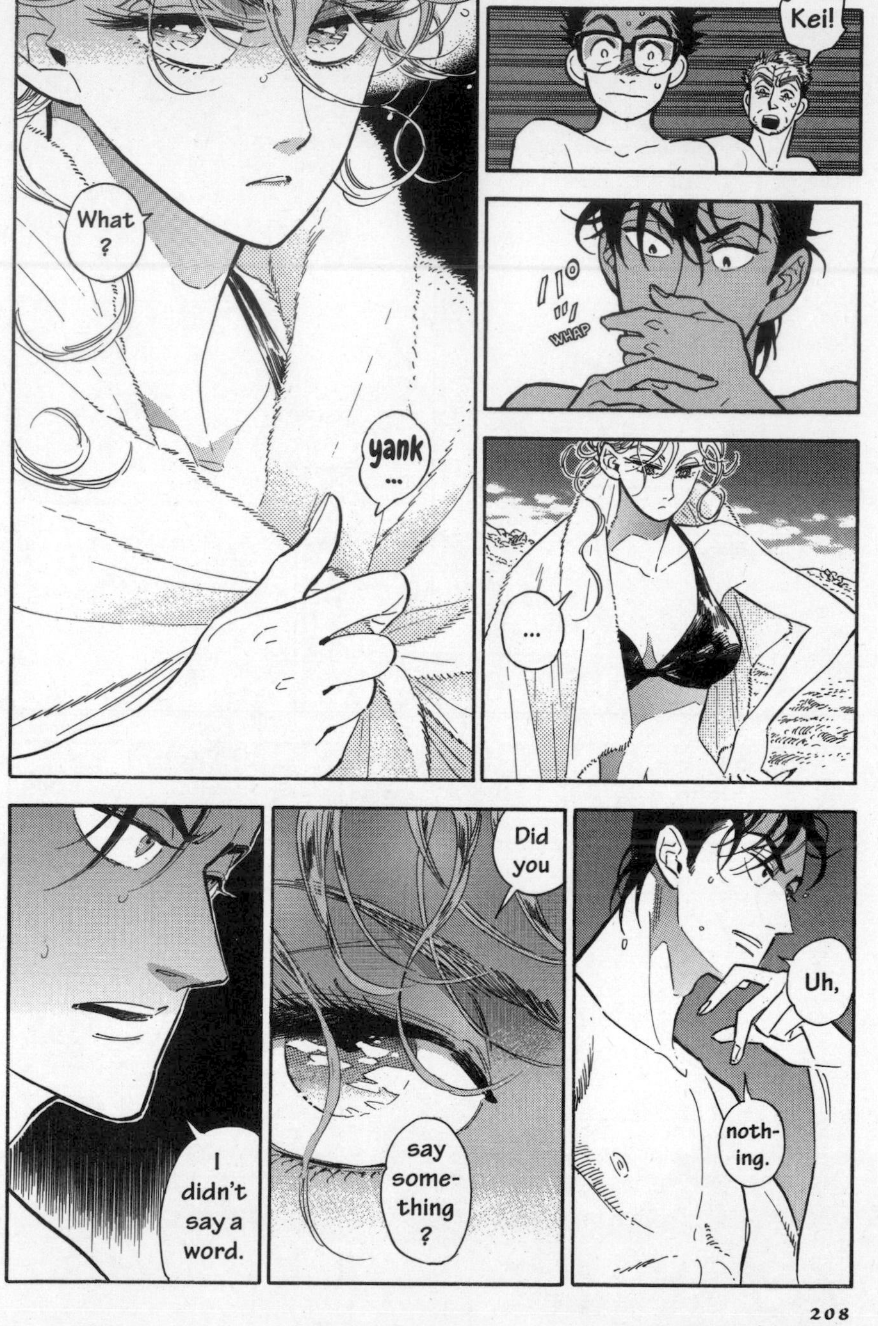
Kei!
WHAP
...
What?
yank ...
Uh, nothing.
Did you say something?
I didn't say a word.

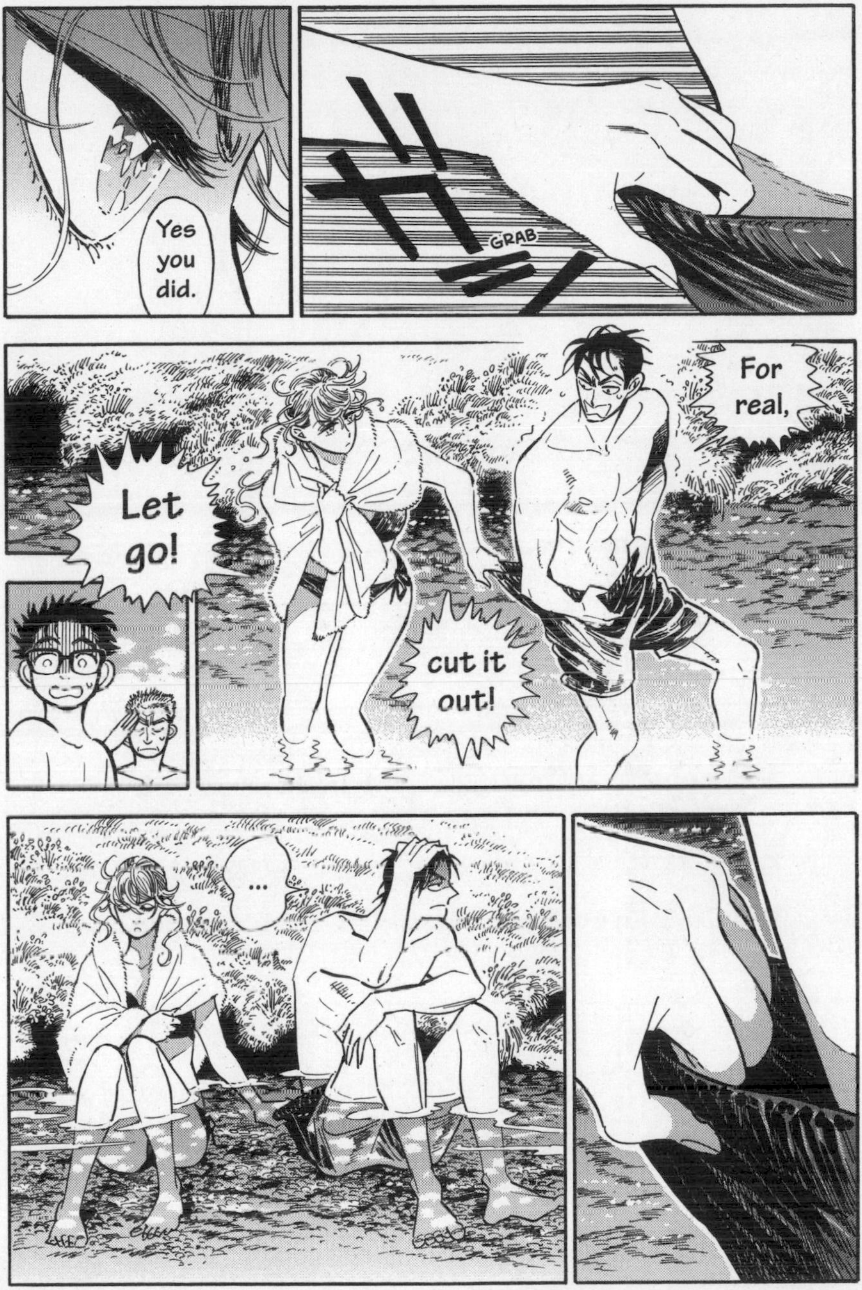
GRAB
Yes you did.
For real,
Let go!
cut it out!
...

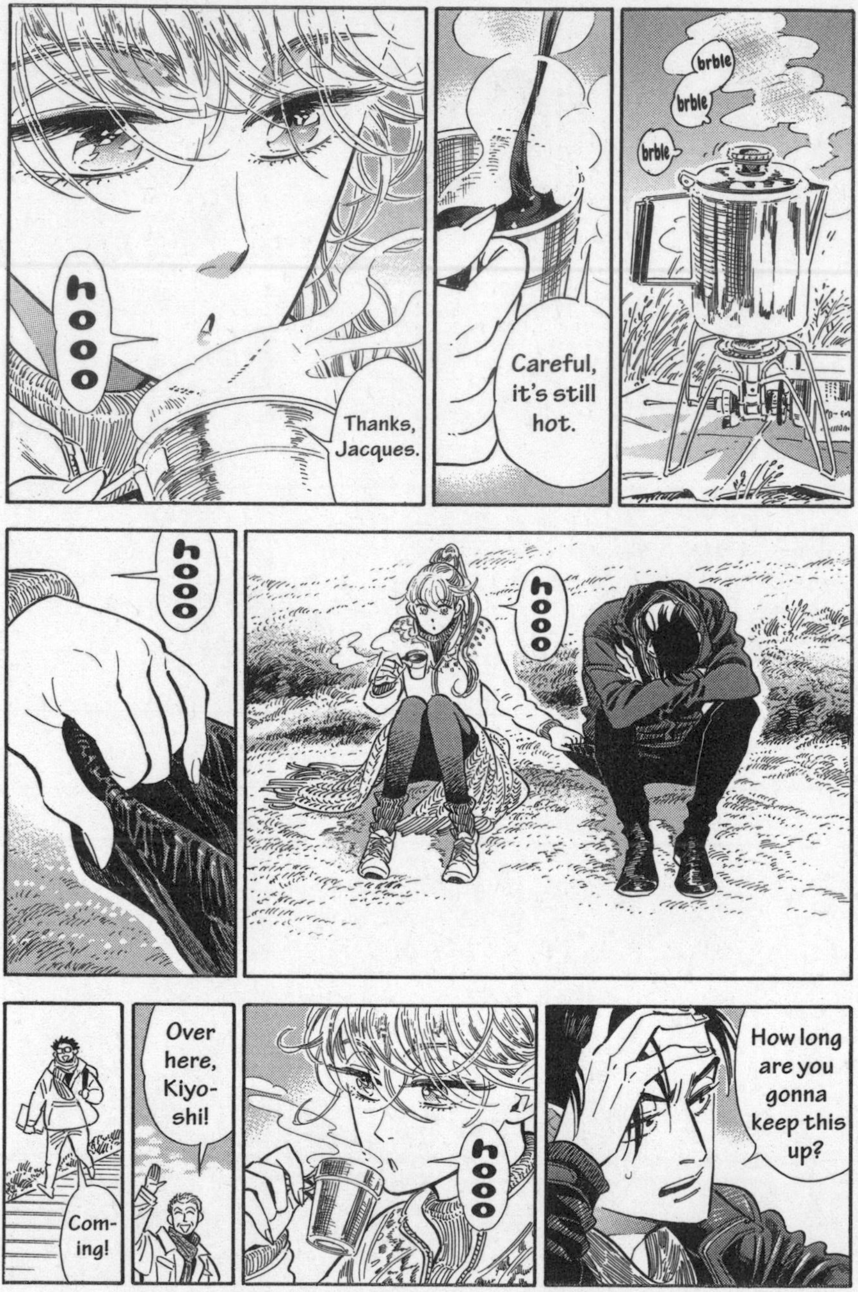
brble
brble
brble
Careful, it's still hot.
Thanks, Jacques.
hooo
hooo
hooo
How long are you gonna keep this up?
hooo
Over here, Kiyo-shi!
Com-ing!

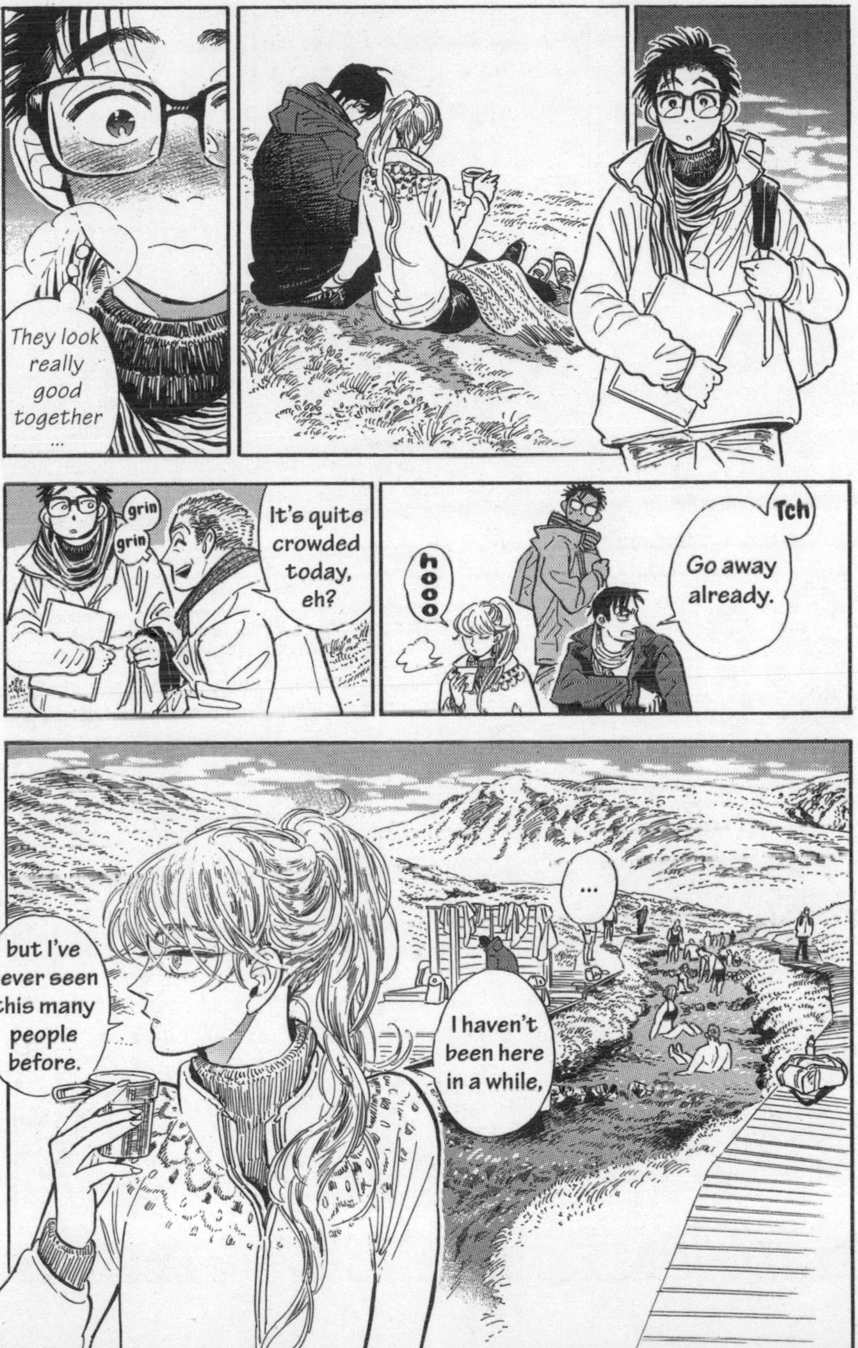
They look really good together ...
Tch
Go away already.
hooo
It's quite crowded today, eh?
grin
grin
...
I haven't been here in a while,
but I've never seen this many people before.

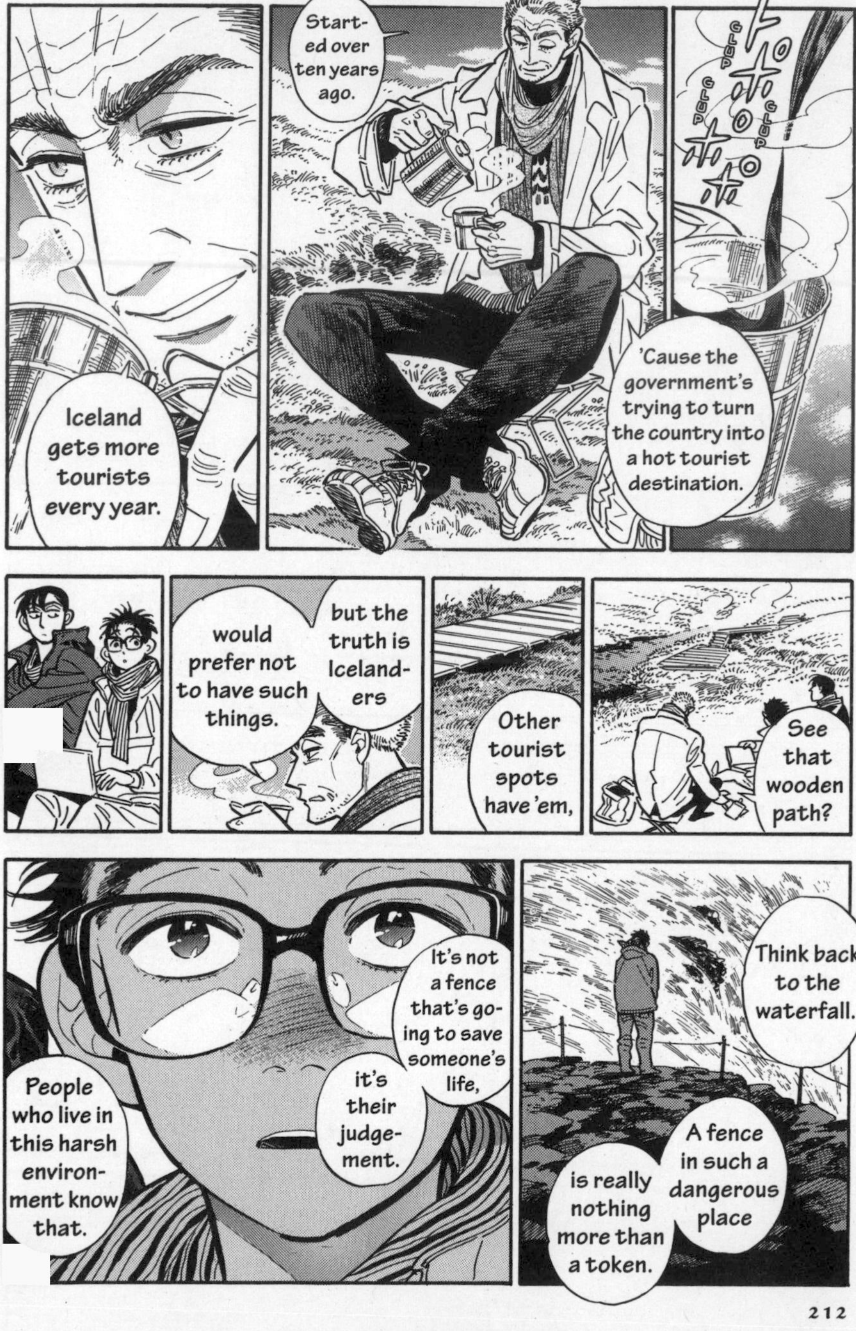
GLUP GLUP GLUP
'Cause the government's trying to turn the country into a hot tourist destination.
Start-ed over ten years ago.
Iceland gets more tourists every year.
See that wooden path?
Other tourist spots have 'em,
but the truth is Iceland-ers
would prefer not to have such things.
Think back to the waterfall.
A fence in such a dangerous place
is really nothing more than a token.
It's not a fence that's go-ing to save someone's life,
it's their judge-ment.
People who live in this harsh environ-ment know that.

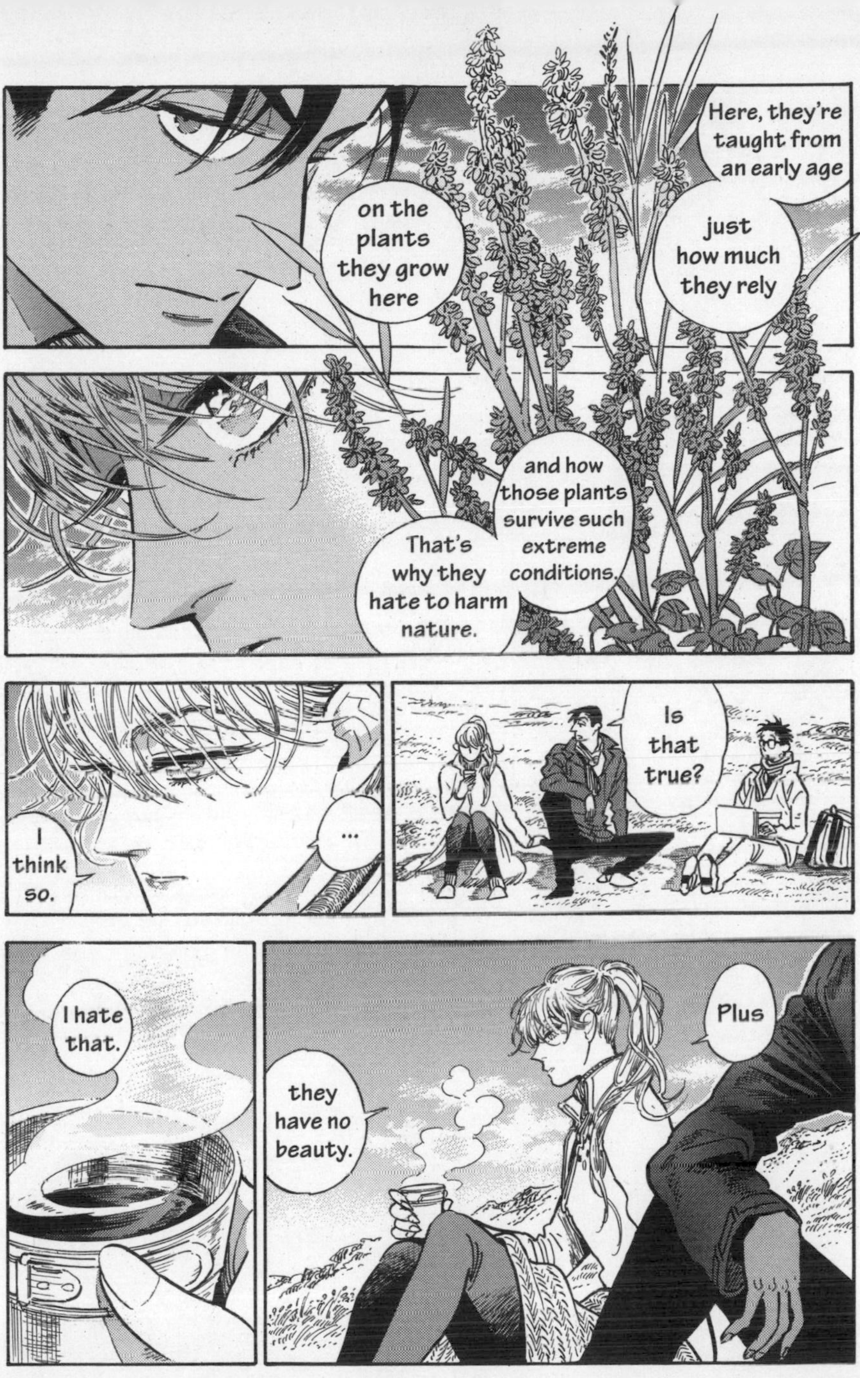
Here, they're taught from an early age
just how much they rely
on the plants they grow here
and how those plants survive such extreme conditions.
That's why they hate to harm nature.
Is that true?
...
I think so.
Plus
they have no beauty.
I hate that.

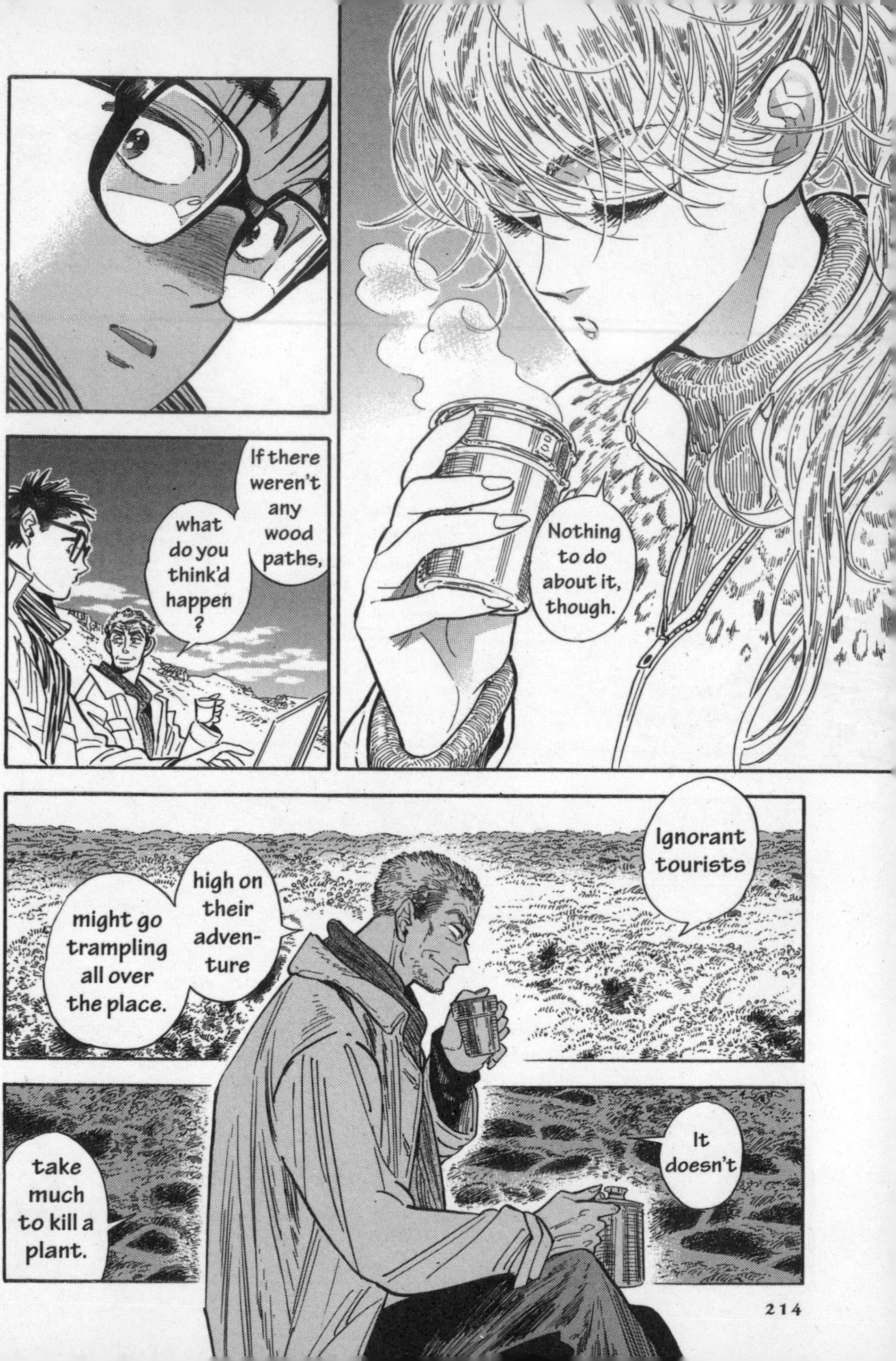
Nothing to do about it, though.
If there weren't any wood paths,
what do you think'd happen?
Ignorant tourists
high on their adven-ture
might go trampling all over the place.
It doesn't
take much to kill a plant.

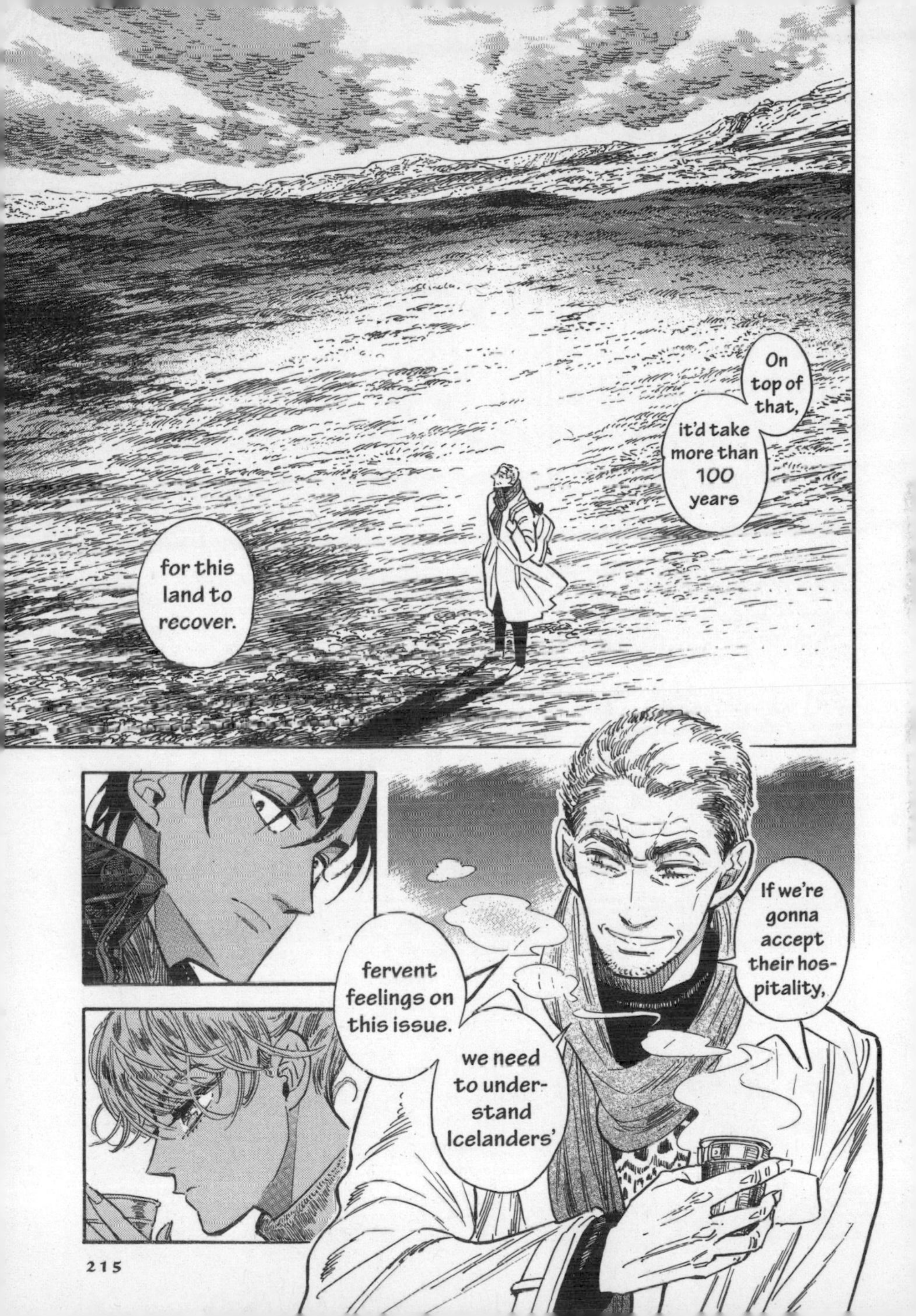
On top of that,
it'd take more than 100 years
for this land to recover.
If we're gonna accept their hos-pitality,
we need to under-stand Icelanders'
fervent feelings on this issue.

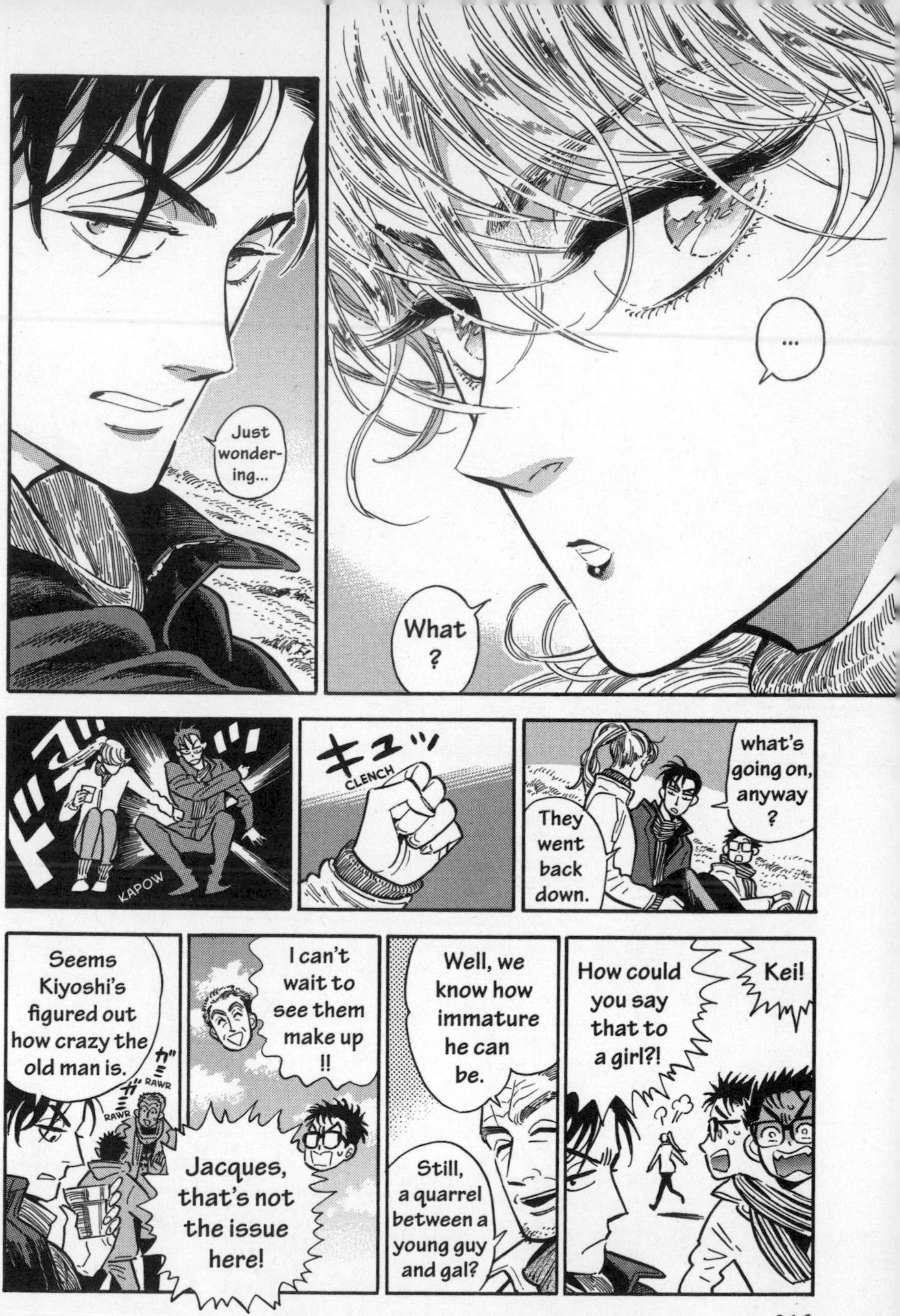
...
What?
Just wondering...
what's going on, anyway?
They went back down.
キュッ
CLENCH
KAPOW
Kei!
How could you say that to a girl?!
Well, we know how immature he can be.
Still, a quarrel between a young guy and gal?
I can't wait to see them make up!!
Jacques, that's not the issue here!
Seems Kiyoshi's figured out how crazy the old man is.
RAWR
RAWR

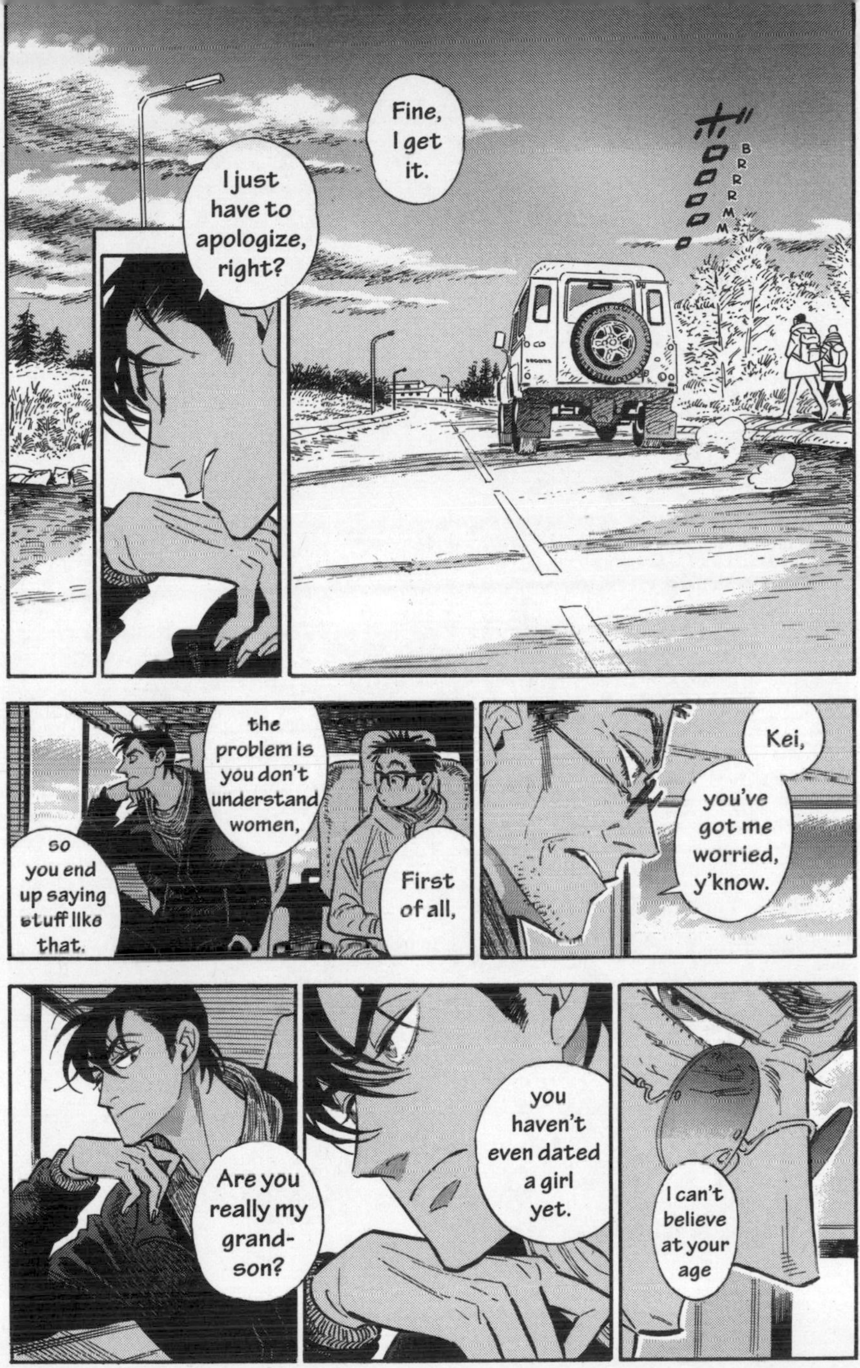

BRRRMM
Fine, I get it.
I just have to apologize, right?
Kei,
you've got me worried, y'know.
First of all,
the problem is you don't understand women,
so you end up saying stuff like that.
I can't believe at your age
you haven't even dated a girl yet.
Are you really my grand-son?

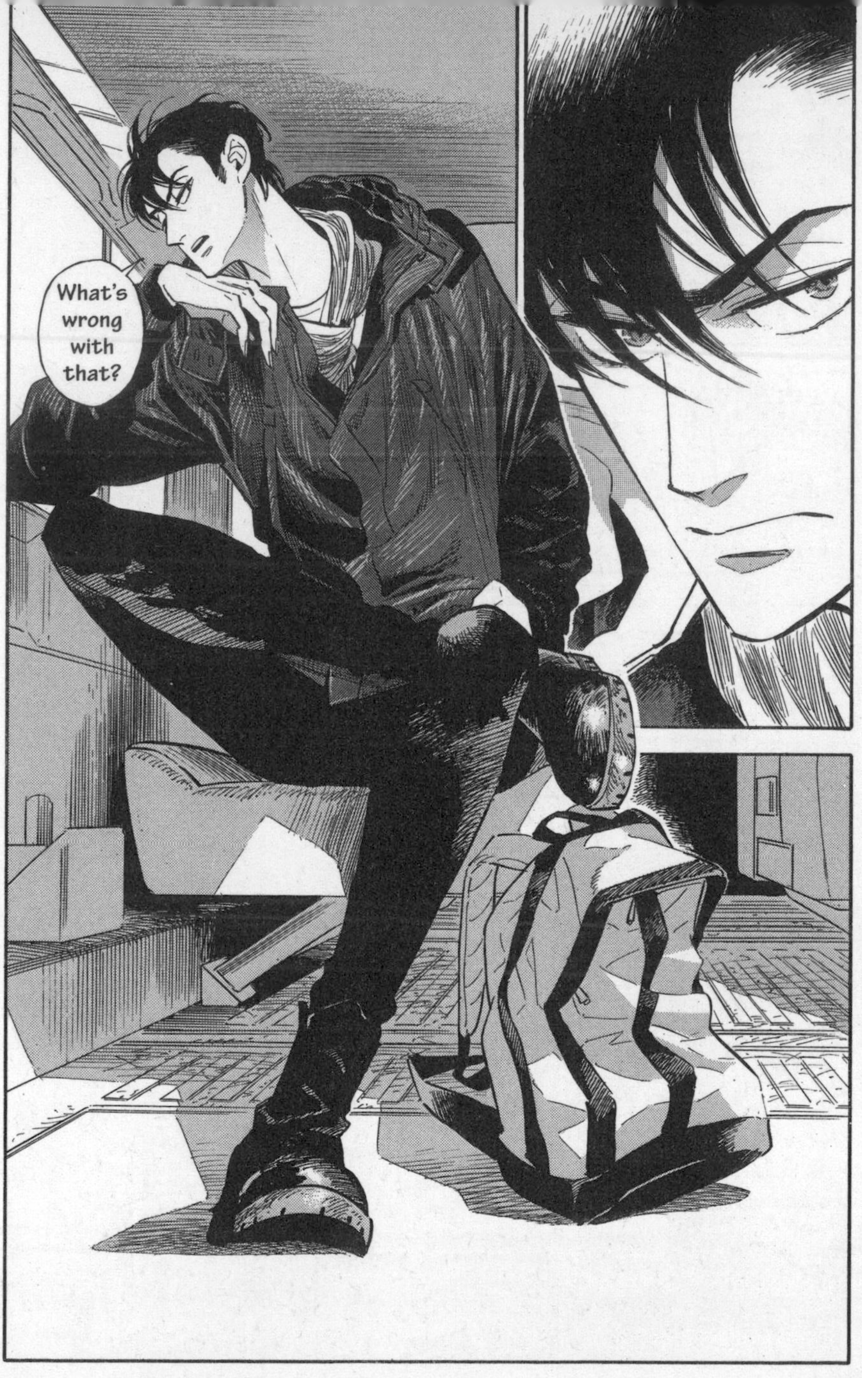
What's wrong with that?

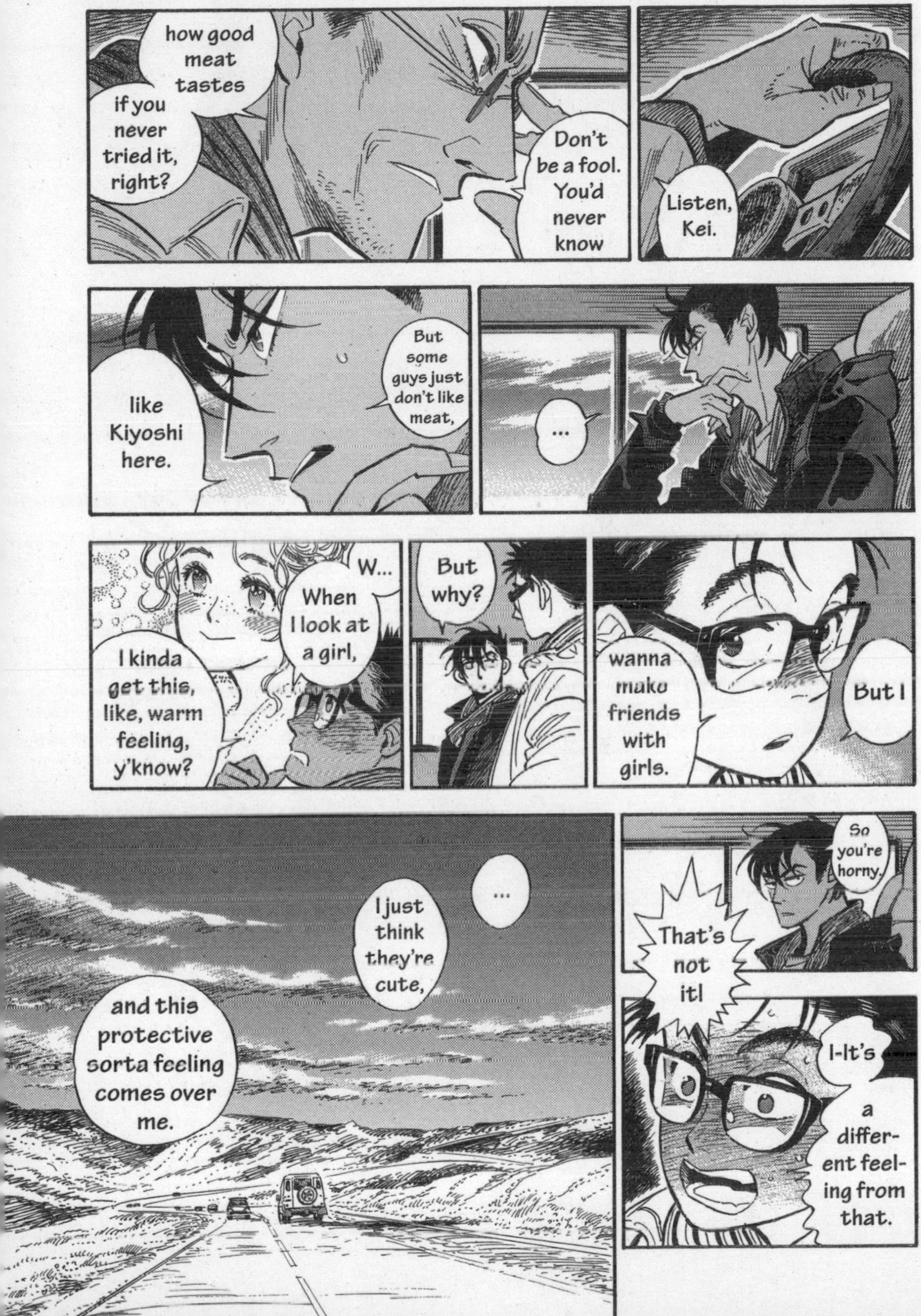
Listen, Kei.
Don't be a fool. You'd never know
how good meat tastes
if you never tried it, right?
...
But some guys just don't like meat,
like Kiyoshi here.
But I
wanna make friends with girls.
But why?
W...
When I look at a girl,
I kinda get this, like, warm feeling, y'know?
So you're horny.
That's not it!
I-It's
a different feeling from that.
...
I just think they're cute,
and this protective sorta feeling comes over me.

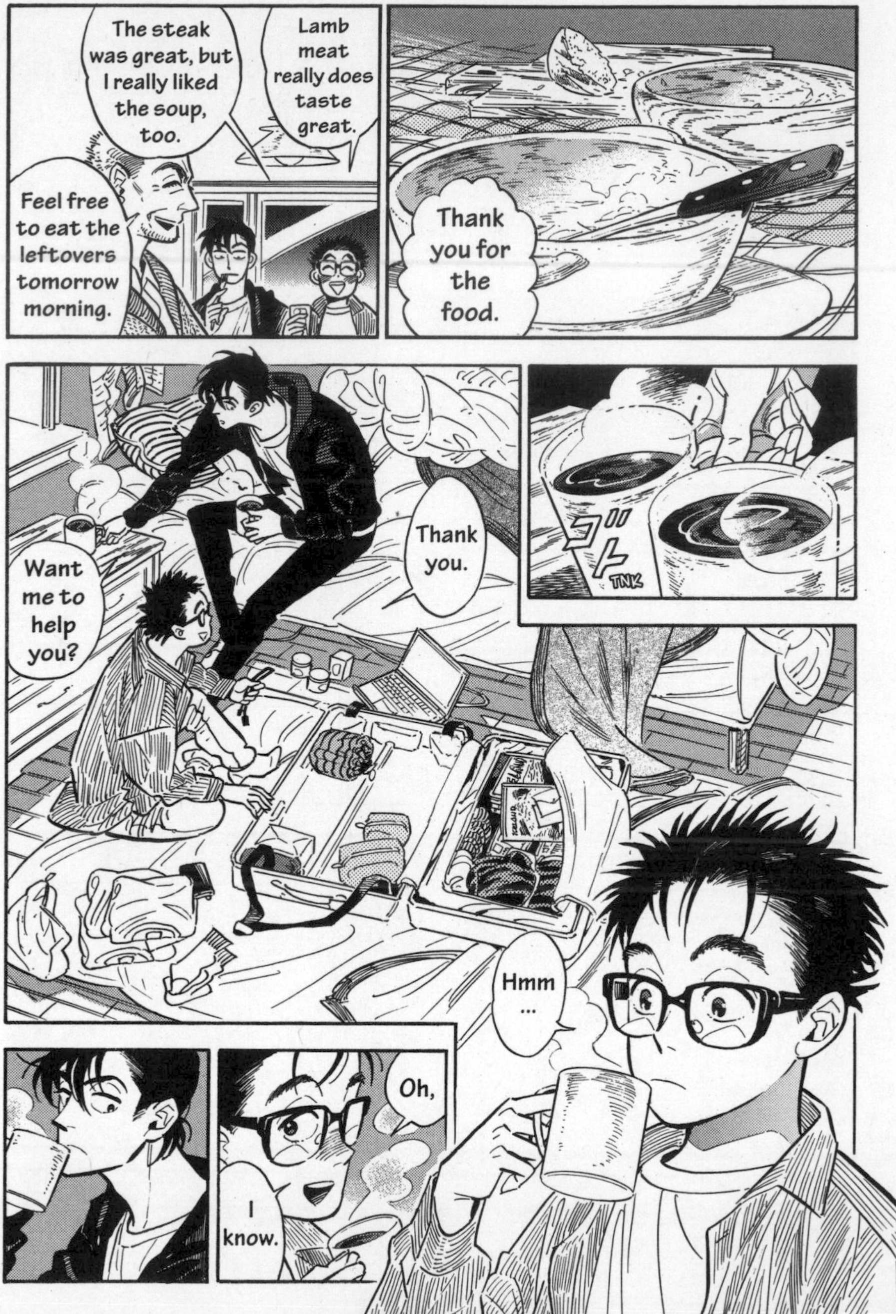

Thank you for the food.
Lamb meat really does taste great.
The steak was great, but I really liked the soup, too.
Feel free to eat the leftovers tomorrow morning.
TNK
Thank you.
Want me to help you?
Hmm...
Oh,
I know.

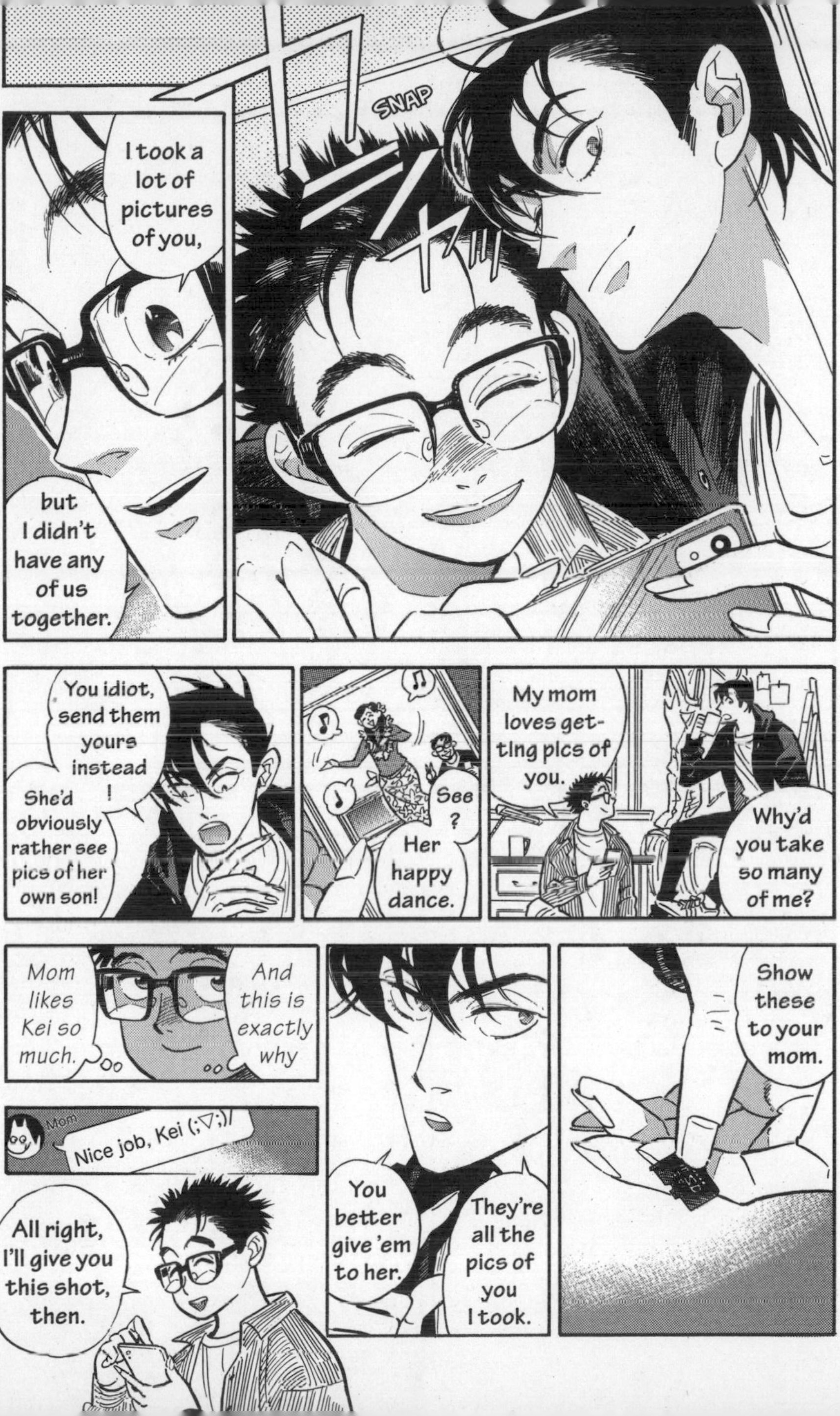
SNAP
I took a lot of pictures of you,
but I didn't have any of us together.
Why'd you take so many of me?
My mom loves getting pics of you.
See? Her happy dance.
You idiot, send them yours instead!
She'd obviously rather see pics of her own son!
Show these to your mom.
They're all the pics of you I took.
You better give 'em to her.
And this is exactly why
Mom likes Kei so much.
Mom
Nice job, Kei (;▽;)/
All right, I'll give you this shot, then.

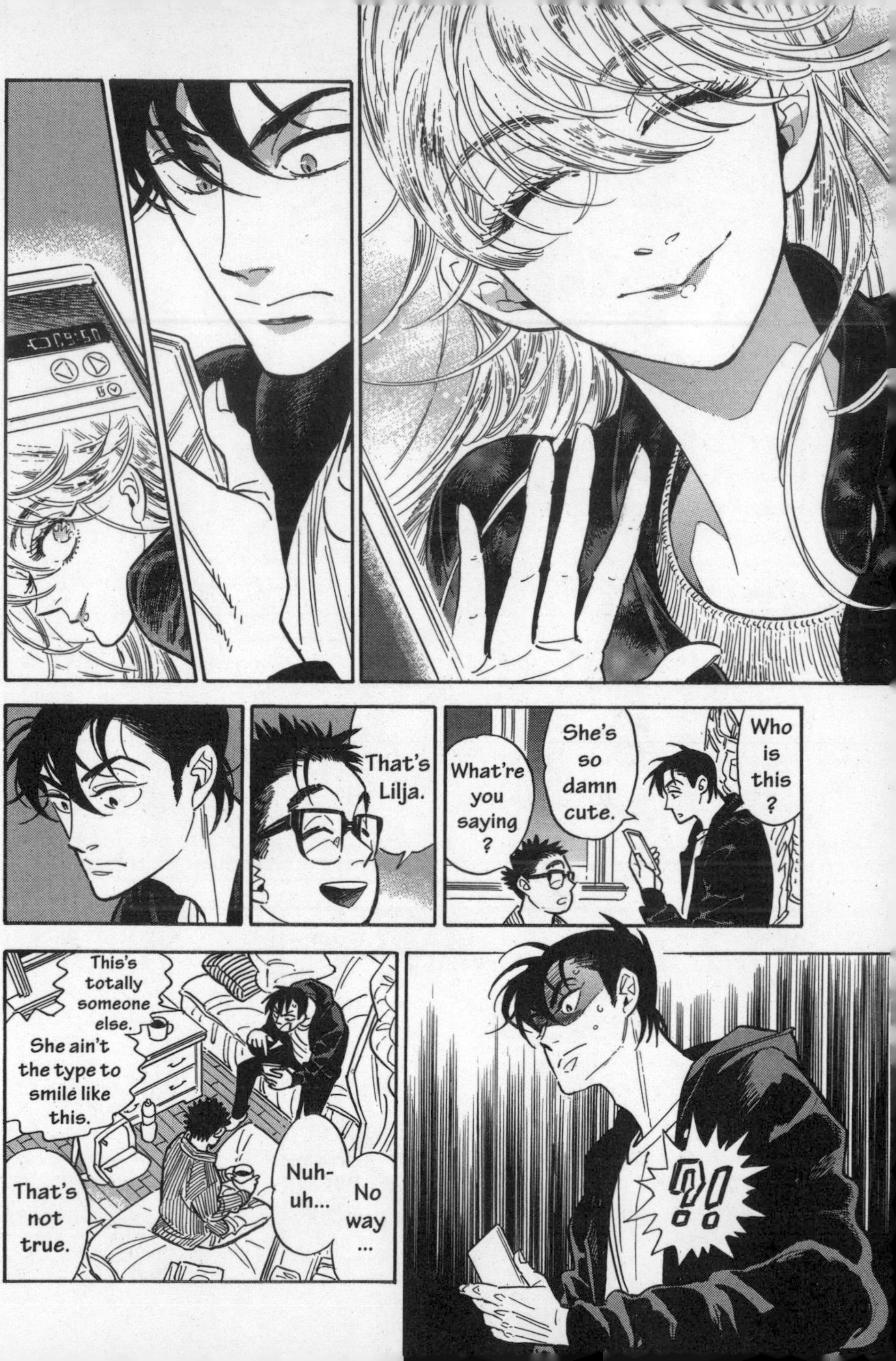
Who is this?
She's so damn cute.
What're you saying?
That's Lilja.
?!
This's totally someone else.
She ain't the type to smile like this.
Nuh-uh...
No way...
That's not true.

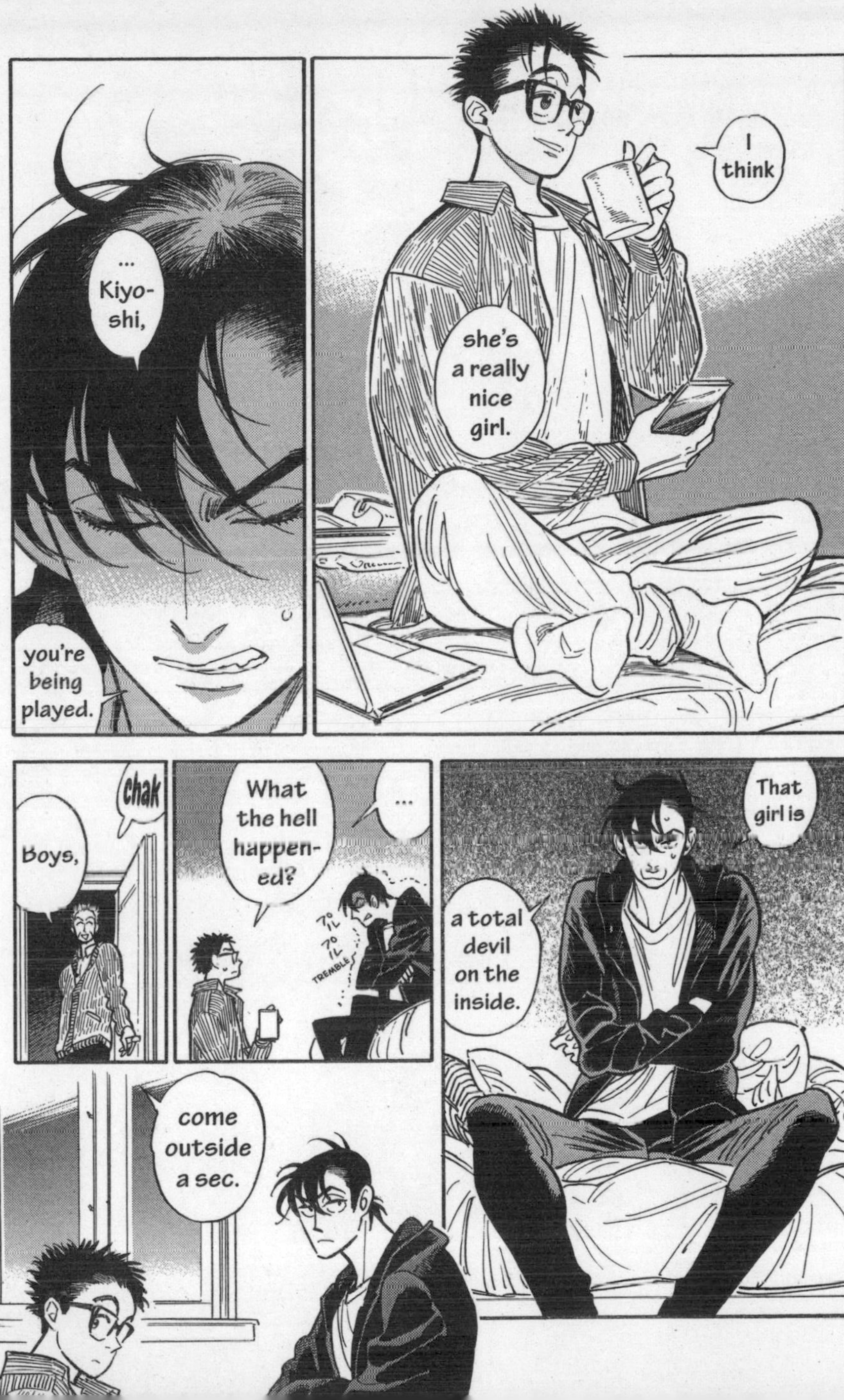
I think
she's a really nice girl.
... Kiyo-shi,
you're being played.
That girl is
a total devil on the inside.
...
What the hell happen-ed?
プルプル
TREMBLE
chak
Boys,
come outside a sec.

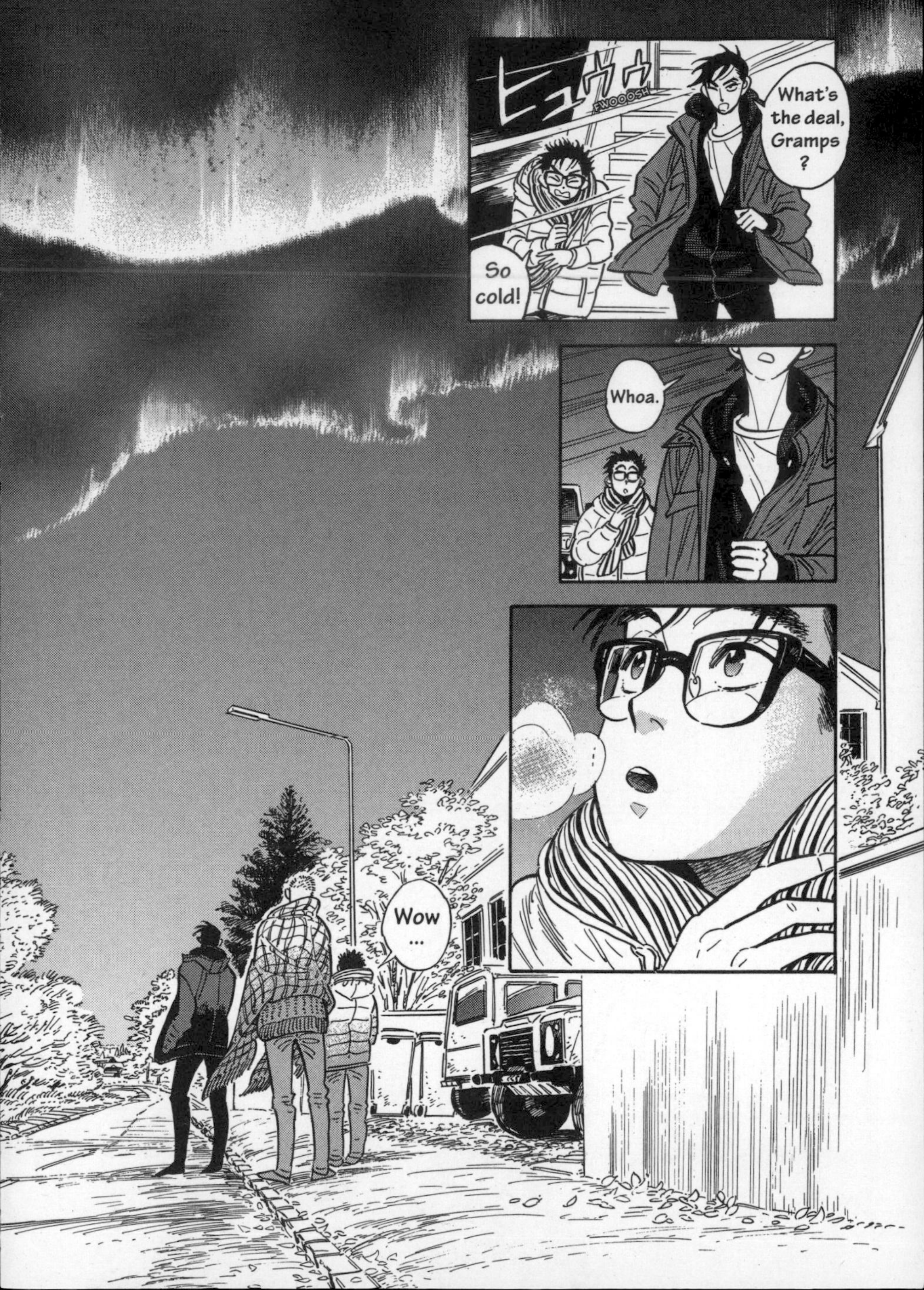
What's the deal, Gramps?
ヒュウウ
FWOOOSH
So cold!
Whoa.
Wow ...

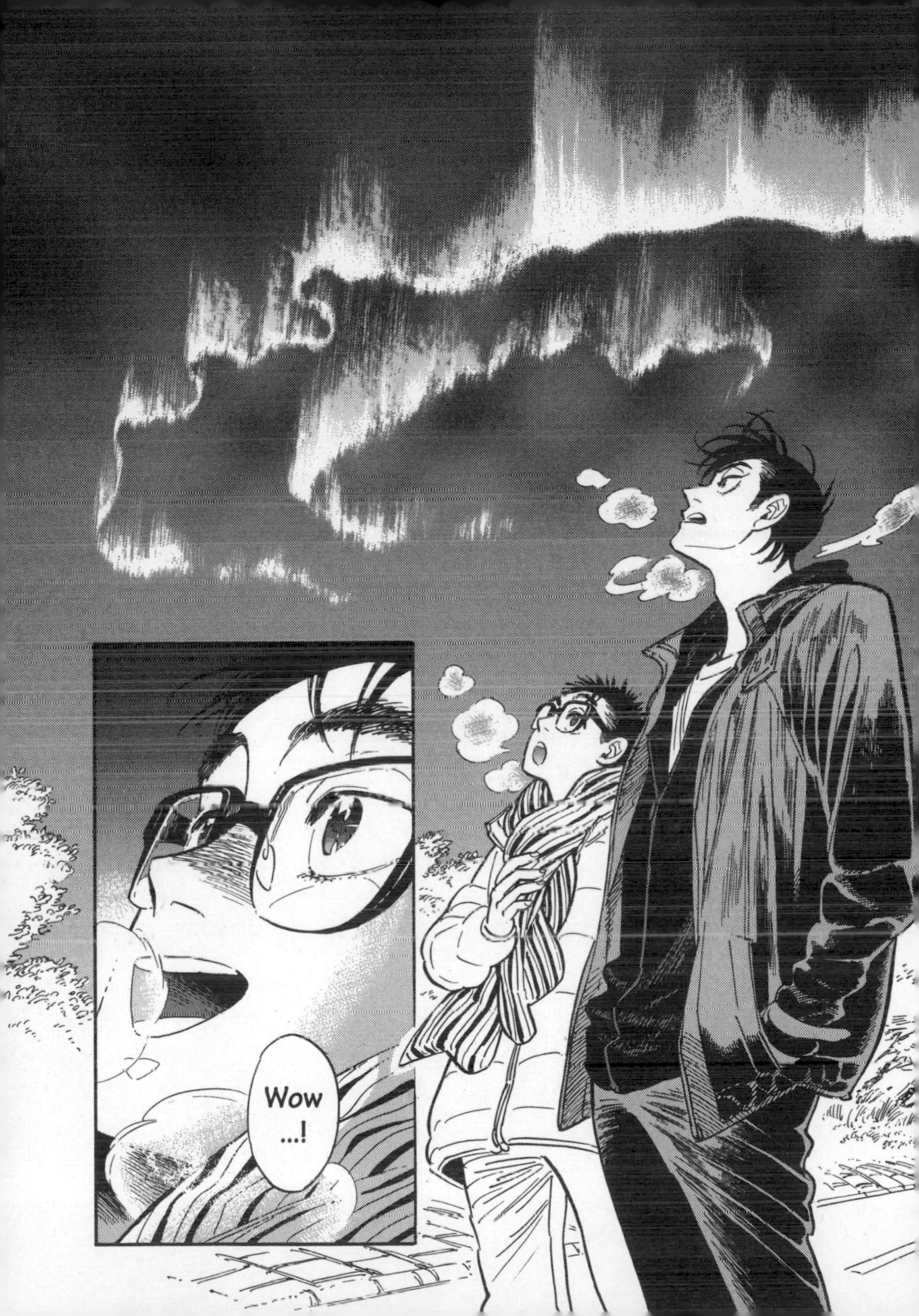
Wow ...!

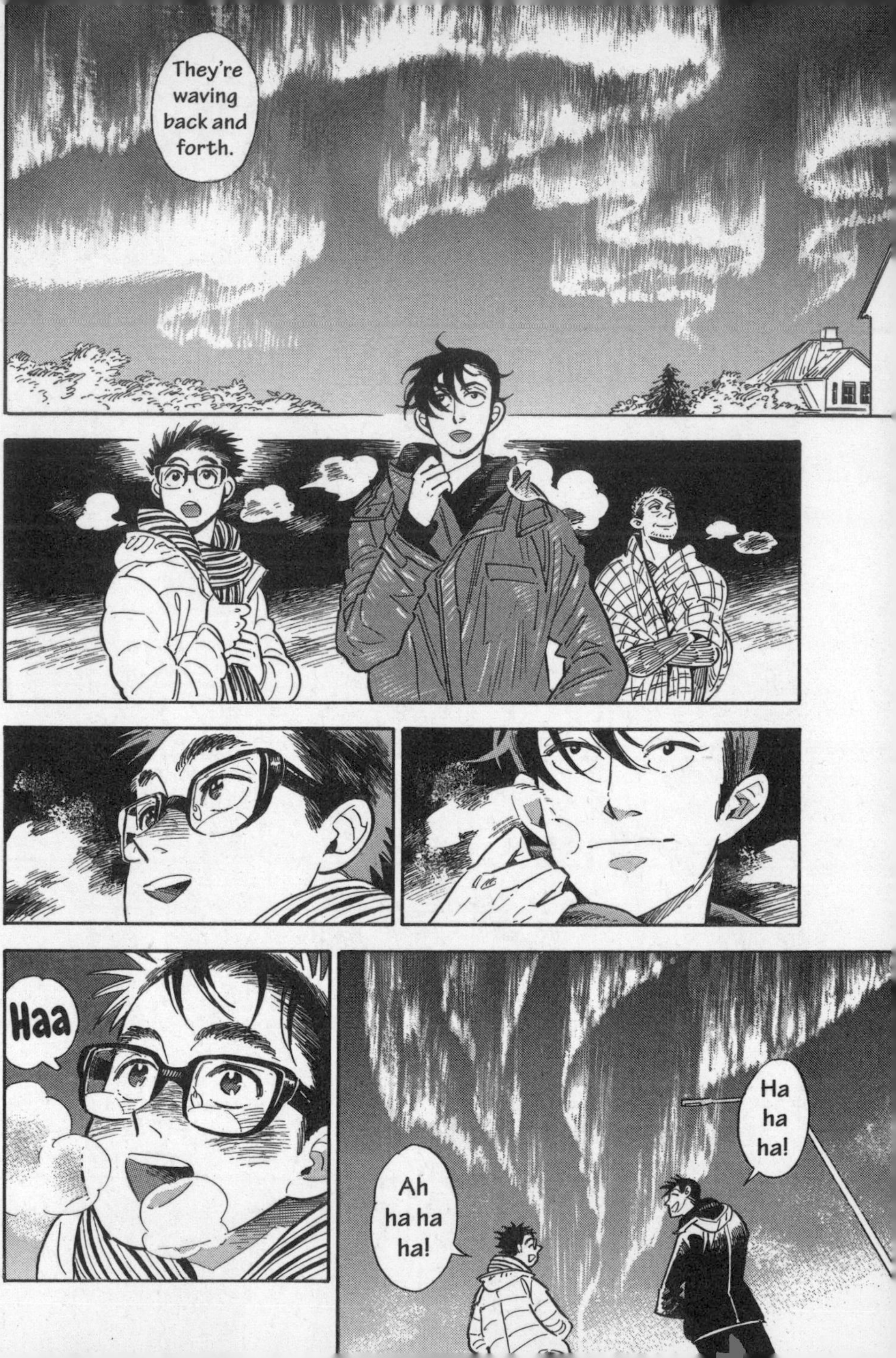
They're waving back and forth.
Ha ha ha!
Ah ha ha ha!
Haa

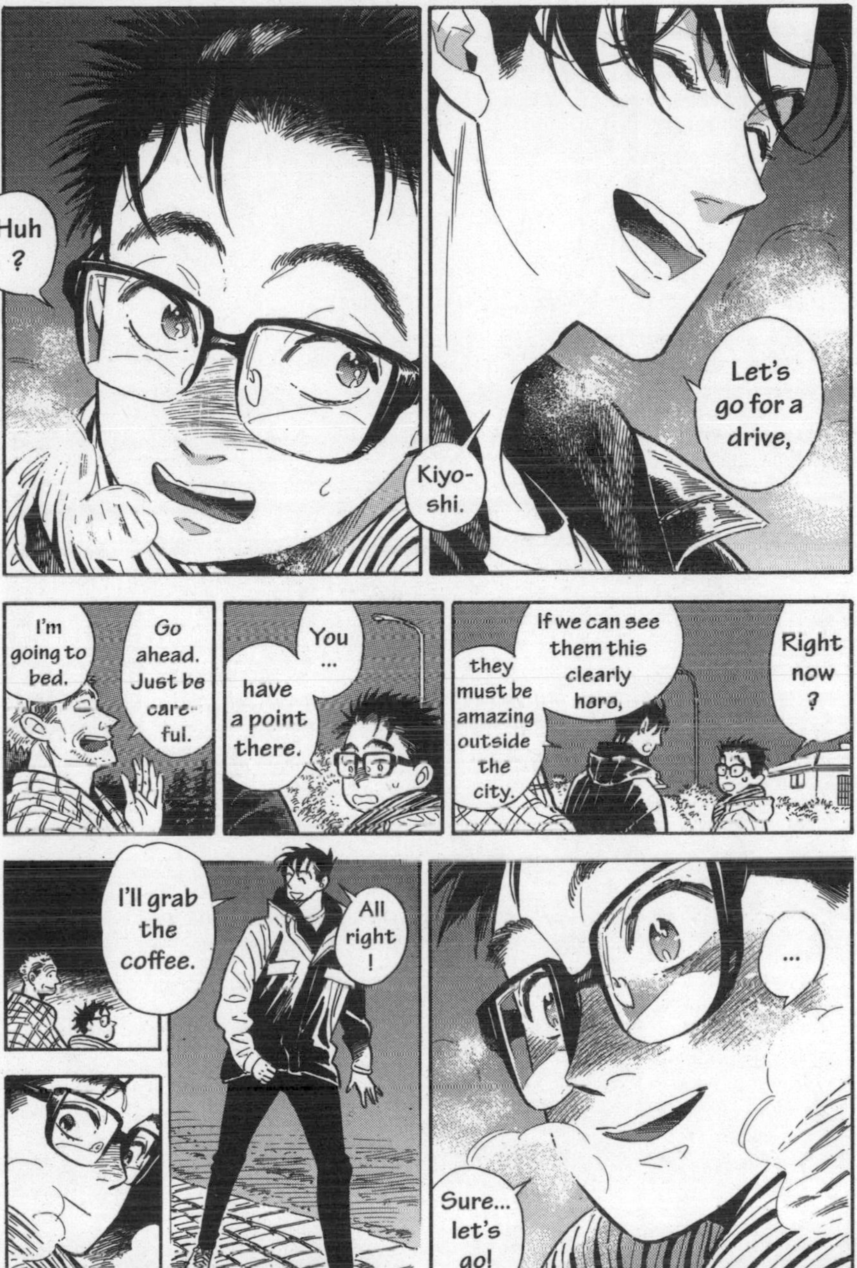
Let's go for a drive,
Kiyo-shi.
Huh?
Right now?
If we can see them this clearly here,
they must be amazing outside the city.
You ... have a point there.
Go ahead. Just be care-ful.
I'm going to bed.
...
Sure... let's go!
All right!
I'll grab the coffee.

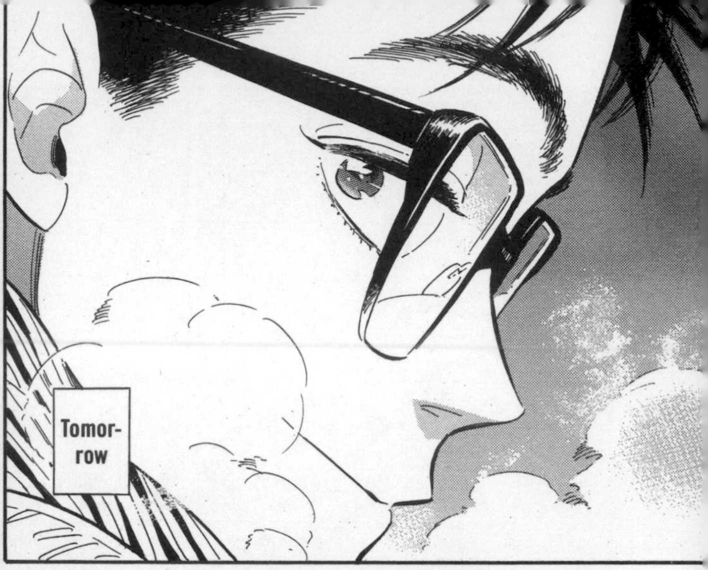
Tomor-
row

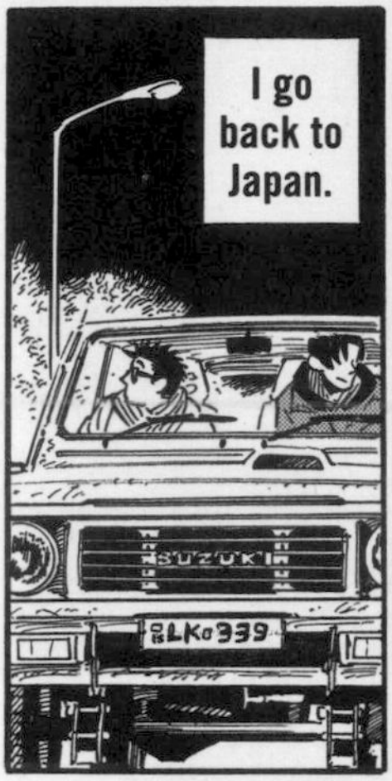
I go back to Japan.

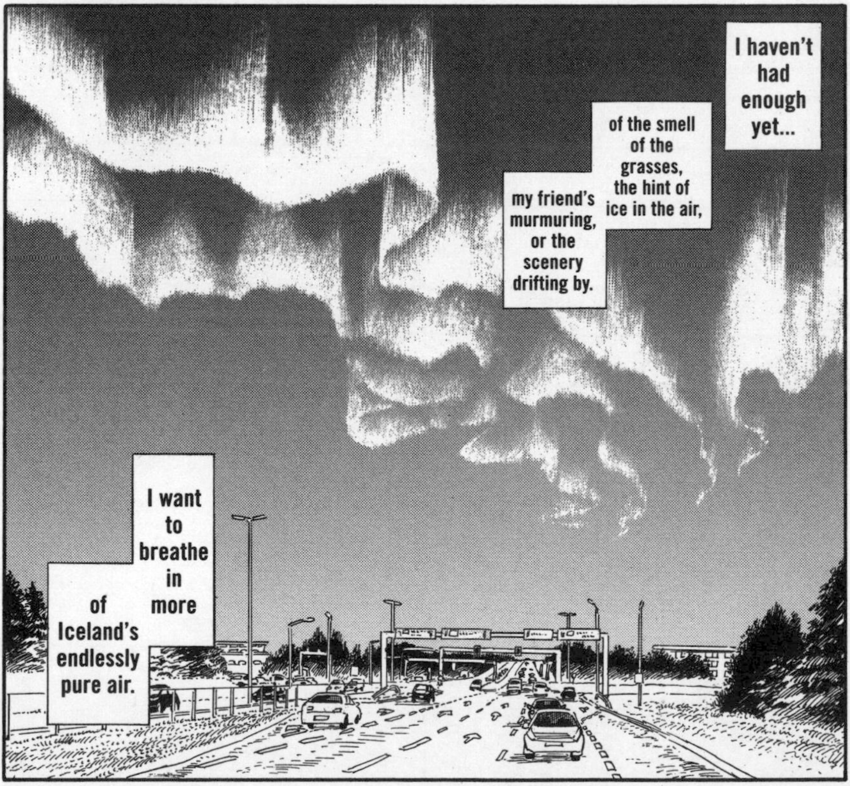
I haven't had enough yet...
of the smell of the grasses, the hint of ice in the air,
my friend's murmuring, or the scenery drifting by.
I want to breathe in more
of Iceland's endlessly pure air.

Go with the Clouds, North-by-Northwest
To be continued in Volume 3

Go with the Clouds
North-by-Northwest 2

A Vertical Comics Edition

Translation: David Musto
Production: Grace Lu
          Tomoe Tsutsumi

© Irie Aki 2018
First published in Japan in 2018 by KADOKAWA CORPORATION, Tokyo.
English translation rights arranged with KADOKAWA CORPORATION, Tokyo
through TUTTLE-MORI AGENCY, INC., Tokyo.
English language version produced by Vertical Comics, an imprint of Kodansha USA
Publishing, LLC, New York

Translation provided by Vertical Comics, 2019
Published by Vertical Comics, an imprint of Kodansha USA Publishing, LLC, New York

Originally published in Japanese as *HOKUHOKUSEI NI KUMO TO IKE* by
KADOKAWA SHOTEN, 2018
HOKUHOKUSEI NI KUMO TO IKE first serialized in *Harta*, 2017-

This is a work of fiction.

ISBN: 978-1-947194-68-7

Manufactured in the United States of America

First Edition

Kodansha USA Publishing, LLC.
451 Park Avenue South
7th Floor
New York, NY 10016
www.vertical-comics.com

Vertical books are distributed through Penguin-Random House Publisher Services.